CW00455360

The Frame of Art

PARALLAX RE-VISIONS OF CULTURE
AND SOCIETY

Stephen G. Nichols, Gerald Prince, and Wendy Steiner
SERIES EDITORS

THE
FRAME
of ART

Fictions of Aesthetic
Experience, 1750–1815

DAVID MARSHALL

The Johns Hopkins University Press
Baltimore

© 2005 The Johns Hopkins University Press
All rights reserved. Published 2005
Printed in the United States of America on acid-free paper
9 8 7 6 5 4 3 2 1

The Johns Hopkins University Press
2715 North Charles Street
Baltimore, Maryland 21218-4363
www.press.jhu.edu

Library of Congress Cataloging-in-Publication Data

Marshall, David, 1953 Dec. 20–
   The frame of art : fictions of aesthetic experience,
1750–1815 / David Marshall.
      p.   cm. — (Parallax, re-visions of culture and society)
   Includes bibliographical references and index.
   ISBN 0-8018-8233-8 (hardcover : alk. paper)
   1. Literature, Modern—18th century—History and
criticism. 2. Literature, Modern—19th century—History and
criticism. 3. Literature—Aesthetics. 4. Criticism—History—
18th century. 5. Criticism—History—19th century. I. Title.
II. Parallax (Baltimore, Md.)
   PN751 M27 2005
   820.9'384—dc22   2005005916

A catalog record for this book is available from the
British Library.

Frontispiece: Thomas Gainsborough, "Study of a Man
Sketching, Holding a Glass." Copyright of the British
Museum, inv. no. Oo, 2-27.

For my parents

Contents

The Frame of Art

The Problem of
Aesthetic Experience

What would it mean to speak about the problem of aesthetic experience in the eighteenth century? Consider these tableaux from eighteenth-century fiction and writing about art: A young woman thinks that romances are true histories and lives her life as if the people and events around her formed the plot of a romance. People repeat in their lives the plots of stories they have read, seen, or experienced. A naïve spectator goes to the playhouse and, thinking that he is watching real life, cries out and tries to warn the characters; a sophisticated spectator goes to the playhouse and, forgetting that he is watching a play, cries out and tries to join the characters. A naïve spectator goes to the theater and sees the actors as people in costumes behaving strangely; a sophisticated spectator views the people around him or her as if they were actors. A play is performed at home rather than in a theater; people in a private house appear before an audience in costumes and pose as figures from paintings.

Consider these tableaux: A man and a woman possess miniature portraits of each other and have intense erotic experiences when viewing these portraits and imagining each other. Readers speak to each other through letters, written representations of their experiences, and feel each other's presence, as if they hear and see each other in person. A sensitive reader forgets that he is reading a book and believes himself to be in another place and time in dialogue with the characters. Readers of literary texts see images and tableaux in their imaginations so vividly that they feel themselves transported to the place described, transformed from readers into spectators. People experience dreams as real events and real events as dreams; real events are experienced as copies of representations. People are moved to ecstasy while listening to music. A garden is designed according to the principles of painting; a natural landscape is dismissed as unworthy of a painting. People arrange or view the world around them, including the other people in it, as if they were beholding a painting, viewing a play, or reading a novel.[1]

Do these tableaux represent aesthetic experience? Before considering why aesthetic experience might be a problem in the eighteenth century, or for whom it might be a problem, there is a problem of definition. The word *aesthetica* was coined in the mid-eighteenth century by Alexander Gottlieb Baumgarten, a German philosopher writing in Latin, and it is not used by the eighteenth-century authors discussed in the chapters that follow. Indeed, although the word was imported into English as "aesthetic" through translations of Baumgarten and Kant, its appropriateness as an English word was still debated well into the nineteenth century.[2] To speak about aesthetic experience in the eighteenth century is in some sense anachronistic but I am interested precisely in authors who felt compelled to describe and represent an experience for which they lacked a name or even a category.

Writing about art flourished in the Enlightenment, which saw the beginning of modern criticism and the demarcation of aesthetics as a modern philosophical discipline distinct from rhetoric and poetics. This professionalization took place simultaneously with a popularization, beginning with the creation of a class of amateurs; influential authors (exemplified by Shaftesbury and Addison) defined the role of the critic and sought to form and reform public taste.[3] I am interested in this story, especially its recurrent concern with the possibility of a standard of taste, and I discuss eighteenth-century writing about art, but my subject in this book is not primarily aesthetics as such or the principles of aesthetic judgment elaborated throughout the century by so many English, French, and German writers. Nor do I aim to rehearse the well-known story of the rise of criticism, connoisseurship, and theories of taste. Yet I invoke these important stories because they form a parallel plot to the stories of aesthetic experience that have intrigued me in the texts discussed in this book. Put another way, the stories about art that interest me here form a kind of counterplot to the narrative about aesthetic experience that is typically associated with the eighteenth century.[4]

The story of the rise of criticism and its efforts to delineate taste and aesthetic judgment begins with the rejection of the a priori rules of classical rhetoric and poetics by writers who privileged the affective responses to works of art characterized by sensibility, sentiment, and sympathy. Reflecting anxieties about how subjectivity and relativism might undermine the possibility of judging and even defining beauty, it is also a story about the concept of the work of art and our ability to recognize it and evaluate it as such; it involves efforts to refine the qualifications of the critic and the criteria for aesthetic judgment. Central to this story is the concept of disinterestedness, present at the beginning of the century in Shaftesbury and culminating in Kant, which becomes a core principle of aesthetic judgment, symbolizing the ability to view the work of art as an object in itself.

Scholars have emphasized the radical character of these efforts to define and understand what M. H. Abrams calls a "uniquely distinctive aesthetic experience."[5] According to Jerome Stolnitz, "When Shaftesbury formulated the concept of 'disinterestedness,' he took the first and crucial step toward setting off the aesthetic as a distinctive mode of experience. That there is such a mode of experience was a radically new idea in Western thought." Describing a "phenomenology, or the beginnings of one," in which the term "disinterested" is used "to denote perception of a thing 'for its own sake'" in an antithesis between "'object-centered' and 'self-centered,'" Stolnitz writes: "It is not surprising, therefore, that in Shaftesbury and in his successors, such experience is defined chiefly by opposition to certain kinds of non-aesthetic behavior."[6] Looking back at this eighteenth-century innovation, Abrams sees the centrality of this aesthetic experience as a defining feature of the concept of the work of art: "What defines a work of art is its status as an object to be 'contemplated,' and contemplated 'disinterestedly'—that is, attended to 'as such,' for its own sake, without regard to the personal interests or possessiveness or the desires of the perceiver, and without reference to its truth or its utility or its morality."[7]

Abrams cites the twentieth-century critic T. E. Hulme, who calls "contemplation" a "detached interest" and continues: "The object of aesthetic contemplation is something framed apart by itself and regarded without memory or expectation, simply as being itself, as end not means, as individual not universal."[8] The culmination of this point of view, according to Abrams, is the museum: "The most prominent institution that functions to confer this status has become the public museum: the exemplary art-of-arts, which over the century has been poetry, has become painting, in which the product is hung on a wall and isolated from its surroundings by a material frame; and the disinterested and absorbed contemplation of an isolated art object—the paradigmatic experience of the theory of art-as-such—is typically a museum experience."[9] Beginning with a point of view, a certain mode of attention or perception that

3

defines the aesthetic, the detachment of the observer seems to end by detaching the work of art, removing it and its contemplation from the everyday world. When we think about aesthetics in the eighteenth century, especially in the contexts of either aristocratic connoisseurship or the emerging professional critic, this is the master-plot that is likely to come to mind.

I cite this characteristic view of the development of aesthetics in the eighteenth century because this is what I do *not* mean in speaking of aesthetic experience. Our notions of the aesthetic as it was invented in the eighteenth century tend to be retrospectively and perhaps retroactively Kantian. It is not wrong to see the end point of the aesthetic when we think about Shaftesbury's sense of disinterestedness or the attempts of Joseph Addison and David Hume to delineate the character of the critic. However, reading the works on taste, beauty, gardening, poetry, theater, criticism, and moral philosophy that we today think of under the general sign of aesthetics, and especially reading works of fiction, the work of art we find described and represented is not generally consigned to a private, isolated, disinterested space. The effect of an aesthetic perspective is not the separation of the realm of art but rather a blurring of the boundaries between the realm of art and whatever is defined in opposition to art: nature, reality, real life.

Enlightenment writers, especially those we today think of as novelists, were preoccupied with the varieties of aesthetic experience and with the effects of works of art in various contexts. In Jane Austen's *Mansfield Park,* we see characters engaged in staging theatrical performances, such as home theatricals in which they act in plays, as in Goethe's *Elective Affinities,* another early nineteenth-century novel that looks back upon eighteenth-century perspectives, in which characters pose in *tableaux vivants* to represent paintings. In Rousseau's *Julie, ou La Nouvelle Héloïse* and Henry Mackenzie's *Julia de Roubigné,* we see characters having intense experiences with portraits, and these paintings are often miniatures that can be held and touched, rather than framed canvases hung on a wall. Their encounters with these works of art seem to transport them, often erotically, through the power of representations that seem to transgress borders and boundaries. Reading, as dramatized in these books, is also a highly charged act; characters have powerful experiences reading works of fiction or letters exchanged in correspondence with other characters. The epistolary novel, central to narrative fiction in the eighteenth century, dramatizes as well as displays the power (and sometimes dangers) of textual representations for authors as well as readers.

Aesthetic encounters such as these take place in domestic settings: characters experience paintings, theatrical performances, or literary representations in salons or "closets." Art is entered into or experienced in everyday life, often with disconcerting effects, especially as the boundaries that appear to separate art and life become blurred. Characters in these texts often experience confusion between reality and representation; hallucinatory images, illusions, and representations appear with a force that compels belief. Often characters are compared to images and representations, but what we see is not merely an extension of the traditional *theatrum mundi* perspective that views people or describes them metaphorically as if they were actors framed in pictures or scenes. Characters seem to become representations, resembling or even seeming to become works of art, even when they are not engaging in performances.

We see characters in these narratives attending performances of plays, but here, even in an officially demarcated space consigned to art, boundaries between art and life are blurred. Eighteenth-century texts by Denis Diderot, Henry Fielding, and Frances Burney, for example, often portray uneducated or naïve spectators, unable to understand or respond to theatrical illusion. Yet the most sophisticated and sensible spectators are also pictured at the moment that, enthralled by theatrical illusion, they forget they are watching a play and try to add a real character to the scene. Both of these responses to artistic illusion are also pictured in novel readers. The figure of Don Quixote presides over much of eighteenth-century fiction, where we often find the naïve quixotic figure who thinks that romances are true histories and interprets the people and events in his or her life as if they formed the plot of a romance.[10] Yet in addition to this comic figure, we also find portrayed a sophisticated reader of the utmost sensibility who weeps while reading Samuel Richardson and cries out in spontaneous dialogue with fictive characters. Readers today may feel superior to Don Quixote figures like Charlotte Lennox's Arabella and even embarrassed by Diderot's descriptions of himself reading *Clarissa*. Tearful, agitated, repeatedly speaking to the characters, Diderot compares himself to a child in the theater who tries to warn the characters in a play of impending danger.[11] Whether objects of satire or exemplars of sensibility, these readers figure extravagant aesthetic experiences in which the borders that are presumed to separate art and life are transgressed. The best and most powerful art is seen to make the most sophisticated spectators respond like naïve spectators.

In the eighteenth century, extravagant claims for the ideal experience of art appear to have been translated into extravagant expectations for and demands upon the experience of art. As the criteria for judging works of art shifted from conformity to classical rules to the power of art to shape the subjective experience of readers and beholders, unprecedented demands were placed on the experience of art. The power of language, images, representations, and stories to create not just verisimilitude but compelling illusions that transported readers and spectators became a recurring theme and preoccupation. Literary texts, for example, were expected to act like paintings and present images and tableaux to the eyes or at least to the imagination, transforming the reader into a spectator who was transported to the scene being described. Texts were expected to convey a sense of spectacle, voice, presence—and, of course, these expectations were finally impossible to fulfill. It is not surprising that apparently hyperbolic claims for aesthetic experience (exemplified by the eighteenth-century versions of the *ut pictura poesis* tradition) are often accompanied by acknowledgments that art lacks the force to achieve the desired sense of presence or illusion.

It is not a coincidence that these claims also coexist with fears about the dangerous effects of art, which was felt to have the power to confuse truth and fiction, stir the passions, and inspire readers and beholders to copy problematic models. Although the condemnation and even the suspicion of art in the eighteenth century grows out of antitheatrical and Puritan traditions, it makes sense that these views would acquire new relevance and even urgency precisely because of the description of aesthetic experience presented by the advocates of art. The texts that I analyze in this book also show a deep investment in—and a great ambivalence about—the power of art and aesthetic experience. These experiences are neither disinterested (indeed, they are often related to appetites, such as sexual desire) nor removed from everyday life. They often represent the ubiquitous presence of art in everyday life in the form of paintings, novels, performances, or music, or in ways of perceiving the world that make art the model that life must copy, in representations that are often compulsive.

"Aesthetic experience" may seem like a misleading or inaccurate phrase to describe the range of experiences and concerns that I have been invoking here if we assume that the concern with aesthetic experience in the eighteenth century was primarily about the invention of a professional, disinterested, isolated contemplation and evaluation of the museum-quality work of art. This, of course, is my point. These intense experiences with and of art (although not always literal works of art) are far from the disinterested "museum experience" that Abrams describes as the paradigm and end point of eighteenth-century aesthetics. Such experiences are difficult to categorize, and eighteenth-century writers seem to have trouble finding a name for them as well. The sense that much eighteenth-century writing about art is trying to describe something new is conveyed by authors' frequent acknowledgments of the problem of describing works of art and people's experiences as they read books, behold paintings, listen to music, and become spectators of plays—and especially as they become readers or spectators of scenes and representations in everyday life. Insofar as the "museum experience" that Abrams describes came to be called "aesthetic experience," it must be read next to and perhaps against texts that represent the insistent insertion of works of art and people's experience of them into everyday life and the blurring of the boundaries of art.

Stolnitz emphasizes the effort to describe the aesthetic as "a distinctive mode of experience" that was defined "chiefly by opposition to certain kinds of non-aesthetic behavior"—especially desire and appetite but including any "moral, religious, instrumental, cognitive" behavior. Even the reflections of the philosopher are seen as "anti-aesthetic."[12] Yet the emphasis on this distinctive experience ultimately undermines the boundaries that it is seeking to delineate by disassociating aesthetic experience from the properties of the work itself and emphasizing the perspective of the judge or beholder. Hans Reiss writes of Baumgarten: "His attention is focused not on the objects themselves, the works of art, whether of literature, fine art or music—or for that matter on the creative process—but on the mode of apprehending them. . . . It is a way of looking at the world different from that of scientific thought."[13] Citing Addison's well-known description of the "man of polite imagination" as someone who "looks upon the world, as it were in a different light," Stolnitz writes: "By contrast to traditional theory, no object is admitted to or excluded from the realm of the aesthetic because of its inherent nature. It is the attitude of the percipient that is decisive."[14] Addison considers both "Works of *Nature* and *Art*," allowing that "the Supreme Author of our Being" has "given almost every thing about us the Power of raising an agreeable Idea in the Imagination."[15] Richard Payne Knight would later describe the picturesque in terms of "modes and habits of viewing."[16]

Discussing the abbé Jean-Baptiste Du Bos in his account of the development of eighteenth-century aesthetics, Ernst Cassirer states, "All aesthetic enjoyment owes its existence to certain reactions called forth in the spectator by the presence of the work of art," but he worries: "Since Dubos seeks movement for its own sake, he makes the intensity of the emotion aroused by the quality and peculiar character of the work of art become definitely a secondary matter; at times indeed he treats them as if they were quite meaningless." Describing Du Bos's "aesthetics of 'pathos,'" in which the "work of art threatens to become a mere spectacle," Cassirer writes: "Dubos characteristically does not interpret his thesis primarily in terms of aesthetic phenomena but rather in a different and broader sense. He does not hesitate to place the impression we gain from the contemplation of a painting or from listening to a tragedy immediately alongside of those other emotions which we feel, for instance, at the execution of a criminal or at gladiatorial combats and bullfights."[17] Cassirer is alluding to the tendency of critics such as Du Bos to emphasize the ability of spectacles to move the passions, but what seems problematic here is the transference of aesthetic experience into other venues of life—or the tendency to understand other kinds of experience through the lens of aesthetic experience. Du Bos is concerned by the theatricality of the gladiators and the attraction of spectacles of suffering for crowds of spectators, but the presence of an aesthetic perspective becomes problematic in more benign settings as well.[18] Once aesthetics is defined by a way of looking, the work of art becomes reinscribed in the world. The focus is not the object of art, the work of art, but rather the experience of art, the perspective or point of view that frames aesthetic experience. The frame of art here identifies an ambiguous and paradoxical place; whereas, as Louis Marin writes, the frame of a painting "renders the work autonomous in visible space" and "the object of contemplation," the act of framing represented by an aesthetic perspective inserts aesthetic distance into everyday life. The frame of art intrudes upon rather than excludes the world.[19]

This is what is so disconcerting about the phenomenon of the picturesque by the end of the eighteenth century, and why the picturesque is seen as a paradigmatic example in this book. Chapter 1, "The Problem of the Picturesque," argues that the picturesque is less a problem *in* aesthetics than a problem *about* aesthetics. Originally described as a mode of viewing nature according to the principles of painting, the picturesque becomes a practice in which landscape gardens and real estate are modeled on paintings. Apparently outside the bounds of art, the natural landscape is judged and even designed in comparison to real and imagined works of art. I begin this chapter about the problem of the picturesque by citing a story told by Uvedale Price about the landscape painter Richard Wilson in the conclusion to his *Essay on the Picturesque*, first published in 1794: "Sir Joshua Reynolds told me, that when he and Wilson the landscape painter were looking at the view from Richmond terrace, Wilson was pointing out some particular part; and in order to direct his eye to it, 'There,' said he, 'near those houses—there! where the *figures* are.'—Though a painter, said Sir Joshua, I was puzzled: I thought he meant statues, and was looking upon the *tops* of the houses; for I did not at first conceive that the men and women we plainly saw walking about, were by him only thought of as figures in the landscape."[20]

Although Reynolds seems to disapprove of a perspective that would regard people as if they were figures in a painting, Price argues that landscape design and gardening should be based on the principles of painting, extending William Gilpin's admiration of "that peculiar kind of beauty, which is agreeable in a picture" or is "capable of being *illustrated in painting*" to a way of looking at the landscape and finally composing the landscape as if it *were* a painting.[21]

What does it mean to see a scene from nature as if it were a work of art—to look at the world through the frame of art? Such questions inform the following chapters. Theories of the picturesque and debates about picturesque gardening often turned upon vertiginous reversals of model and copy, nature and art, reality and representation. Humphry Repton, defending what he calls *"Picture Gardening"* against the advocates of the picturesque, sarcastically suggests that if "the painter's landscapes be indispensable to the perfection of gardening, it would surely be far better to paint it on canvas at the end of an avenue, as they do in Holland, than to sacrifice the health, cheerfulness, and comfort of a country residence, to the wild but pleasing scenery of a painter's imagination."[22] However, the excesses found in the picturesque were represented less by the literal insertion of an actual painting into the natural landscape than by the point of view that framed the world with an aesthetic perspective that insistently focused on—and reproduced—the representations of art. My discussion of the picturesque begins with the shifting "ratio of art to nature"[23] in theories of landscape gardening and then considers the problematic relation between model and copy. It concludes with an analysis of Richard Payne Knight's effort to represent the place of his aesthetic perspective in life through a vertiginous interplay of painting, playacting, and fiction in a remarkable argument by analogy that returns the picturesque to the scene of the novel and the scene of theater. Knight is seen to engage Reynolds in a debate about how to read Fielding's *Tom Jones.*

After considering the presence of the painter's point of view in nature, the illusion that entering a landscape could be like entering a painting, I turn, in chapter 2, to a consideration of Henry Home, Lord Kames, a Scottish critic who dreamed of the power of texts to transform readers into spectators and transport them to the place described, and the better-known German critic Gotthold Ephraim Lessing, whose *Laocoön* announced itself as *An Essay on the*

Limits of Painting and Poetry. This chapter, "The Impossible Work of Art," which examines a translation from art to life rather than a translation from life to art, discusses Kames's adaptation of the principles represented by the phrase *ut pictura poesis* ("as is painting so is poetry," words borrowed from Horace's *Ars Poetica*). Kames is read next to Lessing's definitive refutation of such practices to consider both writers' investment in a powerful experience of art.

I am interested in eighteenth-century theories of *ut pictura poesis* because they make extravagant claims about the effects of aesthetic experience. Arguments about the pictorial properties and powers of literary texts need to be understood in the context of a preoccupation with the effects of the work of art on the senses and the passions. I suggest that we need to take these descriptions seriously to consider the investment of both the advocates and the detractors of *ut pictura poesis* in the claim—indeed, the demand—that texts transport readers by representing images and tableaux. *Ut pictura poesis* represented not so much a doctrine or a formal school of thought as a set of beliefs about the experience of the work of art. In a sense, it is a name for a cluster of aesthetic preoccupations about the effects of art and the power both of art and of the imagination. At stake in this chapter is also the possibility of translating from one art to another, which is also a problem of translation or description for the critic who wants to describe the power of aesthetic experience. I suggest that Lessing, despite his efforts to demarcate the boundaries of art, shared with Kames a deep investment in describing an impossible experience of reading literature.

The next four chapters present readings of works of fiction. Although these readings can stand on their own as they explore various topics and issues, as case studies they cumulatively and collectively demonstrate the argument that I have been staking out in this Introduction, because the authors share a preoccupation with the scenes and experiences of art that I have been describing. The writers I focus on—Charlotte Lennox, Jean-Jacques Rousseau, Henry Mackenzie, and Jane Austen—address varying themes and subjects, but their novels (to use another anachronistic term) share a concern with an aesthetic perspective that views the world through the frame of art. Chapter 3, "True Acting and the Language of Real Feeling," reads Austen's 1814 novel *Mansfield Park,* which, as I have suggested, refers back to these eighteenth-century preoccupations. In *Mansfield Park,* the literal introduction of theater into the domestic scene, like the picturesque principles governing the landscape outside, forms the context for a problematic perspective that frames nature and blurs the boundaries between acting and feeling. Austen's famously antitheatrical heroine is seen to have trouble escaping the play of theater and signification that turns the world into a stage.

Chapter 4, "Fatal Letters," and chapter 5, "The Business of Tragedy," explore the introduction of the work of art and aesthetic experience into the landscape of the sentimental novel. Rousseau's *Julie, ou La Nouvelle Héloïse* (1761) and Mackenzie's *Julia de Roubigné* (1777) use the epistolary genre—in which characters are dramatized as authors and readers who seem to spend their days and nights creating or responding to literary texts—to display characters who repeatedly experience the transports of aesthetic experience through both actual works of art introduced into the domestic scene and an increasingly hallucinatory repertoire of images, reenactments, and representations. Like Lennox's *The Female Quixote* (1752), these texts raise questions about the powers of art and aesthetic experience. *Julie* and *Julia de Roubigné* also portray landscapes populated by the ghostly simulacra, and echoes of prior images and texts, in the context of Mackenzie's creative translation and reenactment of Rousseau and Rousseau's creative translation and reenactment of Richardson—which, I argue, is filtered through the abbé Antonine-François Prévost's translation of *Clarissa*. Repetition compulsion and representation compulsion come together as works of art seem to reproduce other works of art in a vertiginous chain of models and copies.

In chapter 6, "Writing Masters and 'Masculine Exercises' in *The Female Quixote*," I discuss Lennox's ambivalent investigation of female authority and authorship in *The Female Quixote,* in which the paradigmatic Don Quixote plot dramatizes the dangerous power of art and the dangers of viewing the world as if it were a romance. Like the landscape gardeners who design their picturesque landscapes according to the principles of painting, Lennox's heroine Arabella seems to live her life governed by the laws of romances—except Arabella's blurring of the boundaries between art and life comes less from a conscious decision to view the world through the frame of art than from an inability to tell the difference between fiction and reality. The problem of turning one's life into a copy or likeness of the model of fiction is seen both in the novel's anxieties about authority and in its inscription of its heroine in a crisis of imitation that also turns on the problematic relationship between models and copies.

Chapter 7, "Arguing by Analogy," ends the book with a reading of Hume's "Of the Standard of Taste," an essay (first published in 1757) that aims to establish the authority of the critic who would exemplify professional and disinterested aesthetic judgment, yet itself must enter into the realm of likeness.

Hume's philosophical arguments return to the scene of *Don Quixote*. As in *The Female Quixote,* a consideration of art is translated into a consideration of authority as both author and reader consider what it would mean to inhabit a world of likeness. The power of art yields to the power of the critic.

The reader will note that the chapters in this book are not arranged chronologically. This is partly because they are presented more as case studies than as successive steps on a timeline. These chapters were not written to prosecute the position outlined in this Introduction; rather, they exemplify the textual readings and engagements that led me to understand these problems and patterns in the ways that I am proposing. They represent varieties of aesthetic experience, dramatizations of the power of art—the risks and possibilities of art—that often take place in the context of fictions that are *also* about other topics. My point here is in part that these authors did not necessarily set out to write about aesthetic experience per se; their plots and preoccupations seem to take them to the scene of art almost compulsively as they engage the various stories and topics that I pursue in my readings.

My juxtaposition of works that we would today categorize as criticism or philosophy or even "aesthetics" with works of fiction that we would today call novels reflects my belief that some of the most interesting thinking about the experience of art in the Enlightenment takes place in the realm of fiction. The architecture of the chapters also reflects my interest throughout this book in authors who are involved not only in aesthetic arguments with other theorists and critics but also—perhaps reflecting their own aesthetic experience—in intense engagements with textual models, precursors, authorities, and interlocutors: Richard Payne Knight with Reynolds and Fielding, Lessing with Homer, Austen with Shakespeare, Rousseau with Richardson and Prévost, Mackenzie with Rousseau, Lennox with Johnson and Richardson, and finally Lennox and Hume with Cervantes. This book is about shared preoccupations and textual dialogues, as well as the compulsion to rework and work through works of art.[24]

In *The Figure of Theater: Shaftesbury, Defoe, Adam Smith, and George Eliot* and *The Surprising Effects of Sympathy: Marivaux, Diderot, Rousseau, and Mary Shelley,* I focused on authors who explored analogies between the experience of facing people in the world and the experience of beholding paintings, watching plays, or reading texts. This theatrical perspective turned the world into theater and viewed life in terms of spectator-spectacle relations. Theatricality was problematic because it characterized epistemological and moral problems about how we view both self and others and because it figured disconcerting relationships of both sympathy and skepticism. The works I consider in this book share many of these preoccupations, but here I focus more specifically on a point of view that places the work of art in the landscape of everyday life. The characters in these books, viewing the world through the frame of painting, theater, or the novel, often seem motivated by a drive that I have described as a representation compulsion. They seem to design the world as if it were a work of art.[25] The authors of these works of fiction share with the theorists of the picturesque and *ut pictura poesis* an investment in the dramatization and description of aesthetic experience. These texts participate in the ancient debate about the values and dangers of art for readers and beholders, but they also are preoccupied by the pervasive presence of an aesthetic perspective in everyday life in more general and more specific senses. These texts tell stories about intense experiences of art—uncanny, powerful, and never disinterested encounters with works of art faced or created in the landscape of their lives, which seem to be filled with images, simulacra, copies, reenactments, performances, texts, and representations of various sorts.

I have suggested that the readings and interpretations offered in these essays add up to a sort of counterplot to the story of aesthetic experience that is traditionally told about the eighteenth century. This is not to suggest that the story that ends in the triumph of the museum experience of detached and disinterested aesthetic judgment of the work of art framed safely on the wall is completely wrong. One could understand the drive to establish a professional sphere of aesthetic experience as both an effort to establish a new set of rules in an age of sensibility and a reaction against a perception of the disconcerting effects of art and the extravagance of aesthetic experience in everyday life. In this sense, the wish to formulate a disinterested experience of the work of art—displacing the question of whether it is "good" in moral or practical terms with the question of whether it is "good" in "purely" "artistic" terms—is related to a deep interest in removing the work of art from the human landscape in which it is situated in the works considered in this book. The story I am telling runs counter to the stories told by both the guardians of the flame of aesthetic disinterestedness and those who have sought to critique or even attack the supposedly aristocratic (and subsequently bourgeois) values embodied in figures such as Shaftesbury and Addison. I do not mean to refute these accounts but rather to suggest that both views have missed a pervasive aspect of aesthetic experience in the Enlightenment.[26]

This leads to a point about my approach and focus in this book. This is not a social history or an empirical study, except insofar as it aims to scrupulously analyze the textual evidence found in the writings of the novelists, theorists, and critics being studied. My project is historical in the sense that I seek to understand the development of certain concepts, the significance of particular practices and preoccupations, and the ways in which fiction and discussions of art can construe, construct, and deconstruct understandings of aesthetic experience in a particular historical period.[27] I have not sought to incorporate statistics or unpublished contemporary accounts about the experience of "real people" with novels, paintings, home theatricals, and the like. The spread of literacy, the rise of the bookseller and the proliferation of published books, the availability of circulating libraries, new forms of mechanical reproduction of works of visual art, the Grand Tour, the popularity of journals and periodicals, the rise of criticism, debates about fiction and the stage—all of these form an important context for my readings, if not my primary focus here.[28]

Furthermore, although I am interested in why so many eighteenth-century writers are preoccupied with the experience of art, I am not trying to ascertain anyone's actual experience—for example, what Diderot "really felt" when reading Richardson or whether Burke did or didn't see pictures in his mind when reading Milton. Nor would I suppose that eighteenth-century novels, written by definition by authors who were likely to be either self-consciously or unconsciously preoccupied with their art, offer simple reflections of how "real people" experienced works of art in "real life." (I do consider the authors to be "real people" who have mapped a set of shared concerns and preoccupations in the context of ongoing dialogues and debates about art.) We read *The Female Quixote* (or *Northanger Abbey*) as an exaggerated satire rather than as a realistic account of readers in the eighteenth century, but one has to assume that such themes and preoccupations were real, so to speak, and that they can teach us about the hopes and fears that people had about art. One would not assume that eighteenth-century fiction provides a documentary representation of sexual practices in eighteenth-century society, although one would expect to learn something about contemporary attitudes, desires, possibilities, and anxieties. One might ask whether the aesthetic experiences described in *Julie,* for example, or in *Julia de Roubigné,* are in relation to "real people's" experiences with art what *Memoirs of a Woman of Pleasure* or other pornographic novels are to "real people's" sexual experiences in the eighteenth century. It may be easier to explain pornography in terms of sexual fantasies; this book insists that we need to consider what was at stake in fantasies of aesthetic experience.

If my focus does not appear to be the "real world" per se, this is also because my focus is the way that these texts are about the blurring of the boundaries between the real and the imaginary, between art and real life. These questions are complicated by the fact that both the advocates and detractors of fiction at the time were concerned with the prospect that readers of novels copied the models of fiction in their "real lives." One wouldn't assume that the behavior of characters in novels was typical of the behavior of "real people," although both novelists and their detractors seemed to believe that such behavior became "more typical" after "real people" read about it in novels. Works of art and works of pornography were both seen as aesthetically contagious and hard to control. What is interesting to me here is not so much whether readers saw pictures in their minds, people had intense experiences with portraits, or readers took romances to be real histories, but rather why writers at the time repeatedly *described, prescribed,* or *proscribed* such powerful experiences of art.

I am not suggesting that the sorts of experiences of art described in these texts were unique to the eighteenth century or unprecedented. The *theatrum mundi* tradition viewed the world as a stage and the seemingly inevitable self-reflexivity of art means that works from all ages have presented descriptions or allegories of aesthetic experience. I am suggesting, however, through readings of particularly compelling works, that these concerns figured prominently and problematically in Enlightenment writing about art, much of which took place in works of fiction. This is explained in part by a proliferation of actual works of art as more and more people were introduced to new forms of literature, painting, music, and theater, as new classes of people were introduced to principles of criticism and aesthetic judgment and taught to be both consumers and connoisseurs, and as new experiences of reading and beholding were valorized and validated, circumscribed and condemned. The professionalization of aesthetic judgment and criticism may have been a reaction against this democratic diffusion, or the logical development of a category of experience that was being classified and codified, or a reaction against the disconcerting presence of aesthetic experience or aesthetic perspectives in everyday life—an effort to circumscribe the place and experience of art. The texts that I discuss here tell a different story about eighteenth-century aesthetics. Whether encountering actual works of art in the domestic landscape, designing works of art in the natural landscape, or viewing the world through the frame of art, the readers and beholders whose experiences are represented in these texts seem to enter into varieties of aesthetic experience that are particularly intense and problematic. It is the framing of this problem that is my subject in this book.

1 The Problem of the Picturesque

The art that I profess is of a higher nature than that of painting, and is thus very aptly described by a French author. "—il est, à la poèsie et à la peinture, ce que la realité est à la description, et l'original à la copie."

Humphry Repton, *Observations on the Theory and Practice of Landscape Gardening*

The problem of the picturesque in eighteenth-century criticism and aesthetics—and I will suggest why it is a problem—might be approached through a tableau that appears in the conclusion to Uvedale Price's *Essay on the Picturesque,* first published in 1794. In a note, Price recounts the following anecdote: "Sir Joshua Reynolds told me, that when he and Wilson the landscape painter were looking at the view from Richmond terrace, Wilson was pointing out some particular part; and in order to direct his eye to it, 'There,' said he, 'near those houses—there! where the *figures* are.'—Though a painter, said Sir Joshua, I was puzzled: I thought he meant statues, and was looking upon the *tops* of the houses; for I did not at first conceive that the men and women we plainly saw walking about, were by him only thought of as figures in the landscape."

Price's use of this story about Richard Wilson seems odd in the context of his polemic against the "improvement school" of landscape design. Reynolds the portrait painter appears to be somewhat scandalized that Wilson the landscape painter should regard men and women as if they were figures in a painting. Yet Price seems to cite the story approvingly as an illustration of his claim that painting "tends to humanize the mind." Whereas the improvers practice despotism and destruction, he argues, "the lover of painting, considers the dwellings, the inhabitants, and the marks of their intercourse, as ornaments to the landscape."[1] Price is arguing that landscape design and gardening should be based on the principles of painting. In advocating the picturesque both in theory and practice, he is extending Gilpin's admiration of "that peculiar kind

16

of beauty, which is agreeable in a picture" or is "capable of being *illustrated in painting*" to a way of looking at the landscape (and indeed composing the landscape) as if it *were* a painting.[2] Despite Price's identification with Wilson's point of view, however, the story raises the question of what it means to see a scene from nature as if it were a work of art, what it means to look at the world through the frame of art.

Raymond Williams observes that the "very idea of landscape implies separation and observation" and that in the late eighteenth century—a time when "the proscenium frame and the movable flats were being simultaneously developed" in the theatre—the idea that the landscape itself could be a *scene* became inscribed in the language.[3] Writers like Uvedale Price had to refer to "natural scenery" and "real scenery" in order to distinguish the views they were describing from the realm of art, but the terms "scene" and "scenery" implied a theatrical perspective from the outset.[4] In Jane Austen's novel *Mansfield Park* (1814), Fanny Price (who, like Uvedale Price, argues against the improvers and advocates picturesque principles) speaks of her tendency to rhapsodize when she is out of doors, but the speech in which she experiences the "sublimity of Nature" in terms that recall the picturesque is spoken while "standing at an open window" beholding what is described as a "scene."[5] Her stance only literalizes the theatrical metaphor contained in the aesthetic category of the picturesque. The controversy about improvement and landscape design in the novel parallels the controversy about the theatricals, just as in Goethe's novel *Elective Affinities* (1809) characters discuss landscape design *and* pose in *tableaux vivants*.[6]

The picturesque represents a point of view that frames the world and turns nature into a series of living tableaux. It begins as an appreciation of natural beauty, but it ends by turning people into figures in a landscape or figures in a painting. Coinciding with a discovery of the natural world, anticipating an imaginative projection of self into the landscape through an act of transport or identification, it assumes an attitude that seems to depend on distance and separation. Insofar as it represented a sign of sensibility and taste, the picturesque might be seen as a chapter in the history of aesthetics, a moment of intersection between the history of painting, subgenres such as descriptive poetry and the gothic, and what James Dallaway called "the literary history of gardening" in 1827.[7] Insofar as it is accompanied by a hint of discomfort, controversy, or excess, however, the picturesque is less a problem *in* aesthetics than a problem *about* aesthetics. As such, it represents more than a trend in gardening or a footnote to the history of the sublime; the invention of the picturesque represents a complex and at times paradoxical moment in the evolution of eighteenth-century attitudes about art, nature, and aesthetic experience.

In his 1794 *Essay on the Picturesque,* Price complains, "There are few words, whose meaning has been less accurately determined than that of the word picturesque." Rejecting Gilpin's definitions as "at once too vague, and too confined," Price asserts that the word "is applied to every object, and every kind of scenery, which has been, or might be represented with good effect in painting."[8] Gilpin popularized the modern sense of the word "picturesque," using the term "to denote *such objects, as are proper subjects for painting.*" He writes as a "picturesque traveller," touring Great Britain and Scotland with sketchbook in hand, recording the varieties of natural scenery available to the "picturesque eye."[9] Gilpin, and especially Price, want to distinguish the picturesque from the beautiful or sublime. Whereas for Edmund Burke beauty is smooth, for Gilpin the "*smoothness*" of "an elegant piece of gardening . . . offends in picture": "Turn the lawn into a piece of broken ground: plant rugged oaks instead of flowering shrubs: . . . give it the rudeness of a road: mark it with wheel-tracks; and scatter around a few stones, and brushwood; in a word, . . . make it *rough;* and you make it also *picturesque.*" Palladian architecture becomes unpleasingly formal when represented in a painting. For picturesque beauty, explains Gilpin, "we must use the mallet, instead of the chisel: we must beat down one half of it, deface the other, and throw the mutilated members around in heaps. In short, from a *smooth* building we must turn it into a *rough* ruin. No painter, who had the choice of the two objects, would hesitate a moment." The observer with a "picturesque eye" prefers "the elegant relics of ancient architecture; the ruined tower, the Gothic arch, the remains of castles, and abbeys."[10] Not quite a genre or a style, yet related to the sketch, certain styles of architecture, and to landscape painting (especially that of Nicolas Poussin, Claude Lorrain, and Salvator Rosa), the picturesque was, according to Martin Price, "an attempt to win traditional sanctions for a new experience."[11] John Barrell describes "a very different attitude to landscape"—a "way of looking" that became a "way of *knowing*" the landscape.[12] Richard Payne Knight argued in 1805 that the picturesque represented "modes and habits of viewing."[13]

Whereas Gilpin used the term "picturesque" for the most part to appreciate those accidental scenes that might be encountered by the traveler—and increasingly the tourist—passing through the landscape, others were concerned with designing landscape as well as appreciating it. Gilpin wrote essays on "picturesque beauty" and wrote up his tours, but Price indicated the practical aspect of his *Essay on the Picturesque* by declaring in his subtitle that his work was also about *the Use of Studying Pictures, for the Purpose of Improving Real Landscape.* The tendency to admire natural scenery according to the principles of art, to appreciate a landscape the more it resembled a painting, led a certain class of people to redesign the natural scenery around them in order to reproduce the reproductions of landscape painting.[14] In an often-quoted remark reported by Joseph Spence, Alexander Pope declared: "All gardening is landscape-painting." He referred to "clumps of trees" on his estate at Twickenham as being "like the groups in pictures."[15] Horace Walpole, who asserted that an "open country is but a canvass on which a landscape might be designed," claimed that the lawns at Stanstead "recall such exact pictures of Claud Lorrain, that it is difficult to conceive that he did not paint them from this very spot."[16] In his influential treatise on gardening, William Shenstone declared: "Landskip should contain variety enough to form a picture upon canvas; and this is no bad test, as I think the landskip painter is the gardiner's best designer."[17]

From the beginning of the century, the garden becomes an arena in which both theoreticians and practitioners display a complex ambivalence about art and nature. Shaftesbury, Addison, Pope, and others, condemned the formality, symmetry, and artificial order of the classical garden associated with France and Holland. In a pre-romantic effort to embrace a state of nature with the transports of a new enthusiasm that sought out the wild, savage, and sublime, and in an at once ideological and allegorical display that sought to figure English democracy and liberty in contrast to French despotism, the English developed new types of gardens. Much has been written about the literary history of gardening and the picturesque. My focus here is on the ways that the practice of viewing the world through the frame of art gains power and authority in an escalating rejection of art, artificiality, and artifice, and especially in the paradoxical grounding of nature in aesthetic experience.

Shaftesbury, for example, in *The Moralists* (1709), has his rhapsodist prefer the "inmost recesses" of "wildness" and nature "where neither art nor the conceit or caprice of man has spoiled their genuine order by breaking in upon that primitive state" to "the artificial labyrinths and feigned wildernesses of the palace." Yet "glorious nature . . . whose every single work affords an ampler scene, and is a nobler spectacle than all which ever art presented" is nonetheless pictured as spectacle and scene. Shaftesbury's enthusiast's praise of "the rude rocks, the mossy caverns, the irregular unwrought grottos and broken falls of water, with all the horrid graces of the wilderness itself" for "representing Nature more" than "the formal mockery of princely gardens," anticipates the descriptions of Gilpin, Price, and Knight, yet it also anticipates the idea that a natural scene might itself *represent* nature.[18]

Addison's 1712 *Spectator* series on "the pleasures of the imagination" praises nature and attacks formal gardens, juxtaposing "the Works of *Nature* and *Art*" and comparing landscapes to verbal and visual representations of them. Indeed, Addison insists that "we find the Works of Nature still more pleasant, the more they resemble those of Art." This is because "our Pleasure rises from a double Principle; from the Agreeableness of the Objects to the Eye, and from their Similitude to other Objects: We are pleased as well with comparing their Beauties, as with surveying them, and can represent them to our Minds, either as Copies or Originals."[19] He even concludes that words, "when well chosen, have so great a Force in them, that a Description often gives us more lively Ideas than the Sight of Things themselves. The Reader finds a Scene drawn in Stronger Colours, and painted more to the Life in his Imagination, by the help of Words, than by an actual Survey of the Scene which they describe. In this Case the Poet seems to get the better of Nature."[20] In the context of garden design, nature is preferable to the artificial; yet in the larger context of the imagination, art seems to get the better of nature. The natural is simultaneously valued for its avoidance of the artful or artificial and its resemblance to art. The juxtaposition of originals and copies in the representations of nature as well as the representations of the imagination creates a double landscape in which the lines between art and nature are increasingly blurred. The resemblance between works of art and works of nature makes it increasingly difficult to tell the difference between originals and copies.

The evolution of the English garden can be charted according to the changes in what Ronald Paulson has called "the ratio of art to nature."[21] In gardens such as Twickenham and Stowe, the newly declared taste for unadorned nature was displayed in a landscape that was not only appreciated for its spectacles and scenes but actually composed to resemble works of art. The so-called poetic or emblematic garden, emerging precisely as designers sought to make their landscapes more natural, inscribed *with* writing and *as* writing in both figurative and literal senses, was influenced by an iconographic tradition that allowed the garden to be composed (and subsequently read) as a series of emblems, hieroglyphs, and literary allusions. Gardens became complex texts that had to be deciphered.[22] Composed in a private and soon almost illegible language of emblems, influenced by newer principles of association derived from Hobbes and Locke,[23] they were criticized for being unnatural and for failing to provide an aesthetic experience.[24] In a famous passage in his *Observations on Modern Gardening* (1765), asserting that gardens should make an impression rather than appeal to the intellect, Thomas Whately complained that "natural cascades have been disfigured with river gods; and columns erected only to receive quotations. . . . All these devices are rather *emblematical* than expressive . . . they make no immediate impression; for they must be examined, compared, perhaps explained, before the whole design of them is well understood." Allusions should "have the force of a metaphor, free from the detail of an allegory."[25] This move from emblem to expression, from allegory to metaphor, continued to lay the groundwork for the picturesque. Like earlier evolutions and revolutions in landscape design, it took place under the sign of nature at the same time as its critique was figured as the substitution of one literary form for another.

Lancelot "Capability" Brown, who began as the head gardener at Stowe and became one of the first professional landscape designers, is credited with replacing contrived and ordered allusions with "more flexible patterns of association." Brown was praised for his ability to "copy nature"[26] and for being "a great painter";[27] yet if Brown's "Place-making" cleared the way for the picturesque, Price and Knight believed that it cleared away too much with extravagant engineering that literally uprooted the landscape and replaced nature with mass-produced forms and a new artificiality. The remarkably vitriolic debate between the improvers and the theoreticians of the picturesque also focused on the ratio of art to nature, centering on the status of painting and the adherence of the landscape designer to picturesque principles. Brown and Humphry Repton were accused of having betrayed nature because they renounced the principles of painting.[28] Knight declared that "the system" of Brown and his followers "is the very reverse of picturesque; all subjects for painting instantly disappearing as they advance."[29] He called upon Repton to "quit the school of Mr. Brown, and return to that of the great masters in landscape painting."[30] In his didactic poem "The Landscape," first published in 1794, Knight charged that the improvers (with their "charts, pedometers, and rules in hand") had destroyed "the forms of nature, and the works of taste."[31] They had reinstated artificiality and formality because they had abandoned both the forms of nature and the forms of art. Adherence to the principles of painting is the measure of faithfulness to nature.

Repton, who was derided for being a gardener like Brown,[32] boasts of having combined the "powers of the *landscape painter* and the *practical gardener*" in what he terms "*Landscape Gardening*," asserting that landscape design cannot be judged by the principles of painting alone. Like Reynolds describing Wilson, he declares that Knight "appears even to forget that a dwelling-house is . . . for the purposes of habitation; and not merely the frame to a landscape, or the foreground of a rural picture."[33] Evoking discredited gardening practices and pursuing the principles of "*picture gardening*" to their logical conclusion, Repton suggests that if "the painter's landscapes be indispensable to the perfection of gardening, it would surely be far better to paint it on canvas at the end of an avenue, as they do in Holland, than to sacrifice the health, cheerfulness, and comfort of a country residence, to the wild but pleasing scenery of a painter's imagination."[34] At stake is not just comfort but what it would mean to paint the landscape of nature. What seems threatening here is the idea that the scene of painting would have priority over the scene of nature. An actual painting placed in a garden only literalizes the idea that a representation would take the place of nature if landscape gardeners were to copy a natural landscape from the model of painting.[35]

To a great extent this debate centers on the relation between the terms "model" or "original" and "copy"—which is to say, it raises the question of what it means (to borrow Shaftesbury's ambiguous terms) to *represent nature*. Whately had warned in his *Observations on Modern Gardening* that the works of a great painter "are fine exhibitions of nature" that can teach "a taste for beauty; but still their authority is not absolute; they must be used only as studies, not as models; for a picture and a scene in nature, though they agree in many, yet differ in some particulars, which must always be taken into consideration, before we can decide upon the circumstances which may be transferred from the one to the other."[36] Price insists that there are "reasons for studying *copies* of nature, though the *original* is before us."[37] Yet once one enters the picturesque, it is not always easy to make a distinction between the original and the copy, even when the scene of painting is merely a study (and not a model) for the scene of nature. For Whately, gardening is "as superior to landskip painting, as a reality is to a representation."[38] However, one might ask what one is looking at when the original of nature is before one, especially when the real scene of nature is regarded as if it were a representation? What does one compose when one designs a landscape, since, as William Marshall noted in 1785, "Nature scarcely knows the thing mankind call a *landscape*"?[39] The improvers' counterattack on Price and Knight is based on common sense rather than a moral or philosophical argument; yet in challenging the priority of painting in the picturesque point of view, it draws upon an undercurrent of anxiety about aesthetic distance that runs throughout the literary history of gardening as well as the aesthetic of the picturesque.

I have suggested that from the outset the question of aesthetic distance informs the very concept of the picturesque. The construction of amphitheaters, the arrangement of trees to frame natural scenes like the wings of a stage, and the use of mirrors to fill the gallery of nature with tableaux were only literal manifestations of the point of view the beholder of the picturesque was supposed to internalize.[40] Pope's estate at Twickenham contained a famous grotto that incorporated mirrors in which water, light, and various images would be reflected. In 1747, a visitor offered this description: "Plates of Looking glass in the obscure Parts of the Roof and Sides of the Cave, where a sufficient Force of Light is wanting to discover the Deception, while the other Parts, the Rills, Fountains, Flints, Pebbles, &c. being duly illuminated, are so reflected by the various profited Mirrors, as, without exposing the Cause, every Object is multiplied."[41] According to Pope, the grotto was designed "to function as a *camera obscura* on the Walls of which all the objects of the River, Hills, Woods, and Boats, are forming a moving Picture in their visible Radiations."[42] Describing the "very extraordinary Effect" of the "profusion of Mirrors," in a rare moment in which a picturesque landscape is said to be beyond the skill of a master painter, Gilpin wrote: "The prospects without are likewise transferred to the Walls within: And the Sides of the Room are elegantly adorned with landskips, beyond the Pencil of *Titian*."[43]

This is not the sort of transfer between a picture and a scene of nature that Whately warned against. Yet if the transfer of these prospects is somehow more natural, if it could be said to represent nature, it is not clear whether the landscapes projected on the walls represent works of nature or works of art. The visitor explains how, surrounded by these images and reflections, "by a fine Taste and happy Management of Nature, you are presented with an undistinguishable Mixture of Realities and Imagery."[44] This indistinguishable mixture of aesthetic judgment and control of nature is a defining feature of the aesthetic of the picturesque—which not only compares image and reality, not only looks at nature through the frame of art, not only designs the original after the representation, but finally breaks down the distinction between one and the other. Pope may have acted the part of Prospero with machinery that "performs the same part in the Grotto that supernal Powers and incorporeal Beings act in the heroick Species of Poetry,"[45] but the end of his play of light and mirrors is not the renunciation of art. Entering the grotto in Pope's garden, one found oneself immersed, not only in what we might today call a virtual reality, but in the technology of representation that has created it. The landscape of the cave was simultaneously a picture and a camera obscura.

Addison offers a remarkable description of the transformation of a "dark room" into an accidental camera obscura in the same *Spectator* essay in which he asserts that "the Products of Nature rise in value, according as they more or less resemble those of art" and that "artificial Works receive a greater Advantage from their Resemblance of such as are natural." He writes: "The prettiest Landskip I ever saw, was one drawn on the Walls of a dark Room, which stood opposite on one side to a navigable River, and on the other to a Park. The Experiment is very common in Opticks. Here you discover the Waves and Fluctuations of the Water in strong and proper Colours, with the Picture of a Ship entering at one end, and sailing by Degrees through the whole Piece. On another there appeared the Green Shadows of Trees, waving to and fro with the Wind, and Herds of Deer among them in Miniature, leaping on the Wall." Addison ascribes its power to "its near Resemblance to Nature, as it does not only, like other Pictures, give Colour and Figure, but the Motion of the Things it represents."[46] He sees images and pictures projected in miniature upon the wall in light and color; it is as if he had discovered motion pictures. The images projected on the wall are not compared to "other pictures," as one might expect; instead, they are admired for their resemblance to nature itself. Addison does not appear to be interested in looking out the window or actually stepping into the landscape of nature. The prettiest landscape he has ever seen is this natural representation.

Even in the landscape of nature, however, picturesque travelers could introduce representation into the scene. Countless beholders literally framed their acts of looking with instruments such as the camera obscura and especially the Claude-glass. Described as "a plano-convex Mirror of about four inches diameter on a black foil, and bound up like a pocket-book," the Claude-glass was designed to "gather every scene reflected in it into a tiny picture."[47] It allowed one to convert the scene of nature into a miniature picture in a way that increased its resemblance to a Claudian landscape or at least to a painting. "My Convex Mirror," wrote a tourist at Lake Windermere, "brought every scene within the compass of a picture."[48] Thus, outside of the borders of the picturesque scenes contained in the garden and the estate, the traveler, tourist, or *promeneur solitaire* in search of natural beauty was not limited to those scenes that accidentally resembled a landscape by Claude Lorrain. Equipped with a mirror or oval glasses, the picturesque traveler could turn reality into representation; equipped with notebook and sketch pad, he or she could contemplate the natural through its reflection. It was through this mimesis that nature could be fully appreciated. This mediation was multiplied by the tendency to visit well-known picturesque landscapes with well-known descriptions of them in hand.[49]

Paradoxically, the ancient metaphor of art as a mirror that offered a direct reflection of reality is literally introduced into the landscape. In Pope's grotto, the mirror returns the beholder to Plato's cave, regarding a world of images and shadows at several removes. In the shape of a Claude-glass, the mirror inserts mimesis between art and reality, distorting the scene of nature with artistic license. The camera obscura, a prototype of photography meant to create a totally realistic representation of nature, is used as a mechanism that intermixes reality and images and finally turns the picturesque eye away from nature. In the frame of the picturesque, the Claude-glass becomes a mirror of art rather than a mirror of nature. Gilpin remarks that "nature has given us a better apparatus, for viewing objects in a picturesque light; than any, the optician can furnish," but he appears to be rather interested in the use of both colored glasses and the mirror of the Claude-glass, which he calls "the only picturesque glasses."[50] He describes the images of the landscape reflected in that mirror as having "a flatness something like the scenes of a playhouse, retiring behind each other." He also describes the experience of looking out the window of a chaise through a Claude-glass or convex mirror: "A succession of high-coloured pictures is continually gliding before the eye. They are like the visions of the imagination, or the brilliant landscapes of a dream. Forms and colours in brightest array fleet before us; and if the transient glance of a good composition happen to unite with them, we should give any price to fix, and appropriate the scene."[51] In the mind described by Locke and Hume, fleeting images are constantly gliding before the imagination, which is pictured in terms of images. Looking with a picturesque eye, the beholder internalizes the frame and mirror of the Claude-glass and transforms the fleeting images of the world into pictures of art.

As so often happens with eighteenth-century authors, epistemology and aesthetics become superimposed. What is crucial here is not optics or the props and machinery of the picturesque but rather what Gilpin calls "the picturesque eye," which Knight describes in another context as "modes and habits of viewing."[52] Gilpin declares that in viewing the picturesque, the "imagination becomes a camera obscura."[53] This process is not limited to the production of images in the imagination; it appears to take place even when viewing things as they really are in a present scene. In this sense, the imagination of the picturesque traveler or beholder becomes a Claude-glass, transforming the scene of nature with the framing perspective of art. The problem of turning objects as they really are into representations by regarding them through the mirror of the picturesque is, of course, compounded when the objects of nature themselves have been designed according to the rules of art—when the landscape before the eye is a vision of the imagination from the outset: the brilliant landscape of a dream of painting. Gilpin at one point suggests that "the more refined our taste grows from the *study of nature,* the more insipid are the *works of art,*"[54] yet the perspective of the picturesque, which depends on an "undistinguishable Mixture of Realities and Imagery," places the work of art in the scene of nature.

Repton insists on trying to separate what Addison calls "Works of *Nature* and *Art.*" In his *Observations on the Theory and Practice of Landscape Gardening,* in resisting the idea that the principles of landscape painting should govern the landscape designer, Repton denies that "art is to be the standard for nature's imitation." He continues: "neither does it disgrace painting, to assert that nature may be rendered more pleasing than the finest picture; since the perfection of painting seldom aims at exact or individual representations of nature." In the curious context of defending the sketches that illustrate his books—insisting that they should be judged not as paintings but rather as a "sort of panorama, or *fac-simile,* of the scenes they represent"—he boasts: "The art that I profess is of a higher nature than that of painting, and is thus very aptly described by a French author. '—il est, à la poèsie et à la peinture, ce que la realité est à la description, et l'original à la copie'" (—it is to poetry and to painting what reality is to description and what the original is to the copy).[55] In terms that are no less problematic for being familiar, Repton asserts the priority of reality over description, the original over the copy, nature over art—or at least his imitation of nature over a painter's imitation. The passage recalls Whately's assertion that gardening is "as superior to landskip painting, as a reality is to a representation."[56] Yet in speaking of his *art* as being of a higher *nature* than the art of painting, Repton's claims for a more natural art do not escape the problem of similitude, even if both his art and his facsimiles are supposed to transcend the representation of painting. In a proliferation of analogies and almost syllogistic similes in which the act of comparison at the center of the picturesque is itself at stake, Repton inserts a French quotation about description to "describe" his natural art, apparently unconcerned by any instability in his terms and concepts—or by the fact that the unnamed and unnoted French author he quotes is actually a proponent of the picturesque. Repton does not acknowledge that his quotation is taken from the preface to René Louis de Gérardin's *De la Composition des paysages*.[57]

Gérardin's preference for nature over copies is expressed in the context of his advocacy of what he calls *l'effet pittoresque* (picturesque effect) in garden design. The lines Repton quotes follow a suggestion that the invention of landscape design came about after centuries of representations of nature by painters and poets in order to "réaliser ces descriptions & ces tableaux, dont tout le monde avoit sans cesse le modèle sous les yeux" (to realize these descriptions and these tableaux, of which everyone constantly has the model under his eyes). Gérardin advocates the "art" of embellishing the countryside around one's home, which he defines as "de développer, de conserver, ou d'imiter la belle Nature" (developing, conserving, or imitating beautiful Nature). This art, he writes, "est à la Poèsie et à la Peinture, ce que la realité est à la description, & l'original à la copie" (is to poetry and painting what reality is to description and the original is to the copy); Gérardin, who constantly compares "le tableau sur le *terrein*" (the tableau on the ground) with "le tableau sur *la toile*" (the tableau on the canvas) insists that to design an estate one must hire a landscape painter. "Ce n'est donc ni en Architecte, ni en Jardinier, c'est en Poëte & en Peintre, qu'il faut composer des paysages" (It is thus neither as architect nor as gardener but rather as poet and as painter that one must compose landscapes), Gérardin writes. Insisting that the estate designer and the landscape painter must work from sketches and paintings as well as from the principles of composition, he argues against the objection that "commencer par faire un tableau, avant que le local soit arrangeé, ce seroit commencer par la copie avant l'original" (to begin by making a tableau before the area is arranged would be to begin with the copy before the original).[58]

The terms of these analogies and comparisons (and their implications for questions of reference and priority) are both confronted and complicated in Richard Payne Knight's avowedly painterly aesthetic. In a note added to the second edition of *The Landscape: A Didactic Poem*, Knight might seem in agreement with Repton's position when he suggests that the landscape gardener is capable of surpassing artistic imitations of nature. Knight asserts that "by carefully collecting and cherishing the accidental beauties of wild nature; by judiciously arranging them, and skillfully combining them with each other, and the embellishments of art; I cannot but think that the landscape gardener might produce complete and faultless compositions in nature, which would be as much superior to the imitations of them by art, as the acting of a Garrick or a Siddons is to the best representation of it in a portrait."⁵⁹ Like Addison, Knight imagines the landscape gardener as an artist creating compositions in nature, suggesting that the designer not only mixes nature and art but composes nature as if it were a work of art. Yet here the seemingly formulaic analogy that we see in Whately and Repton sets up a chain of terms that complicates the relationship of nature to art even further. It is possible for the landscape designer to use his art to create a flawless composition in nature that would be superior to any artistic imitation; but Knight asserts the potential superiority of the supposedly natural art of the landscape designer over the imitations of art not by invoking the superiority of reality to a representation or the superiority of the original to a copy; rather, introducing a startling new term, he compares its superiority to the superiority of *acting* over painting.

Knight does not claim that the landscape composition is to its imitation in art as a person—for example, the famed actors David Garrick and Sarah Siddons—is to the portrait of that person. It is "the acting of a Garrick or a Siddons" that is better than "the best representation of it in a portrait." In asserting the superiority of the natural, the point of his comparison is not even the superiority of theater's representation of a person over painting's representation of a person. Knight's ultimate praise here asserts that the artfully designed natural landscape (which, of course, is not the same as nature itself) is to an imitation of it what the acting of Garrick or Siddons is to a portrait of Garrick or Siddons acting. The referent is fixed in the realm of representation—and indeed since the actor interprets or embodies a text (Garrick playing Hamlet, for example, or Siddons playing Hermione) the referent is already at two removes. The composition in nature is as superior to an imitation as the actor's representation of a playwright's representation of a character is to a painting that represents an actor representing a playwright's representation of a character. There is a difference in degree, in the number of removes recoiling in the representation, but in Knight's schema both the work of nature and the work of art seem inextricable from the realm of imitation. Furthermore, as a picturesque composition, the work of nature presumably is designed according to the rules of painting to begin with, so the imitation of it in painting is an artistic imitation of a natural imitation of an artistic imitation of nature. Even the terms of the first half of the analogy radically undermine the poles that writers such as Repton wish to keep apart.

Knight's remarkable footnote continues to press the analogy still further through an apparent digression into literary criticism that underlines the significance of the scene of theater for the picturesque. Continuing the attack on Repton and the improvers made in both poem and notes, Knight declares: "The refined delicacy of that art, which conceals itself in its own effects, is above the reach of such critics; who, looking only for the artifice of imitation, are pleased in proportion as that artifice is glaring and ostentatious; in the same manner as Partridge approves the actor most who never conceals his skill in the easy expression of nature, but performs his part throughout with such stiff pomposity that *every one might see that he was an actor.*"[60] Alluding to the well-known scene in *Tom Jones* in which Partridge and Jones watch Garrick performing in a production of *Hamlet,* Knight accuses the improvers of preferring artifice to nature because they don't have the taste to understand or even recognize a more subtle use of art. Once again, theater is the key term in an analogy that seeks to calibrate the ratio of art to nature in the landscape; and after comparing an actor to a representation of the actor in a portrait, Knight extends his first analogy by offering his own portrait of the actor; he presents a portrait representing Garrick's acting as represented by Fielding through the frame of Partridge's perspective. At issue here is finally less a portrait of a Garrick or a Siddons than a portrait of Partridge. Knight's comparison of a good actor and a portrait of the actor acting shifts to a comparison of a good actor and a bad actor, which leads to a comparison of a good spectator with a bad spectator. This comparison takes place within a comparison of a good portrait of Partridge by Knight himself with a bad portrait of Partridge by "the best writer on art, as well as the best artist of the present age," Sir Joshua Reynolds.

Arguing that "this admirable scene in Fielding's most excellent novel has been misunderstood, and consequently misrepresented" by the great portrait painter Reynolds, Knight insists that Partridge does not (as Reynolds supposes) "mistake, for a moment, the play for reality: on the contrary, he repeatedly says, *that he knows it is but a play, and that there is nothing at all in it;* and as *imitation* was all that he looked for, the most glaring and obvious imitation of the most dignified and imposing personage, was, to him, the most undoubted test of excellence in acting." According to Knight, when Partridge sees Garrick as Hamlet display fear of the ghost "with such unaffected truth and simplicity, that all artifice of imitation disappears, his own feelings overpower his understanding, and he sympathizes involuntarily with what he sees expressed, though he knows that all the circumstances which excite it are fictitious." Against Reynolds's assumption that Partridge momentarily forgets that he is in a play, Knight insists that such involuntary sympathy "suspends, for the moment, the operation of every other faculty," causing Partridge to fear a "ghost he knows to be *only a man in a strange dress.*"[61]

Reynolds (in his thirteenth Discourse) faults Fielding for depicting Partridge "mistaking Garrick's representation of a scene in Hamlet, for reality" when "there is not one circumstance in the whole scene that is of the nature of deception." No one, Reynolds argues, especially an "ignorant man" such as Partridge, would mistake such a theatrical performance for reality. "[T]he best stage-representation appears even more unnatural to a person of such character, who is supposed never to have seen a play before," he insists.[62] Knight agrees, and points out that Fielding agrees as well. Knight maintains that Fielding represents a scene in which the spectator (who recognizes the "man in the strange dress" not as a ghost but rather as something "like" what he has seen in a "picture") himself becomes a portrait of the actor in the involuntary mirroring that takes place in the representations and enactments of sympathy—"the same passions which succeeded each other in Hamlet succeeding likewise in him."[63] In this sense, the actor's acting is not forgotten but, rather, multiplied. Partridge finds himself taking Hamlet's part in spite of an almost Brechtian awareness of theater and the mediation of the actor representing Hamlet's passions.

What is important in this context, however, is the analogy that places the improvers in the role of the spectator who is taken with artifice yet ignorant of the real powers of art. Using Fielding's "perfectly natural and exact picture of the effects" that can be exercised by "different kinds of imitative expression," Knight portrays those who "admire extravagantly every artifice of imitation, which is sufficiently gross for them to perceive and comprehend"; like Partridge, "when it is so refined as no longer to appear artifice, they entirely disregard it,"[64] unless it somehow takes them by surprise. Delineating this vulgarly theatrical yet paradoxically naïve point of view, Knight explicates his analogy to the scene of theater: "[I]n landscape gardening, as well as landscape painting, there are many such critics as Partridge is represented to have been in acting; and, in *their* estimation, the stiff and tawdry glare of a modern improved place will appear as much preferable to the easy elegance and unaffected variety of natural scenery, as the stately strut and turgid declamation of the mock monarch of the stage did in *his,* to the easy dignity of deportment and grace of utterance, which a good actor would have given to the same character."[65]

After asserting that a well-designed picturesque landscape is to an imitation of it in art what the performance of a good actor would be to the representation of that actor in a portrait, Knight uses Fielding's natural picture to compare good and bad portraits of a spectator that in effect represent portraits of good and bad acting. Tom Jones, who anticipates "entertainment in the criticisms of Partridge, from whom he expected the simple dictates of nature, unimproved, indeed, but likewise unadulterated, by art," asks him, "Which of the players he had liked best?"[66] In Knight's analogy, Partridge stands for the improver of nature who misunderstands both nature and art. Entering the novel's debate about good and bad acting, Knight asserts that a place transformed by improvers is to natural scenery what the artificial performance of a bad actor is to the unaffected performance of a good actor. Once again we see that the best landscape gardening is neither reality nor nature nor the original that is only copied by art but rather good theater; and good theater is acting that "conceals itself in its own effects." The picturesque designer embraces the principles of art and creates compositions in natural scenery; the art that the improver professes claims the status of reality, yet in disregarding art, it embraces artifice and affectation. The choice is not between art and nature but rather between good acting and bad acting. The concept of the natural has been absorbed into the aesthetics of the picturesque.

Knight's insertion of his debate with Reynolds into the debate with the improvers that he conducts in the notes to *The Landscape* is overdetermined as it evokes a scene about the murder of an authoritative father; he competes with the greatest portrait painter in representing a portrait of acting and stakes out an emblematic scene of theater in constructing his analogies about the relation between nature and art in the picturesque.[67] The thirteenth Discourse, however, also includes discussions of landscape painting and gardening and enters into the analogies that we have seen at play in discussions of the picturesque. Reynolds's general argument in the Discourse is that "Painting is not only not to be considered as an imitation, operating by deception, but that it is, and ought to be, in many points of view, and strictly speaking, no imitation at all of external nature." Exploring an "analogy" with "other Arts," he argues for a "general system of deviation from nature"[68] in theater, painting, and landscape gardening. Within these comparisons and analogies, he presents a series of arguments by comparison and analogy.

First, Reynolds states that painting should be "as far removed from the vulgar idea of imitation, as the refined civilized state in which we live, is removed from a gross state of nature";[69] second, in a paragraph about Nicolas Poussin, Sebastian Bourdon, and Claude Lorrain—seen as models for the picturesque sensibility—he claims that "a view of nature represented with all the truth of the *camera obscura*" would be inferior to "the same scene represented by a great Artist"; and finally, discussing landscape painting of the sort created by Claude, Titian, or Salvator Rosa, Reynolds asserts that "a landskip thus conducted, under the influence of a poetical mind, will have the same superiority over the more ordinary and common views, as Milton's *Allegro* and *Penseroso* have over a cold prosaick narration or description; and such a picture would make a more forcible impression on the mind than the real scenes, were they presented before us." It is at this point that he introduces the question of theater—which, he says, alluding to Hamlet's advice to the players, "is said *to hold the mirrour up to nature.*"[70]

A radical advocate of the priority of the principles of painting in landscape design, Knight might agree with Reynolds's Addisonian position that a landscape painting by Rosa or Claude is as superior to a common view, and even to the real scene of nature itself, as two poems by Milton (often associated with the picturesque) are superior to prose descriptions. Reynolds could be invoked here to argue against the more naïve comparisons and analogies in Repton's claims that his real landscape is as superior to painting and poetry as reality is to description and the original is to the model. In fact, Reynolds explodes the concept of the original and the model, arguing that "the true test of all the arts, is not solely whether the production is a true copy of nature." Throughout the *Discourses,* although he characterizes servile and "general copying as a delusive kind of industry," Reynolds argues that "a painter must not only be of necessity an imitator of the works of nature . . . he must be as necessarily an imitator of the works of other painters"; great works of art are "the means of teaching him the true art of seeing nature." In a declaration that would undermine the ground of Repton and the improvers, Reynolds writes, "*The art of seeing Nature,* or in other words, the art of using Models, is in reality the great object, the point to which all our studies are directed."[71] In this sense, introduced into the subtext of Knight's footnotes, Reynolds's thirteenth Discourse serves as an authority for Knight's polemic against the improvers. Although Reynolds's painterly aesthetic is developed in the context of the theoretical and pedagogical project of the *Discourses,* which aims to teach painters how to look at as well as make paintings, it offers Knight a model for his argument about the art of seeing nature and making compositions in nature according to the rules of painting. I suggest, however, that Reynolds goes too far for Knight in his discussion of gardening.

After discussing Partridge and the question of "unnaturalness in theatrical representations," Reynolds writes: "So also Gardening, as far as Gardening is an Art, or entitled to that appellation, is a deviation from nature; for if the true taste consists, as many hold, in banishing every appearance of Art, or any traces of the footsteps of man, it would then be no longer a Garden." Knight would agree that the spectator in the garden, like the spectator in the theater, does not forget the frame of art in looking at the garden, although the advocates of the picturesque do want a garden that doesn't look like a garden. Yet Reynolds goes on to raise a paradox that challenges the basic principles of the picturesque. Citing Pope's well-known line from the *Essay on Criticism,* he writes of the garden: "Even though we define it, 'Nature to advantage dress'd,' . . . it is however, when so dress'd, no longer a subject for the pencil of a Land-skip-Painter, as all Landskip-Painters know, who love to have recourse to Nature herself, and to dress her according to the principles of their own Art; which are far different from those of Gardening, even when conducted according to the most approved principles, and such as a Landskip-Painter himself would adopt in the disposition of his own grounds, for his own private satisfaction."[72] Although the designer (who might even be a painter himself) might design a garden according to the principles of painting, the result (clearly a garden and not nature itself) would not be a subject suitable for painting. In other words, designed according to picturesque principles, the picturesque landscape would no longer be (strictly speaking) picturesque. It might resemble or even be modeled after a scene that a painter wanted to paint, but insofar as it was a scene designed by picturesque principles, no painter would want to paint it.

In addition to his skepticism about the art of gardening and the principles of painting, Reynolds concludes his comparisons and analogies (and introduces his discussion of gardening) by proposing as a "general rule, that no Art can be engrafted with success on another art." He states that "each has its own peculiar modes both of imitating nature, and of deviating from it"; the deviations, he writes, "more especially, will not bear transplantation to another soil."[73] Such a position might threaten any version of the doctrine of the sister arts; but the implication that the art of painting could not be engrafted or transplanted into the soil of landscape design would be particularly threatening to the advocates of the picturesque—especially coming from the "best artist of the present age." Furthermore, Reynolds's explicitness about gardening as a deviation from nature, and his suggestion that even the most picturesque and painterly garden would not be a suitable model for painting, threaten to disrupt the loop that endlessly cycles between art and nature in picturesque aesthetics. What is at stake is not only skepticism about the possibility of transplanting the principles of landscape painting into the literal ground of the picturesque, but finally the difficulty of delineating a hybrid that seems to embody both nature and art, model and copy, reality and representation. In the picturesque scene, in the art of seeing nature according to the model of painting, the borders between nature and art are designed to be blurred.

The idea that art should be concealed was, of course, a commonplace in eighteenth-century landscape design, as it was in earlier aesthetic traditions. Theorists and practitioners such as Whately recognize gardening as one of the "imitative arts" yet warn that "the consciousness of an imitation, checks the train of thought which the appearance naturally suggests." (Whately also suggests that the "art of gardening aspires to more than imitation: it can create *original* characters, and give expressions to the several scenes superior to any they can receive from allusions.")[74] Joseph Spence, who directs the landscape designer to "follow Nature," writes that "Gardening is an imitation of 'Beautiful nature', and therefore should not be like works of Art. Wherever art appears, the gardener has failed in his execution."[75] Shenstone insists: "Art should never be allowed to set a foot in the province of nature, otherwise than clandestinely and by night."[76] Repton (who at times seems to disregard the "imitative" status of gardening) himself asserts that "in defining the shape of land or water, we take nature for our model; and the highest perfection of landscape gardening is, to imitate nature so judiciously, that the interference of art shall never be detected." It is one of the basic "requisites" of landscape gardening that it "studiously conceal every interference of art, however expensive, by which the scenery is improved; making the whole appear the production of nature only."[77]

In their attack on the alleged artificiality and theatricality of the improvers, Knight and Price follow these conventional formulas. Knight advocates "art clandestine, and conceal'd design" in *The Landscape.*[78] Price insists that "wherever there is any thing of natural wildness and intricacy in the scene, the improver should conceal himself like a judicious author, who sets his reader's imagination at work, while he seems not to be guiding." He should be like Homer, who, Price notes, following Aristotle, "scarcely ever appears in his own person."[79] In a note to the first edition of the *Essay on the Picturesque* in 1794 that he deleted from the revised *Essays,* Price contrasts Homer's refusal to appear *in propria persona* with Fielding's tendency to appear "sometimes ostentatiously"—which is said to be "a striking defect."[80] "There are indeed certain words in all languages," writes Price in his conclusion to his *Essays,* "that have a good and a bad sense: such as *simplicity* and *simple, art* and *artful,* which as often express our contempt as our admiration." Even Brown and Repton would have agreed with Price that "art" when "used in a good sense" implies "contrivance that is not obvious" and "with regard to improving" is "employed in collecting from the infinite varieties of *accident* (which is commonly called *nature,* in opposition to what is called *art*) such circumstances as may happily be introduced, according to the *real* capabilities of the place to be improved."[81] Yet the literary history of gardening and picturesque aesthetics involves such ambivalence about both nature and art—such contempt as well as admiration—that formulas about the concealment of art cannot be dismissed as mere convention.

Furthermore, Reynolds's comments about landscape gardening point to another paradox. Insofar as the picturesque depends on the *recognition* of art, the recognition of the resemblance between a scene and a work of art that either has or might have been composed by an artist, the idea that the art of the design should be invisible becomes complicated. One might wish for a natural landscape that accidentally looked as though a painter had composed it, but in Knight's terms, the ideal would be good theater as opposed to bad theater, not the absence of theater. Knight's positions in particular raise this problem, since his most important contribution to the theory of the picturesque is his application of associationism. Far from the post-Lockean theories of the proponents of the emblematic garden's obelisks and inscriptions, Knight uses associationism to argue a more radical epistemology of the picturesque that is mostly directed against his ally Price. In his *Analytical Inquiry into the Principles of Taste,* Knight declares:

> The sensual pleasure arising from viewing objects and compositions, which we call picturesque, may be felt equally by all mankind in proportion to the correctness and sensibility of their organs of sight; for it is wholly independent of their being picturesque, or *after the manner of painters.* But this very relation to painting, expressed by the word *picturesque,* is that, which affords the whole pleasure derived from association; which can, therefore, only be felt by persons, who have correspondent ideas to associate; that is, by persons in a certain degree conversant with that art.

Focusing on those who are "in the habit of viewing, and receiving pleasure from fine pictures," who will "naturally feel pleasure in viewing those objects in nature, which have called forth those powers of imitation," Knight declares: "The objects recall to the mind the imitations, which skill, taste, and genius have produced; and these again recall to the mind the objects themselves, and show them through an improved medium—that of the feeling and discernment of a great artist."[82]

Here again we have a Claude-glass of the imagination: objects in nature remind us of paintings, and we view the objects before our eyes through the medium of an absent representation, through the eyes of the painter who might have beheld them. What is crucial here is Knight's insistence that objects themselves do not possess picturesque properties independent of the associations of the beholder: "All these extra pleasures are from the minds of spectators; whose pre-existing trains of ideas are revived, refreshed, and reassociated by new, but correspondent impressions on the organs of sense; and the great fundamental error, which prevails throughout the otherwise able and elegant *Essays on the Picturesque,* is seeking for distinctions in external objects, which only exist in the modes and habits of viewing and considering them."[83] In insisting that the picturesque does not come from "the necessary and inherent qualities of the objects,"[84] Knight is to some extent returning to Gilpin's emphasis on the picturesque eye. However, whereas Gilpin spoke of gardens that are "a very good Epitome of the World" in that they are "calculated for Minds of every Stamp, and give free Scope to Inclinations of every kind,"[85] Knight's theory is by definition elitist. Only "a mind richly stored"[86] will be able to appreciate the picturesque; indeed, Knight might suggest further that to the beholder who is not equipped with the necessary associations, the picturesque will be virtually invisible: "To all others, however acute soever may be their discernment, or how exquisite soever their sensibility, it is utterly imperceptible."[87] When witnessed by the "eye of the uninformed observer, the sublime spectacle of the heavens presents nothing but a blue vault bespangled with twinkling fires," Knight insists. "Show either picturesque, classical, romantic or pastoral scenery to a person, whose mind, how well soever organized, is wholly unprovided with correspondent ideas, and it will no otherwise affect him than as beautiful tints, forms, or varieties of light and shadow would, if seen in objects, which had nothing of either of these characters."[88]

The perspective of the "eye of the uninformed observer," to whom the picturesque, however pleasing or moving, might be "utterly imperceptible," returns us to the central example of Partridge. Eighteenth-century writers interested in the experience of theater are especially drawn to the figure of the naïve spectator—the provincial or foreigner brought to the playhouse for the first time who can't understand why the people on stage are speaking and behaving so unnaturally, or the beholder who believes the illusion of theater and mistakes the play for reality. A figure of particular interest for many writers is the more sophisticated spectator who in the transports of art momentarily forgets that he or she is in a theater and tries (in Diderot's words) to "ajouter un personnage réel à la scène" (add a real character to the scene).[89] Evelina, in Fanny Burney's 1778 novel, describes herself watching Garrick perform and reports, "I almost wished to have jumped on the stage and joined them."[90] Knight's portrait of Partridge, however, might lead us to question the difference between those "minds just cultivated enough to have their judgments perverted, without having their feelings destroyed," and "the minds of spectators" that are storehouses of skill, taste, and genius. Like the sophisticated spectator, Partridge is aware that he is watching a play; Knight insists that even when he shares Hamlet's passions in the involuntary transports of sympathy, he doesn't lose what Whately calls "the consciousness of an imitation." It is this double consciousness—and not the forgetting of theater—that Knight wants from art.

Partridge's parodic portrait of the spectator also raises the more subversive question of what the difference is between his (or Repton's) point of view and Knight's picturesque perspective. Like the improver, in Knight's portrait, Partridge prefers glaring and ostentatious artifice to the concealed and natural art represented by Garrick; he prefers imitation that is recognizable as imitation. Yet Partridge's vulgar admiration of the actor whose ostentatiousness and affectation ensures that "Anybody may see he is an actor"[91] in some ways resembles (or, however comically, differs from only by degree) Knight's more subtle and refined admiration of the picturesque landscape garden. However much it rejects artificiality, the picturesque depends on the recognition of art and imitation. According to Knight, the improvers "admire extravagantly every artifice of imitation, which is sufficiently gross for them to perceive and comprehend"; like Partridge, "when it is so refined as no longer to appear artifice, they entirely disregard it."[92] Yet in Knight's view, the most subtle beholder also disregards the landscape that cannot be seen through the frame of art—that is invisible without the associations and "reassociations" of painting. Although its art is supposed to be clandestine and concealed, the landscape is valued in proportion to its status as an imitation of imitations. In Knight's associationism, the picturesque landscape does not exist except insofar as the beholder perceives its relation to painting in a relay of resemblances in which the "objects recall to the mind the imitations . . . and these again recall to the mind the objects themselves, and show them through an improved medium— that of the feeling and discernment of a great artist."[93]

Partridge parodically embodies this sort of mediation: insofar as Knight's portrait of a good actor and a bad actor is really a portrait of a good spectator and a bad spectator, it focuses on Partridge beholding Garrick's performance of Hamlet's reaction to the spectacle of the ghost. As Knight insists, Partridge's response is not fear of the ghost, which he insists is "only a man in a strange dress," but rather sympathy with the man who sees the ghost. In Fielding's description, "he sat with his eyes fixed partly on the ghost and partly on Hamlet . . . the same passions which succeeded each other in Hamlet succeeding likewise in him."[94] Like Partridge, the beholder of the picturesque identifies with another beholder, experiences someone else's point of view, mediates his perception of the landscape through a double perspective that is divided between a sight and someone else's view of it.

Earlier forms of associationism in landscape design were abandoned because they relied on increasingly private and inaccessible codes. Appealing to emotions, moods, and more general acts of imagination, later forms were more inclusive; depending on correspondent ideas, they look forward to the writings of the romantics. Yet in the context of the picturesque, Knight's theories raise the possibility of the end of the picturesque. If the picturesque exists only in the mind of the designer or beholder and not in the properties of objects themselves, it is possible that the picturesque might become too invisible. Depending on an act of recognition, the picturesque takes place in the vertiginous space of a comparison that associates a composition in nature with a composition in art in an unending relay of representations, imitations, and reflections. Knight complained that the improvers "disregarded" art when it was concealed and not ostentatious; but insofar as the picturesque depends on an act of looking that resonates between the absent and the present, between works of art and nature, it is possible that the place between concealment and ostentatiousness might become increasingly difficult to design.

Ironically, perhaps, the fate of the picturesque was to become too recognizable. Depending on a sense of déjà vu, the picturesque became recognizable as a style in itself, so that a picturesque landscape—even one accidentally created in and by nature—did not resemble a painting as much as it resembled a picturesque landscape. Once recognized, the picturesque garden, like the earlier poetic garden, risks becoming a stage set. Eighteenth-century garden design is famous for its excesses: the artificial ruins, temples, and even hermitages inhabited by hired hermits in costumes—or, if necessary, "stuffed dummies that gave the right emblematic effect at twenty yards."[95] The picturesque garden may have aimed to be less theatrical, but it aimed no less to be theater. Like the garden designs and theories that preceded it, then, it also was fated to feel artificial the more its art was recognized and consequently revealed. In a sense, however, it was both the contribution and the curse of the picturesque to inscribe the place of nature in the realm of art. It is precisely in the uncanny wavering between art and artifice, between reality and representation, that the aesthetics of the picturesque take place. By hiding or erasing the boundaries between nature and art, by insisting that those boundaries were never very clear to begin with, the picturesque eye foregrounds our ambivalent investment in aesthetic experience.

2 The Impossible Work of Art

Kames, Pope, Lessing

One thinks that one is tracing the outline of the thing's nature over and over again, and one is merely tracing round the frame through which we look at it.
Ludwig Wittgenstein, *Philosophical Investigations*

Words, when well chosen, have so great a Force in them, that a Description often gives us more lively Ideas than the Sight of Things themselves. The Reader finds a Scene drawn in Stronger Colours, and painted more to the Life in his Imagination, by the help of Words, than by an actual Survey of the Scene which they describe.
Joseph Addison, *The Spectator,* No. 416 (June 27, 1712)

In his *Philosophical Enquiry into the Origin of Our Ideas of the Sublime and Beautiful,* Edmund Burke argues that the effect of words "does not arise by forming pictures of the several things they would represent in the imagination." Insisting that "on a very diligent examination of my own mind, and getting others to consider theirs, I do not find that once in twenty times any such picture is formed," Burke asserts: "Indeed, so little does poetry depend for its effect on the power of raising sensible images, that I am convinced it would lose a very considerable part of its energy, if this were the necessary result of all description."[1] As Burke's appeal to empiricism suggests, however, it was not at all uncommon in 1757 (the year the *Enquiry* was published) to assume that words, especially words in literary texts, could represent and even present pictures. Nine years later, in 1766, when Lessing set out to delineate the effects of painting and poetry in his *Laocoön: An Essay on the Limits of Painting and Poetry,* he announced his intention to counteract the "false taste" and "unfounded judgements" that had converted Simonides' assertion that paintings were silent poems and poems were speaking pictures into a set of rules for artists and critics.[2] Like Burke, Lessing insisted that when reading texts (a poem by Arisoto, for example), "I see nothing, and I am annoyed by the futility of my best efforts to see something" (108).

Both Lessing and Burke sought to refute different aspects of the tradition known as *ut pictura poesis*—those famous words that were taken out of context from Horace's *Art of Poetry* to stand for the belief that poetry and painting were or should be alike.[3] *Ut pictura poesis* overlapped with several related traditions, most importantly the tradition of viewing literature and painting as "sister arts."[4] The Renaissance search for "parallels" between the visual and verbal arts and its elevation of painting to the ranks of the liberal arts were given new energy in the eighteenth century by the Enlightenment desire to discover universal principles and by the popularity, diffusion, and reproduction of paintings through prints and engravings. Concepts of vivid illusion (such as *enargeia*) taken from prescriptions of classical rhetoric and poetics that orators should speak with such vivid images that their listeners would see the objects they described were reinvigorated by an epistemology that repeatedly described perception and imagination in terms of fictions, images, pictures, and paintings.[5] Literary descriptions inspired by *ut pictura poesis* set out to rival paintings, following in the traditions of ekphrastic poetry (in which poems attempted to give voice to a work of graphic art)[6] and Renaissance *paragoni,* or contests between the arts. When the abbé Jean-Baptiste Du Bos chose the words "Ut Pictura Poesis" as the epigraph for his influential *Réflexions critiques sur la poésie et sur la peinture,* published in 1719, he summarized and prefigured much eighteenth-century writing about art.[7] By 1746, in *Les Beaux Arts réduits à un même principe,* the abbé Charles Batteux could suggest that after having written a chapter on poetry, he hardly needed to write a chapter on painting. It would be almost enough, he wrote, for the reader to re-read his first chapter, substituting the word "painting" wherever the word "poetry" appeared.[8]

Eventually, arguments that denied the power of description to produce images and downplayed analogies between poetry and painting—as well as a weariness with descriptive poetry—would lead to the demise of the *ut pictura poesis* tradition. If Lessing won the day, however, at least until the modernist experiments of the twentieth century,[9] this does not mean that we should merely dismiss the claims of Du Bos or others as misguided. Nor is it finally adequate to explain descriptions or prescriptions about the representation of pictures by words by locating them in the context of the *ut pictura poesis* and ekphrastic traditions. Eighteenth-century accounts of the effects of literature and the experience of reading often strike twentieth-century readers as excessive, hyperbolic, or simply wrong. Yet efforts to explain and thereby dismiss such accounts by invoking traditions, conventions, or experience ignore the question of why critics and readers made such extravagant claims about the experience of literature. Arguments about the pictorial properties and powers of literary texts need to be understood in the context of eighteenth-century descriptions of the effects of the work of art. We need to take such descriptions seriously, not to ask whether Burke or Lessing or their contemporaries really saw pictures while reading texts but rather to consider the investment of both the advocates and the detractors of *ut pictura poesis* in the claim—indeed, the demand—that texts transport readers by representing images and tableaux.[10] What is at stake is finally the power of description in criticism as well as in literature: the power of language to describe the experience of art itself.

In 1762, about midway between the publication of Burke's *Enquiry* and Lessing's *Laocoön,* Henry Home, Lord Kames, published his *Elements of Criticism,* which contains an articulation of the eighteenth-century principles of *ut pictura poesis.* Although especially interesting, this book is less original than representative of the critical conventions and commonplaces of its time. In sections organized around such topics as "Emotions and Passions" rather than literature and painting, Kames focuses not on the parallels between the arts but rather on the power of words to act like paintings. In a section titled "Emotions Caused by Fiction," Kames insists that "the power of language to raise emotions, depends entirely" on the production of "lively and distinct images."[11] In "Narration and Description," he writes: "In narration as well as in description, objects ought to be painted so accurately as to form in the mind of the reader distinct and lively images. . . . The narrative in an epic poem ought to rival a picture in the liveliness and accuracy of its representations" (2: 232).

Kames follows the influential prescriptions of Du Bos, who asserts that the writer must "place the objects of which he speaks before our eyes through paintings" (mettre sous nos yeux par des peintures, les objects dont il nous parle). According to Du Bos, the representations of the poet should contain "images that form tableaux in our imagination" (des images qui forment des tableaux dans notre imagination); "it is necessary that the style of poetry be filled with figures that paint the objects described in verse so well that we cannot hear them without having our imagination continually filled with tableaux that follow there one after another" (il faut que . . . le stile de la Poësie soit rempli de figures qui peignent si bien les objets décrits dans le vers, que nous ne puissions les entendre, sans que notre imagination soit continuellement remplie des tableaux qui s'y succedent les uns aux autres). Du Bos declares:

"We must believe that we see, so to speak, in listening to verse: *Ut Pictura Poesis,* says Horace" (Il faut donc que nous croïions voir, pour ainsi dire, en écoutant des Vers: *Ut Pictura Poesis,* dit Horace).[12]

Like Du Bos, Kames begins with metaphors that prejudge the question (it is the *painting* of objects in the mind that forms images, and images that form tableaux), but his descriptions push the limits of figurative language. For Kames, "Writers of genius, sensible that the eye is the best avenue to the heart, represent every thing as passing in our sight; and, from readers or hearers, transform us as it were into spectators" (2: 248). The textual representation, in picturing things as if we saw them, in acting like a visual representation, transforms us into spectators, as it were. "A lively and accurate description . . . raises in me ideas no less distinct than if I had been originally an eye-witness: I am insensibly transformed into a spectator; and have an impression that every incident is passing in my presence" (1: 86). Not only is the reader *like* a spectator, with ideas and impressions that can be compared to those of an eyewitness; as Kames portrays him, the reader *is* a spectator, so strong is his sense of sight.

"The force of language," Kames writes, "consists in raising complete images; which have the effect to transport the reader as by magic into the very place of the important action, and to convert him as it were into a spectator, beholding every thing that passes" (2: 232). If the reader seems to be transported by magic and is converted into a spectator, this is because language has raised images. The transformation of the text into a spectacle transports the reader and transforms him into a spectator. The word *transport* (a key term in eighteenth-century aesthetics associated with the sublime) suggests the force of this experience. In his treatise on the sublime, Longinus (in Leonard Welsted's English translation) speaks of an "extraordinary Transport of Mind" through which "we seem to view the things we speak of, and . . . place them in their full light, before those who hear us."[13] Kames seems to borrow more directly from Roger de Piles, who writes that both poetry and painting "are intended to deceive; and if we do but give attention to them, they will transport us, as it were, magically, out of one country into another."[14] He seems to be describing a transport of body and not just of mind. If Kames focuses less on the vertigo or ecstasy of the sublime, he insists on the "power" and "force" of the transport of readers who appear to be carried away by images. He describes a reader who seems to find himself placed before the objects depicted in the text by a force that must be described as magic. In order for the text to become a spectacle, its images must transport the reader in a supernatural or a religious sense; these images compel his belief, literally *converting* him to a spectator.

Kames's description reads as a secular or aesthetic version of the conversion that St. Augustine experiences while reading a book. Augustine's famous account of his conversion in book 8 of the *Confessions* would have remained compelling in the eighteenth century not just for its resonance in the tradition of spiritual autobiography but also for its account of a particularly powerful experience of reading.[15] Reading here makes the reader someone—or at least somewhere—else. After this conversion (or at least for its time and space), the reader, "forgetting himself," according to Kames, is "thrown into a kind of reverie" in which he is described as "forgetting that he is reading" (1: 87). In an earlier version of this passage, the man in "reverie" is said to be "losing sight of himself"; in the reverie brought about by language, he loses "the consciousness of self, and of reading, his present occupation."[16] Losing himself, the reader finds himself in the time and place of the spectacle that the text has become: transported in both mystical and physical senses by the transformations effected by the text's conversion into a spectacle. In other words, the power of language seems to have effaced reading and the text as the reader beholds everything that passes. Kames describes this experience as *ideal presence*.

Kames introduces his concept of ideal presence in a description of the power of memory in "Emotions Caused by Fiction" (1: 83). It is his first example of what he calls a "fiction of the imagination."[17] Wanting to distinguish presence *in idea* from "real presence," he describes the sense of presence that is the ideal consequence of the power of language. Kames depicts an act of memory that is stronger than a "slight recollection" in which "the thing is not figured as in our view, nor any image formed." Here, where the mind "is not satisfied with a cursory review," he says, "I am imperceptibly converted into a spectator, and perceive every particular passing in my presence, as when I was in reality a spectator. For example, I saw yesterday a beautiful woman in tears for the loss of an only child, and was greatly moved with her distress: not satisfied with a slight recollection or bare remembrance, I ponder upon the melancholy scene: conceiving myself to be in the place where I was an eye-witness, every circumstance appears to me as at first: I think I see the woman in tears, and hear her moans" (1: 84). In a conscious recollection that recalls the *Spiritual Exercises of St. Ignatius* in its act of imagination (especially if we see in the image of the woman a Madonna figure), Kames rejects a cursory review, insisting on a review that really would mean viewing again—complete with a perception of presence: a sense of contemporaneousness with someone with whom he seems to stand face to face.[18]

Recalling a woman he beheld, Kames performs an act of memory, presented to us as if it were happening before our eyes. Insisting on the woman's tears and cries, Kames conceives himself in the place again, at the scene, as we imagine the spectacle to which he seems an eyewitness. Not coincidentally, a scene of loss, mourning, and absence is translated into an aesthetic experience for the beholder of the "beautiful woman," collapsing the distance of time and space between a present and past event. "Hence it may be justly said," Kames writes, "that in a complete idea of memory there is no past or future: a thing recalled to the mind with the accuracy I have been describing is perceived as in our view, and consequently as existing at present" (1: 84). In this conception, absence seems to disappear as all sense of the past disappears; according to Kames's description, the sense of sight returned to this act of recalling (and retelling) seems to result in *presence*—both in time and space.[19] It is at this point that Kames proceeds to describe how reading can effect this transport to another realm of presence and the present—a transport to ideal presence that is also termed "*a waking dream*" (1: 85).[20]

Kames notes that man is "so remarkably addicted to truth and reality, one should little dream that fiction can have any effect upon him." Yet basing his argument on "the power of fiction to generate passion" (1: 83), he presents a waking dream of fiction—a dream that fiction could have an effect, a dream that fiction could act upon us like reality and satisfy our addiction to the truth. Everything appears to us "as passing in our sight" when we are "first . . . lulled into a dream of reality" (2: 356); but what in reality *is* before our eyes when we experience ideal presence? Kames accompanies his descriptions of the power of fictions of the imagination with qualifications and acknowledgements that perception in ideal presence is more "faint and obscure"[21] than in real presence. What is remarkable, however, is the extent to which he seems to insist upon the sense of sight, transport, and presence that he describes. Reviewing a memory of a tree and a river, Kames asks how he recalls these objects to mind: "Do I endeavour to form in my mind a picture of them or a representative image?" he asks. "Not so," he responds. "I transport myself ideally to the place where I saw the tree and river yesterday: upon which I have a perception of these objects similar in all respects to the perception I had when I viewed them with my eyes, only less distinct. And in this recollection, I am not conscious of a picture or representative image, more than in the original survey; the perception is of the tree and river themselves, as at first" (2: 360). Once again, a memory moves from a picture to a presence, from a perception that is like a perception of things to a perception of things themselves, from a fiction to a reality.

This description of memory appears in the context of Kames's disagreement with metaphysical theories of phantasms or simulacra that threaten to "annihilate totally the material world" (2: 361n). This context suggests the significance of the revival of theories of *ut pictura poesis* at a time when writers such as Berkeley and Hume, following Descartes, Hobbes, and Locke, developed theories of perception that gave new, complex, and even technical meanings to terms such as "mental vision," "imagination," "representation," and, especially, "images." Memory and the ability to combine and change remembered images and thereby create new images are both examples of what Hobbes calls a "fiction of the Mind."[22] Berkeley, who also speaks of "fictions of the mind," writes of "ideas imprinted on the senses by the Author of Nature" (called "real things") and those less vivid ideas "excited in the imagination" called "'ideas' or 'images of things' which they copy and represent."[23] What is most relevant in this context is the idea that we know and perceive the world around us through images in the mind.[24] Both epistemological and aesthetic discussions of perception and imagination in the eighteenth century commonly make the distinction that the images generated by the imagination are more faint and obscure—less vivid and lively—than the things we actually perceive when they are present to us. Yet despite these disclaimers, eighteenth-century advocates of *ut pictura poesis, enargeia,* and description repeatedly stress the vividness of fictions of the mind.

Addison's distinction in the *Spectator* between primary and secondary pleasures of the imagination is surprisingly unhierarchical. Following Locke, who writes of "secondary perception" in discussing the retention of ideas ("the Power to revive again in our Minds those *Ideas* which after imprinting, have disappeared, or have been as it were laid out of Sight"),[25] Addison writes about "Primary Pleasures of the Imagination, which entirely proceed from such Objects as are before our Eyes" and "Secondary Pleasures of the Imagination which flow from the Ideas of visible Objects, when the Objects are not actually before the Eye, but are called up into our Memories, or form'd into agreeable Visions of Things that are either Absent or Fictitious."[26] Addison is interested in the pleasures of the imagination that come from "visible Objects, either when we have them actually in our view, or when we call up their Ideas into our Minds by Paintings, Statues, Descriptions" but his descriptions of these experiences are located somewhere between primary and secondary pleasures precisely because he is interested in images.

Although Addison follows conventional formulations in asserting that "*Description* runs yet further from the things it represents than Painting; for a Picture bears a real Resemblance to its Original, which Letters and Syllables are wholly void of," in describing the power of language, he elevates the status of the images that can be produced by words: "Words, when well chosen, have so great a Force in them, that a Description often gives us more lively Ideas than the Sight of Things themselves. The Reader finds a Scene drawn in Stronger Colours, and painted more to the Life in his Imagination, by the help of Words, than by an actual Survey of the Scene which they describe." Taking the conventional terms "strength," "vividness," and "liveliness," Addison seems to reverse the conventional comparison of images produced by objects and images re-presented in the mind: "In this Case the Poet seems to get the better of Nature; he takes, indeed, the Landskip after her, but gives it more vigourous Touches, heightens its Beauty, and so enlivens the whole Piece, that the Images which flow from the Objects themselves appear weak and faint, in Comparison of those that come from the Expressions."[27] In Addison's view, the painting of a real thing on the imagination might not be as forceful as the images painted in the colors of art. Comparing two types of representations, copies, or paintings, he ascribes greater force to those in the poet's descriptions.

In his 1748 *Enquiry Concerning Human Understanding,* Hume warns that a "blind and powerful instinct of nature" leads us to "always suppose the very images, presented by the senses, to be the external objects, and never entertain any suspicion, that the one are nothing but representations of the other."[28] However, he might be arguing against Addison's essays when he differentiates between the images of perception and those of imagination: "These faculties may mimic or copy the perceptions of the senses; but they never can entirely reach the force and vivacity of the original sentiment. The utmost we say of them, even when they operate with greatest vigour, is, that they represent their object in so lively a manner, that we could *almost* say we feel or see it." Hume insists, however, that "except the mind be disordered by disease or madness, they never can arrive at such a pitch of vivacity, as to render these perceptions altogether undistinguishable. All the colours of poetry, however splendid, can never paint natural objects in such a manner as to make the description be taken for a real landskip. The most lively thought is still inferior to the dullest sensation."[29] It is as if Hume were trying to reclaim a set of epistemological principles from an aesthetic tradition that has carried the power of images too far. Although he is associated with those accused of reducing the real world to images, he resists the conflation of the fictions of art with the perceptions and even the fictions of the mind.

Dedicated to exploring our fictions of the world, Hume is a skeptic when it comes to the world of fiction. He concedes the power of imagination: "Nothing is more free than the imagination of man . . . in all the varieties of fiction and vision. It can feign a train of events, with all the appearance of reality, ascribe to them a particular time and place, conceive them as existent, and paint them out to itself with every circumstance, that belongs to any historical fact, which it believes with the greatest certainty." However, when he asks what the difference is "between such a fiction and belief," despite the similarity on some level of the images and representations produced in the mind by perception and imagination, Hume insists on the differences in the power of these images: "[B]elief is nothing but a more vivid, lively, forcible, firm, steady conception of an object, than what the imagination alone is ever able to attain. This variety of terms, which may seem so unphilosophical, is intended only to express that act of mind, which renders realities, or what is taken for such, more present to us than fictions." For Hume, the imagination "may conceive fictitious objects with all the circumstances of place and time. It may set them, in a manner, before our eyes, in their true colours, just as they might have existed. But as it is impossible that this faculty of imagination can ever, of itself, reach belief, it is evident that belief consists not in the peculiar nature or order of ideas, but in the *manner* of their conception, and in their *feeling* to the mind." It is belief that "distinguishes the ideas of the judgement from the fictions of the imagination."[30]

For a believer in the power of language such as Addison, who thinks that a description could present "more lively Ideas than the Sight of Things themselves," it is possible to imagine believing in fiction. Advocates of the eighteenth-century versions of *ut pictura poesis,* partially founding their theories on a view of the world determined by post-Lockean epistemology, focused on what Hume describes as the "utmost" power of the imagination to "mimic or copy the perception of the senses": "they represent their object in so lively a manner, that we could *almost* say we feel or see it." Transformed by what one might call the *ut pictura poesis* effect, belief is no longer "a more vivid, lively, forcible, firm, steady conception of an object, than what the imagination alone is ever able to attain."[31] Kames, in particular, is invested in the space of the *almost* that Hume evokes. Whereas Hume wants to establish the difference between our belief in fiction and our belief in realities, Kames is interested in an act of mind that blurs the distinctions between them. He situates the chapter in which he articulates his version of *ut pictura poesis* in relation to the terms and categories of eighteenth-century epistemology with the announcement that he will consider "fictions of the imagination";[32] yet allying himself with

Addison rather than Hume, Kames insists that fictions of the mind or imagination can be as lively and vivid as the presence of things themselves, not more faint and obscure.[33]

For Hume, "The thinking on any object readily transports the mind to what is contiguous; but it is only the actual presence of an object, that transports it with a superior vivacity"[34]; for Kames, as we have seen, images "transport the reader as by magic into the very place of the important action" and "convert him as it were into a spectator"; a "lively and accurate description" can create a fiction of the imagination that "raises in me ideas no less distinct than if I had been originally an eye-witness: I am insensibly transformed into a spectator; and have an impression that every incident is passing in my presence" (2: 232; 1: 86). Fictions of the imagination, working through images presented to the mind, can compel belief by seeming to present (rather than represent) things themselves to the reader turned spectator. Rejecting skepticism, Kames seems to believe in the world of fiction as much as he believes in the fiction of the world. I am focusing here on the devoutness with which Kames believes in the materiality of the world of fiction in his conversion from reader to spectator because I want to underline the "unphilosophical" terms to which he is drawn, both what he says and what he *almost* says about the *utmost* power of the imagination. What is remarkable is the *extravagance* of his claims.

Kames rationally admits that objects presented by fictions of the imagination are not identical to objects actually present in his sight, but he frequently acts as if they were or could be—almost saying as much, even literally saying as much, at least for a moment. His transfer of the conditions of sight and presence to the experience of reading finally describes precisely what books are *not*. Kames denies the material conditions of the book—which, after all, literally presents to one's eyes only print on the page. What does it mean, then, to say that texts can produce or reproduce images, views, tableaux, and even objects? Du Bos displays a strong sense of the formal and material conditions of the book, referring to "la peine de lire" (the trouble of reading) and the "travail pour nos yeux" (work for our eyes) since we must read "comme on dit, l'oeil sur le papier" (as we say, with eyes on the paper).[35] How could a book present sight and transport one to its presence and present, how could it grant one the sense and tense of presence, when its very conditions dictate that its events (like its author) are sealed off from one's view, removed in time and place? To say that Kames or Du Bos writes in the tradition of *ut pictura poesis* explains very little.

Obviously, one should not be too literal-minded in reading Kames or take his demands and assertions about reading at face value. Throughout *Elements of Criticism,* in describing the experience of reading, Kames repeatedly says "as," "as if," and "as it were"; just as Du Bos, throughout his *Réflexions critiques,* repeatedly says "pour ainsi dire" (so to speak). In raising the flag of *ut pictura poesis,* Du Bos, as we have seen, declares, "Il faut que nous croïions voir, pour ainsi dire, en écoutant des Vers" (We must believe that we see, so to speak, in listening to verse).[36] Kames typically insists that the reader must be "converted, as it were, into a spectator" (1: 184). However, despite these markers of figurative language, despite occasional acknowledgements that (rationally) they couldn't really mean what they say, Kames and Du Bos frequently act as if they do mean what they say. In their descriptions, readers often seem to become spectators who really see spectacles and even "things themselves." Ideal presence comes to feel like real presence.

In his long chapters on comparisons and figures, Kames speaks of a simile being "converted into a metaphor" when we abandon the "like" that indicates the "resemblance" of a hero to a lion and instead "feign or figure the hero to be a lion" (1: 195). Paradoxically, the phrases that mark the similes in Kames's claims stop his similes from becoming metaphors and instead cling to the literal sense of his expressions. In reading Kames's and Du Bos's descriptions of the power of language, one senses that they make their claims literally, as it were, not figuratively. Du Bos, who uses phrases like "métaphoriquement parlant" (metaphorically speaking), in addition to "pour ainsi dire" (so to speak), at one point concedes: "Je parle peut-être mal, quand je dis que la peinture employe des signes; c'est la nature elle-même que la peinture met sous nos yeux" (I perhaps speak badly when I say that painting employs signs; it is nature itself that painting places before our eyes).[37] Yet if speaking of painting as using signs is to speak badly or incorrectly, how does one speak when one asserts that painting doesn't use signs at all but instead presents nature itself? The problem here is not Du Bos's distinction between natural and artificial signs; it is rather the sort of speech one must use in order to say that painting presents nature itself or that the words in a text present things themselves before the eyes of the reader. The recurrence of expressions like "pour ainsi dire," "so to speak," "as if," and "as it were" in these descriptions of the power of language serve to locate rather than dismiss the problem of how Du Bos and Kames mean what they say.

One says "so to speak" in order to speak. "So to speak" signals that one doesn't really mean what one is saying but has no other way to say what one means. Even if one's statement doesn't quite make sense, even if one doesn't quite mean the sense that it makes, one says it that way just so that one will be able to speak. In other words, "so to speak" signals the limits of language. Kames finds himself faced with a failure of language when he tries to describe ideal presence and the power of fiction. He writes:

> Lamentable is the imperfection of language, almost in every particular that falls not under external sense. I am talking of a matter exceedingly clear in the perception: and yet I find no small difficulty to express it clearly in words; for it is not accurate to talk of incidents long past as passing in our sight, nor of hearing at present what we really heard yesterday, or at a more distant time. And yet the want of proper words to describe ideal presence, and to distinguish it from real presence, makes this inaccuracy unavoidable. When I recall any thing to my mind in a manner so distinct so as to form an idea or image of it as present, I have not words to describe that act, but that I perceive the thing as a spectator, and as existing in my presence; which means not that I am really a spectator, but only that I conceive my-self to be a spectator, and have a perception of the object similar to what a real spectator hath. (1: 85)

Kames identifies his problem as the imperfection or inaccuracy of language; he cannot express his sense clearly in words. Yet he also describes his problem as a lack of words: "I have not words to describe this act"; more specifically, he laments "the want of proper words to describe ideal presence." "Proper" in this phrase means more than appropriate. Kames is referring to a lack of words whose proper meaning or *sens propre* could describe ideal presence. When he writes earlier that "ideal presence may properly be termed *a waking dream;* be-cause, like a dream, it vanisheth the moment we reflect upon our present situ-ation" (1: 85), he really means that it may *figuratively* be termed a dream: it is *like* a dream. As Kames tries to describe description, he wants words whose lit-eral sense will say what he means; so he must turn to figurative language—or frame his literal statements with words like "as if" and "like": the signals of po-etic language. These words allow him to describe by framing his statements with invisible quotation marks, as it were; they set off his descriptions from the rest of the text like the border around a picture. Yet led by his lack of proper words into unavoidable inaccuracies, which he must then try to frame with the verbal gestures of figurative language, Kames himself seems to have trouble telling how the figures in these pictures are to be separated from the supposedly literal statements that form a background.

In the passage in which Hume compares fiction and belief, resorting to "unphilosophical" terms to explain why "it is impossible that this faculty of imagination can ever, of itself, reach belief," he begins with an acknowledgement that "a *definition* of this sentiment" would be a "difficult, if not an impossible task" and goes on to suggest that it "may not, however, be improper to attempt a *description* of this sentiment; in hopes we may, by that means, arrive at some analogies, which may afford a more perfect explication of it." Hume warns that he can approach his perhaps impossible subject only through description and analogy, whether or not his words are proper or improper, philosophical or unphilosophical. Yet even after this warning, he is forced to make a confession about the failure of his language: "I confess, that it is impossible perfectly to explain this feeling or manner of conception. We may make use of words which express something near it. But its true and proper name, as we observed before, is *belief;* which is a term that every one sufficiently understands in common life." It is here that he asserts that "in philosophy, we can go no farther than assert, that *belief* is something felt by the mind, which distinguishes the ideas of the judgement from the fictions of the imagination."[38] Kames feels compelled to make a similar confession, but this is because he wants to believe in the fictions of his imagination and the power of words to describe. He wants to believe that the language of description and analogy—words that say what something is *like*—could attain the power of the true and proper names that appear to be near objects themselves.

Kames prefaces his *Elements of Criticism* by stating that "the design of the present undertaking . . . is to examine the sensitive branch of human nature, to trace the objects" (1: xxi) that affect us. Rather than composing a treatise on the fine arts, he says, he wants only "to exhibit their fundamental principles" (1: xxvi). Later, in speaking of his "design" to "delineate" (1: 41) the relations between emotions and passions, he proposes to "take a survey of human nature, and to set before the eye, plainly and candidly, facts as they really exist" (1: 42). He offers an example as an "illustration" (1: 85) of an idea. In introducing an example from the *Iliad* in which "we may observe how the writer" presents things to the reader "as a spectator," he instructs: "Witness the following passage" (1: 91). He speaks of an "insight" that "unfolds" a "mystery" (1: 87). However, as Kames designs, delineates, traces, examines, surveys, unfolds, and places before the eye so his readers can observe, witness, and gain insight—as he tries to describe the visual powers and effects of description—he must come to terms with his own language.

At the end of his first volume, in depicting what he pejoratively calls "the language of description," Kames worries: "Looking back upon what is said, I am in some apprehension of not being perfectly understood; for it is not easy to avoid obscurity in handling a matter so complicated; but I promise to set it in the clearest light" (1: 357). The obscurity, however, does not lie in the subject itself. "I have been only describing what passeth in the mind of everyone," Kames writes; yet, he continues, "however clear in the internal conception, it is far from being so when described in words" (1: 88). It is as if description itself stands in the way of description. Kames wants to present before the eyes of his readers facts as they really exist: in describing what he expects from description, he wants to enact the very act of description he dreams of. But he realizes that he must *enter* description to describe it; and consequently, he can't describe what description *is;* he can only describe what description is *like.* Description lacks proper words.

What is at stake is the power of language to describe: the possibility that language might form, shape, trace, mark, represent, portray, or imagine pictures, speak to the sense of sight. When Kames laments "the want of proper words to describe ideal presence," he is not only worrying about the figurative character of his descriptions; he also wants the literal sense that they make. Kames wants the sense of sight in reading because this is precisely what he lacks—or rather what a book lacks. "Ideal presence," he writes earlier, "supplies the want of real presence" (1: 87). Kames wants language to efface itself and present the object of its representation, as if the object were really there; he wants the veil to fall from the eyes of the reader. He notes that "a thing ill described is like an object seen at a distance, or through a mist; we doubt whether it be a reality or a fiction" (1: 93). In Kames's terms, however, this description of what description is like must describe "good" description as well as "bad" description. All description must render things at a distance or through a mist; description is itself the distance or the mist that it resembles, and its reality must always be its fiction. Placed at a remove in a book that figures mediation and absence, description can render a thing or experience only *as it were,* not as it is. This is what description is like: it places readers at two removes, with a dream of transport, sight, reality, and presence both promised and denied.

Like Du Bos, Kames writes with the force of a desire that would embrace the meaning of what he says; yet in speaking the desire that language be powerful, he must face the imperfection of words and what he calls "the poverty of language" (2: 364–65). Kames may believe that language "has not arrived at greater perfection than to express clear ideas" and he warns that "ambiguity in the signification of words is a great obstruction to accuracy of conception"; but the poverty of language is his condition. This is the realm of *ut pictura poesis,* which must itself enter into simile simply by stating that poetry is "like" or "as" painting. This is the moment that tells us that we have crossed the border into figurative language: transported through the transfer of sense enacted by comparison. Kames is forced to enter this territory and to acknowledge his transport of sense in trying to describe the impossible work of description and its impossible power of representation.

Arguments about the parallels between the arts are established in part by translations that move between the literal and the poetic as well as between the languages of painting and literature. Dryden's "Parallel Between Painting and Poetry," the introduction to his influential 1695 translation of Charles-Alphonse Dufresnoy's *De arte graphica,* or *The Art of Painting,* draws attention to the status of the work as a "*Prose Translation* of the *Poem,*" yet Dryden worries not about his knowledge of Latin but rather whether he is "sufficiently versed in the *Terms of Art,*" asserting that if the translation is "not free from Poetical Expressions," some of which are "at least highly metaphorical," this is a "fault" in the original. Using formulations such as "To make a Sketch, or a more perfect Model of a Picture, is in the language of Poets, to draw up the Scenery of a Play" and "*Expression,* and all that belongs to Words, is that in a *Poem,* which *Colouring* is in a *Picture,*" Dryden notes that he has not "Leisure to run through the whole Comparison of Light and Shadows, with Tropes and Figures"—but part of the enterprise of establishing parallels depends on the language of comparison and the ability to use tropes and figures in translating between the terms and languages of the arts.[39]

Pope's "Observations on the Shield of *Achilles,*" the brief essay that accompanies his translation of book 18 of the *Iliad,* also confronts the necessity of translation between the literal and the figurative as well as between languages and mediums in its defense of Homer's "Genius for Description."[40] Taking up an emblematic example for eighteenth-century debates about *ut pictura poesis,* Pope sets out to refute the charges that the shield as described by Homer represents an impossible work of art. Stating that he will "attempt what has not yet been done, to consider it as a Work of *painting,* and prove it in all respects conformable to the most just Ideas and establish'd Rules of that Art," Pope advances an argument about both the design of the poem and the design of the shield. He asserts that the famous passage in book 18 is an ekphrastic tour de force in which Homer, "intending to shew in its full Lustre, his Genius for Description," demonstrates his powers. Yet he also argues that the description of the shield should be taken as a realistic description of a painting that is it-self a tour de force: "His intention was no less, than to draw the Picture of the whole World in the Compass of this Shield." Pope ultimately concedes that the description of the shield could be considered "as a complete *Idea of Paint-ing,* and a Sketch for what one may call an *universal Picture*" (363), and that a genius might have "design'd to give a Scheme of what might be perform'd, than a Description of what really was so" (364); but his defense of the descrip-tion of the shield is based on the supposition—indeed the "ocular Demon-stration" (362)—that the description realistically represents a plausible and imaginable work of art.

Pope's defense of Homer's description and his design to consider it as a work of painting against the objections of critics "that 'tis impossible to repre-sent the Movement of the Figures" (358) on the shield must begin by address-ing translations and transports of literal and figurative reading. The represen-tation seems impossible, he argues, only if one takes the description too literally. "'Tis certain that *Homer* speaks of the Figures on this Buckler, as if they were alive; And some of the Ancients taking his Expressions to the Strict-ness of the Letter, did really believe that they had all sorts of motion." Pope notes that Eustathius goes to the extreme of imagining detached figures that "'mov'd by Springs, in such a manner that they appear'd to have Motion'" but he suggests that Eustathius himself solves the false dilemma by emphasizing that Homer, "'to shew that his Figures are not animated, as some have pre-tended by an excessive Affection for the Prodigious, took care to say that they *moved and fought, as if they were living Men*'" (359). If we recognize the simile in Homer's description, suggests Pope, and don't take his words too literally, we can recognize a work of art that might actually be designed.

This objection is followed by the complaint that Homer "describes two Towns on his Shield which *speak different Languages.*" Pope responds that the problem here is "the *Latin* Translation" and the Greek word in question indi-cates only that they had "*an articulate voice*" and that the towns would have spoken "the same Language." This explanation does not solve the problem of speech or translation, however. To the objection that Homer says "that *we hear the Harangues of two Pleaders,*" Pope reminds us that "he only says, *Two Men pleaded,* that is, were represented pleading"—just as Pliny said that Nico-machus "painted two *Greeks,* which spake one after another." At the center of Pope's defense of Homer's description is the question of the speech of painting and our ability to translate between the language of painting and the language of description. The determination of the possibility or impossibility of

Homer's representation—both the representation supposedly on the shield and the representation of that representation—turns on our ability to speak of painting, to represent verbally a visual representation.

> Can we express ourselves otherwise of these two Arts, which tho' they are mute, yet have a Language? Or in explaining a Painting of *Raphael* or *Poussin,* can we prevent animating the Figures, in making them speak conformably to the Design of the Painter? But how could the Engraver represent those young Shepherds and Virgins that dance first in a ring, and then in Setts? Or those Troops which were in Ambuscade? This would be difficult indeed if the Workman had not the Liberty to make his Persons appear in different Circumstances. All the Objections against the young Man who sings at the same time that he plays on the Harp, the Bull that roars whilst he is devoured by a Lion, and against the musical Consorts, are childish; for we can never speak of Painting if we banish those Expressions.

If we are to speak of painting, if we are to give speech to its mute language through the translation of description, we must make use of figures of speech that animate the figures of painting. Pliny even said that Apelles "painted those things which could not be painted, as Thunder." Such common expressions, according to Pope, excuse Homer's descriptions of the shield.

What is striking is that Pope's defense rejects the idea that only a god could make the shield Homer describes and minimizes the argument that the shield is only an ideal work of art. After insisting that Homer's description should not be taken too literally, Pope goes on to demonstrate through words and illustrations how the shield of Achilles that Homer represents could really be executed and reproduced. The overcharged example of the shield represents more than another skirmish in the battle to defend Homer's reputation as a great artist; it raises the question of the impossible meeting of verbal and visual representation. Despite Pope's assertion that "there is a great deal of difference between the Work itself, and the Description of it," to consider the shield as "a work of *Painting*" is to consider the extent to which the description itself acts like a painting. Throughout his preface Pope speaks of Homer's images, pictures, and paintings and (as Jean Hagstrum points out) his translation indulges in the mode of *ut pictura poesis* more than the original. Thinking about the description of the shield, Pope must address the language of description and the possibility of translating the mute language of painting into the figurative expressions of speech. He wants to insist that the painting on the shield is not an impossible work of art, but he acknowledges that to speak of painting, one might have to describe it painting things that cannot be painted.

This is also the predicament that Lessing finds himself in when describing the shield of Achilles in the *Laocoön* in his famous attack on attempts to represent Homer's representation of the shield and (in general) the advocates of *ut pictura poesis*. Despite his claim in the preface that the chapters "were written as chance dictated" and "as unordered notes for a book" (5), Lessing's placement of his pivotal discussion of book 18 of the *Iliad* in chapter 18 of his treatise suggests the strategic importance of this example in his battle to "counteract" the "false taste" and "unfounded judgments" (5) of his time. As a crucial moment in an argument that aims to separate the arts, this description of a visual representation that appears in verse is also a highly charged and complex example.

In chapter 16, after arguing that "bodies with their visible properties are the true subjects of painting" and "actions are the true subjects of poetry," Lessing notes that "Homer represents nothing but progressive actions" (78–79). In chapter 17, he refers to the "Homeric device for transforming what is coexistent" in "depictions of physical objects" into "what is really consecutive" (89). Finally, in chapter 18, Lessing explains in detail what caused Homer "to be considered by the ancients a master of painting [*ein Lehrer der Malerei*]" (94/133). He writes: "Homer does not paint the shield as finished and complete, but as a shield that is being made. Thus, here too he has made use of that admirable artistic device: transforming what is coexistent in his subject into what is consecutive, and thereby making the living picture of an action out of the tedious painting of an object. We do not see the shield, but the divine master as he is making it" (95). This method is contrasted with Virgil's description of the shield of Aeneas in which, according to Lessing, "the action comes to a standstill." In a critique that can be read as an attack on eighteenth-century descriptive poetry, Lessing writes: "By its eternal 'here is' and 'there is,' 'close by stands' and 'not far off we see,' the description becomes so cold and tedious that all the poetic beauty which a Virgil could give it was required to keep it from becoming intolerable" (96).

Insofar as Lessing is offering advice to authors who might succumb to the contemporary "mania for description" (5), this lesson from the masterpiece of the master teacher of painters makes sense; but as a description of what happens in book 18 of the *Iliad,* Lessing's account is inaccurate, or at best incomplete. Insisting that we see the process of making the shield rather than the shield itself, Lessing refrains from his usual method of quotation and instead describes the actions of Hephaestus at some length in his own words: "He steps up to the anvil with hammer and tongs, and after he has forged the

plates out of the rough, the pictures which he destines for the shield's orna-
mentation rise before our eyes out of the bronze, one after the other, beneath
the finer blows of his hammer. We do not lose sight of him until all is finished.
Now the shield is complete, and we marvel at the work. But it is the believing
wonder of the eyewitness who has seen it forged" (95). Homer does give some
fifteen or sixteen lines describing Hephaestus at work as he fires the bellows
and prepares bronze, tin, and gold on his anvil. However, after we read how
"with all his craft and cunning / the god creates a world of gorgeous immortal
work," the actual descriptions of the scenes depicted begin and continue for
about 150 lines, punctuated by only a few interruptions of "he forged" to remind us that the description applies to a shield that is in the process of being
made.[41] The action doesn't stand still in the famous lines that actually represent the shield, but we do lose sight for the most part of the maker, the process
of creation, and indeed even the object being made. If the reader is transformed into an eyewitness by the description, it is an eyewitness to the events
represented, not to the artist's work.

What is remarkable about the descriptions of the shield of Achilles is that
Homer transforms "what is coexistent in his subject into what is consecutive"
not by keeping Hephaestus and his work before our eyes but rather by drama-
tizing a series of scenes, embedding extended narratives within the depiction
of the various images. In the depiction of the decorations on the shield, we see
pictured a wedding feast, a market scene, a trial, battle preparations, fighting,
fields, vineyards, plowing, harvesting, banquets, dancing—all with sequence,
action, histories, plot, characters, and events that are described unfolding over
time. In the first tableaux, for example:

> And he forged on the shield two noble cities filled
> with mortal men. With weddings and wedding feasts in one
> and under glowing torches they brought forth the brides
> from the women's chambers, marching through the streets
> while choir on choir the wedding song rose high
> and the young men came dancing, whirling round in rings
> and among them the flutes and harps kept up their stirring call—
> women rushed to the doors and each stood moved with wonder.
> And the people massed, streaming into the marketplace
> where a quarrel had broken out and two men struggled
> over the blood-price for a kinsman just murdered.
> One declaimed in public, vowing payment in full—
> the other spurned him, he would not take a thing—

so both men pressed for a judge to cut the knot.
The crowd cheered on both, they took both sides,
but heralds held them back as the city elders sat . . .
and each leapt to his feet to please the case in turn. (18.572–90)

In other words, these verses leave Hephaestus and his anvil behind to represent visual representations that appear to be everything that pictures can't be, and, according to Lessing, everything that the visual arts shouldn't try to be.

This, of course, is part of the point that Lessing is trying to make. Deriding readers who sought to explain how all of these scenes could be represented on one shield and artists who tried to create an exact replica of the shield Homer describes, he argues that an artist depicting the public lawsuit, for example, would have to choose "one single moment" to represent. "Obviously," Lessing writes, "not everything Homer says can be combined into a single picture; the accusation and denial, the presentation of witnesses and the shouts of the divided crowd, the attempts of the heralds to still the tumult, and the decision of the judges are events which follow one another and cannot exist side by side at the same time." The poet, he explains, simply has made use of the "peculiar advantages" of his medium: "The liberty to extend his description over that which preceded and that which followed the single moment represented in the work of art; and the power of showing not only what the artist shows, but also that which the artist must leave to the imagination." Only by seizing upon these advantages can the poet "raise himself to equality with the artist" (99–100).

In arguing that poetry and painting should each respect the borders of its own province, Lessing suggests that neither should be constrained by the limits of the other: "the poet, even when he speaks of works of art, is not compelled to confine his description within the limits of art." Lessing makes this comment, which he claims is a "further example of the observation" that he has made about the shield of Achilles, after discussing a poem by Anacreon that instructs an artist how to paint the picture of his mistress. Lessing makes the point that Anacreon, in figuratively demanding that "the artist make all the graces hover around her soft chin, her marble neck," is "demanding an impossibility of the painter," who can't "literally" accomplish what "is impossible to do in painting" (113–14). If, however, in delineating the boundaries separating the arts, Lessing suggests the ways in which painting and poetry can mutually taunt each other, as it were, with what the other is powerless to do, with what is possible in one art but impossible in the other, he is no more interested in staging a *paragone* in which the (allegedly) sister arts vie for superiority than he is in separating poetry and painting into separate but equal spheres. Lessing's example of the shield, like the example of Anacreon, is striking precisely because his account does not depict two parallel (or not so parallel) alternatives for describing an event or person, one appropriate for poetry and one appropriate for the visual arts. Lessing focuses not on two representations of an event or scene from "nature" but rather on a verbal representation of a visual representation, a work of art in which a poet is allegedly copying scenes from the visual arts. The poet in this case has not confined his description of a work of art within the limits of that art. Homer has represented what amounts to an impossible work of art.

I am suggesting that the shield of Achilles is an overdetermined example for *Laocoön* because it goes beyond a lesson about two alternative modes of representation in a *paragone* in which each art will win only if it uses the powers and liberties that belong to it alone. Lessing places before our eyes a representation of a representation that on one level violates all the rules that he is outlining. He asks us to imagine an impossible transgression of the borders that he is surveying in his book as he draws our attention to static pictures on a two-dimensional surface in the process of becoming narratives that dramatize characters in time and space. When we read this description of a scene pictured on a shield—

> Detached from the ranks, two scouts took up their posts,
> the eyes of the army waiting to spot a convoy,
> the enemy's flocks and crook-horned cattle coming . . .
> Come they did, quickly, two shepherds behind them,
> playing their hearts out on their pipes—treachery
> never crossed their minds. But the soldiers saw them,
> rushed them, cut off at a stroke the herds of oxen
> and sleek sheep-flocks glistening silver-gray
> and killed the herdsmen too. Now the besiegers,
> soon as they heard the uproar burst from the cattle
> as they debated, hurdled in council, mounted at once
> behind their racing teams, rode hard to the rescue,
> arrived at once, and lining up for assault
> both the armies battled it out along the river banks—
> they raked each other with hurtling bronze-tipped spears.
> And Strife and Havoc plunged in the fight, and violent Death—
> now seizing a man alive with fresh wounds, now one unhurt,
> now hauling a dead man through the slaughter by the heels,

the cloak on her back stained red with human blood.
So they clashed and fought like living, breathing men
grappling with each other's corpses, dragging off the dead. (18.608–28)

—we are no longer in the realm that Lessing has carefully circumscribed for the visual arts. As he tries to separate the realms, techniques, and effects available to verbal and visual representation, Lessing draws our attention to a vivid fantasy of pictures that seem cinematic rather than photographic. Homer is shown to have made not a *tableau vivant* but a "living picture [*lebendige Gemälde*] of an action out of the tedious painting of an object" (95/134). If pictures seem to come alive, it is not, for example, because they represent skies so realistic that birds try to fly into them, but rather because they deny stasis and assume the powers and liberties of story. Like Kames, Lessing asks his reader to imagine an exceptionally vivid work of art. Whereas Kames dreams of an impossible text that will act like painting, presenting tableaux before the eyes of readers who feel transported to the presence and present of the scenes described, Lessing directs his reader's attention to pictures that—at least in the time and space of Homer's fiction—break all the rules and act like texts. Homer may observe the limits of poetry and avoid the temptation to compose his representation like a painting, but he represents a painting that acts like a narrative.[42]

I have no stake in whether Lessing is right or whether his general argument is ultimately persuasive; my point is that his central example does not work in the way that he initially suggests. Homer's account of Achilles' shield at the least illustrates Lessing's argument in a more complicated and complicating way than Lessing at first suggests: it demonstrates how poetry depicts events unfolding over time *not* by showing the creation of the shield but rather by entering unreservedly into narratives that multiply at a dizzying rate. Lessing does not acknowledge just how radical and ultimately problematic his example is. He argues that poetry can achieve the power and effects of the visual arts only by translating the visual into its own terms through an example that shows the visual arts acting like epic poetry—and in doing so, I suggest, he displays his own ambivalent investment in the powerful image of an impossible work of art that does not respect the borders or limitations of its own medium. Lessing's alternate title for *Laocoön* is *Über die Grenzen der Malerei und Poesie* (*On the Limits of Painting and Poetry*), and his book is about borders, boundaries, frontiers, edges, limits, extremities, thresholds. Indeed, despite his intention to separate the realms of poetry and painting, Lessing is drawn to examples that confuse them. He seems compelled, as it were, to imagine representations that confront the limits of their art, no matter how cannily they observe the laws of their medium.

Lessing's use of the example of Anacreon "demanding an impossibility of the painter" by asking him to paint his mistress and "make all the graces hover around her soft chin, her marble neck" (113) evokes the ekphrastic tradition, yet it cites a poet who calls upon a painter to paint an impossible painting by assigning him, as it were, a line of poetry that he could never execute literally, by asking him to depict what lies "beyond his powers" (über seine Kräfte) (113/158).[43] Lessing cites the example of Anacreon in the preceding chapter as well, but here he is interested in the device of the poet instructing the painter because the poet senses "the inadequacy of verbal expression" (die Unfähigkeit des wörtlichen Ausdrucks). He remarks that at the end of the poem the poet "sees not her picture [*das Bild*] but herself and believes that she is about to open her mouth to speak," although the lines he quotes ("Stop now—for I see her: / soon, image of wax, you will even begin to speak")[44] suggest that the final apostrophe addresses the work of art and not the woman depicted, like Pygmalion beholding his statue before it is turned into the living Galatea. Indeed, Lessing suggests that Anacreon composes his song more as "a hymn of praise to art than to his mistress," just as the poem instructing the painter to depict the boy Bathyllus is "so interwoven with the praise of art and the artist that it becomes doubtful in whose honor Anacreon really composed the song." Both passages imagine an impossible space in which poetry and painting seem to join forces, not so much to represent a beautiful object of desire as to confront the limits and possibilities of their respective powers.

The second example, in which Anacreon borrows "parts of various pictures [*Gemälden*]" to represent Bathyllus, reminds Lessing of Lucian, who, he argues, refers to statues in describing the beauty of Panthea in "an admission that language in itself is powerless [*ohne Kraft*] here; that poetry falters and eloquence grows mute unless art [*Kunst*] serves as an interpreter in some degree" (109–10/154–55). Lessing's acknowledgement that the painter's task is finally impossible makes it clear that he is not suggesting the inferiority of poetry to painting. If language and poetry need art to be an interpreter, painting, too, is presented with a task of translation that threatens to mute its silent eloquence. Just as the painter can't take the poet's instructions literally in Anacreon's ode, in Lucian's *Essays in Portraiture,* the painters that Lycinus invokes to contribute fragments and aspects to an imaginary representation of Panthea must incorporate and translate Homer's similes: "But stay! We have Homer, the best of all painters, even in the presence of Euphranor and Apelles. Let her be throughout of a colour like that which Homer gave to the thighs of Menelaus when he likened them to ivory tinged with crimson; and let him also paint the eyes and make her 'ox-eyed.'"[45] The artists who would follow these instructions in representing Panthea, joining with as much as imitating Homer, are not asked to paint the statue either ivory and crimson or the color of Menelaus's thighs when the "the fresh blood went staining down"—which is the referent of Homer's simile. Panthea should be colored like the color that Menelaus's wound is likened to in Homer's simile. Furthermore, the simile instructs the reader, "Picture a woman dyeing ivory blood red" in a picture that frames the woman as an artist.[46]

Essays in Portraiture Defended, the dialogue of Lucian's that follows his *Essays in Portraiture,* suggests how overdetermined Lessing's example is in the context of these translations between both literal and figurative and painting and poetry. Panthea's modest protests that she does "not recognize the likeness" of the composite and manifold pictures that Lycinus and Polystratus imagine elicits a defense of comparisons and similes. Polystratus indicts his interlocutor by insisting that "to liken a female human being to Aphrodite and to Hera, what else is it but downright cheapening of the goddesses? In such matters the less is not made greater by the comparison"; and he illustrates his point with a simile about comparisons. Describing a tall and a short person walking together, he asserts: "[I]f they are to look alike in size, the latter will stoop and make himself appear shorter. Just so in such comparisons."[47] Lycinus defends himself with a discussion of Homer's "use of comparisons and similes" and with the argument that he compared Panthea not with goddesses but with the likenesses of them represented in works of art, "with masterpieces of good craftsmen, made of stone or bronze or ivory."[48] The composite representation of Panthea imitating aspects of works of art and comparing her to the likenesses of paintings and statues is, of course, impossible. Not only is this statue almost impossible to imagine, it is meant to be "gifted with speech" (in another Homeric description) and to represent Panthea's soul.[49] What is a stake here, however, is an impossibly powerful work of art.

In one sense, Panthea is a representation from the outset. In response to Polystratus's request to "sketch her appearance in words as best as you can," Lycinus declares: "It is not in the power of words, not mine, to call into being a portrait so marvelous," comparing her to "the Gorgon" and insisting that "if you get but a distant view of her she will strike you dumb."[50] Yet Polystratus eventually identifies the beautiful woman Lycinus saw reading a scroll as the emperor's mistress—and more specifically as someone whom Lycinus has encountered in his own reading, in Xenophon's description. Lycinus notes: "[I]t makes me feel as if I saw her when I reach that place in my reading; I can almost hear her say what she is described as saying, and see how she armed her husband and what she was like when she sent him off to battle."[51] Whereas Hume would later evoke such terms to demarcate the limits of representations—"The utmost we say of them, even when they operate with greatest vigour, is, that they represent their object in so lively a manner, that we could *almost* say we feel or see it"—the *almost* here indicates a Kamesian belief in the power of art. Like the poet who exclaims at the end of Anacreon's poem about representing his mistress, "Stop now—for I see her: / soon, image of wax, you will even begin to speak," Lycinus claims a powerful experience of reading in which description seems to convey sight and sound, even if the power of his words seems inadequate to his task of description. Yet Panthea "herself" seems lost in the dizzying accumulation of representations, descriptions, similes, comparisons, paintings, and statues that are called upon to picture her.

Bathyllus, too, seems caught in what we might anachronistically call a loop of representations. After being described, like Panthea, as a composite of works of art, Bathyllus is posed, at the end of Anacreon's ode, as himself the model for the painter: "taking down that Apollo / make this Bathyllus. / And if you ever come to Samos / paint Phoebus from my Bathyllus").[52] Although Bathyllus can be represented only in copies of various works of art, the reader is left with a picture of him as the model for a work of art, in the reverse of the terms of the comparisons to gods that trouble Polystratus in Lucian's dialogue. Lessing's references to Lucian's *Essays in Portraiture* and Anacreon's poems introduce into *Laocoön* a vertiginous play of comparisons and imitations in which representations reflect and reflect back on representations; the borders between model and copy are blurred in the translations that move between image and reality as well as between poetry and painting. Painting may be called in to interpret when poetry falters and eloquence grows mute, but what is at stake for Lessing is the experience of a composite work of art in which painting and poetry reflect back on each other in a play of comparisons that can't really be described. "Can we express ourselves otherwise of these two Arts, which tho' they are mute, yet have a Language," asked Pope, "for we can never speak of Painting if we banish those Expressions." The failure of language here—the necessity of similes, comparisons, and hyperboles—may have less to do with the limits of poetry or painting than with the difficulty of expressing the power of representation in words, and the problem of describing hybrid works of art that transgress the limits of painting and poetry not to imitate each other but to call attention to their impossible joining.

Lessing's examples, and the examples to which they allude, are about desire. Lucian begins his dialogue with a sexual joke about Lycinus being "struck stiff" and "turned into stone" upon seeing Panthea, which surprises Polystratus since the spectacle that engages him was "only a woman" and not the boys of whom Lycinus is enamoured. Describing a statue of Aphrodite, Lycinus recalls "the story that the natives tell about it—that someone fell in love with the statue, was left behind in the temple, and embraced it to the best of his endeavours."[53] However, by evoking Ovid's account of Pygmalion, the artist who creates a statue of a woman and falls in love with the simulacrum that Venus miraculously transforms into a living woman, Lessing's accounts of men who turn the objects of their love into representations suggest that he understands the Pygmalion myth as a story about aesthetic experience as much as erotic experience. In shrewdly remarking that Anacreon's poems are really hymns to art and the artist, he draws attention to the triangulation that underwrites these works and mediates them through the reflection of art at the same time that it makes them narcissistic. The obscure object of desire is finally the work of art itself, which seems always already an imitation of an imitation, poised between poetry and painting in a shifting exchange of model and copy. Repeatedly in Lessing's examples, what is behind the work of art is not the "thing itself," the referent of the representation, but rather another representation.

In chapter 11, in discussing the relative merits of invention and representation in painting and poetry, and the comte de Caylus's assertion that the artist should imitate Homer, Lessing allows that "sometimes the merit of the artist is greater when he has imitated nature by following the poet's imitation." Describing the difficult task of a painter who copies a landscape from the "description of a Thomson" rather than "directly from nature," he contrasts the one who must create "something beautiful out of indefinite and weak images of arbitrary symbols" (jener aus schwanken und schwachen Vorstellungen willkürlicher Zeichen) with the one who has the "original model [*Urbild*] directly before him" (63/94). (Of course, in the eighteenth century, copying a landscape directly from nature might mean copying a picturesque prospect that was itself composed according to the principles of painting and the poetry of descriptive poets such as James Thomson.)[54] Lessing's point in this chapter is about how we understand and value invention and originality differently in painting and poetry; he is not actually advocating that the painter use Thomson as his model rather than a real landscape. Yet this is another example of Lessing trying to work out what it would mean for painting or poetry to take the other for its model, another example in which the borders between image and reality, model and copy, seem less than clear.

Lessing's chapter 7 begins: "When we say that the artist imitates the poet or the poet the artist, we can mean one of two things: either that the one takes the other's work as his model, or that both work from the same model and one borrows his manner of presentation from the other." Addressing in part the question of whether or not Virgil copied the statue of Laocoön, Lessing distinguishes between two examples in distinguishing between these two types of imitation: "When Virgil describes the shield of Aeneas, he is 'imitating' the artist who made it, in the first meaning of the term. The work of art, not what is represented in it, is his model, and even if at the moment he describes what we see represented in it, he is only describing it as a part of the shield and not as the thing itself. But if Virgil had imitated the statue of Laocoön, this would have been an imitation in the second meaning of the term. For he would have imitated not the statue, but what the statue represents." Lessing insists that the "work of the poet" is original when he describes the shield, but that it is only "a copy" if he imitates the statue. The first case is "that general imitation which is the essence of his art . . . whether his subject is a work of other arts or a work of nature"; in the second case, however, imitating "not the statue, but what the statue represents," the poet would be devoid of originality: "Instead of representing the thing itself, he imitates an imitation and gives us lifeless reflections of the style of another man's genius rather than his own" (45). Paradoxically, the effort to represent "the thing itself" (die Sache selbst) in the sense of the object of the sculptor's representation, rather than "the thing itself" (der Dinge selbst) in the sense of the work of art, would condemn the poet to imitate an imitation; whereas the imitation of the work of art itself—the copy of the representation rather than the subject or referent of that representation—saves the poet from lifeless reflections. The work of art in this context is like or indeed *is* a work of nature. In Lessing's scheme, Virgil's representation is at one remove from the shield, whereas the suffering of Laocoön would be at two removes if Virgil had taken the statue as his model—like the landscape described by Thomson represented in the painter's copy of a copy. Again privileging a work of art that takes as its subject another work of art, that imitates an imitation, Lessing lays the groundwork for his argument about Homer, although he goes on to claim that Homer avoids the static description of the shield that in Virgil's poem brings the action "to a standstill" by instead representing the creation of the god's works of art.

We have seen, however, that the famous lines describing the shield of Achilles at the end of book 18 of the *Iliad* ask us to imagine an impossible work of art: a series of images that leave not only painting but also poetry behind as they depict action, sight, and sound. We also have seen that Homer's artistic device in describing the shield, which, according to Lessing, transforms what is coexistent into what is consecutive, finally does represent the subject that the paintings on the shield represent. The example of Homer's representation of the shield illustrates Lessing's theory about temporal and spatial signs, but it also embodies an example in which one art imitates another that seems to violate Lessing's own laws about the proper provinces of painting and poetry. I suggest that what compels Lessing to place it at the center of his discussion, regardless of the argument it supposedly illustrates, is its status as a hybrid imitation of an imitation that somehow describes what the experience of a work of art is like.

It is not a coincidence that the descriptions of the images on the shield, as they open up into narrative and the successive movement of temporality, resemble the similes that throughout the *Iliad* transform the static images of description into consecutive actions. This comparison might remind us, however, that paradoxically, in the context of the epic narrative, Homer's famous similes also turn what is consecutive into what is coexistent. The Homeric simile causes the reader to swerve from the progressive plot of the epic, threatening to derail or at least to sidetrack the train of events and actions that propel the narrative forward. Throughout the *Iliad,* for brief or not so brief moments, the reader is turned away from the linear sequence and destination of the epic narrative. By opening up into time in this way and transforming description into narrative, the simile actually stops narrative time and brings the epic to a standstill. This, in a sense, is what the description of the images on the shield do at the end of book 18; although they avoid the static description that Lessing condemns in Virgil's depiction of the shield of Aeneas in their almost flamboyant entry into narrative, these images repeatedly escape from and consequently eclipse the process and action that ostensibly are the subject of the narration. By swerving into temporality through the path of description, by turning into time, these images use the consecutive to create coexistent or parallel moments that we are asked to imagine side by side. Homer's representation of the shield of Achilles, then, is a complicated and overdetermined example both because it represents an impossible work of art that transgresses the borders separating poetry and the visual arts and because it represents the ways in which the *Iliad* challenges our understanding of narration and description.

As with Kames's discussion of fictions of the imagination, Lessing's discussion turns upon the status of a simile: the question of whether poetry and painting are alike. Kames embraces the simile governing *ut pictura poesis,* entering into simile himself in order to describe what the power of description is like. Lessing devotes himself to dismantling the simile in *ut pictura poesis,* to separating the arts, yet he makes his point that verbal and visual arts must make use of different techniques of representation by foregrounding an example that represents one art acting like the other. Focusing on an example that from the outset blurs the borders dividing the arts—a representation of a representation, a depiction of the visual arts in an epic poem—he leads us to imagine the mirror image of Kames's dream of a text that would act like a painting. In doing so, he leads the reader into various examples of works that themselves compare poetry and painting (or sculpture) and ask us to think about likeness itself and the power of art to present vivid copies of reality. Lessing foregrounds an example in which a poet understands the limits and properties of his art, yet in doing so, he frames a description of a work of art that would seem impossible if we were to take its author literally. As a description of a work of art, Homer's account of the shield is finally more extravagant than any of Kames's descriptions.

The work of art, as both Kames and Lessing see it, is poised between power and impossibility. The terms used to describe the work of art in the eighteenth century are adapted from commonplaces of classical rhetoric and poetics and the newly developed languages of empiricism and sensibility; yet the critic who would describe the effects and experience of the work of art seems to be presented with an almost impossible task of description. To some extent, the dream of all realistic or mimetic art is impossible, and increasing expectations of verisimilitude and naturalism raised the stakes for mimesis; but the problem for readers such as Kames is more specific. Eighteenth-century advocates of *ut pictura poesis* (and other eighteenth-century readers in general) demanded an experience of reading that books in particular threaten to refuse. The absence, mediation, blindness, and muteness that Kames and others want to deny—or at least forget—are embodied in and by books. One way to understand the excesses of Kames's version of *ut pictura poesis* is to locate them in his desire to transgress the borders and boundaries of the book. In this sense, one could see

Kames's extravagant account of the experience of reading as a kind of reaction formation developed in response to the situation of the published book. As a cultural fact and artifact, the book was present and multiplying as never before; and the novel brought both new expectations and new challenges for aesthetic experience as it replaced drama as a popular art form with its private theater of the mind.[55] Kames ascribes powers to description precisely at the moment when texts and language itself seem less and less likely to deliver.

Kames actually shares Lessing's distrust of description. In *Elements of Criticism,* Kames attacks "the language of a spectator" and warns against the "very humble flight of imagination" that will "convert a writer into a spectator; so as to figure, in some obscure manner, an action as passing in his sight and hearing. In that figured situation, being led naturally to write like a spectator, he entertains his readers with his own reflections, with cool description, and florid declamation; instead of making them eye-witnesses, as it were, to a real event." Going beyond classical rhetorical theories about *enargeia* in oratory, Kames asserts that if the writer himself becomes a spectator, the reader won't see the scene.[56] Hugh Blair would echo Kames's formulations in his warning, in his *Lectures on Rhetoric and Belles Lettres,* that "we have reason always to distrust an Author's descriptive talents, when we find him laborious and turgid amassing common-place epithets and general expressions, to work up a high conception of some object, of which, after all, we can form but an indistinct idea." For Blair, when a "second-rate Genius" tries to describe nature, he "gives us words rather than ideas; we meet with the language indeed of poetical description, but we apprehend the object described very indistinctly. Whereas, a true Poet makes us imagine that we see it before our eyes . . . he places it in such a light, that a Painter could copy after him."[57] For Blair and Kames, the "language of poetical description" finally presents itself to the sight of the reader rather than the things it is supposed to describe. The attempt to transcend the arbitrary signs of language and present unmediated nature can itself lead to the failure of *ut pictura poesis.*

Lessing, of course, insisted that he saw nothing in reading, and he called for poetry to "raise its arbitrary signs to natural signs,"[58] but paradoxically, he is the one who finally seems most interested in the language of description. Although Lessing rejects the principles of critics who called upon painters and poets to imitate each other, he is finally deeply invested in the scene of representation, particularly in the poet who would represent a painting in language. Taking the work of art as if it were a work of nature, Lessing's ideal poet does not imitate an imitation, yet he takes a copy for his model, bringing before our eyes the artist in the act of representation itself. In this sense, he would be like Hephaestus, creating a shield with pictures on it, if not like Homer, describing pictures that seem to transport the reader to the scene itself. Lessing's topic, as stated in his book's title, is "the limits [*Grenzen*] of painting and poetry," yet despite his most practical advice to painters, poets, readers, and beholders, he, too, seems compelled to imagine representations that challenge their limits.

Drawn to works of art that represent or themselves demand an impossible representation, Lessing, too, writes with the force of desire; but unlike Kames, who wants the work of art to disappear, Lessing seems to desire the work of art itself—like Anacreon, in Lessing's description, composing a hymn to art and the artist that somehow begins where "language in itself is powerless" and "poetry falters and eloquence grows mute." This is also the place where the critic, wanting proper words, fears that he will never be able to speak of painting or poetry, especially if he has to banish figurative or unphilosophical expressions. The perspective of empiricism, combined with the psychological aesthetics of authors following Locke and Addison, calls upon the critic, too, to undertake description—not to anatomize the work of art or to reconstruct its rules but rather to describe an experience that is "exceedingly clear in the perception" yet still presents "no small difficulty to express it clearly in words." Critics trying to understand what the work of art is like find themselves trying to describe the nature of aesthetic experience.

Looking back on his own work, Wittgenstein writes: "A *picture* held us captive. And we could not get outside it, for it lay in our language and language seemed to repeat it to us inexorably."[59] In his *Philosophical Investigations,* a series of remarks that are, he says, "as it were, a number of sketches of landscapes," an "album" of "pictures," Wittgenstein suggests that the goal of philosophy is to describe: "We must do away with all *explanation,* and description alone must take its place."[60] Philosophy should not make assertions such as "This is how things are," Wittgenstein suggests. When one says, "*this* is how it is," he writes, "I feel as though, if only I could fix my gaze absolutely sharply on this fact, get it in focus, I must grasp the essence of the matter."[61] For Wittgenstein, this would be a deceptive view, because what we see is what a thing looks like, not what it is. When one says, "This is how things are," "One thinks that one is tracing the outline of the thing's nature over and over again, and one is merely tracing round the frame through which we look at it."[62] Kames wants to "trace the objects" that we see, to "set before the eye, plainly and candidly, facts as they really exist" (1: 42); and he wants to do this to show us how description could efface itself and present us with things themselves, as if they were really there, as if we were really there. Despite his demystifying criticism, Lessing also wants the artist to present the thing itself, although he repeatedly pictures moments in which the thing itself is a work of art trying to represent the thing itself. Both Kames and Lessing want to deny the frame that offers one visions yet renders one distant and absent; but they keep finding themselves focused on the frame that lies in their language. They cannot step outside of the language of description that they want to describe. Eighteenth-century criticism begins and ends with the frame of art.

3

True Acting and the Language of Real Feeling

Mansfield Park

> *What signifies a theatre?*
> Jane Austen, *Mansfield Park*

Contemporary critics have been troubled by the significance of the private theatricals staged in *Mansfield Park*. Lionel Trilling observes that "it is never made clear why it is so very wrong for young people in a dull country house to put on a play." The novel's apparent moral condemnation stands in contrast with Austen's own enjoyment of theater and experience in home theatricals.[1] Scholars have debated the literary and historical relevance of *Lovers' Vows,* the play that the characters rehearse, but Trilling has set the terms for the discussion of the theatricals in influential essays that focus the problem on what he calls "the integrity of the real self." Calling the novel Austen's *Letter to d'Alembert,* he invokes Plato in explaining the "traditional, almost primitive, feeling about dramatic impersonation that pervades the novel's distrust of playacting."[2] It is Fanny Price's opposition to the dangerous impersonation of the theater—particularly, the Crawfords' threat to the integrity and stability and fixity of the self that ostensibly exemplifies her almost allegorical embodiment of sincerity, authenticity, integrity, self-sufficiency, single-mindedness, transparency, truth to oneself, fixity of self, and genuine feeling.[3]

Fanny Price is presented in *Mansfield Park* as the one character who both experiences and expresses real feelings. At the end of the novel, for example, Fanny's feelings about her cousin's illness are contrasted with the sentiments expressed in a letter from her aunt: "Fanny's feelings on the occasion were indeed considerably more warm and genuine than her aunt's style of writing. She felt truly for them all." Lady Bertram's writing, we are told, is "a sort of playing at being frightened" until she witnesses the gravity of her son's illness and then writes "in a different style, in the language of real feeling and alarm" (416–17). A. Walton Litz claims that "the distinction between genuine emotion and the impersonation of feeling is never more clearly before us than" in this comparison.[4] Most readers have seen the Crawfords, of course, as the representatives of playing at feeling in the novel. Henry and Mary are cast as models of insincerity, bad faith, hypocrisy, role-playing and impersonation, while Fanny is regarded as the model of real, true, and genuine feeling. Fanny insists that she "cannot act," that acting for her "would be absolutely impossible" (168–69), and critics mostly have taken her at her word, assuming that, like Cordelia, she cannot feign.[5]

However, despite the antitheatrical sensibilities that make her dread being "called into notice" in a "public" manner (172) or finding "that almost every eye was upon her" (169), Fanny's insistence on being audience, auditor, and spectator inscribes her in theatrical relations. She positions herself as the "spectator" and "only audience" (185) to the rehearsals of *Lovers' Vows,* the "quiet auditor of the whole" production both on and off stage. Fanny is not opposed to theater. She looks forward to the production of the play, and although she disapproves of the shocking subject matter of *Lovers' Vows,* she is "not unamused" (156) to watch the human comedy being played out by her family circle. She admires Henry Crawford as an actor, if not as a man. Fanny simply prefers to experience theater as a spectator.

This theatrical perspective is underlined by Fanny Price's association in the novel with what Austen elsewhere calls "picturesque principles."[6] Throughout the extensive discussions about landscape design that take place in *Mansfield Park,* Fanny's stand against the improvers places her firmly on the ground of the picturesque. Critics have noted Austen's fondness for William Gilpin but they seem to have overlooked the fact that the heroine of this novel about place and landscape design bears a name—Price—that the educated public immediately would have associated with the picturesque.[7] The most famous spokesman of the picturesque school in the decade in which Austen wrote *Mansfield Park* was Sir Uvedale Price, whose three-volume *Essays on the Picturesque* was first published in 1810, four years before the 1814 publication of her novel.[8]

Although Fanny speaks of her tendency to engage in "rhapsodizing" when she is "out of doors," the only time we witness her experiencing what she calls "the sublimity of Nature" occurs when she is "standing at an open window . . .

looking out on a twilight scene" (139, 135). The word "scene" is used three times to describe what Fanny sees as she views nature through the frame of a window as if she were beholding a painting or a scene on a stage:

> Fanny spoke her feelings. "Here's harmony!" said she. "Here's repose! Here's what may leave all painting and all music behind, and what poetry only can attempt to describe. Here's what may tranquillize every care, and lift the heart to rapture! When I look out on such a night as this, I feel as if there could be neither wickedness nor sorrow in the world; and there certainly would be less of both if the sublimity of Nature were more attended to, and people were carried more out of themselves by contemplating such a scene."

After Fanny speaks of "rapture," Edmund labels her monologue with the technically accurate term "enthusiasm"—and, indeed, Fanny also seems to be quoting Shaftesbury when she later characterizes this sort of experience as "rhapsodizing" in a "wondering strain" (223). After Edmund pities those who "have not been taught to feel in some degree as you do," Fanny responds: "You taught me to think and feel on the subject," and Edmund replies, "I had a very apt scholar" (139).

Edmund's role as Fanny's teacher is certainly tinged with irony in the novel, yet the question of what it might mean that Fanny has been "taught to feel" resonates in a passage in which she speaks her feelings with an almost self-conscious command of the technical vocabularies of sentimentalism and the picturesque. As the usually austere or ironic narrative voice indulges in a restrained poetic register in describing "the scene without, where all that was solemn and soothing, and lovely, appeared in the brilliancy of an unclouded night, and the contrast of the deep shade of the woods," and as the usually silent printing press provides "nature" with a capital "N" in Fanny's description of the "sublimity of Nature," the terms and topoi of eighteenth-century aesthetic and sentimental categories read as if they were already in quotation marks.

Edmund's characterization of Fanny as his "scholar" in this scene recalls the description of Catherine Morland as a "scholar" in *Northanger Abbey* when after a "lecture on the picturesque" she "voluntarily rejected the whole city of Bath as unworthy to make part of a landscape." Fanny's picturesque rhetoric also might recall Marianne Dashwood's complaint in *Sense and Sensibility* that "admiration of landscape scenery is become a mere jargon" in a discussion about "picturesque principles" and whether people "really feel" what they profess to feel when they admire a landscape. Certainly, Fanny is a more serious "scholar" than Catherine; and if Fanny inadvertently lapses into the jargon of the picturesque or the rhetoric of the sublime as she tries to speak feelings that "poetry only can attempt to describe," we might recall Marianne's confession that "sometimes I have kept my feelings to myself because I could find no language to describe them in but what was worn and hackneyed out of all sense and meaning."9

My point is that Fanny's position as a spectator and a proponent of the picturesque may frame her own sentiments as theater, turning moments such as her poetic description of the sublimity of nature into self-consciously theatrical set pieces. The frame that positions Fanny looking at "the scene without" (139) as she speaks her own feelings places Fanny and the reader at more than two removes from both real feelings and the language in which feelings are described. The frames of the window, the book, and the page also set off Fanny as an actor who reads aloud from (what are by 1814) the scripts of eighteenth-century aesthetic and sentimental experience. Perhaps it is the legacy of Fielding that readers of the nineteenth-century novel must view characters' feelings through a frame—or the combined legacy of Sterne's irony and Richardson's sentimentalism—that readers must view characters viewing their own feelings through a frame: speaking feelings that are always already in quotation marks. Unlike Catherine or Marianne, Fanny may not have learned her feelings from gothic or sentimental novels; but if she is less susceptible to romance, it is precisely her distance from the real feelings she has been taught to feel that might remind us that the frame of the picturesque inscribes Fanny as a spectator to herself as well as to others.

If I seem to be perversely skeptical in questioning the language of Fanny's feelings, my point is not that Fanny is supposed to be insincere or affected. Rather, I want to suggest that Fanny is implicated as both a spectator and an actor in the world of play and theater that is dramatized in *Mansfield Park.* Despite everyone's confidence in the genuine and true character of what Fanny really feels, the novel asks us to speculate about what it would mean for Fanny as well as the Crawfords to play at feeling. The crisis of the novel occurs not when Mansfield is turned into a theater but when the Crawfords call into question Fanny's understanding of the roles of player and spectator, forcing her to reexamine the place and position that she has staked out for herself. Mary and Henry Crawford challenge Fanny's privileged point of view, attacking the presumption that one could refuse to act, breaking the frame that defines her theatrical perspective. They challenge the distinction between genuine emotion and the impersonation of feeling that many readers have seen as the cornerstone of the novel's moral statement.

The challenge posed by the Crawfords turns on what the narrative describes in another context as "true acting" (198). The phrase is used to describe the unexpected encounter of Mr. Yates and Sir Thomas, who finds himself "upon the stage of a theatre . . . making part of a ridiculous exhibition" when he unexpectedly returns home and interrupts the rehearsals. But the phrase resonates outside of this comic context. Edmund, who praises "real acting" (150), is at one point described as being "between his theatrical and his real part" (183). Mary Crawford asks Fanny, "Is not there a something wanted, Miss Price, in our language—a something between compliments and—and love" (292). I suggest that *Mansfield Park* is concerned with something between playing at feeling and real feeling, something between a theatrical part and a real part, something that might be called true acting. As the plot seems to turn on the problem of telling the difference between acting and true feeling, between play and real and genuine feeling, the novel asks whether acting could be true and whether real feeling could be acted.

As the possibility of true acting threatens distinctions between play and authenticity, both the inhabitants of Mansfield and the reader must confront the question that Henry Crawford poses early in the novel: "what signifies a theatre?" (149). The immediate context here is whether they need to construct a stage in order to produce their play, but again the question reverberates throughout the narrative, as the Crawfords demonstrate that playing and acting do not require a stage set. Reading the question "what signifies a theatre?" we must ask: what signifies or stands for theater—and, more important, what does a theater signify? *Mansfield Park* turns on the question of what theater signifies, and to understand the significance of true acting and the language of real feeling for Fanny Price, we need to understand her relation to both theater and signification. What is at stake in the novel's overdetermined game of speculation is, I suggest, nothing.

When Fanny is called upon to play a part in *Lovers' Vows,* she vehemently refuses, but at the moment that she insists, "I really cannot act," it is already too late: she is "shocked to find herself at that moment the only speaker in the room, and to feel that almost every eye was upon her" (168–69). If Fanny fears that the "attack" of being "called into notice" in "so public" a manner is only a "prelude to something so infinitely worse, to be told that she must do what was so impossible as to act" (172), the language of her feelings acknowledges that she already has been placed on stage, cast as a player in a prelude that is itself theatrical. It is ironic that she thinks of Mary Crawford as her protector in this dilemma, for although Mary has intervened to save Fanny from the theatrical board's entreaties and Mrs. Norris's cruel reminder to Fanny of "who and what she is" (170), Mary is the first to succeed in leading her from prelude to play.

In one of the strangest scenes of *Mansfield Park,* Mary asks Fanny to rehearse a scene from *Lovers' Vows* that Mary and Edmund are supposed to play together: apparently the scene in which Amelia rather scandalously declares her love to the clergyman Anhalt. Mary professes to be embarrassed at the prospect of speaking such lines to Edmund, and she tells Fanny: "You must rehearse it with me, that I may fancy you him, and get on by degrees. You have a look of his sometimes." Chosen for her family resemblance, Fanny finds herself "representing Edmund . . . but with looks and voice so truly feminine, as to be no very good picture of a man" (188–89). The dynamics of this piece of forced acting are complex. Fanny is ostensibly chosen for the ease afforded by her uncanny embodiment of identity and difference, both her ability and her failure to personate Edmund, but it is precisely such unstable acts of identification that place her in an awkward and even torturous position. In personal terms, Fanny is asked to play a love scene with Mary in which she must not only witness her rival speak the lines that she herself would like to say to Edmund but also take Edmund's place and imagine him receiving and reciprocating Mary's lover's vows. It is hard not to read a finely tuned sadism in Mary's disingenuous casting.

Mary may understand that she must seduce Fanny in order ultimately to seduce Edmund. Such mediated desire and displacement are also at work when Mary plays a role in the seduction of Fanny on behalf of her brother Henry. There are also homoerotic currents in the veiled and mediated incestuous energies that circulate between Edmund, Fanny, Mary, and Henry. After a point, as Fanny stands in for Edmund with Mary, Mary takes the part of Henry with Fanny, and each woman becomes increasingly invested in her brother's or cousin's desire for the other, both the objects and the subjects of desire become confused. In this context, Mary's assertion that Fanny would not be embarrassed to play this love scene with Edmund because "he is your cousin, which makes all the difference" (188) must read as a joke about the problem of desire and difference in a novel in which endogamy wins the day and a marriage that was supposed to be "morally impossible" because cousins would be "like brothers and sisters" (44) is the happy ending.

If the psychological implications of this scene are complicated, however, it is the ontology of the theater that makes the rehearsal vertiginous. To begin with, the entire production of the play has called into question the difference between actor and role for all of the characters in the novel. Critics have observed that what is most scandalous about the play is that the actors aren't acting at all.[10] Edmund first declines to play the role of the clergyman, suggesting that a clergyman would be "one of the last who would wish to represent it on the stage" (168), but he soon agrees to a role that places him "between his theatrical and his real part" (183). Thus, Fanny—chosen for her simultaneous resemblance to and difference from Edmund—must represent Edmund representing a role that is almost identical to his own.

The performance is painful for Fanny because Mary makes it clear that she is not to play Anhalt but rather Edmund playing Anhalt; and what she fears most about "the idea of representing Edmund" is that she is representing someone who is only pretending to playact; she must represent an actor for whom acting is only an act. The impossibility of Fanny's position is augmented when Edmund makes an "entrance" and interrupts the "scene"; he, too, "was seeking Fanny, to ask her to rehearse with him" (189). Fanny is then forced to watch Edmund and Mary play the love scene before her—on the one hand, deprived of the opportunity to represent herself in the scene and declare her lover's vows for Edmund, yet on the other hand, spared the dilemma of being asked to play Mary in the scene, thereby being forced to act the sentiments she really feels. After refusing to accept a role in the play and insisting that it is impossible for her to act, Fanny finds herself in an overdetermined game of "true acting" in which she must experience her own sentiments spoken in quotations from a book in the middle of an uncanny play of doubles and reflections that carries her outside of herself in frightening ways.

Adding to this multiplication of parts and persons is the possibility of an overlay of theatrical texts. *Lovers' Vows* is obviously relevant: like Edmund with Fanny, Anhalt is represented as the teacher who has taught Amelia everything from "geography" and "language" to "love."[11] Furthermore, Henry Crawford tells us that Shakespeare is to be found "in half the books we open"; "we all talk Shakespeare," he says, "use his similes, and describe with his descriptions" (335). Readers have noted the presence of *King Lear* in *Mansfield Park*—for example, in the name Edmund; but it has not been recognized that Edmund shares his rather more improbable last name, Bertram, with the protagonist of *All's Well That Ends Well*.[12]

In this play, a young nobleman named Bertram avoids fulfilling the lover's vows he makes to a virtuous maiden who has been taken into his home to be raised by his mother. Helena, who rejects the description of Bertram as her brother because she wants to marry him, is abandoned by Bertram after he has given her his vow. Encouraged by a "counterfeit module" named Paroles who "deceived [him] like a double-meaning prophesier," he pursues a young virgin named Diana rather than the woman who should be his wife. Finally, in a turn of plot that will be repeated in *Measure for Measure* when Mariana appears in the "imagined person" of Isabella and makes love with Angelo,[13] Bertram is tricked into making love with Helena, who secretly appears in the place of Diana in a rendezvous with him. All finally ends well, with Bertram accepting Helena as his wife.

Surely there is irony in the supposedly pious Edmund's relation to the irresponsible Bertram, just as there is irony in the allusive act that names him Edmund rather than Edgar. The relevance of the allusion to Shakespeare's Bertram is underlined by the reversals, replacements, and substitutions that we have been examining in the rehearsal of *Lovers' Vows*. In his pursuit of Mary, Edmund Bertram is avoiding a love scene with his cousin Fanny. Paradoxically, although he is substituting Mary for Fanny, when he makes his entrance in the rehearsal scene, he is trying to get Fanny to stand in for Mary; and if Mary hadn't gotten there first, he would have tricked himself into receiving Fanny's vow of love while trying to play a love scene with Mary.

In *All's Well That Ends Well*, an act of impersonation is meant to correct an improper switching of parts. When Helena appears in the imagined person of Diana, she is in fact playing the role that is properly hers, the role in which Bertram improperly wants to cast Diana. Fanny almost gets to assume her proper place by appearing in the imagined person of Mary. The theatrical acts of personation and impersonation in which a character must play someone else in order to reclaim the role that is properly hers but has been assigned to someone else are both replayed and reversed in the substitutions of the rehearsal of *Lovers' Vows*. Fanny's love scene, however, removes her further from her own part; and after being asked to impersonate both Edmund and Mary in their love scene, she finally must experience lovers' vows as audience and voyeur. Both acting and not acting become impossible for her as she is plunged into vertiginous acts of identification and impersonation.

These intertextual and interpersonal displacements are complicated even further by the possibility that Austen is rehearsing in this scene aspects of the plot of Goethe's novel *Die Wahlverwandtschaften*, or *Elective Affinities*, which was published in 1809, five years before the publication of *Mansfield Park*. In *Elective Affinities*, characters stage extravagant private theatricals—in the form of *tableaux vivants*—in a home theater constructed by an architect. At the center of these performances is a vivacious young woman named Luciane, who is known for her "excellent acting"; she is continually contrasted with her "inarticulate" cousin Ottilie, the representative of sensibility in the novel; at one point, the timid Ottilie identifies with the suffering of a girl who is "dragged from the refuge of her room by Luciane, who tried to force her to take part in games and dancing." In the course of this scandalous novel about adultery, a character named Eduard excels at dramatic recitation and "reading aloud"; characters have long discussions about landscape design, English parks, and the picturesque; and the already quiet Ottilie refuses to speak.[14]

What is especially relevant, however, is the complicated lovers' foursome that in the elective affinities of the plot pairs Eduard with Ottilie and his wife Charlotte with the character called the Captain. In perhaps the most scandalous scene in the novel, as Eduard and Charlotte make love, "their passions and their imaginations asserted their rights over reality. It was Ottilie who was closed in Eduard's embrace, while the Captain's image . . . hovered before Charlotte. The absent and the present, strangely interwoven, blended in their blissful ecstasy." The child born from this act of "double adultery" turns out to have a "double resemblance" to Ottilie and the Captain.[15] It is this play of double images, this interplay of the absent and the present, that seems to resonate in the rehearsal scene in *Mansfield Park*. The plot of Austen's novel is filled with lovers' triangles, foursomes, and elective affinities that shift with varying degrees of intensity. In the chapter recounting this rehearsal, however, we are asked to imagine a love scene that takes place both alternately and simultaneously between Amelia and Anhalt, Mary and Edmund, Fanny and Edmund, and Mary and Fanny—with the odd elective affinities that intermix Henry and Mary with Fanny and Edmund in the background. It is finally impossible to know whose image is closed in whose embrace as absent and present images are interwoven by the already double substitutions of playacting, by the lovers' triangles and foursomes, and finally by the idea of Fanny representing Edmund—which leads to the phantasmagoric possibility that in Fanny's imaginative projections, the Edmund she represents is actually embracing an image of herself.

Acting may be impossible for Fanny; but what we behold in this scene is precisely a kaleidoscope of impossible situations, all of which inscribe Fanny in acts of theatrical representation, impersonation, role-playing, substitution, identification and projection. At the least, the scenes of *All's Well That Ends Well* and *Elective Affinities* teach us how to read the levels of true acting that are dramatized in Austen's rehearsal scene. I believe that these scenes also point to a network of texts of and about the theater that show us the extent to which Fanny's real feelings are always already framed by theatrical scenarios that threaten to cast people as characters in interchangeable roles. Fanny's forced immersion in the scene of play is traumatic not only for psychological reasons but also because it calls into question her understanding of her role in the theater of *Mansfield Park*.

The climax of the scene occurs when Edmund makes his "entrance" and replaces Fanny in the roles of Anhalt and himself. Fanny is "wanted only to prompt and observe them," and as Mary and Edmund rehearse with zeal, we read, she "felt herself becoming too nearly nothing to both, to have any comfort in having been sought by either." We may sympathize with Fanny as she realizes that "their performance would, indeed, have such nature and feeling in it . . . as must make it a very suffering exhibition to herself," but we must recognize—along with Fanny—that she finally suffers in this scene when she is assigned the role that she has chosen for herself from the outset: prompter, auditor, audience. By forcing her to play a role, Mary makes Fanny come face to face with the part she wants to play. In miscasting her, Mary shows Fanny what it is like to lose one's place, to abdicate one's part to someone else. By the time Fanny resumes her customary position in the audience, wanted only as prompter, she is reduced to nothing. "In watching them," we read, "she forgot herself and . . . closed the page and turned away exactly as [Edmund] wanted help" (189). Fanny loses her place in the book—the text of *Lovers' Vows*—just as she risks losing her place in *Mansfield Park*.

Within a few hours, as the group prepares to rehearse the three first acts, Fanny accepts a part in the play. She agrees only "to read the part," but that is all she did in rehearsing with Mary Crawford, and in this book we know that reading aloud can be "truly dramatic" (335). Why does she accept the impossible here? She may feel that she already has lost her customary position as spectator, or that it is too nearly nothing to satisfy her. In accepting the role, Fanny feels that she is "properly punished" (191), perhaps for having been seduced into acting earlier that afternoon, perhaps for having recognized her own desire. Fanny also has recognized, as if for the first time, that the scene between Edmund and Mary in *Lovers' Vows* has "nature and feeling in it" (190), that the actors speak in the language of real feeling, even if their dialogue is framed as play. All of these realizations change Fanny's understanding of theater and her place in it.

Fanny is saved from this performance by the *deus ex machina* of Sir Thomas's return from Antigua; but despite the ensuing demise of the theatrical production, Fanny's entrance into the scene of the theater continues, again prompted by Mary and (especially) Henry Crawford. Fanny thinks of Henry's return to the neighborhood as the return of a spectator to her everyday performances: "The idea of having such another to observe her, was a great increase of the trepidation with which she performed the very aweful ceremony of walking into the drawing-room." She hopes that an additional guest will make it easier for her to "sit silent and unattended to" (234) but Henry's presence places her in play. Henry soon teaches Fanny how to play Speculation and we read that after the game Henry "sat silently observing" Fanny while he is "observed" by Sir Thomas (256). Next, Sir Thomas gives a ball, at which Fanny makes "her first appearance" and is "regarded as the Queen of the evening" (273). Fanny is no Roxana; yet this dance marks the point of no return in the Crawfords' plan to draw Fanny into play.

The central prop in this elaborate game is the necklace that Fanny takes from the Crawfords. Since she has "nothing but a bit of ribbon" (262) with which to wear a cross she has received from her brother, Fanny accepts from Mary a necklace that Henry apparently once gave her; Mary calls it "nothing but an old necklace" (265). When Edmund also gives Fanny a chain to wear with the cross, Fanny is ready to return the necklace but Edmund insists that this would have "the air of ingratitude, though I know it could never have the meaning" (270). The necklace is thus immediately inscribed in the play between meaning and appearance—and it becomes clear that Fanny will not be able to control either. Fanny's acceptance and display of the necklace at the dance that represents her "first appearance" (273) is later taken to mean that she has accepted and acknowledged Henry's affections. Although, in making the gift, Mary reproaches Fanny for suspecting a "confederacy" (266) between the Crawfords, she later insists: "And then before the ball, the necklace! Oh! you received it just as it was meant. You were as conscious as heart could desire." Contradicting what she earlier led Fanny to believe, Mary declares that the gift was Henry's "doing entirely, his own thought. . . . I was delighted to act on his proposal" (357). Fanny insists, "had I had an idea of it, nothing should have induced me to accept the necklace." As for Henry's attentions, she says, "I considered it as meaning nothing. . . . I could not but see that Mr. Crawford allowed himself in gallantries which did mean nothing" (358).

"Nothing" indeed induces Fanny to accept the necklace. She believes that what is "nothing but an old necklace" simply means nothing, is meant as nothing; but as she should have suspected when Edmund warned her about the appearance and meaning of returning the necklace, this prop has irrevocably introduced her into an act of signification: an extended performative speech act that resonates beyond intentionality. This argument about appearance, meaning, and intentionality is at the center of the crisis that Fanny is thrown into by the Crawfords' insistence that she act, their insistence that she is already acting. We should recall here that despite the trick of the necklace, Fanny is never really the dupe of the Crawfords; she is not fooled by hypocrisy, not mystified by false claims to truth, not misled by playacting that misrepresents real feeling. Fanny is, so to speak, the first poststructuralist reader of the Crawfords: to her, as to Leo Bersani, they are "ontological floaters." She may not like what D. A. Miller calls Henry's "semiological equivocation" or what Joseph Litvak calls Henry's "semiotic promiscuity," but to Fanny it's all the free play of signifiers. She does not like Henry Crawford "as a man," we read, "but she must admit him to be the best actor" (185). For most of the novel, Fanny simply assumes that Henry and Mary Crawford mean nothing.[16]

After the visit to the chapel in which Fanny finds "nothing awful . . . nothing melancholy, nothing grand" (114) and Mary Crawford declares that "a clergyman is nothing," Edmund remarks, "The nothing of conversation has its gradations, I hope" (120). Conversations in *Mansfield Park* are riddled with the word "nothing"—it appears more than 150 times in the novel in a remarkable array of gradations, ranging from conversational to Shakespearean—and the Crawfords seem to be particularly associated with both word and concept. At one point, Fanny disagrees with Mary about her preference for calling Edmund "Mr. Bertram," declaring: "To me, the sound of Mr. Bertram is so cold and nothing-meaning" (224). In general, everything that Mary or Henry says is to Fanny "nothing-meaning." When Henry declares his love to her, Fanny insists: "I know it is all nothing" (305). She understands Henry's avowal as "nonsense." He speaks "in words so plain as to bear but one meaning even to her," but what Fanny finds "incomprehensible" (305) is that what Henry says has meaning, that Henry means what he says, that what he says does not mean nothing. Fanny later tells her uncle that she would have rejected Henry's proposal immediately "if I had been quite certain of his meaning any thing seriously," but she feared "imputing more than might be intended. I thought it might all pass for nothing with him" (315). She tells Edmund, "I had not an idea that his behaviour to me before had any meaning," suggesting that even Henry's sisters must have supposed "he had meant nothing" (349).

Certain that Henry is not "serious," assuming that he will "think nothing of what had passed," Fanny is doubly perplexed by a letter from Mary that seems to second Henry's proposal and "even to appear to believe it serious."

Fanny thinks: "There was every thing in the world against their being serious, but his words and manner." Henry gives her looks that "she did not know how to class among the common meaning; in any other man at least, she would have said that it meant something very earnest." What she is most concerned about in responding to the Crawfords is "wishing not to appear to think any thing really intended." Puzzled by an *air* that she knows could never have a *meaning,* she wants to avoid the *appearance* that she thinks that it is *meant.* She thanks Mary for her comments about William and insists, "The rest of your note I know means nothing" (308–10). Fanny does not think that Henry is trying to deceive her; she assumes that he is only playing, that his words and acts are to be taken as play. She is mortified that the playful Crawfords will think that she takes them seriously.

What throws Fanny into a crisis is the Crawfords' insistence that they do not mean nothing after all. The necklace that Fanny wears at the ball becomes a floating signifier that seems to change meaning and cast Fanny in a speech act that she has not meant to perform, but its threat is not really its uncertainty or semiological instability. Paradoxically, the Crawfords insist on its presence as a symbol, on the referentiality and intentionality inscribed in its exchange in a community of shared meaning. Fanny's view of the world depends on her belief that this "nothing but an old necklace" means *nothing,* was meant as *nothing,* and was taken as *nothing.* At stake is the difference between lovers' vows spoken in play and in the language of real feeling; at stake is the meaning of theater.

When Yates and Tom Bertram first introduce their project of home theatricals, Edmund asks, "You are not serious, Tom, in meaning to act?" In response to Edmund's questions about propriety, Tom says, "You take up a thing so seriously! . . . We mean nothing but a little amusement among ourselves." A moment earlier, when Henry asks, "and for a theatre, what signifies a theatre?" and Yates claims that aside from some scenery "nothing more would be necessary . . . we should want nothing more," Edmund sarcastically insists, "Let us do nothing by halves. . . . If we do not out do Ecclesford, we do nothing" (149–51). Despite the colloquial and contextual gradations of these "nothings of conversation," the debate about the theatricals at Mansfield Park turns on the question of whether theater signifies nothing—whether, to borrow Edmund's words, one is serious in meaning to act, whether in acting one means seriously.

When the actors try to persuade Fanny to act, Tom insists "it is a nothing of a part, a mere nothing . . . and it will not much signify if nobody hears a word you say"; Mrs. Norris reproaches, "What a piece of work here is about nothing" (168–69). The moral of the novel, of course, is that such playacting does not mean nothing; it is not about nothing, any more than parts are mere nothings. My point, however, is that it is above all Fanny who must learn this lesson. She may be offended by the impropriety of *Lovers' Vows* or Henry's flirtations or Edmund's bad faith, but Fanny seems to believe for much of the novel that playacting means nothing seriously. To her, the poor player that struts and frets his hour upon the stage tells a tale full of sound and fury, signifying nothing. Her assumption that Henry Crawford means nothing is integral to her view of him as the best actor at Mansfield Park. Henry and Mary could not be serious, they could not intend or mean anything in earnest, because everything they say and do takes place for Fanny under the sign of play. They mean nothing because theater means nothing. The crisis of meaning that the Crawfords cause for Fanny is a crisis about theater: they force Fanny to confront the possibility that theater might not signify nothing. By the time that Mary preemptively insists to Fanny that Henry's scandalous behavior means nothing—"Say not a word of it," she writes, "hear nothing, surmise nothing, whisper nothing, till I write again" (426)—Fanny no longer believes that nothing will come of nothing.[17]

Although Fanny ultimately is judged to have been right in her reading of Henry's character, the novel leaves the crux of the crisis unresolved. Tony Tanner may be right in saying that Henry is "trying to play the most difficult role of all—the role of sincerity" but the novel leaves open the possibility that, following the eighteenth-century theories of acting that Henry echoes, Henry has really become the part he plays.[18] The Jamesian epistemological crisis that Fanny experiences in the second and third volumes of the novel is related to her inability to tell the difference between the language of real feeling and playing at feeling, between vows that mean something and vows that mean nothing.

In the last volume, we read that Fanny's "heart was softened for a while toward [Henry]—because he really seemed to feel" (360); and that "it was pleasing to hear him speak so properly; here, he had been acting as he ought to" (397). The language here is not so reassuring—what does it mean that Henry is acting properly, that he really seems to feel?—but the ambiguity comes from the possibility that Henry might be acting truly rather than truly acting: his "true acting" suggests that *even for the speaker of feelings,* it may not be easy to tell the difference between real feelings and play. This possibility is more threatening than the dilemma that "how Miss Crawford really felt—how she meant to act, or might act without or against her meaning . . . were subjects for endless conjecture" (407–8). Fanny is forced to enter a realm in which real feelings, acting, meaning and intention are vertiginously confused and undermined, not because people can't know each other's feelings, but because the category of *real feeling* itself is thrown into doubt by the speculation of play.

Fanny's situation is still more complicated, however, because the Crawfords' success in drawing her into the realm of play challenges her own attempts to mean nothing. We saw that despite her insistence that she cannot act, Fanny is cast in Mary's bizarre rehearsal scene, agrees to read the nothing of a part that she earlier refused, and is tricked into playing a role in the game of signification surrounding the necklace. After Henry declares his lover's vows and he and Mary appear to think themselves serious, Fanny becomes "more silent than ever . . . speaking only when she could not help it" (307–8). Earlier, Mary has complained to Fanny (who, we know, prefers to sit "silent and unattended to" [234]), "You don't speak, Fanny—Miss Price—you don't speak" (293). Henry will not allow Fanny to maintain this silence.

After Henry's "truly dramatic" reading of Shakespeare, which brings "all his acting before [Fanny] again," she desperately tries not to participate in the scenario of Henry's courtship. He relentlessly entreats "to know her meaning," asking, "Did you speak? . . . I saw your lips move." As Fanny reproaches herself "for not having been as motionless as she was speechless," Henry repeatedly demands: "What did that shake of the head mean? . . . What was it meant to express? . . . What did that shake of the head mean?" After she is "wearied at last into speaking," he has "always something to intreat the explanation of" (338–40). Soon thereafter, insisting that Fanny took the necklace "just as it was meant" (357), Mary asks Fanny for the favor of her "correspondence. You must write to me," she says, and we read: "it was impossible for her to refuse" (359). Later, she feels that she has been "compelled into a correspondence" (370). As in the episode of the necklace, Fanny is forced into conversation with the Crawfords.

Perhaps Fanny suspects that she cannot control the play of appearance and meaning in her words and gestures. In the previous chapter, we read: "Fanny knew her own meaning, but was no judge of her own manner" (326). Confronting Henry Crawford, whom earlier she experiences as her spectator and who in this scene reasserts himself as an actor, Fanny is aware that she has once again been drawn into the Crawfords' dangerous play of signification. Her response is to try to sit silent and motionless, to refuse to speak or gesture, to attain a kind of "degree zero" of signification. Faced with Henry's claim of meaning, Fanny wants to mean nothing. It is as if she wants to say, echoing Edgar in *King Lear*, *Fanny I nothing am*.[19] But Henry interrogates her every gesture, demands the explanation of her every look, asks the meaning of her words and silence, compels her into an exchange of words and letters. He insists that she speak, that she mean. As she listens to a discussion about theater and reading aloud, Fanny is not permitted to be a passive spectator watching from the audience or beholding through the frame of a window. She must act, and she is not allowed a mere nothing of a part in the true acting that pervades Mansfield Park.

If acting is not impossible for Fanny Price—if, indeed, it is inevitable—then we might wonder if, finally, Fanny can play Cordelia, if she can love and be silent. Cordelia speaks nothing at the risk that nothing will come of nothing, while Fanny learns that even *nothing* can signify. By the end of the novel, however, Fanny seems to have triumphed not only as Cordelia but as the Cordelia in the eighteenth-century version of *King Lear*: resurrected from tragedy to marry the good brother (in this case, Edmund), after the stage is littered with the corpses of every character with a moral flaw. If, as many readers have observed, the dangerously subversive play represented by the Crawfords is purged from both estate and novel, does this mean that Fanny can return to the position she sought to occupy outside of the frame of theater, outside of the language of play?[20]

Toward the end of the novel, while in exile at Portsmouth, Fanny joins "a circulating library." We read: "She became a subscriber—amazed at being any thing in *propria persona*, amazed at her own doings in every way; to be a renter, a chuser of books!" (390–91). Fanny may be amazed that she is playing the role of Edmund as she educates her sister Susan; but what Fanny seems most amazed about is the act of subscribing herself as herself, the act of signing her name. When Richardson's Pamela marries Mr. B., she waits for her new husband to sign her name. Pamela narrates: "He then took a pen himself, and wrote, after Pamela, his most worthy surname; and I underwrote thus: Oh rejoice with me . . . that I am enabled . . . thus to write myself!" Pamela is exultant that she has become "a poor worthless creature . . . a mere cipher on the wrong side of a figure" who, "though nothing worth in myself, shall give signification by my *place*."[21] Although Fanny Price has yet to marry her Mr. B. at this point, the contrast with Pamela is striking. Soon to be considered priceless rather than worth nothing, Fanny underwrites herself, gaining (at least temporary) possession of books by signing her own name.

Yet if Fanny seems momentarily to approach the role of an author here, to seize the authority of self-inscription, we must acknowledge that to subscribe oneself "in *propria persona*" is an ambiguous act, since this obvious quotation from Aristotle's famous praise of Homer places Fanny's signature under the sign of an absent author; it alludes to an author who said very little "in *propria persona*," who did not sign his name. The italicized citation is in effect the signature of the absent author, the author who won't say "I."[22] The phrase undermines Fanny's self-inscription in other ways as well. It might make us wonder whose *persona* she has been in for the last 390 pages if not her own, reminding us that in this novel about impersonation, playacting, and *personae* it is not always easy to know the difference between a true self and a mask. This question might also alert us to the paradox that the same Fanny who has been portrayed as the model of self-integrity and stable identity has been experienced by readers as "too nearly nothing." In Leo Bersani's words, Fanny is "a negative presence": "she almost is not."[23] The inscription of Fanny's identity reminds us of the strange absence of her identity: the novel that dramatizes her sensibilities so acutely ends up removing her from sight and presenting even the language of real feeling under the sign of play.

Fanny begins to fall in love with Edmund when he helps her write a letter to her brother. He serves as her interpreter; when her "motives had been often misunderstood," Edmund had "explained her meaning" (173). He urges her "to speak for yourself" (61) and reproaches her for being "too silent" (213); yet in the conversation in the last chapter of the narrative proper (what comes as close to a display of their lovers' vows as the novel gives us), we see Fanny communicating by silence. "You do not wish me to be silent?" Edmund asks; "if you do, give me but a look, a word, and I have done." Then, set off by itself like a line of dialogue, we read: "No look or word was given" (441). Fanny's wish for Edmund to continue his narrative and not be silent is expressed by complete stillness and silence. As in her torturous conversation with Henry, every look is given meaning; but Fanny succeeds with Edmund where she failed with Henry in being able to communicate from a "zero degree" of signification. Fanny's lover's vow is delivered when she does and says nothing.

Indeed, we should recognize that when Fanny subscribes her name "in *propria person*," she is signing herself not as an author but as a reader. Her subscription to the circulating library recalls her presence as a reader in the novel. Throughout the rehearsals of the play, Fanny is the prompter: the keeper and guardian of the book who watches the performances of others with text in hand. The Crawfords challenge her ability to remain as audience and spectator; by forcing her to read a part, to read aloud, to enter into the dangerous circulation of floating signifiers and speculation, they refuse her the safety of the reader's position. However, by the end of the novel, Fanny seems to be able to declare herself a silent reader once again. Despite her triumph, or because of her triumph, she is able to love and be silent. Like Pamela, she must retreat from authority, even—or especially—if she gets everything she wants.

Paradoxically, it is this contradictory position that finally may inscribe Fanny in the position of author. Readers have complained about the novel's last chapter, in which a Fieldingesque narrator suddenly appears to clean up the plot and lower the curtain on the characters.[24] This abrupt assertion of narrative authority reminds us, however, that for virtually all of *Mansfield Park,* the author does not appear *in propria persona.* The dramatic narrative and indirect discourse keep author and narrator hidden from view—except insofar as we might see her in the woman acting as auditor and spectator, "judge and critic" (189) of the novel's characters, holding the book in her hand as they rehearse and enact the novel's plots.

In this sense, we might see in Fanny not so much a figure for the reader as an ambivalent self-portrait of the absent author: the supervising author who would not speak *in propria persona.* Mary at one point complains about the brevity of her brother's letters and asserts: "That is the true manly style" (90). By the end of *Mansfield Park,* however, as we speculate on the style and language of real feeling in a character cast as a sentimental heroine in a post-sentimental novel, we must wonder if the style of silence (if not of brevity) is for Austen the true womanly style—or whether, rather, the style or *persona* of silence must mask the true womanly style.

It is not generally noticed, as far as I can tell, that the first-person singular that abruptly begins the last chapter and closes the book in the voice of a narrator also makes an earlier appearance in *Mansfield Park.* In chapter 24, in the middle of a convoluted fifteen-line sentence that might have been dictated late in life by Henry James, an "I" appears, spoken by the voice of the narrative. We read: "for although there doubtless are such unconquerable young ladies of eighteen (or one should not read about them) as are never to be persuaded into love against their judgment . . . I have no inclination to believe Fanny one of them" (241). Here, without warning and for the only time before the epilogue-like conclusion, an "I" speaks out of nowhere. Not only does it occur next to a comment about reading: this is the chapter in which the Crawfords plan the plot to make Fanny fall in love with Henry that generates so much of the novel. One could suggest that Austen nodded here and forgot the style in which she was writing; but it might be more appropriate to say that here Austen wakes up, or that here she tries to wake up her reader.

A moment before the narrator suggests a lack of absolute knowledge about Fanny's character, Henry exclaims, "I do not quite know what to make of Miss Fanny. I do not understand her. . . . What is her character?—Is she solemn?—Is she queer?—Is she prudish? Why did she draw back and look so grave at me? I could hardly get her to speak" (240). Perhaps we can hear the voice of the reader in the exasperated comments of Henry Crawford as he tries to figure out the character of the recalcitrant and silent heroine. But if Henry's complaints about the silent and disapproving woman whose character can't be understood and who can't be made to speak apply to Fanny, they also apply to the character of the author, whose presence is indeed conjured up momentarily on the next page.

The glimpse of the "I" on this page, like the flaunted first-person singular in the last chapter, reminds us that Austen, like Fanny, has lost her place in the book. She may wish to speak her feelings, but she chooses to write and be silent. The appearance of the "I" acknowledges her decision to absent herself from the pages of the novel. *Mansfield Park* teaches us about the difficulty of appearing *in propria persona*. Even the language of real feeling and the integrity of the true self must be spoken *in persona,* personated in the mask of true acting. Yet *Mansfield Park* also teaches us about the difficulties of not appearing at all; even when masked by silence and absence, one cannot avoid entering into the play of signification.

4 ❘ Fatal Letters

Clarissa and the Death of Julie

> *[T]out me retrace une scène imaginaire avec plus de force que les*
> *événements qui me sont réellement arrivés.*
>
> Jean-Jacques Rousseau, *Julie ou La Nouvelle Héloïse*

In *Lettres angloises, ou Histoire de Miss Clarisse Harlove,* the abbé Prévost's 1751 translation of Richardson's *Clarissa,* there is a particularly striking illustration of the heroine's deathbed scene (fig. 1).[1] Jacques Pasquier's design (which follows the novel's carefully delineated literary tableau in which Belford promises to "peindre la scène qui s'est présentée à moi" (paint the scene that presented itself to me)[2] pictures Clarissa in a canopied bed with the curtains pulled back while several attendants, afflicted with grief and in tears, gather around her. Mrs. Lovick leans over the bed, Mrs. Smith clasps her hands together, a nurse holds a cordial, and a servant girl raises her hand to her face; Morden is on his knees taking Clarissa's lifeless hand, while Belford stands toward the foot of the bed with his back turned three-quarters toward the spectator. Rousseau's *Julie ou La Nouvelle Héloïse,* published ten years after Prévost's *Lettres angloises,* contains a similar illustration designed by Gravelot (fig. 2).[3] Here, in what Wolmar describes as an "extravagante scène" (723), the corpse of Julie also lies in a canopied bed with the curtain pulled back, while Claire lifts a veil to cover her. Several servants stand to the side in various poses of sorrow: one woman with her hands to her eyes, another with her hands clasped together; a man kneels on the floor next to Claire.

Unlike an illustration that appears earlier in Rousseau's novel, "L'Inoculation de l'amour," a deathbed scene that Julie survives, where St. Preux kneels next to a curtained bed kissing Julie's hand, here Claire stands at the center of the scene holding the veil. In the text, before she gets the veil, Claire is positioned "au chevet du lit" (725) (at the head of the bed), just as Mrs. Lovick is

Fig. 1. Engraving by Jacques Pasquier in Antonine-François Prévost, *Lettres angloises, ou Histoire de Miss Clarisse Harlove* (London, 1751–52), vol. 6, plate 7. Beinecke Rare Book and Manuscript Library, Yale University.

Fig. 2. Engraving by Gravelot (Hubert-François Bourgignon) in Jean-Jacques Rousseau, *Julie ou La Nouvelle Héloïse* (Amsterdam, 1769), vol. 3. Beinecke Rare Book and Manuscript Library, Yale University.

described with her head "contre le chevet du lit" (against the head of the bed).[4] Yet most strikingly, the image in Rousseau's text also contains a figure—the spectator and narrator of the *scène*—whose presence and pose internalize the beholder within the frame.[5] Like the representation of Belford, Wolmar stands at the foot of the bed, slightly at an angle, with his back to the beholder.

In his early plans for *Julie,* Rousseau apparently intended to drown his heroine.[6] The vestiges of this scenario may be seen in the letter that ends part 4, in which St. Preux describes his expedition with Julie to his former retreat at Meillerie. St. Preux, "dont l'imagination va toujours plus loin que le mal" (499) (whose imagination always exceeds the damage [423]), twice imagines the death of Julie. First, frightened by an accident in their boat, St. Preux writes, "je croyais voir de moment en moment le bateau englouti, cette beauté si touchante se débattre au milieu des flots, et la pâleur de la mort ternir les roses de son visage" (499) (I pictured the boat swallowed up from one moment to the next, that touching beauty flailing amidst the waves, and the pallor of death fading the roses of her face [423]). Then, when they return, St. Preux follows his vision of Julie's face in death with the fantasy of a murder-suicide: "je fus violemment tenté de la précipiter avec moi dans les flots, et d'y finir dans ses bras ma vie" (504) (I was violently tempted to hurl her with me into the waves, and there in her arms to put an end my life [428]). Julie ultimately leaps into the water in part 6 to save her child from drowning, and this accident eventually kills her, but only after she is allowed the literary luxury of a protracted death in bed. Death by drowning would have precluded the deathbed scenes that figure so importantly in the novel. Rousseau instead follows the example of Richardson in displaying his heroine's death in an elaborate series of spectacles and tableaux. Indeed, in an era in which such scenes were popular in paintings, engravings, and novels, it is difficult to imagine that Rousseau would have been able to resist a pathetic *tableau à la Greuze* as he sacrificed his heroine at the end of a novel that was seen as Richardsonian from the outset.

Clarissa's status as a precursor to *Julie* was obvious to readers from the moment Rousseau published his novel in 1761.[7] It is likely that when he wrote *Julie,* Rousseau knew *Clarissa* only in Prévost's original abridged translation.[8] The letters containing Clarissa's will and the accounts of her funeral were not added to the French translation until 1762,[9] although Rousseau may have been aware of them earlier from public discussion about Prévost's abridgments while he was writing *Julie* (for example, in the *Correspondance littéraire*)[10] and from his friendship with Prévost while the abbé was working on his translation.[11] It is evident, however, that in imagining Julie's deathbed scene,

Rousseau would have had the image of the dying Clarissa before him—perhaps even literally on his writing table.[12] Obviously, the deathbed scenes of Clarissa and Julie, in both their written and engraven versions, participate in a tradition with recognizably formulaic elements. Pasquier and Gravelot, like Richardson and Rousseau, composed familiar set pieces in these scenes. Yet both Rousseau and Gravelot would have known the illustrations in Prévost's translation of *Clarissa*. Gravelot and Pasquier together had designed the illustrations for Prévost's *Manon Lescaut* in 1753; and although it is often noted that Rousseau originally wanted François Boucher as the illustrator of *La Nouvelle Héloïse,* in understanding Rousseau's designs it is perhaps more significant that Gravelot was well known as the illustrator of Richardson's *Pamela.*[13]

Rousseau provided elaborate written instructions for each illustration (in addition to the text of his novel) in a text called "Sujets d'estampes." These literary tableaux, first written as descriptions of imaginary engravings representing scenes depicted in the novel, were printed alongside the illustrations in the original *Recueil d'estampes*. Rousseau also wrote letters critiquing and demanding revisions in the illustrations, most extensively in the deathbed tableau.[14] The resemblances between the depictions of the deathbed scenes of Clarissa and Julie thus may be explained by a variety of factors in addition to literary and artistic formulae: the influence of Pasquier's illustration on Gravelot's illustration, the influence of Pasquier's illustration on Rousseau's text, the influence of Richardson's text on Rousseau's text, and the influence of Rousseau's texts (the novel, the "Sujets d'estampes," and the instructions) on Gravelot's illustration. One cannot know which factor or combination of factors determined the overdetermined relations apparent in the series of translations transacted between model and copy—between text and text, image and image, text and image, and image and text. What interests me here, however, are the ways in which these relations are inscribed and interrogated within the texts of the novels themselves, especially in *La Nouvelle Héloïse.*

Both Richardson and Rousseau create self-consciously theatrical spectacles in imagining the deaths of their heroines. Rousseau, in particular, locates his heroine in a series of literary, visual, and imaginary images and tableaux that extends back to the images and tableaux of *Clarissa*. Throughout his novel, Rousseau is concerned with the relations between real scenes and imagined scenes, and between representations—especially letters—and events. The extravagant scenes and performances in which Rousseau poses his dying heroine seem charged with a sense of déjà vu whether or not we read them next to the spectacles and images of Clarissa's death. In this chapter, in focusing on Julie's deathbed scenes and related images and representations, I keep in mind the double sense of déjà vu that comes from reading *Julie* next to *Clarissa*. My subject is neither influence nor originality in the terms of the traditional study of literary sources.[15] In a sense, I am interested in the ghost of Clarissa in Rousseau's tableaux of Julie's death—the traces of which, I suggest, become more visible if we work through the medium of Prévost's translation. To understand *Julie*, we must keep the language of Prévost's *Clarissa* before us. The relations between these images, tableaux, and texts help to illuminate Rousseau's preoccupation with both the prediction and the reenactment of deathbed scenes, as well as the status of the epistolary novel as a collection of posthumous texts sent, as it were, from the grave.

> *Ce n'est plus moi qui te parle; je suis déjà dans les bras de la mort.*
> *Quand tu verras cette lettre, les vers rongeront le visage de ton amante,*
> *et son coeur où tu ne seras plus.*—Rousseau, *Julie ou La Nouvelle Héloïse*[16]

In Clarissa's will, one of the numerous posthumous letters that she leaves to be read after her death, Clarissa expresses the desire that she "may not be unnecessarily exposed to the view of any-body" besides her relations. She stipulates in particular that Lovelace "might not be permitted to see my corpse" and then proceeds to describe (and prescribe) a strange fantasy about a final epistolary exchange.

> But if, as he is a man very uncontroulable, and as I am Nobody's, he insist upon viewing *her dead* whom he ONCE before saw in a manner dead, let his gay curiosity be gratified. Let him behold, and triumph over the wretched Remains of one who has been made a victim to his barbarous perfidy: But let some good person, as by my desire, give him a paper, whilst he is viewing the ghastly spectacle, containing these few words only—"Gay, cruel heart! behold here the Remains of the once ruined, yet now happy, Clarissa Harlowe!—See what thou thyself must quickly be;—and REPENT!—"[17]

In the aftermath of the rape, Clarissa seeks to avoid the "shock of *public shame*" and the publicity of a trial that would expose her to "the world's eye."[18] In her first letter to Lovelace after the rape, she asks to be "locked up in some private Madhouse . . . never more to be seen," pleading, "don't let me be made a shew of."[19] In particular, she seeks to avoid being seen by Lovelace (who never does see her again after her final escape). In this fantasy, however, Clarissa becomes invested at least momentarily in the image of Lovelace beholding the spectacle of her dead body. Writing on her deathbed, or perhaps on the coffin that she "writes and reads upon . . . as others would upon a desk or table,"[20] Clarissa seeks to stage a deathbed scene that would also be the scene of a posthumous letter. It is a scene that would teach Lovelace a lesson about the spectacle, the body, and the text of Clarissa.

Although Clarissa goes on to insist that she does "most sincerely forgive Mr. Lovelace the wrongs he has done me,"[21] her fantasy can be seen as a Gothic or even a Jacobean scenario of revenge, in which she seems to rise from the dead or appear as a ghost to admonish Lovelace with both the image of his crime and the specter of his own death. In addition, by comparing Lovelace's imaginary encounter with her corpse to the scene of the rape (thereby inscribing the encounter as a repetition of a scene of death that has already occurred), Clarissa makes the point that Lovelace has not possessed her in possessing her body. Indeed, in her description Clarissa seems to disappear before his (and our) very eyes as she shifts from the first-person singular to the third person within one sentence. The phrase "as I am Nobody's," which shifts to the phrase "*her dead*," recalls Clarissa's sentiments after the rape that "I am no longer what I was in any one thing. . . . I don't know what my name is!"[22] Although she can name herself in the third person as "Clarissa Harlowe," Clarissa (as if anticipating Frances Burney or even Emily Dickinson) seems to declare her body to be "Nobody" as well as "Nobody's." A moment later, she refers to her body as "*what will be Nothing when this writing comes to be opened and read.*"

Lovelace has argued that Clarissa's unconsciousness at the time of the rape has meant her "Triumph" rather than his: "her will is unviolated," he insists.[23] Yet in allowing and even commanding that Lovelace should look at her corpse ("Let him behold . . . ") Clarissa envisions that in violating her will, Lovelace will misread her body. His wishful misreading of her allegorical letter about her journey to her father's house already has demonstrated his error of reading too literally. Although not even Clarissa (who instructs that her corpse not be "opened") anticipates his literalizing wish to have her "opened and embalmed" so that he can "have possession of her dear heart,"[24] she plans to stage a scene in which Lovelace would be caught in an act of misreading if he beheld the spectacle of her body.

The fantasy that Clarissa imagines and enacts in all of her many posthumous letters is that of speaking from the grave. "Hear me therefore, O Lovelace! as one speaking from the dead," she apostrophizes in the posthumous letter and call to repentance that she actually sends to him.[25] However, what is at stake here is what Anna Howe describes as "writing as from the dead."[26] Lovelace, Clarissa instructs, "as by my desire," is to be given "a paper, whilst he is viewing the ghastly spectacle, containing these few words only— 'Gay, cruel heart! behold here the Remains of the once ruined, yet now happy, Clarissa Harlowe!'" As he fixates on the spectacle of her body, he is to be tapped on the shoulder, as it were, and handed a letter that instructs him to "behold *here* the Remains" of Clarissa: focused on the body, he is to be confronted with a text containing Clarissa's words, declaring in effect that he is mistaken in trying to see her in her body.

Faced with both body and text, he is told that she is "here" in the text— which is to say that as he tries to satisfy his "curiosity" and see her spectacle, he must confront the fact that she is not there. Clarissa gives orders "with great presence of mind, about her body," Belford notes earlier.[27] Here, she instructs Lovelace, through the medium in which he knows her best, that despite the presence of her body, she is absent. In both the fantasy and the reality of her will, the body that she insists should not be "opened" after her death "*will be Nothing when this writing comes to be opened and read*" because her body has been replaced or displaced by her writing. Despite the physical suffering of Clarissa as a character within the realistic plot of the novel, this has been the case from the moment the reader opened the book and read Clarissa's first letter.

The lesson that Clarissa stages about her absence is also demonstrated in the extensive deathbed scenes that actually do take place in the plot of the novel. In these scenes, Clarissa is described at the center of carefully constructed tableaux. We read how Morden and Belford "beheld the Lady, in a charming attitude" asleep in an "elbow-chair": "In this heart-moving attitude she appeared to us when we approached her, and came to have her lovely face before us."[28] (Although presented in a different light, this scene recalls Lovelace's description, shortly after the rape, of how he "looked through the key-hole of my Beloved's door" and "beheld her in a sweet slumber" in her "elbow-chair" in "a sleepy lifelessness.")[29] In his account of Clarissa's "happy Exit," Belford describes "the woeful scene that presented itself to me," carefully noting the position of everyone in a deathbed scene that reads like a description of an illustration. At first "moving her lips without uttering a word," after she speaks, Belford notes, "She *looked* what she said."[30] After they have "seen the last scene closed," they "could not help taking a view of the lovely corpse, and admiring the charming serenity of her noble aspect. The women declared, they never saw death so lovely before."[31]

Each of these tableaux is in its way highly theatrical, especially for the reader who beholds the scenes self-consciously framed and described by Belford, yet each contains the classic antidotes used by eighteenth-century writers and painters to neutralize theatricality. When Clarissa wakes from her sleep, Morden is hiding behind the "Screen" that conceals the coffin, "unseen by his Cousin."[32] Just before she dies, Clarissa exclaims, "My sight fails me!"[33] She acknowledges that her death is "worse to beholders, than to me,"[34] but sleeping, unaware that she is being watched, almost blind, and finally dead, Clarissa seems oblivious to the beholders who witness her death and to the spectacle in which she is playing a part (just as she is oblivious to Lovelace's voyeurism in her "sleepy lifelessness").[35] Despite her edifying last words and saintly apotheosis, at these moments Clarissa is not there. As in the rape scene, in which she is "in a manner dead," she is in a sense absent in these tableaux, absent to them, even as she embodies their ghastly or lovely spectacles.[36]

This absence also characterizes the scene of the funeral. Belford, who witnesses this scene only as a reader through a letter that "so naturally describes all that passed, that I have every scene before my eyes," pictures himself near the "eye-attracting coffin": "Now, thro' the buz of gaping, eye-swoln crouds, do I descend into the clammy vault, as a true Executor, to see that part of her Will performed with my own eyes."[37] Yet despite the theatrical terms that Richardson prescribes for the reader, the "last mournful Rite" must focus on the absence of Clarissa. She is, of course, concealed in the coffin covered with the "plates, and emblems, and inscription" that "set every one gazing upon it"—in what Terry Castle has described as "a concretized metaphor for textuality itself," "a coffin-text" that is "a sign of absence."[38] Those mourners who "wished to be permitted a sight of the corpse" but rather "satisfied their curiosity, and remarked upon the emblems"[39] must (like Lovelace as he seeks to satisfy his curiosity in Clarissa's fantasy) see the spectacle of Clarissa's corpse replaced by a text.

Furthermore, at the funeral, the cynosure of the crowd (transfigured by prosopopeia into "the face of All") is literally nobody. When the preacher "pointed to the pew where" Clarissa "used to sit or kneel, the whole auditory, as one person, turned to the pew with the most respectful solemnity, as if she had been herself there."[40] The auditory presumably looks at an empty pew or a place where the presence of someone else reveals Clarissa's absence, beholding Clarissa only "as if" she were there. Earlier, Mrs. Norton, one of the few people to satisfy her desire to "see the corpse," is said to kiss Clarissa's face "as if she were living." Mrs. Norton insists, "It was *She* indeed . . . Her very Self! Nor had death, which changed all things, a power to alter her lovely features!"[41] We read several times that the corpse has not decayed, even without Lovelace's embalming fluids; but the lesson of Clarissa's death is that one can see her only *as if* she were there. Clarissa is present only in the image that embodies her absence, only in the text through which we imagine her. The deathbed scene that Clarissa imagines in the posthumous text of her will stages the delivery of a posthumous letter that speaks or writes from the grave to tell us about the posthumous character of all of the letters in Richardson's epistolary novel. Juxtaposing the spectacle of her corpse, the sight of her "in a manner dead," and the "paper" in which she writes from the grave—all within the imagined images of a fantasy—Clarissa pictures the scene of death inscribed within the scene of representation.

> *But why should I, who have such* real *evils to contend with, regard* imaginary *ones?*
>
> *I said that whatever we strongly imagined was, in its effects, at the time, more* than imaginary, *although to others it might not appear so.*
> —Richardson, *Clarissa*[42]

The illustration of Julie's deathbed scene in which Claire covers Julie's face with a veil—this final illustration in the novel, according to Rousseau's instructions, is the only engraving to appear without an inscription—represents the corpse of Julie, but it does not (strictly speaking) represent the moment of her death. It is only one moment in a series of tableaux that recounts Julie's death. Indeed, despite (or perhaps because of) this proliferation of images, it is not so easy to locate Julie's deathbed scene in the pages of the novel. We know that Clarissa's death occurs "exactly at 40 minutes after Six o'clock, as by her watch on the table."[43] (Pasquier actually includes this watch in his illustration of the scene although, following Prévost's translation, it is "suspendue" rather than "on the table.")[44] The moment of Julie's death is more indeterminate; as Wolmar, in a Richardsonian climax of "writing to the moment," describes how he is awakened by groans in the night to open the curtain of Julie's bed just as she dies in Claire's arms, the moment of death seems almost lost in the shift from breathless present tenses to a past imperfect: "J'accours, j'entre, j'ouvre le rideau . . . je vois les deux amies sans mouvement et se tenant embrassées, l'une évanouie et l'autre expirante. Je m'écrie, je veux retarder ou recueillir son dernier soupir, je me précipite. Elle n'était plus" (721–22) (I run, I enter, I open the curtain . . . I see the two friends motionless, locked in each other's embrace; the one in a faint, and the other expiring. I cry out, I want to delay or to receive her last breath, and I rush forward. She was no more [602]).[45] The deathbed scene witnessed by Wolmar recasts an earlier moment described by St. Preux. Returning to Clarens unexpectedly, Claire surprises Julie, running towards her crying "avec un emportement impossible à peindre: 'Cousine, toujours, pour toujours, jusqu'à la mort!'" (in a rapture impossible to paint, "Cousin, forever, forever until death!"). In the passion of the moment, Henriette is knocked down, and Claire and Julie both begin to faint; Wolmar, in what St. Preux describes as a rare display of sentiment, "se jeta sur un fauteuil pour contempler avidement ce ravissant spectacle" (threw himself into an armchair to contemplate avidly this ravishing spectacle). He explains that "ces scènes de plaisir et de joie n'épuisent un instant la nature que pour la ranimer d'une vigueur nouvelle" (585) (these Scenes of pleasure and joy exhaust nature for a moment only to reanimate her with a new vigor [490]). The emotional reunion evoking death and the spectacle of the two lifeless women to which Wolmar voyeuristically positions himself as a beholder prefigures the scene he witnesses when he opens the curtains on Julie's deathbed.

Nature cannot be reanimated, however, in the repetition of the scene that is enacted with Julie's corpse, although Claire "se jetait sur son corps, le réchauffait du sien, s'efforçait de le ranimer" (722) (threw herself upon her body, warmed it with hers, endeavored to reanimate it [602]). These details recall the scene in *Clarissa* in which Anna Howe tries to wake Clarissa's corpse, crying: "Let thy Anna Howe revive thee; by her warm breath revive thee, my dear creature! And kissing her again, Let my warm lips animate thy cold ones!" (or in the French: "laisse-moi te rappeller à la vie; partage le souffle qui m'anime . . . que la chaleur de mes levres réchauffe les tiennes!").[46] Anna speaks these lines after having "pushed aside the lid" of Clarissa's coffin and "impatiently removed the face-cloth" (translated by Prévost as "le voile qui couvroit le visage").[47] The scene with the *voile* that Rousseau chooses for his illustration of the death of Julie is the culmination of the "extravagante scène" represented for the reader by Wolmar. The day after Julie's death, after visiting Julie's father, Wolmar returns to find "tout le monde dans le transport" (everyone transported) insisting that "Madame n'est pas morte" (Madame is not dead). Wolmar recounts, again writing to the moment:

> Je monte à pas précipités dans l'appartement de Julie. Je trouve plus de vingt personnes à genoux autour de son lit et les yeux fixés sur elle. Je m'approche; je la vois sur ce lit habillée et parée; le coeur me bat; je l'examine . . . Hélas! elle était morte! Ce moment de fausse joie sitôt et si cruellement éteinte fut

le plus amer de ma vie. Je ne suis pas colère: je me sentis vivement irrité. Je voulus savoir le fond de cette extravagante scène. Tout était déguisé, altéré, changé. (723)

I climb with hurried steps to Julie's apartment. I find more than twenty people on their knees around the bed with their eyes fixed on her. I approach, I see her on the bed dressed up and made up. My heart pounds, I examine her . . . Alas! she was dead! This moment of false joy so quickly and so cruelly extinguished was the most bitter in my life. I am not an angry sort; I felt intensely irritated. I wanted to get to the bottom of this extravagant scene. Everything was disguised, altered, changed. (603–4)[48]

Everything is altered and changed, but the horror of this scene is "l'horreur de la perdre une seconde fois" (the horror of losing her a second time). Once again, Wolmar approaches the moment of death and finds that Julie's presence has already passed. He must live through a repetition of Julie's death not only because of the false report that she is alive but also because he must become a spectator to a restaging of her deathbed scene. Here, however, in an embodiment of theatrical disguise, both the spectacle of her death and "scènes de plaisir et de joie" (scenes of pleasure and joy) are replayed as a "moment de fausse joie" (moment of false joy).

Wolmar learns that the old valet of Julie's father had imagined that he saw the dead Julie move:

[I]l se met à genoux au pied de son lit, il la regarde, il pleure, il la contemple . . . les yeux toujours collés sur ce visage, il crut apercevoir un mouvement: son imagination se frappe; il voit Julie tourner les yeux, le regarder, lui faire un signe de tête. . . . Bientôt la défunte n'avait pas seulement fait signe, elle avait agi, elle avait parlé, et il y avait vingt témoins oculaires de faits circonstanciés qui n'arrivèrent jamais. (724)

He kneels at the foot of her bed, he looks at her, he cries, he contemplates her . . . his eyes still glued to that face, he believed that he perceived a movement. His imagination strikes him; he sees Julie turn her eyes, look at him, make him a sign with her head. . . . Soon the deceased not only made a sign, she had acted, she had spoken, and there were twenty eyewitnesses to detailed facts that never took place. (604)[49]

Finally, after repeatedly trying to revive her ("la ranimer"), persisting in their "erreur," Julie's attendants dress her: "elles lui prodiguèrent la parure; ensuite l'exposant sur un lit, et laisant les rideaux ouverts, elles se remirent à la pleurer au milieu de la joie publique" (they made her up prodigiously; then exposing her on the bed, and leaving the curtains open, they went back to crying in the midst of the public joy). It is this staged scene that Wolmar stumbles upon when he returns. He is worried, on the one hand, that he will be considered a murderous husband who has buried his wife alive and, on the other hand, that "les chairs commençaient à se corrompre" (the corruption of the flesh was beginning). There are even some "signes d'altération" (signs of alteration) in the face. He confides his fears to Claire, who has indulged in this "mortel spectacle" (deathly spectacle) despite the fact that she is not "la dupe d'une illusion" (the dupe of an illusion). Claire returns with a veil, with which she covers her friend's face, crying: "Maudite soit l'indigne main qui jamais lèvera ce voile! maudit soit l'oeil impie qui verra ce visage défiguré" (724–25) (Cursed be the wretched hand that ever lifts this veil! Cursed be the sacrilegious eye that ever looks on this disfigured face! [606]). The "spectateurs" are struck by these words, and they bury the body without daring to touch the veil.[50]

The spectacle represented here is a *tableau vivant,* a deathbed scene that tries to make a living tableau out of a corpse displayed as if it were alive before an audience of spectators and eyewitnesses whose eyes are fixed upon it. In *Romeo and Juliet,* Shakespeare's heroine is made up and costumed as if she were dead in a deathbed scene that turns out to be prophetically convincing for a spectator who has accidentally missed the messenger sent to inform him of the playacting. Unlike Juliet, Julie is costumed and made up as if she were alive after a valet who missed a messenger carrying news of death imagines that he sees in her a sign of life. Like Lily Bart in Edith Wharton's *The House of Mirth,* a literary heroine who might be seen as a descendant of both Juliet and Julie, at the end of the novel, Rousseau's heroine is presented as both a *tableau vivant* and a *nature morte.*[51] Diderot praises his own Richardsonian novel *La Religieuse,* which he describes as "rempli de tableaux pathétiques" (filled with pathetic tableaux), by calling it "un ouvrage à feuilleter sans cesse par les peintres" (a work for painters to leaf through incessantly).[52] By deciding that the illustration of Julie's death should represent not the actual moment of death but rather the *tableau pathétique* in which Julie is posed as if she were alive, Rousseau prescribes a tableau within a tableau within a tableau. By the time Gravelot designed the illustration based on Wolmar's description of the scene in the novel and Rousseau's description of what the illustration should look like, the deathbed scene representing Wolmar beholding the posed, costumed, and made-up body of Julie framed by the curtains of her bed had already been translated into a spectacle—an illustration, a scene, a work of art—several times over within the narrative of the novel itself. It is not just that this scene is self-consciously imagined and framed as an illustration in the original description of the scene in the letter, or that it rehearses other deathbed scenes. Within the scene itself, Julie is already an illustration; posed as a representation of herself, her corpse plays the role of her living body.

Whether or not the image of Claire covering the dead Julie's face suggests Rousseau's awareness of Morden's letter describing Anna Howe and Clarissa's "face-cloth"—"le voile qui couvroit le visage"[53]—we can recognize in the "extravagante scène" in which Wolmar loses Julie a second time a more elaborate reenactment of the double moment of Clarissa's death. Like Wolmar, if on a smaller scale, Belford and Morden must witness the moment of Clarissa's death twice. After she utters what appear to be her last words, Clarissa appears to die, only to revive and then die again. In Prévost's version:

> [S]a tête s'est appesantie sur son oreiller; ses mains ont quitté les nôtres, & la pâleur de la mort s'est répandue sur son visage. Nous avons cru qu'elle venoit d'expirer, & la douleur nous a fait pousser un cri. Mais quelques signes de vie, qu'elle a recommencé à donner, ont rappellé aussi tôt notre attention.

> Her head sunk upon her pillow; her hands had left ours, and the paleness of death spread on her face. We believed that she had just expired, and grief made us let out a cry. But some signs of life that she again began to give, just as soon recalled our attention.[54]

(The "pâleur de la mort . . . sur son visage," which echoes in Claire's hallucinatory "je crois voir sur son visage la pâleur de la mort," is Prévost's invention.) Whereas Clarissa, after seeming to die, shows "signs of returning life" only to expire a moment later, the "signe" witnessed on Julie's face is a false sign and it leads to the macabre spectacle that Wolmar describes: "Il fallait qu'elle ressuscitât pour me donner l'horreur de la perdre une seconde fois" (560) (She had to be resussicated to inflict on me the horror of losing her a second time [602]). Clarissa's deathbed scene is, of course, hundreds of pages longer than Julie's; but these details suggest that the two moments of Clarissa's death are translated, repeated, and expanded in the two scenes of Julie's death beheld by Wolmar.

In one of the footnotes to this scene, written in the persona of what he describes in the Second Preface as "l'éditeur de ce livre" (753) (the editor of this book [19]), Rousseau acknowledges that the image of the veil has been seen before—specifically in St. Preux's dream about Julie's death in part 5. There, amidst "images funèbres" (deathly images), St. Preux imagines the deathbed scene of Julie's mother: "cette scène," he writes to Claire, "que vous m'avez autrefois dépeinte" (this scene you depicted to me years ago). He continues:

> Je vis Julie à sa place; je la vis, je la reconnus, quoique son visage fût couvert d'un voile. . . . Toujours ce spectacle lugubre, toujours ce même appareil de mort, toujours ce voile impénétrable échappe à mes mains, et dérobe à mes yeux l'objet expirant qu'il couvre. (603–4)

> I saw Julie in her place; I saw her, I recognized her, although her face was covered with a veil. . . . Again this lugubrious spectacle, again the same trappings of death; again this impenetrable veil eludes my hands and conceals from my eyes the expiring object it covered. (505)

As regrets and death "se peignirent dans mes songes" (painted themselves in my dreams), St. Preux is pursued "de fantôme en fantôme" (from phantom to phantom) by "apparitions." He imagines a deathbed scene based on Claire's earlier description of the "plus attendrissant de tous les spectacles" (302) (the most moving of all spectacles [264]) and then substitutes Julie for the character at its center. Claire's epistolary painting of a deathbed scene is translated into St. Preux's dream images of Julie's deathbed scene, which are translated into the "fatale lettre" he writes to Claire, which causes her troubling visions: "à chaque instant je crois voir sur son visage la pâleur de la mort" (607) (at every moment I think I see on her face the pallor of death [508]). These images are finally enacted in the strange dramatic reprise of Julie's deathbed scene when Claire places the veil over Julie. Rousseau's footnote argues that the dream caused but did not predict Claire's use of the veil: "L'événement n'est pas prédit parce qu'il arrivera; mais il arrive parce qu'il a été prédit" (705) (The event is not predicted because it will happen; but it happens because it has been predicted [606]).[55] At the level of plot, as he attempts to control the interpretation of his plot, Rousseau insists on a psychological rather than a supernatural explanation; but in doing so, he acknowledges a sense of *déjà vu* here, a sense of *déjà dit* that might lead one to think that an event has been *prédit*. Image, representation, model, and letter precede and in some sense prescribe the events they describe. The event seems to take place because it has been written in a letter.

Among the letters that precede and prefigure the visionary displays in which Julie seems to appear in the place of someone else in the center of someone else's deathbed scene—"tristes pressentiments" that have been seen before—are the dreams about death recounted by Lovelace and Clarissa. Once again, although the plot and the characters are different, Richardson's language and images (mediated through Prévost) seem to be recycled in Rousseau's text. St. Preux dreams of Julie's death, with its "spectacle lugubre" (lugubrious spectacle) and sees "toujours ce même appareil de mort" (again the same trappings of death); "toujours ce voile impénétrable échappe à mes mains, et dérobe à mes yeux l'objet expirant qu'il couvre" (again this impenetrable veil eludes my hands and conceals from my eyes the expiring object it covered [505]). The scene recalls the dream in which Lovelace imagines Clarissa's apparent ascension into heaven. In his "misérable vision" (as rendered by Prévost), "Le plat-fond, qui s'est fermé aussi-tôt, m'a dérobé la suite du spectacle. Je me suis trouvé, entre les mains, une robe de femme, d'un fond bleu, toute parsemée d'étoiles d'or, que j'ai reconnue pour celle de Miss Harlove, & par laquelle je m'étois efforcé de la retenir: mais c'est tout ce qui resté de cette adorable fille" (The ceiling, which soon was closed, hid from me what followed of the spectacle. I found myself with a woman's dress in my hands, with a blue background, completely studded with stars of gold, that I recognized as Miss Harlow's, by which I tried to hold on to her, but this is all that remained of this adorable girl).[56]

The *robe* that conceals (*dérobe*) the sight of Clarissa is "parsemée d'étoiles d'or" (studded with stars of gold); the veil that conceals (*dérobe*) Julie's face is "un voile d'or brodé de perles" (725) (a golden veil embroidered with pearls [606]). Lovelace awakens "inondé d'une sueur froide" (drenched in a cold sweat) as "toutes ces images ne m'ont pas été moins présentes que des réalités" (all these images were not less present to me than realities). St. Preux awakes "trempé de sueur. . . . croyant me voir environné de fantômes" (603–4) (drenched in sweat. . . . I could see myself surrounded by phantoms [505]). In Prévost's version, Lovelace later boasts to Belford, "mon songe prophétique n'est-il pas bien expliqué?" (hasn't my prophetic dream been well explained?).[57] Although he completely misinterprets his "misérable vision," it is more prophetic than he realizes. Rousseau tries to explain away the "tristes pressentiments" (sad presentiments) in the "rêve funeste" (deadly dream) of his "visionnaire" (visionary) when they appear to come true; but what is at stake here is not prophecy but rather the relation between prediction and event, between an imaginary or literary model and its copy in "reality."

Lovelace's dream itself reiterates Clarissa's dream, in which she imagines that Lovelace "stabbed me to the heart, and then tumbled me into a deep grave ready dug, among two or three half-dissolved carcases." Once again we might retrospectively recognize St. Preux's "images funèbres" (deadly images) and "imagination troublé" (troubled imagination) as Clarissa recounts her awakening, especially if we attend to the language of Prévost's translation:

> Je me suis réveillée dans une terreur inexprimable, baigné d'une sueur froide . . . Ces affreuses images ne sont pas encore sorties de ma mémoire. Mais pourquoi m'arrêter des maux imaginaires, lorsque j'en ai de si réels à combattre? Ce songe est venu, sans doute, du trouble de mon imagination.

> I awoke in an inexpressible terror, bathed in a cold sweat. . . . These terrible images are not yet gone from my memory. But why should I stop on imaginary evils when I have real ones to combat? The dream came, no doubt, from my troubled imagination.[58]

This confusion between what is real and what is a product of a troubled imagination, between (in the words of Prévost's Lovelace) "images" and "réalités," also recalls another deathbed scene that is simultaneously dream and event.

Writing to Claire after she has almost died of smallpox, Julie describes "un délire" (a delirium) in which she thought that she saw St. Preux "à genoux" (on his knees). (The imagined pose recalls Morden at Clarissa's deathbed in both text and illustration.) She describes how "il prit un de mes mains" and "la couvrait de baisers et de larmes" (he took one of my hands . . . he was covering it with kisses and tears) and she represents the effect of "sa présence" (his presence) and the after-images of the dream: "Je ne puis te représenter l'effet étonnant que ce rêve a produit sur moi" (I cannot represent for you the astounding effect this dream has had on me), she writes, representing "impressions" in her "imagination" that she can't "effacer" (erase). The tableau that Rousseau selects for the fifth illustration ("L'inoculation de l'amour") seems to repeat itself in Julie's imagination: "A chaque minute, à chaque instant, il me semble le voir dans la même attitude. . . . tout me retrace une scène imaginaire avec plus de force que les événements qui me sont réellement arrivés" (308–9) (At every minute, at every instant I imagine I am seeing him in the same posture . . . everything retraces to me an imaginary scene with more force than the events that have actually befallen me [270]). The "vision" that Julie fears is "un pressentiment de la mort" (a presentiment of death) as it repeats itself in her imagination turns out to be a scene that really did take place. Claire explains: "Apprends donc que ton rêve n'est point un rêve; que ce n'est point l'ombre de ton ami que tu as vue, mais sa personne, et que cette touchante scène, incessamment présente à ton imagination, s'est passée réellement dans ta chambre"

(310) (Know then that your dream is not a dream; that it is not the ghost of your friend that you have seen, but his person; and that this touching scene constantly present to your imagination actually took place in your room [271]).[59]

Julie tries to represent to Claire the sentiment that Clarissa notes, that "tout ce qu'on s'imagine fortement produit dans le temps plus d'effet qu'une simple imagination" (all that we imagine strongly produces at the time more of an effect than something simply imagined);[60] like Lovelace, for whom "toutes ces images ne m'ont pas été moins présentes que des réalités" (all these images were not less present to me than realities), Julie experiences an imaginary scene that represents itself with the force of reality. Yet in a novel in which images, dreams, and imaginary tableaux seem to attain the status of reality, this is a real event that seems like a dream rather than a dream that seems like a real event. In the "scène imaginaire" of this deathbed scene, strangely narrated from the point of view of the dying heroine, the persons and not merely the shadows of characters apparently were present. However, in assuring Julie that the event really took place, Claire herself frames it as a "touchante scène, incessamment présente à ton imagination" (touching scene constantly present to your imagination), just as Julie represents how "tout me retrace une scène imaginaire" (everything retraces to me an imaginary scene). Both Julie and Claire describe the representation of an event that seems to have been always already a *tableau pathétique;* the deathbed scene that occurs before Julie's death, like the one that occurs after her death, seems to have been an illustration from the outset. This is not to say merely that Rousseau, like many of his contemporaries, composed a literary tableau, but rather that the scene is experienced by the characters themselves as an illustration or spectacle. Although Julie is told that her dream was not a dream, its immediate translation into a "scène imaginaire" is repeatedly reiterated as its touching tableau is retraced in the imagination.

> Quelque rôle qu'on ait pu faire durant sa vie, on ne doit point jouer la comédie à sa mort.   —Rousseau, *Julie ou La Nouvelle Héloïse* [61]

Like the spectacle of Julie posed and costumed in the deathbed scene at the end of the novel, the tableau of Julie's dream is located somewhere between the real and the imaginary. This ambiguity also characterizes Julie's face, which is the other subject of the exchange of letters between Claire and Julie about the imaginary deathbed scene. In addition to focusing on the scene that has retraced itself in Julie's memory and imagination, these letters also focus on the traces marked upon the person and "figure" of Julie. Confessing her attachment to the "image chérie" of her past with St. Preux, Julie hopes that her illness will preclude her unwanted marriage. She suggests that unlike St. Preux, whose "goût ne se bornait pas aux traits et à la figure" (307–8) (taste was not restricted to features and to countenance [269]), Wolmar will be put off by the "aspect" of her scarred face. Reminding Julie that she already has "renoncé à la personne de ton ami" (renounced your friend's person), Claire assures her: "ton visage a été épargné. Ce que tu prends pour des cicatrices ne sont que des rougeurs qui seront bientôt éffacées" (313) (your visage has been spared. What you take for scars are only a rash that will soon be effaced [274]). Just as Claire hoped to "effacer" the traces of an "apparition" in which Julie saw retraced the "personne" she has renounced, she promises Julie that the marks on her face will be effaced or erased. Julie is not merely a beholder or an actor in an imaginary scene; she is a tableau herself.

After this deathbed encounter, St. Preux, who is "de plus fort marqué de la petite vérole" (409) (much scarred by smallpox [352]), agonizes over the image of Julie's face when he returns from his long absence. He writes to Édouard: "Mon imagination me refusait opiniâtrement des taches sur ce charmant visage; et sitôt que j'en voyais un marqué de petite vérole, ce n'était plus celui de Julie" (401) (My imagination obstinately resisted marks on that charming face, and the minute I saw one marked with smallpox, it was no longer Julie's [344]). Although it turns out that the smallpox has left only "quelques légères traces presque imperceptibles" (403) (a few slight, almost imperceptible traces [347]), he still has trouble picturing the same Julie. The anticipated "entrevue" (interview), he writes, "se présentait à mon esprit sous mille tableaux différents" (401) (presented itself to my mind in a thousand different tableaux [344]). He tries to "voir sous un autre point de vue ce même objet qui m'était jamais sorti de mon coeur" (see from a different point of view that same object that had ever remained in my heart) and he imagines seeing "Julie mariée, Julie mère, Julie indifférente" (Julie married, Julie a mother, Julie indifferent) instead of the "sa figure" (400–401) (her face [343–44]), which he has identified with their love.

As he approaches her, he writes, "Je ne voyais plus Julie; mon imagination troublée ne me présentait que des objets confus" (I no longer saw Julie; my troubled imagination presented only blurry objects to me). Finally, when he does see Julie accompanied by her children, he sees a spectacle that seems to make her disappear: "Que devins-je à cet aspect? . . . O spectacle! . . . Je voyais, pour ainsi dire, multiplier celle qui me fut si chère. Hélas! je voyais au même instant la trop vive preuve qu'elle ne m'était plus rien, et mes pertes semblaient se multiplier avec elle" (403–4) (What became of me at this sight? . . . O spectacle! . . . I was, so to speak, seeing her whom I so cherished multiplied. Alas! I was seeing at the same instant the only too vivid proof that she was nothing more to me, and my losses seemed to be multiplied with her [347]). Multiplied even before St. Preux recognizes the traits of her face in the "physionomie" of her children, Julie seems lost amidst a kaleidoscope of anticipated, recollected, and imagined images as tableaux, spectacles, aspects, and points of view seem to proliferate. Once again, at stake here is not merely Julie's presence in a scene or a series of images. Julie's face itself is the spectacle in question; and remarkably, after he has imagined all of these aspects of Julie, St. Preux experiences the sight and presence of the "real" Julie as loss and absence.

This experience recalls the letters about Julie's portrait. Julie intends the portrait to operate as a sort of "talisman" that will allow them to communicate across distance and absence. When he opens the package containing the portrait, St. Preux experiences revelation: "Julie! . . . ô ma Julie! le voile est déchiré . . . je te vois . . . je vois tes divins attraits!" (Oh my Julie! . . . the veil is torn away . . . I behold you . . . I behold your divine charms!). He then vacillates between moments of belief in "le magique effet de ces traits" (the magical effect of these features) and moments of disillusionment. On the one hand, he writes, "Je crois, en le voyant, te revoir encore" (When I look at it, I think I am beholding you once more), with the emphasis of the oddly redundant "revoir encore." On the other hand, he writes, "un instant me désabuse, toute la douleur de l'absence se ranime et s'aigrit en m'ôtant l'erreur qui l'a suspendue" (I am instantly disabused; all the pain of absence is reanimated and sharpened when it dispels the error that had relieved it [229]). St. Preux's desire to "transmettre" (transmit) to her senses the "délire et l'illusion" (258) (delirium and illusion [229]) that he experiences seems to succeed; Julie writes: "Je m'imagine que tu tiens mon portrait, et je suis si folle que je crois sentir l'impression des caresses que tu lui fais et des baisers que tu lui donnes" (268) (I imagine that you are holding my portrait, and I am so crazy that I think I am feeling the touch of the caresses and the kisses you are giving it [236–37]). Yet Julie's sensual hallucination of transcending distance and absence is actually a fantasy about St. Preux and her portrait. She imagines him kissing and caressing a painting, not herself.

After describing how she pictures St. Preux facing her portrait, Julie gives an almost Platonic account of the composition of the painting, explaining that she secretly commissioned the painter to make a "seconde copie" of the portrait. She writes: "Ensuite, sans m'embarrasser de copie ni d'original, je choisis subtilement le plus ressemblant des trois pour te l'envoyer" (Then without minding which was the original or the copy, I adroitly chose the best likeness of the three to send to you). Julie suggests that it would be "une espèce d'in-fidélité" (a sort of infidelity) if St. Preux gave his fetishistic devotion to "une autre figure que la mienne" (269) (a face other than mine [237]) but it is not clear which copy of her "figure" is her own. We don't know whether Julie sends her lover the first copy, the second copy, or the original portrait—which, of course, is itself only a copy of the original "figure" that is itself repeatedly pic-tured as a tableau. This situation is compounded when St. Preux—who writes that he reproaches the portrait "de te ressembler et de n'être pas toi" (269) (for resembling you without being you [237])—has another painter make a copy of his copy: "j'espère te voir bientôt plus semblable à toi-même. De peur de gâter le portrait, nous essayons les changements sur une copie que je lui en ai fait faire, et il ne les transporte sur l'original que quand nous sommes bien sûrs de leur effet" (272) (I hope soon to see you more like yourself. For fear of spoiling the portrait, we try out the alterations on a copy I had him make, and he trans-ports them to the original only once we are quite sure of their effect [239]).

Among St. Preux's complaints, in addition to his insistence that the portrait is too revealing, is that the first artist has gotten her coloring wrong and has omitted a "tache presque imperceptible" (an almost imperceptible mark) and a "petite cicatrice" (270) (little scar [238]) on Julie's face. We can see that when he imagines Julie from every point of view and in countless tableaux and is re-lieved that her illness has left only "quelques légères traces presque impercep-tibles" (403) (a few slight, almost imperceptible traces [347]) on her face rather than "taches" or "cicatrices," he is retracing in his imagination a gallery of im-ages that includes these copies of copies. The original Julie, although the model for these copies, represents one portrait among many. When, after their reunion, St. Preux is asked to return the portrait, Claire reports to Julie that he swears "qu'il consentirait plutôt à ne te plus voir qu'à se dessaisir de ton portrait" (418) (he would sooner consent never to see you again than surrender your por-trait [359]). It is as if the portrait is more real than the image of Julie herself.[62]

The appearance of Julie's face again becomes an issue at the end of the novel when the servants stage the macabre *tableau vivant* of Julie's corpse. Wolmar's letter describing these deathbed scenes notes that Claire uses the veil to put an end to "ce mortel spectacle" (this deathly spectacle), which Wolmar says he tolerates so he won't be accused of burying his wife alive, when he points out that after thirty-six hours and extreme heat, "les chairs commençaient à se corrompre; et quoique le visage eût gardé ses traits et sa douceur, on y voyait déjà quelques signes d'altération" (725) (the corruption of the flesh was beginning; and although the face had retained its features and its sweetness, one already saw some signs of alteration [604]). The introduction of the corruption of the flesh is surprising here. Despite Wolmar's assurance about the "traits" (features) and "douceur" (sweetness) of Julie's face, Claire emphasizes the physical signs of death where earlier the servant thought he saw a sign of life. As she covers "la face de son amie" (her friend's face) she proclaims: "maudit soit l'oeil impie qui verra ce visage défiguré" (725) (cursed be the sacrilegious eye that ever looks on this disfigured face! [606]). This disfigurement is reiterated in a strange image in the posthumous letter that Julie, like Clarissa, writes from the dead: "Quand tu verras cette lettre, les vers rongeront le visage de ton amante, et son coeur où tu ne seras plus" (731) (When thou seest this letter, worms will gnaw thy lover's face, and her heart where thou shalt no longer dwell [610]). Although the reference to St. Preux's presence in her heart moves into the realm of the figurative, the image of worms gnawing upon Julie's face seems painfully literal, especially after St. Preux's preoccupation with her portraits and images and every mark on her face.

One might read in the servants' desire to dress and make up Julie as if she were alive a more benign (if still grotesque) version of Lovelace's insane orders to remove Clarissa's heart and embalm her in order to "preserve the Charmer from decay"—in Prévost's version, "pour garantir ses précieux restes de toute altération" (to preserve her precious remains from all alteration).[63] Although Lovelace never gets to enact this fantasy, it is in one sense unnecessary, because, as Richardson repeatedly reminds us, Clarissa's body shows no signs of decay. Mrs. Norton finds, when she admires Clarissa's "aspect" in death, that "la mort, qui défigure tout, n'avoit point eu le pouvoir d'altérer ses aimables traits" (death, which disfigures everything, had not had the power to alter her amiable features).[64] When Morden has the coffin lid removed and some "aromatics and flowers" put in, he finds the corpse "very little altered. The sweet smile remained."[65] Clarissa's body in death is obviously contrasted with the disgusting "spectacle" of the "huge quaggy carcase"[66] of Mrs. Sinclair in her deathbed scene—a scene that Prévost declined to translate. He explains that this "tableau est purement Anglois" (this tableau is purely English), an "étrange peinture" (strange painting) represented in colors that are "si contraires au goût de notre nation, que tous mes adoucissemens ne le rendroient pas supportable en françois" (so contrary to the taste of our nation that all my polishing would not make it tolerable in French).[67] Indeed, by the time that Clarissa becomes a corpse, there does not seem to be much left to her body.

In his translation and transfiguration of the plot and characters of Richardson's sentimental novel, however, Rousseau allows his tableau of Julie's body to frame a carcass. Unlike the corpse of Clarissa, where "la mort, qui défigure tout, n'avoit point eu le pouvoir d'altérer ses aimables traits," Julie's "visage défiguré" (disfigured face) shows "signes d'altération" (signs of alteration). Paradoxically, after hundreds of pages that aestheticize Julie—refusing, as it were, any disfiguring marks on the image of her face—Rousseau leaves St. Preux (and the reader of the novel) with a portrait of her face decomposing and finally being eaten by worms. The final deathbed tableau represented for the readers and the beholders of the scene simultaneously frames Julie as an aesthetic object and insists upon her physical presence as a corpse. The representations of the posthumous deathbed scene that preserves Julie in a *tableau vivant* and the posthumous letter that speaks or writes from the grave both deny and declare Julie's death.[68]

Instead of leaving the reader with the image of Julie framed by the sentimental spectacle in which she expires in Claire's arms, Rousseau prolongs both her life and death in a series of representations that recalls the proliferation of images of Julie in the multiple copies of her portrait. Earlier in the letter describing Julie's death, in another context, a footnote declares: "quelque rôle qu'on ait pu faire durant sa vie, on ne doit point jouer la comédie à sa mort" (699) (whatever role one may have played in life, one must not playact at one's death [584]). Yet Rousseau continues, as if obsessively, to restage the scene of Julie's death in this letter. The spectacles of these deathbed scenes and the related images that appear both before and after Julie's death suggest a sort of repetition compulsion that might more accurately be understood as a representation compulsion: an extravagant multiplication of images that seem to retrace and reproduce reproductions that increasingly act to stage the scene of death even as they compose wishful tableaux of life.[69]

After Wolmar succeeds in ending the "mortel spectacle" that preserves the disfigured Julie and buries his wife's body, he tries to keep the almost hysterical Claire and the children apart. He explains:

> [L]e spectacle des passions violentes de toute espèce est un des plus dangereux qu'on puisse offrir aux enfants. Ces passions ont toujours dans leur excès quelque chose de puéril qui les amuse, qui les séduit, et leur fait aimer ce qu'ils devraient craindre.* Ils n'en avaient déjà que trop vu. (726)

[T]he spectacle of violent passions of all kinds is one of the most dangerous one can put before children. There is always something puerile about these passions in their excesses that entertains them, seduces them, and makes them like what they should fear.* They had already seen only too much of that. (606–7)

This paragraph is interrupted by an asterisk that refers the reader to the ninth of the editorial footnotes that punctuate the second half of this letter, which further explains: "Voilà pourquoi nous aimons tous le théâtre, et plusieurs d'entre nous les romans" (726) (That is why we all like the theater, and quite a few of us novels [607]). This statement recalls the famous first line of the preface—"Il faut des spectacles dans les grandes villes, et des romans aux peuples corrompus" (3) (Great cities must have theaters; and corrupt peoples, novels [3])—as well as the *Lettre à d'Alembert sur les spectacles,* which was written as Rousseau was completing *La Nouvelle Héloïse.* These remarks of Wolmar and Rousseau's editorial persona situating the extravagant scenes that we have witnessed within the arena of violent passions identified with both theater and novels would seem to end the elaborate reproduction of deathbed scenes with a warning about the excesses of art and the imagination. However, no sooner does the severe and austere Wolmar seem to close the curtain on extravagantly sentimental scenes that threaten to decompose before the eyes of their eyewitnesses, he himself becomes the producer of yet another dangerously excessive *tableau vivant.*

In order to get the grieving Claire to eat after she becomes disconcerted by the "place vide" (empty place) at the table where Julie used to sit, Wolmar formulates the following plan with Claire's young daughter:

Vous savez que sa fille ressemble beaucoup à Mme de Wolmar. . . . Je fis donc habiller Henriette le plus à l'imitation de Julie qu'il fût possible, et, après l'avoir instruite, je lui fis occuper à table le troisième couvert qu'on avait mis comme la veille. . . . Henriette, fière de représenter sa petite maman, joua parfaitement son rôle, et si parfaitement que je vis pleurer les domestiques. (727)

You know that her daughter greatly resembles Madame de Wolmar. . . . I therefore had Henriette dressed as much as possible in imitation of Julie, and after instructing her carefully, I had her take the third place at table, which had been set as the day before. . . . Henriette, proud of representing her petite-Maman, played her role perfectly, and so perfectly that I saw the domestics weep. (607)

Henriette is so pleased with her impersonation of Julie that she suddenly improvises her script and addresses her mother in character. According to Wolmar, "Le geste et le ton de voix furent imités au point que sa mère en tressaillit" (The gesture and tone of voice were imitated so well that it made her mother quiver). When Claire begins to eat too excitedly, he fears that she might go mad, and he stops the performance: "Dès ce moment je résolus de supprimer tous ces jeux, qui pouvaient allumer son imagination au point qu'on n'en serait plus maître" (726–27) (From this moment, I resolved to suppress all this playing, which could inflame her imagination to the point where it would no longer be controlled (608)]. What is bizarre here, however, especially after the excesses of the previous *tableau vivant,* is that Wolmar should have ever decided to stage this extravagant scene in which a child who resembles Julie is dressed up and instructed to imitate his recently deceased wife in an explicitly theatrical representation designed to impose on a susceptible imagination.

After the dead Julie is made to "jouer la comédie à sa mort" (playact at her death), Wolmar stages a macabre theater that repeats, reproduces, and retraces the *tableau vivant* of the earlier scene. Whereas Julie had been made up and costumed to resemble herself, as if her body could be a portrait that figured rather than disfigured her, here a miniature actress is brought on stage to represent her in another living tableau. As in the earlier "mortel spectacle" in which Claire participates, despite the fact that she is not "la dupe d'une illusion si grossière" (the dupe of such a gross illusion), Claire is not exactly fooled by this performance. It is indeed the recognition of the performance, which so moves the servants who witnessed the earlier tableau of the dead Julie, that is perhaps most dangerous to the beholder. Like the performance of *Le Fils naturel* that Diderot represents in the narrative frame of his *Entretiens,* where the performance of a *comédie larmoyante* breaks down when an old man appears to play the role of the dead father, the uncanny performance produced by Wolmar is brought to a halt when the dead mother is impersonated by a child.[70] In all of these scenes, the presence of a performance comes to represent the absence of death. Henriette sits at the "place vide" that has earlier troubled Claire, but it is precisely her bodily presence representing Julie that finally must stand for Julie's absence. The bizarrely cute representation of Julie by Henriette and the grotesque representation of Julie by her own decaying corpse both bring the beholder to the same conclusion: like Clarissa after her death, Julie is not there.

These extravagant scenes are simultaneously uncanny and excessively theatrical. They convey a sense not only of *déjà vu* but also of what (following

Wolmar's formulation) one might call *déjà trop vu:* the spectators of these scenes see and have already seen too much. Indeed, the actual scene of Julie's death seems overshadowed by the proliferation of images that either prefigure or disfigure it. Even Wolmar seems governed by the repetition and representation compulsions that govern the plot of the novel, as if imagination itself—the faculty that traces and retraces images—were out of control. These scenes rehearse prior spectacles, scenes, and letters that turn on the relation between originals and copies and between real and imagined scenes, circulating in an economy of images that operates not only within *La Nouvelle Hélöise* but also between Rousseau's novel and the texts of Richardson and Prévost that it transfigures. Rousseau's editorial footnotes situating these pages in the context of the *scènes imaginaires* of Julie's death and the fictive realm of novels and theater underline the sense that these scenes represent the scene of representation itself. However, if these deathbed scenes stage the scene of representation, such tableaux suggest that representation itself stages the scene of death. The deadly images of the dream that seems to predict Julie's death suggest that representations might lead to death, even if they don't predict them; and the extravagant tableaux of the dead Julie and the actress portraying her in miniature—tragedy repeating itself as farce—show representations revealing the death of the figure they mean to embody.

> *L'événement n'est pas prédit parce qu'il arrivera; mais il arrive parce qu'il a été prédit.* —Rousseau, *Julie ou La Nouvelle Héloïse*[71]

St. Preux and Julie's visit to the retreat at Meillerie is framed by two images of Julie's death, imagined moments that bear the traces of Rousseau's early plan to drown his heroine and prefigure the event that causes her death at the end of the novel. The scene that is demarcated by these acts of imagination, however—the return to the place where ten years earlier St. Preux had written letters to his lover—also belongs to the series of real and imagined scenes that depicts the death of Julie. St. Preux's experience in returning to the site of his past engagement with Julie itself relates this letter to the letter describing the dream of Julie's death, which involves a return to another place that St. Preux visited ten years earlier. The dream is preceded by St. Preux's imagining the earlier time and an act of comparison that places two different moments in juxtaposition. At first, he writes, "le rapport des circonstances me fit songer à d'autres temps; et, comparant ce départ à celui dont il me rappelait l'idée, je me sentis si différent de ce que j'étais alors" (the similarity of the circumstances carried me back to other times, and comparing this departure with the one it re-minded me of, I felt so different from what I was then"). However, when he finds himself in the same room he stayed in before, he recounts, "je crus rede-venir à l'instant tout ce que j'étais alors; dix années s'effacèrent de ma vie, et tous mes malheurs furent oubliés. Hélas! cette erreur fut courte, et le second instant me rendit plus accablant le poids de toutes mes anciennes peines. . . . Quelles comparaisons douloureues s'offrirent à mon esprit!" (601–2) (I seemed instantly to revert to all I was then: ten years of my life were effaced and all my misfortunes were forgotten. Alas! this error was short-lived, and the second in-stant made the weight of all my former sufferings more overwhelming. . . . What painful comparisons came to my mind! [502–3]). This moment of error in which a brief illusion leads to a realization of loss also recalls St. Preux's first sight of Julie's portrait in which, after thinking that he sees her, "un instant me désabuse, toute la douleur de l'absence se ranime et s'aigrit en m'ôtant l'erreur qui l'a suspendue" (258) (I am instantly disabused; all the pain of absence is re-animated and sharpened when it dispels the error that had relieved it [229]). St. Preux's return to Meillerie after ten years with Julie—"celle dont l'image l'habitait jadis avec moi" (500) (the one whose image formerly dwelled there with me [424])—involves a moment of comparison that juxtaposes not only different times but also Julie and her image.

St. Preux describes how he brings Julie to a place that already seems marked with her presence:

> "Quoi! dis-je à Julie en la regardant avec un oeil humide, votre coeur ne vous dit-il rien ici, et ne sentez-vous point quelque émotion secrète à l'aspect d'un lieu si plein de vous?" Alors, sans attendre sa réponse, je la con-duisis vers le rocher, et lui montrai son chiffre gravé dans mille endroits, et plusieurs vers de Pétrarque ou du Tasse relatifs à la situation où j'étais en les traçant. En les revoyant moi-même après si longtemps, j'éprouvai combien la présence des objets peut ranimer puissamment les sentiments violents dont on fut agité près d'eux. (502)

> What! I said to Julie, looking at her with a tear in my eye, does your heart tell you nothing here, and do you not feel some secret emotion at the sight of a place so full of you? Then without waiting for her answer, I led her to-ward the cliff and showed her her initials carved in a thousand places, and several lines of verse of Petrarch and Tasso relative to the situation I was in

when I traced them. Seeing them again myself after such a long time, I experienced how powerfully the presence of objects can reanimate the violent sentiments with which one was formerly seized in their presence. (425)

Looking at Julie, St. Preux expects her to feel her presence in the aspect of a place that he had previously invested with meaning, where (he says, speaking of himself in the third person), "ta chère image faisait son bonheur" (502) (your dear image was all his happiness [425]). Yet remarkably, what he finds in Julie's presence is neither Julie herself nor a copy of her image nor the ghostly apparition of a dream but rather the traces of her manifested by the signs of writing. The return to Meillerie constitutes a return to the scene of writing. In the letter that he writes in and from the place in the first part of the novel, St. Preux explains: "J'ai pris tant de goût pour ce lieu sauvage que j'y porte même de l'encre et du papier; et j'y écris maintenant cette lettre sur un quartier que les glaces ont détaché du rocher voisin" (65) (I have taken such a fancy to this wild spot that I even carry ink and paper there with me, and am now writing this letter on a boulder which the ice has detached from the neighboring cliff [74])—writing to the moment in an ambiguous site of *énonciation* in which the indeterminate French "y" vacillates between a *here* and *now* and a *there* and *now*.

In this early letter, St. Preux recounts acts or imagined acts of voyeurism in which he sees or thinks he sees Julie's house through a telescope. Writing to Julie, St. Preux fantasizes himself daring to "en secret pénétrer jusque dans ta chambre" (in secret penetrate right into your room [74]), imagining that he sees Julie reading and responding to his letters: "je vois tes yeux attendris parcourir une de mes lettres; je lis dans leur douce langueur que c'est à ton amant fortuné que s'adressent les lignes que tu traces" (65–66) (I see your tearful eyes scanning one of my letters; I read by their sweet languor that the lines you trace are being addressed to your fortunate lover [75]). Like the unmediated vision of mediation in which Julie imagines St. Preux caressing her portrait, St. Preux's bedroom fantasy focuses on mutual moments of reading in which he seems to read in Julie's eyes what she is reading and writing. When St. Preux revisits the scene ten years later, we learn that not only does he bring ink and paper to the place to record his voyeuristic fantasy of their epistolary communion for Julie, he literally inscribes the place *with* as well as *in* writing. Pointing out the rock where he wrote the earlier letter and the "cailloux tranchants" (sharp stones) that served as "burin pour graver ton chiffre" (my burin to carve your initials), he shows Julie the verses that he traced in the landscape in the tradition of Petrarch and Tasso, as well as her "chiffre gravé dans mille endroits" (502) (initials carved in a thousand places [425]).[72] Reading this writing, he feels the "présence des objets" (presence of objects) reanimating his prior sentiments, but Julie herself does not seem reanimated; it is as if she pales in comparison to the place and the texts that record the traces of her former (imagined) presence. St. Preux explains that he had imagined that "un instant de sa présence effacerait toutes mes peines" (504) (an instant of her presence would efface all my sufferings [428]) but like Claire with the "scène imaginaire" of Julie's dream of real events, St. Preux can't control what is erased, traced, or retraced in this scene. Describing bird songs "me retraçant les plasirs d'un autre âge" (reminding me of the pleasures of another time), he writes: "Tous les sentiments délicieux qui remplissaient alors mon âme s'y retracèrent pour l'affliger" (503) (Every delightful sentiment that then filled my soul now retraced [itself] there to torment it [427]). Most important, Julie's presence itself has been erased—or at least displaced—by the traces of the writing that have preceded her.

Early in the novel, Julie writes, "Le moment de la possession est une crise de l'amour" (25) (The moment of possession is a crisis for love [42]); here, St. Preux experiences possession as a crisis because visiting the place inscribed with her image and presence, he feels Julie to be more remote than if she were absent or dead: "Il me semblait que j'aurais porté plus patiemment sa mort ou son absence, et que j'avais moins souffert tout le temps que j'avais passé loin d'elle" (It seemed to me that I would have borne her death or absence more patiently, and that I had suffered less during all the time I had spent far from her). Instead of the instant of presence that he envisaged, St. Preux writes, "la voir, la toucher, lui parler, l'aimer, l'adorer, et, presque en la possédant encore, la sentir perdue à jamais pour moi; voilà ce qui me jetait dans des accès de fureur et de rage" (504) (to see her, touch her, speak to her, love her, worship her, and, while nearly possessing her anew, to feel she was forever lost to me; all this cast me into fits of fury and rage [427–28]). It is this rage that tempts him to drown Julie; but she is, in a sense, already dead. When they leave, after Julie says, "l'air de ce lieu n'est pas bon pour moi" (the air in this place is not good for me), St. Preux notes, "je quittai pour jamais ce triste réduit comme j'aurais quitté Julie elle-même" (503) (I left forever this sad nook, as I would have left Julie herself). When Mrs. Norton views Clarissa's corpse, she repeats over and over, "C'étoit elle-même" (It is herself), finding that "la mort, qui défigure tout, n'avoit point eu le pouvoir d'altérer ses aimables traits" (death, which disfigures everything, did not have the power to alter her amiable features).[73] Yet here St. Preux views the place of writing as if it were "Julie elle-même" and looks upon Julie as if she were dead. "La topographie est grossière-ment altérée en plusieurs endroits" (3) (The topography is grossly altered in several places [3]), Rousseau writes in the preface; in this letter, the writing of the place, having taken the place of Julie, seems to alter Julie more than death itself.

This experience to some extent confirms the analysis behind Wolmar's strategy in managing St. Preux's emotions. After St. Preux refuses to return the portrait to Julie, Wolmar explains to Claire: "Ce n'est pas de Julie de Wolmar qu'il est amoureux, c'est de Julie d'Étange . . . Il est vrai qu'elle lui ressemble beaucoup et qu'elle lui en rappelle souvent le souvenir. Il l'aime dans le temps passé" (It is not Julie de Wolmar he is in love with, it is Julie d'Étange . . . It is true she much resembles her and that she often recalls his memory of her). According to Wolmar, "Lui découvrir le véritable état de son coeur serait lui ap-prendre la mort de ce qu'il aime" (Revealing to him the true state of his heart would be to apprise him of the death of his beloved). However, "les traits de sa Julie ne sont pas tellement éffacés en Mme de Wolmar" (the features of his Julie are not so effaced in Mme de Wolmar); so Wolmar seeks to "effacer" (ef-face) St. Preux's past ideas by "donnant le change à son imagination" (tricking his imagination). Wolmar writes: "À la place de sa maîtresse, je le force de voir toujours l'épouse d'un honnête homme et la mère de mes enfants: j'efface un tableau par un autre, et couvre le passé du présent" (In the place of his mistress I force him to see always the spouse of an honorable man and the mother of my children: I efface one tableau with another, and cover the past with the present).[74] Wolmar seems to borrow St. Preux's own strategy of painting over Julie's portrait, of replacing one tableau with another as he tries to compare copies and originals. Wolmar argues that "l'erreur qui l'abuse et le trouble est de confondre les temps" (the error that deludes him and troubles him is to confuse the time frames), and he hopes to lead St. Preux and Julie to under-stand "leur erreur en comparant ce qu'ils sentiront avec ce qu'ils auraient autrefois senti dans une situation pareille" (492–94) (their error in comparing what they feel with what they once would have felt in a similar situation [417–19]). St. Preux describes his problem in similar terms when he describes the "erreur" and "comparaisons" that he succumbs to before his dream of Julie's death and his comparison of "l'image de mon bonheur passé" (the im-age of [my] past happiness) with the present time at Meillerie. At Meillerie, however, St. Preux is not spared the recognition of "la mort de ce qu'il aime" (the death of his beloved). The image of Julie, traced and retraced in the land-scape, is not erased or covered over. The power of images to retrace themselves in the imagination with greater force than events that have really taken place—or that will take place—juxtaposes one tableau with another, causing a real event to feel like an imperfect copy of the original representation.

The anticlimatic character of this encounter between St. Preux and Julie, in which writing seems to replace or displace person and event, recalls the almost comically anticlimatic moment of the consummation of their affair in the first part of the novel. Here, in what would read as a parody of what Richardson called "writing to the moment" if it were found in Henry Fielding's *Shamela*, St. Preux writes to Julie while waiting for her in her bedroom: "me voici dans ton cabinet, me voici dans le sanctuaire de tout ce que mon coeur adore" (Here I am in your dressing room, here I am in the sanctuary of all my heart worships). Just as he later describes the spot at Meillerie as "un lieu si plein de vous" (a place so full of you), this place is "plein de toi" (full of you). He explains that he has had the good fortune "d'avoir trouvé de l'encre et du papier! J'exprime ce que je sens pour en tempérer l'excès; je donne le change à mes transports en les décrivant" (to have found ink and paper! I express what I feel to temper its excess, I hold my transports in abeyance by describing them). Yet St. Preux's erotic fantasy, as he fetishistically inventories the strewn pieces of Julie's clothing and the various parts of her body that they "présentent à mon ardente imagination" (present to my ardent imagination), seems far from tempered, erupting into a "spectacle de volupté" (voluptuous spectacle) as he once again imagines that he sees Julie: "je te vois, je te sens partout" (I see you, I feel you everywhere). The fantasy that takes place as St. Preux writes this letter to Julie seems more and more masturbatory, until finally at the climatic moment of Julie's arrival, St. Preux refers to her in the third person rather than the second person and inscribes himself rather than his imagined lover as the *destinataire* of his apostrophes: "c'est elle! c'est elle! je l'entrevois, je l'ai vue . . . mon faible coeur, tu succombes à tant d'agitations" (121–22) (it is she! It is she! I glimpse her, I have seen her . . . my weak heart, thou succumbest at such turbulence! [119–20]).[75]

In this context one might speculate that if St. Preux has engraved Julie d'Étange's initials (her "chiffre") in a thousand places on the rocks, he most likely has engraved the capital letters *J* and *E*—once again transforming his love letters into the narcissistic monogram of the first-person singular: *JE*. Presumably St. Preux is able to engage Julie when she appears in her bedroom in the flesh rather than the spectacle of his imagination; the erotic fantasy that he writes "to the moment" is presumably only foreplay and—like the smallpox deathbed scene that takes place in the same room—a "scène imaginé" (imaginary scene) is replaced by a scene that "s'est passée réellement" (really took place). In the return visit to Meillerie, however, the moment of recognition expressed in "c'est elle" (it is she) is the recognition that the very presence of Julie seems to declare her absence. The imagined scene has neither prescribed nor predicted the ultimate event, as with the deathbed scene that follows part of the script of St. Preux's dream. Here, the imagined scene seems to preempt the real scene, causing it to be experienced as loss.

Like her own corpse, and like Henriette in the extravagant scenes staged at the end of the novel, Julie cannot resemble herself enough; she cannot sufficiently resemble the portrait of herself originally engraved by St. Preux to adequately perform the role in which she has been cast. In the imaginary confrontation that Clarissa fantasizes between her corpse and Lovelace, her posthumous letter instructs him that she is to be found in her writing, not in her body. Here, returning to the scene of writing, the place in which he enacted and imagined their epistolary dialogue, Julie seems to be a bystander as St. Preux discovers that she is present only in his writing. Clarissa, who declares after the rape, "I am no longer what I was," describes her body as "*what will be Nothing when this writing comes to be opened and read.*" Returning at last with a corporeal Julie to the place where he had only imagined her, St. Preux finds her *chiffre* engraved in writing. This *chiffre* is not exactly the "*cypher*" Clarissa describes herself reduced to when she laments, "I am but a *cypher,* to give him significance, and *myself* pain" (Prévost translates "cypher" as "zero" in this letter),[76] yet for the pained St. Preux, it signals the fact that somehow Julie has been reduced to nothing. The self-signifying writing that has momentarily embodied her must end by disembodying her; the writing itself renders Julie posthumous. An editorial footnote describes Julie's last letter (aside from the posthumous letter) as "le chant du cygne" (682) (the swan's song [570]). We might hear in Julie's last letters not only her swan song but also a *chant du signe,* an echo of the signs and cyphers that compose and discompose her. The signs of St. Preux's writing, in seeking to make her present and give her presence, have turned her into a cypher.

When, in the posthumous letter forwarded to St. Preux at the end of the novel, Julie writes, "Ce n'est plus moi qui te parle; je suis déjà dans les bras de la mort" (731) (It is no longer I who speak to thee; I am already in death's embrace [610]), the strange moment that she writes to is anticlimatic from the outset. On her deathbed, insisting that "l'instant de la mort n'est rien" (the moment of death is nothing), Julie refuses the trappings that usually surround the dying: "personne ne me reconnaîtra plus; je ne serai plus la même" (no one will recognize me any more; I will no longer be the same), she explains, "j'aurai, moi vivante, l'affreux spectacle de l'horreur que je ferai, même à mes amis, comme si j'étais déjà morte" (706) (I will have before me, while still alive, the awful spectacle of the horror I inspire even in my friends, as if I were already dead [589]). Yet Julie, who will be framed in a spectacle as if she were alive after she is dead, has already been seen as if she were dead while she is still alive. The instant of death—so difficult to locate or confine in the last pages of the novel—has already been seen, already been prefigured in writing. Indeed, the scene at Meillerie suggests that if writing has not predicted her death, its presentiments, prefigurations, representations, and images have somehow caused it.

Complaining about the "images funèbres" (603) (deathly images [505]) of St. Preux's dream of Julie's death, Claire calls the letter in which he represents her deathbed scene "votre fatale lettre" (607) (your fatal letter [508]). This is not the only letter in the novel that seems fatal, just as Julie's last letter is not the only one that seems posthumous. It is not merely that these letters picture Julie's death; all the letters speak of (as well as from) the grave. Indeed, when Julie in her posthumous letter writes, "Quand tu verras cette lettre, les vers rongeront le visage de ton amante" (When thou seest this letter, worms will gnaw thy lover's face [610]), the strange image in which she pictures worms ("les vers") devouring her face suggests that she is disfigured by verse, just as the traces of verses ("vers") of poetry cut into the face of the rock at Meillerie seem to have effaced her. (The repetition sounded between "tu verras" and "les vers" underlines the presence of this unexpected word.) Similar verbal associations might be at play in the last words of the novel, where a footnote juxtaposes Julie's coffin or "cercueil" (coffin) with "ce recueil" (733) (this collection), the collection of letters we have just read. Wolmar's description of Julie's death notes that he wanted to "recueillir son dernier soupir" (722) (collect her last breath [602]), and the title page notes that the letters in the text have been "recueillies" (collected) by Rousseau. While Clarissa's coffin becomes a text, inscribed with a posthumous message to be read and copied after her death, the text of Rousseau's *recueil* becomes a *cercueil,* a collection of fatal letters. If Clarissa's coffin comes to feel like her book, Julie's book comes to feel like her coffin.

Postscript

The novel's last words, in the footnote that ends *La Nouvelle Héloïse,* suggest that Richardson was on Rousseau's mind as he finished rereading his novel:

En achevant de relire ce recueil, je crois voir pourquoi l'intérêt, tout faible qu'il est, m'en est si agréeable. . . . c'est qu'au moins ce faible intérêt est pur et sans mélange de peine; qu'il n'est point excité par des noirceurs, par des crimes, ni mêlé du tourment de haïr. Je ne saurais concevoir quel plaisir on peut prendre à imaginer et composer le personnage d'un scélérat, à se mettre à sa place tandis qu'on le représente. . . . Je plains beaucoup les auteurs de tant de tragédies pleines d'horreurs, lesquels passent leur vie à faire agir et parler des gens qu'on ne peut écouter ni voir sans souffrir. (733)

As I complete my rereading of this collection, I think I see why the interest, as feeble as it is, appeals to me so. . . . It is because this feeble interest is at least pure and unmixed with pain; because it is not driven by villainy, by crimes, nor mixed with the torment of hate. I cannot conceive what pleasure one can take in imagining and assembling the character of a villain, in putting oneself in his place as one goes about representing him . . . I very much pity the authors of tragedies full of horrors, who spend their lives lending acts and speech to people one could not see without suffering. (612)

Rousseau notes these authors' zeal for "l'utilité publique" (public good) and declares his gratitude that he has not been given the talent or genius to carry out "un travail si cruel" (733) (such cruel work [612]). It is difficult not to hear in this ironic commentary a condemnation of the creator of Lovelace, who is also alluded to in a somewhat derogatory manner in a note to letter 18 in part 3 and in the so-called second preface.[77] Perhaps Rousseau anticipated the comparisons that would judge his novel next to Richardson's from the moment it was published. Yet by ending his novel with this note, Rousseau calls attention to his epistolary precursor as he inscribes himself as a reader—a rereader—of his own letters.

Like Joyce's *Ulysses, La Nouvelle Héloïse* inscribes repetition and rewriting in its title, although except for the basic premise of an illicit love affair between tutor and student, the plot of Rousseau's text ultimately bears little resemblance to the events enacted in the letters of Abélard and Héloïse.[78] The plot of *Clarissa* resembles the plot of Rousseau's novel even less. Yet what is at stake here is not plot but rather the ghostly repetitions that leave the novel with an uncanny sense of déjà vu, especially in its tableaux of Julie. Like Julie after her death, the text of *Clarissa* is *déguisé, altéré, changé* in Rousseau's text, present in images, tableaux, reenactments, textual phantoms and verbal echoes mediated through Prévost's translation. The ghostly shadow of *Clarissa* helps to account for the sense in *Julie,* especially in regard to Julie's death, that scenes have been foreshadowed, prefigured, predicted, and prescribed; as we have seen, this sense of déjà vu is reflected upon by the characters themselves as it is translated into the plot of the novel.

The presence of *Clarissa* as a textual model for *Julie* helps us to understand Rousseau's preoccupation in the novel with models, copies, dreams, repetitions, reenactments, and the priority of the written and the imaginary. However, it does not follow that this textual relation necessarily caused either Rousseau's preoccupations or his plot. Rather, I imagine that Richardson's novel, especially its representations of Clarissa's death, became important in *Julie* because Rousseau's experiment of writing an epistolary narrative became increasingly concerned with the ways in which writing and representation seem to take precedence over experience. The epistolary novel in some sense must always be about the relation between writing and event. Through his method of "writing to the moment," Richardson seeks the sense of presence conveyed by the present tense, as if narration could be contemporaneous with the events it describes. Laclos's *Les Liaisons dangereuses*, a diabolical transfiguration of both *Clarissa* and *La Nouvelle Héloïse*, demonstrates a type of speech act theory (implicit in his models) in which writing itself becomes event. As Rousseau reflects on the relation between the real and the imaginary and the dangerous power of images and representations, he investigates the way in which writing seems to cause events to take place—and subsequently, by taking their place, causes them to be experienced as loss, absence, and death. It is not only that the plot of the novel is displaced by writing, that the generation of the epistolary text becomes the plot. Rather than seeming to represent, recall, or recapture a past event, or even to become contemporaneous with a present moment, writing seems to anticipate events, which then seem always already imagined in and by writing. The event itself—displaced, preempted, and replaced by writing—must always seem anticlimatic, as if it bore the burden of having to reenact and recreate the scene of writing and representation.

In this context, the presence of *Clarissa* becomes important for reasons beyond its powerful precedent as a virtuous, didactic novel of sensibility. Both authors were interested in the stories told by writing in their novels—in both the power and the inability of writing to embody their characters, to bring their heroines to life or make them speak from the grave. One could speculate further that Rousseau sensed in the relation of *Julie* to *Clarissa* a figure for the complex ways in which scenes of writing and scenes of representation seem inevitably to become inscribed as scenes of death. Clarissa's death does not predict Julie's death; yet Julie's death is somehow prescribed in Clarissa's death, which causes Julie's repeated death to be a double loss from the outset. In retrospect, one might say that Richardson's fatal letters, in repeatedly picturing Clarissa's death, lead to Julie's death; but the scene of Julie's death is already foretold from the moment that Rousseau imagines his heroine in the act of writing.

5 The Business of Tragedy
Accounting for Sentiment in *Julia de Roubigné*

The business of tragedy [is] to exhibit the passions, that is, the weaknesses of men.
Henry Mackenzie, *The Lounger*, No. 27 (1785)

Vengeance is the only business I have left.
Henry Mackenzie, *Julia de Roubigné*

Like Rousseau's *Julie, ou la Nouvelle Héloïse*, Henry Mackenzie's *Julia de Roubigné* declares its relation to a specific textual model in its title. Rousseau, as we saw in the previous chapter, is less interested in rewriting *Abelard and Eloise* than in re-imagining aspects of Richardson's *Clarissa* in a complex dialogue that is mediated through the abbé Prévost's French translation of *Clarissa*. These textual relations take place in the context of an extended meditation on the play of models and copies, images, phantoms, simulacra, representations, and reenactments that situates writing between life and death. Mackenzie's epistolary novel, in turn, stands as a sort of miniature version of *Julie*, presenting itself as an English translation of a packet of letters originally written in French and delivered to the "editor" by a Frenchman.

Published in 1777, sixteen years after the publication of *Julie* and seven years after the publication of *The Man of Feeling*, *Julia* evokes Rousseau's novel in its story of a young woman who is separated from her first love, her "master in literature, her fellow-scholar in music and painting,"[1] and compelled to marry an austere, older man whom she does not love in order to save her father from financial ruin. The story of sentiment and suffering ultimately veers off into a Shakespearean tragedy about a jealous husband who murders his wife after imagining her infidelity. *Julia de Roubigné* borrows only moments and motifs from Rousseau's *Julie* as it translates a Richardsonian plot back into English; it is most related to Rousseau in its concern with the power of art. Translating Rousseau's excessive novel of sensibility into the literary landscape of the Scottish Enlightenment, *Julia* tells an ambivalent tale about aesthetic experience. Finally, its story about sensibility and imagination is translated into an account of business transactions that turns on the failure of transmission. Mackenzie's interest in the power of sensibility and imagination also turns upon the value of art.

Although *Julia de Roubigné* is identified on its title page as *A Tale,* as if to warn the reader to expect a work of imagination, the introduction contains a conventional account of how a "*Series of Letters*" fell into the hands of "The Author of The Man of Feeling, and The Man of the World," who presents himself as translator, editor, and publisher. This simultaneous admission and denial of the imaginary character of the work is, of course, a defining tension in the texts that we have come to think of as the eighteenth-century novel; in *Julie,* for example, Rousseau refrains from the elaborate claims that earlier authors made for the text's authenticity but still refuses to fully admit the text's fictive status. The introduction to *Julia de Roubigné* serves to establish the provenance of "the records of private life," the "memoirs of sentiment, and suffering" (1: viii) that a young Frenchman supposedly brings to the editor from France, yet its "account of the following papers" (1: vii) inscribes the text somewhat uneasily in the tradition of sensibility that the novel would appear to embrace in reworking the plot, form, and style of *Julie.*

Describing the papers, the editor confesses: "I found it a difficult task to reduce them to narrative, because they are made up of sentiment, which narrative would destroy" (1: x). This opposition between sentiment and narrative reappears in the "Advertisement" to the second volume; the editor, while considering how the "papers" are "relating a story," asserts that "it is not so much on story, as sentiment, that their interest with the reader must depend" (2: vi–vii). Indeed, in a footnote in volume 2, in one of his rare editorial asides, the editor that Mackenzie impersonates feels it necessary to "apologize to the reader for introducing a letter so purely episodical" (2: 46).[2] Julia herself seems to stumble over the apparent incompatibility of story and sentiment: "I am bewildered in sentiment again.—In truth, my story is the story of sentiment," she explains while noting that the marks of "the progress" of her love for Savillon, the beloved childhood friend and St. Preux figure from whom she has been separated, "are too little for description" (1: 82). After her marriage to the austere and older Count de Montauban, she warns her correspondent that her new life "admits not of much description. Comedies and romances, you know, always end with a marriage, because, after that, there is nothing to be said"

(2: 79). Montauban tells his correspondent that he feels a "happiness that would not figure in narration," admitting "that of facts I have nothing to write, and of sentiments almost as little" (2: 88). He earlier describes his life as being "of a sort that produces nothing," explaining, "I mean in recital. To myself it is not vacant" (1: 61).

Of course, as with *Julie,* as with *Clarissa,* it is not for the plot that one reads Mackenzie's Rousseauian story of a young woman compelled to marry a man she does not love in an implicit financial transaction that sacrifices a romantic "master in literature" and "fellow-scholar in music and painting" (2: 133). (In the end, Mackenzie's economical plot becomes dramatic when he imports elements of *Othello* into his sentimental story.) Mackenzie avoids the challenging length of *Clarissa* and the extravagant philosophical and moral reflections of *Julie,* yet the problem of how to have a *narrative* of sensibility remains. The question of what figures in a narration, what produces nothing (or something) in the account of a life, signals more than a tension between story and sentiment. In raising the question of what the reader's interest depends on in the novel of sensibility, *Julia de Roubigné* asks whether sentiment could be described, represented, narrated, and accounted for without being destroyed, but it also locates "the story of sentiment" in a ledger of economic interests and transactions. Mackenzie once wrote a comic poem called "Poetry and Business: A Moral Tale";[3] in the tragic "tale" of *Julia de Roubigné,* the problematic relation of plot and sensibility turns upon the relation of business and art.

The terms of this literary business are made explicit from the outset in the editor's introduction, in which he transcribes the account that the young Frenchman gives of the acquisition of the papers containing the letters. If the origins of *Julia de Roubigné* can be traced to France and the traditions of the novel of sensibility, they also are located in a "grocery-shop." Describing how his father made the "acquisition" of the manuscript by a "whimsical accident," the Frenchman recounts that "a little boy passed him, with a bundle of papers in his hand, which he offered for sale to the master of the shop, for the ordinary uses of his trade; but they differed about the price, and the boy was ready to depart, when my father desired a sight of the papers, saying to the lad, with a smile, that, perhaps, he might deal with him for his book; upon reading a sentence or two, he found a style much above that of the ordinary manuscripts of a grocery-shop, and gave the boy his price, at a venture, for the whole" (vii–ix).

This recalls the introduction to *The Man of Feeling,* in which the editor describes how he acquired the manuscript by rescuing a "bundle of papers" from a curate who found them "excellent wadding" when he went shooting.[4] In both introductions, these comic stories satirize and thereby deflate the romantic fictions of prefaces that conventionally recount stories of manuscripts discovered in old country houses or armoires. However, in the context of *Julia de Roubigné,* this "account of the following papers" (1: vii) needs to be taken seriously precisely because the status of the narrative as an account is increasingly at issue.

"I hold myself entirely accountable" (1: xii), writes the editor of his publication; this concern with accounts, accountability, and accounting circulates throughout the narrative in both figurative and literal senses. The opposition between sentiment and narrative, sensibility and plot, threatens to bring the story to a standstill, reduce it to nothing; but paradoxically, one alternative to narrative that the series of letters produces (along with the proto-romantic collection of fragments produced in "memoirs of sentiment, and suffering" [1: viii]) is accounting. When Julia offers her confidante Maria "an account of correspondence," it is to say, "You are now, in the account of correspondence, I do not know how deep, in my debt" (1: 36). Montauban writes to his confidant in the same terms: "I am now three letters in your debt; yet the account of correspondence used formerly to be in my favour" (2: 88). When the narrator offers his "account" of the papers to the reader who presumably has purchased his book, then, although the "style" of the letters may be "much above that of the ordinary manuscripts of a grocery-shop," he is explicitly accounting for the "price" of papers "offered for sale" and purchased "at a venture."

The reader, too, is drawn into this speculation, and not just because (in the first edition) the last page of the tragedy is face to face with an advertisement for three books "Published by the same Author," offered at "3s.," "6s.," and "1s. 6d.," respectively. Eighteenth-century authors typically use the fiction of epistolary form (either the collection of letters, exemplified by Richardson's works, or the public letter, exemplified by Rousseau's *Lettre à d'Alembert sur les spectacles*) to deny the place of their books in the public, commercial sphere of books published for readers. Shaftesbury, for example, distances himself from "certain merchant-adventurers in the letter-trade, who in correspondence with their factor-bookseller are entered into a notable commerce with the world." Insisting that his private manuscripts have been copied by the printer for the sake of convenience, he insists that if his writing is "worth any one's purchasing, much good may it do the purchaser. 'Tis a traffic I have no share in, though I accidentally furnish the subject-matter. And thus am I nowise more an author for being in print."[5] Mackenzie maintains the fiction that denies his authorship as well as the theatricality of the book's public address, but he nevertheless inscribes his book in an economy of exchange and speculation from the outset, even before his characters begin accounting for their correspondence in economic terms. The epistolary manuscript that we learn is purchased in the grocery shop by someone who might be described as an adventurer in the letter trade is transmitted to the editor by the man's son; he recounts that he found the son "to inherit all that paternal worth, which had fixed my esteem, about a dozen years ago, in Paris" (1: vi).

This aside itself inscribes the transmission of the book in the economic account that both motivates and structures the plot of the novel. The "facts" that occasion the memoirs of suffering are related to a breakdown in paternal inheritance, a crisis concerning the transmission of paternal worth. Julia is separated from Savillon because he leaves France, "where Fortune had denied him an inheritance" (1: 87). Savillon must seek his fortune in Martinique, where he becomes "worth a power of money, which his uncle left him" (2: 137). Julia is brought together with Montauban, who rescues her father from financial ruin, because he left Spain to "return to the country of his birth, to the inheritance of [his] fathers" (1: 38). Her predicament and vulnerability are caused by her father's loss of a "momentous law suit" (1: 4) which has forced him to "sell his paternal estate" (1: 42). Indeed, insofar as the novel has a plot in the first two-thirds of the letters, it concerns the family crisis brought about by Roubigné's loss of his paternal inheritance, his inability to pass on his paternal worth, and his willingness to trade his daughter in a thinly veiled economic exchange.

Before this plot is revealed, the reader of the novel is implicated in the problems of transmission that will be central to the book as the French father passes on his speculative purchase to his son, who transmits them to the editor, who translates, publishes, and sells them to the reader who, presumably in the market for style or sentiment, himself or herself purchases them at a venture. The epistolary novel is, of course, formally preoccupied with the transmission of its narrative. *Julia de Roubigné* is somewhat odd in this respect, in that (unlike the characters in *Julie*) the interested parties, so to speak, do not correspond; virtually all of the letters are addressed to third parties, whose more or less disinterested position parallels that of the reader. Yet it is precisely the reader's position in the transmission and transactions of the narrative, which is preoccupied with failed transmissions and suspect transactions, that becomes important in the novel. In his ostensible translation of the letters into English from French, the editor chooses not to translate currency; the novel refers to *livres*, not *pounds*. At stake, then, is the value of *livres*. On one level, the novel is concerned with the value of people, the prices that one pays in the transactions of both sentiment and business; but on another level, Mackenzie asks us to consider from the outset the worth and cost of *livres*—that is to say, *books*—and the problem of how to settle accounts between authors and readers.

In trying to understand how narrative might destroy sentiment, then, in *Julia de Roubigné,* we need to consider the translation of the story of sentiment into the language of accounting. At times resembling the double-entry book-keeping of Defoe's Robinson Crusoe or Roxana more than the pathetic self-examinations of Julie or Clarissa, the letters are punctuated with the language of accounting: "I find time to settle accounts with myself" (1: 4); "there is one account which I wish to settle with you" (2: 192); "they close the account, and set down mirth for happiness" (2: 64); and "our pride naturally balances the account" (2: 89). The sentimental transactions of the characters are not merely expressed in occasional economic metaphors; they are framed as and framed by economic transactions. In *Julie,* Julie's father gives his daughter to Wolmar because Wolmar has *lost* his fortune, not so much to compensate him as to insist that his actions are not dictated by economic motives. Julia's father feels compelled to give his daughter to Montauban because he cannot tolerate being in anyone's debt—or to put the most generous construction on it, he allows his daughter to sacrifice herself because she knows that he cannot bear being in anyone's debt.

Montauban describes his initial proposal to Julia as a "suit" (1: 133), the same word used for the legal process that has destroyed her paternal estate and paternal worth. He renounces her hand when he discharges her father's debts, because he claims not to be able to "bear the appearance of purchasing it by a favour"; but this causes Julia to offer her "hand to his generosity," although, she says, "she will not conceal the small value of the gift. . . . If he shall now reject it, that ugly debt, which his unhappiness lays us under, will be repaid in the debasement she endures" (1: 151–53). Although Roubigné insists, as he hands over his "last treasure" to Montauban, that "[f]allen as his fortunes are, not the wealth of worlds had purchased it," and Montauban responds, "I know its value . . . and receive it as the dearest gift of Heaven and you," the conventionally benign exclamations of the betrothed—"I am Montauban's forever!" and "Julia is mine" (155–57)—are soon translated into Julia's acknowledgement that "this bosom is the property of Montauban" (2: 121).

Montauban himself, when he discovers Julia's past attachment to Savillon, says, "I purchased her consent, I bribed, I bought her" (2: 131). Even when Savillon is reunited with Julia (in the "interview" in which he has "to dispatch this one great business" [2: 161]), he takes the opportunity to conduct a financial transaction, giving Julia "a will, bequeathing his fortune" to her. When he says, "I never valued wealth, but as it might render me, in the language of the world, more worthy of thee" (2: 173), the worldly language of accounting is once again literalized. The story of sentiment has been displaced by a financial transmission that is meant to be transacted through an exchange of paper: "let me deposit in your hands this paper. It is a memorial of that Savillon, who was the friend of Julia!" (2: 173). The account of the papers, the records of private life and memoirs of sentiment and suffering, in a sense lead to this one great business.

It is worth remembering that Savillon's fortune, inherited from his uncle in Martinique after "Fortune had denied him an inheritance" in France, derives from a plantation in Martinique that profits from the labor of black slaves. One of the surprising turns of plot in *Julia de Roubigné* when volume 2 shifts to Savillon's letters (after the editor has once again explained that the letters' interest lies in sentiment rather than story) is the lengthy indictment of the treatment of the slaves. "To a man not callous from habit," writes Savillon, "the treatment of the negroes, in the plantations here, is shocking. I felt it strongly, and could not forbear expressing my sentiments to my uncle" (2: 30). Shifting the location of the novel from the romantic landscape of the French countryside, this letter contains a description of Savillon's efforts to "try a different mode of government in one plantation" (2: 30) and his experiment with a slave named Yambu, who had apparently been a prince in Africa. Savillon in effect turns Yambu and his comrades from slaves into sharecroppers, making Yambu the overseer of the others. He tells them that they are free, but rather than returning them to their country, he arranges for them "to help me raise sugars for the good of us all" (2: 39), allotting them a portion of land if they work satisfactorily. Savillon makes a strong argument against slavery, "talking only as a merchant," arguing (like Adam Smith) that his arrangement is finally more cost-effective than slavery.[6] Talking "as a man," however, he evokes "the many thousands of my fellow-creatures groaning under servitude and misery" (2: 41–42).

When Savillon first learns from the overseer that Yambu "had been accounted valuable, yet from the untractable stubbornness of his disposition, was worth less money than almost any other in my uncle's possession," recognizing that "this was a language natural to the overseer," he answers him "in his own style, that I hoped to improve his price some hundreds of livres" (2: 32). As we have seen, however, this is also a language and style natural to the entire novel. One could read the extended account of Yambu (which, of course, is not at all necessary to the plot) as a moral and economic argument against slavery that Mackenzie, writing in the climate of the British and more specifically Scottish abolitionist movement, decided to include in his sentimental novel; in terms of the preoccupations present from the very first pages, it also stands as an indictment of the transformation of Julia into Roubigné's "treasure" and Montauban's "property." The traffic in women that takes place between men in the narrative is made ironically explicit when the maid's account of the wedding notes that during the ceremony, "two happier hearts were not in France, than [Roubigné's] and the count de Montauban's" (1: 168). The novel's own recurrent images and preoccupations suggest that it is not anachronistic to see Yambu's situation as a literalization of Julia's. Indeed, no character in the novel escapes the novel's system of accounting.[7]

Montauban, for example, offers an extended comparison concerning people preoccupied with "the little cordialities of life": "Somebody, I think, has compared them to small pieces of coin, which, though of less value than the large, are more current amongst men; but the parallel fails in one respect: a thousand of those *livres* do not constitute a *louis*." He notes that he doesn't consider the acquaintance under discussion to be "in this number" (2: 91–92). However, Montauban himself is included in one of these numbers. In fact, the man who sends a "letter," "a paper, discharging the debt" (1: 142–43) of Roubigné and makes Julia his own is first introduced as "the count *Louis de Montauban*," a man whose "worth is universally acknowledged" (1: 27), and he is frequently referred to throughout the novel simply as the "count." In the count's metaphoric accounting, people are not only (like Yambu) worth *louis* or *livres*; they are the currency of exchange.

Even the plot of tragedy that is overlaid onto the story of sentiment intersects with the business transactions of the novel. When Roubigné returns from one of his dreadful appointments with the procurer—Julia feels "there is something terrible in that man's business" although she is "ignorant of their transactions"—he finds his daughter reading her "favourite Racine. 'Iphigenia! (said my father, taking up the book) Iphigenia!' He looked on me piteously as he repeated the word. I cannot make you understand how much that single name expressed" (1: 98–99). When she offers to give herself to Montauban following his payment of her father's bills, Julia describes herself as "the silent victim of the scene;" acknowledging the word "victim," she asks her correspondent, "why should I score through that word when writing to you?" (1: 155). Montauban later refers to his wife's death as "the sacrifice" (2: 154). The last line of the novel, alluding to both father and husband, refers to "sacrifices of mistaken honor" (2: 202). If Julia plays Iphigenia in her father's tragedy, she is sacrificed as a silent victim of his business—not his lawsuit but rather his need to balance accounts with Montauban. Mackenzie subsequently wrote in another context that it is "the business of tragedy to exhibit the passions, that is, the weaknesses of men."[8] In *Julia de Roubigné,* the weaknesses of men—and the weakness of women—turn the business of tragedy into business.

If Julia plays Desdemona in her husband's tragedy, it is because by the end of the novel he comes to believe that "vengeance is the only business I have left" (2: 140). He wishes for some "luxurious vengeance" (2: 145), but his revenge finally takes care of business, not luxury. Like the sentimental story, the tragic plots imported into the novel are incorporated into the narrative of accounting. Indeed, if Mackenzie playing the role of editor wants to deny that the novel has a plot, or if he fears that narrative will destroy sentiment, it is perhaps because he fears that the narrative is in sum an account, a series of paper transactions calculating debt, exchange, and human sacrifice. If the scene in the grocery shop recounted in the Introduction inscribes the origins of the manuscript in comedy, the narrative rewrites the account of the papers as tragedy because it rewrites tragedy as an account.

Like the commercial transactions that ultimately lead to the purchase of the book, this account also implicates the reader. One reason that the story of Yambu is central to *Julia de Roubigné* is that it locates tragedy at the crossroads of the story of business and the story of sentiment and suffering. When in his letter about slavery, Savillon thinks of "the many thousands of my fellow-creatures groaning under servitude and misery," he exclaims to God that "the refinements of man, ever at war with thy works, have changed this scene of profusion and luxuriance, into a theatre of rapine, of slavery, and of murder!" Imagining that his uncle "would smile at my romance, and tell me that things must be so," Savillon, formerly a "master in literature" (2: 133), asserts that the "master of slaves has seldom the soul of a man." He concludes: "This is not difficult to be accounted for; from his infancy he is made callous to those feelings, which soften at once and ennoble our nature."

Savillon experiences his feelings (his recognition of "Negroe" slaves as "fellow-creatures") "as a man" rather than "as a merchant," but he also speaks as the spectator of scenes of abundance that form part of a theater of enslavement and destruction; he imagines that the expression of such feelings will sound like a "romance," presumably because they seem improbable and fantastic. (Some years later, in the account he wrote about the parliamentary debate over the slave trade in 1784, Mackenzie would paraphrase the rhetoric of the opponents of abolition, who warned of "the dangerous consequences which the legislature's yielding to this momentary ebullition of romantic humanity might produce.")[9] Yet it is precisely the perspective of a sympathetic spectator in the theater or a reader of romances that is opposed to the perspective of the merchant and slaveholder. In contrast to the callused feelings learned from childhood by the white colonists, Savillon imagines the feelings of European children who are nurtured on moving stories: "Among the legends of a European nursery, are stories of captives delivered, of slaves released, who had pined for years in the durance of unmerciful enemies. Could we suppose its infant audience transported to the sea-shore, where a ship laden with slaves is just landing; the question would be universal, 'Who shall set these poor people free?'— The young West-Indian asks his father to buy a boy for him, that he may have something to vent his spite on when he is peevish" (2: 43–44). Like Savillon, who is appalled by the theater of slavery and suffering in a romantic reaction, children who read or hear stories, who become an audience to romantic adventures, react with compassion—unlike children who grow up beholding the scene of slave ships. Having learned stories of freedom, when transported to a real scene of servitude and suffering, this audience would look for the plot of romance.[10]

An aesthetic response is juxtaposed to the business of slavery; rather than distancing the imagined reader or beholder from the scene, the audience (in the characteristic language of eighteenth-century aesthetics) is "transported" to the time and place in what feels like (in the characteristic language of eighteenth-century moral philosophy) a transport of sympathy.[11] Writing in *The Lounger* in 1785, Mackenzie suggests that "romance and tragedy may be very usefully employed" to combat "indifference and selfishness." Although he warns of the "dangers" of reading novels and tragedy, he asserts: "The region of exalted virtue, of dignified sentiment, into which they transport us, may have a considerable effect in changing the cold and unfeeling temperament of worldly minds; the indifferent and selfish may be warmed and expanded by the fiction of distress, and the eloquence of feeling."[12] Savillon's liberal schemes, his ability to feel compassion and recognize the slaves as fellow creatures, are related to his ability to respond to aesthetic experience. His imaginary tableau of the romantic audience witnessing the slave ship leads him to recall his own position in regard to the Roubignés. Thinking of the more familial relationships people have with the "ancient, the tried domestic" (in particular, Roubigné's servant Le Blanc), he thinks of the "shipwreck" of

Roubigné's fortunes and tells his correspondent, "I sometimes sit down alone, and transporting myself into the little circle at Roubigné's, grow sick of the world, and hate the part which I am obliged to perform in it" (2: 41–45). Like the infant audience transported from the scene of stories to the seashore, Savillon's imaginative transport to the shipwreck of the Roubigné family positions him as a sympathetic witness to their suffering.

Although this vision underlines the language of theater, reading, romance, and aesthetic experience in this letter, the juxtaposition of this aesthetic and sympathetic transport at the seashore with Savillon's transport to the Roubignés' shipwreck raises the question of what part Savillon is "obliged to perform." Even if one were to disregard the origins of the fortunes that Savillon will inherit (and try to transmit to Julia) in the theater of rapine, slavery, and murder, even if Savillon renounces his role in this theater, there is no answer to the question asked by the imagined infant audience: "Who shall set these poor people free?" As Rousseau would argue (and here the *Lettre à d'Alembert* is more important than the second *Discours*), the heightened sympathy that comes from the scenes of tragedy, romance, legend, and story finally leaves the audience with no part to perform:

> En donnant des pleurs à ces fictions, nous avons satisfait à tous les droits de l'humanité, sans avoir plus rien à mettre du nôtre. . . . Au fond, quand un homme est allé admirer de belles actions dans des fables et pleurer des malheurs imaginaires, qu'a-t-on encore à exiger de lui? . . . Ne s'est-il pas acquitté de tout ce qu'il doit à la vertu par l'hommage qu'il vient de lui rendre? Que voudroit-on qu'il fît de plus? Qu'il la practiquât lui-même? il n'a point de rôle à jouer: il n'est pas comédien.

> In shedding our tears for these fictions, we have satisfied all the claims of humanity, without having to give any more of ourselves. . . . Finally, when a man has gone to admire fine actions in fables, and to weep over imaginary misfortunes, what more can one demand of him? . . . Has he not acquitted himself of all he owes to virtue by the homage he has just rendered it? What more would one have him do? . . . he has no role to play: he is not an actor.[13]

In the same remarks on tragedy in *The Lounger* in which he praises the effects of romance and tragedy, Mackenzie writes:

> The high heroic virtue we see exemplified in tragedy, warms the imagination, and swells the mind; but being distant from the ordinary feelings and exertions of life, has, I suspect, but little influence upon the conduct. On the contrary, it may be fairly doubted, whether this play of the fancy, in the

walks of virtue and benevolence, does not lessen the exertion of those qualities in practice and reality. . . . In stage misfortunes, in fancied sufferings, the drapery of the figure hides its form; and real distress, coming in a homely and unornamented state, disgusts the eye, which had poured its tears over the hero of tragic misery, or the martyr of romantic woe.[14]

Mackenzie goes further in another *Lounger* essay, which also reiterates Rousseau's critique of aesthetic response:

In the enthusiasm of sentiment there is much the same danger as in the enthusiasm of religion, of substituting certain impulses and feelings of what may be called a visionary kind, in the place of real practical duties, which in morals, as in theology, we might not improperly call good works. In morals, as in religion, there are not wanting instances of refined sentimentalists, who are contented with talking of virtues which they never practice, who pay in words what they owe in actions.[15]

The story of Yambu seems to offer an aesthetic perspective as an alternative to the account of human relations in terms of property and financial transactions; yet it also suggests the failure of an aesthetic response, the inability of a romantic argument to respond to the story of sentiment and suffering. One could argue that in his treatment of Yambu and in his attempt to give his fortune to Julia that Savillon tries to pay in actions as well as words, although his offer to free Yambu is really an empty speech act: he offers to pay for Yambu's work on the plantation rather than his passage home, and his actions in regard to Julia help to precipitate her death. Aesthetic response may have a payoff, but it is not clear how much it is worth. Indeed, although it may serve to counter the cold, unfeeling, and selfish temperament of worldly minds, aesthetic response may come at too high a price, becoming in the end itself responsible for tragedy. Especially as the narrative of *Julia de Roubigné* shifts from "memoirs of sentiment, and suffering" to the thicker plot of tragedy, eclipsing Rousseau with Shakespeare and Racine, the question of the characters' and the reader's role as beholders of tragedy becomes both more important and more problematic.

Although the last part of the novel seems to find its interest in narrative as well as sentiment, entering into plots of missed communications, adultery, madness, revenge, and murder, the plot of the novel is increasingly motivated by—and finally located in—acts of imagination and aesthetic experience. As the count de Montauban begins to suspect Julia's emotional attachment to the love of her youth, he follows the model of Othello, driving himself to madness and murder in a jealous rage based on unfounded accusations, rather than the model of Wolmar, who, omnisciently aware of Julie's past, incorporates St. Preux into his utopian family circle. At the level of plot—what actually happens in the narrative—Julia is more innocent than Julie; Julie was in fact St. Preux's lover, while Julia and her childhood friend Savillon have never so much as declared their love for each other. According to Sir Walter Scott, in *Julia de Roubigné*, Mackenzie set out to compose a story "in which the characters should be all naturally virtuous, and where the calamities of the catastrophe should arise, as frequently happens in actual life, not out of schemes of premeditated villainy, but from the excess and over-indulgence of passions and feelings." Yet despite her virtue, this overindulgence of passions and feelings that may be "in themselves blameless" makes Julia less than innocent.[16] She is more guilty than Desdemona, who is the unknowing victim of false appearances and Iago's devious plotting. Although she ultimately agrees to a secret interview with Savillon in compromising circumstances in a scene of renunciation that is misinterpreted by Montauban as proof of her infidelity, Julia is guilty of what her husband calls "the adultery of the imagination." Hearing "old stories" in which "Savillon was a person of the drama," Montauban becomes more and more suspicious of his wife's imaginative life: "The name of Savillon never mentioned, except in guilty dreams? while his picture was kept in her chamber for the adultery of the imagination!" (2: 134).

Montauban refers here to a scene of art and aesthetic experience that in fact (or in fiction) makes Julia herself feel guilty. Savillon has what he calls "a little remembrancer, . . . a picture, which has hung at my bosom for some years past, that speaks such things!" (2: 69). Julia and Savillon had their portraits made "by the same hand" and "exchanged resemblances" (1: 173), and it is the companion piece to this picture of Julia, a portrait of Savillon that she possesses, that leads to the tragedy of the novel. Alarmed by his wife's melancholy disposition (she has learned that reports of Savillon's marriage in Martinique are untrue), Montauban finds himself looking at "some loose papers on her dressing-table," where he discovers "the picture of a young man in miniature, the glass of which was still wet with the tears she had shed on it." As his servant enters the room, he exclaims, "look there! . . . holding out the picture without knowing what I did; he held it in his hand, and turning it, read on the back, Savillon" (2: 126). Remarkably, given the "high sense of honour" that the partly Spanish Montauban is said to carry "to a very romantic height" (1: 32), he tries not to leap to conclusions: "It may be I wrong her; but to dream of Savillon, to keep his picture, to weep over it" (2: 128). Julia, however, although innocent of the crime that her husband imagines, has already confessed her guilt earlier in the novel.

After her marriage to Montauban, Julia asks her correspondent and confidante Maria to forget the "history of this poor heart," to erase, as it were, the narrative of the letters that Maria and the reader of the novel have read up to the point of the marriage. "You must assist me," Julia writes, "by holding it a blank, which recollection is no more to fill up" (1: 172)—recalling her earlier instructions to Maria in anticipation of her wedding day, "Set down *Tuesday* next for your Julia—but leave its property blank—Fate will fill it up one day" (1: 165). Despite this desire to make her past a blank, to erase her past history of sentiments in order to avoid "the risk of calling up ideas, which were once familiar, and may not now be the less dangerous" (1: 172), she keeps the portrait of Savillon, which does indeed seem capable of calling up dangerous ideas. In the very same letter, Julia recounts how looking through a drawer, she accidentally found the picture: "I shut the drawer as if it had contained a viper; then opened it again; and again the countenance of Savillon . . . met my view! Was it a consciousness of *guilt* that turned my eye involuntarily to the door of the apartment? . . . I fear I looked too long, and too impassionedly on this miniature." Calling Maria "my own best monitor," Julia wonders "how I should like that my husband had seen this" (1: 174–75). She realizes that there is danger in her imaginative engagement with this work of art. Finding herself met by its gaze, seeing and seen after she has tried to reduce her past narrative to a blank, Julia imagines the gaze of both her husband and her reader, thereby imagining herself as a spectacle as well—either caught guiltily in the act of beholding the picture or even returning the picture, which she suggests would "look like a suspicion of myself" (1: 176).

Julia's suspicion that "keeping this picture is improper" (1: 175) seems to be confirmed by another guilty interview in which she comes face to face with the portrait in volume 2. "That picture, Maria, that picture!" she exclaims, "Why did I not banish it from my sight? too amiable Savillon!" Alternating between an address to her correspondent and an apostrophe to her beloved— or is it more precisely an apostrophe to his portrait?—Julia seems to refer to herself (in both the second and the third person) as well as her reader in a command to look: "Look there, look there! in that eye there is no scorn, no reproach to the unhappy Julia." This address recalls Montauban's command to "look there" when he sees the portrait, but it enters into an act of writing to the moment that seems to join Savillon himself in an imagined present tense: "Thinks't thou, Maria, that at this moment—it is possible—he is gazing thus on the resemblance of one, whose ill-fated rashness has undone herself and him! Will he thus weep over it as I do?" (2: 121–22). Julia suspects that there is "guilt" in her tears as she reminds herself that "this bosom is the property of Montauban." It is after she is "interrupted by the voice of [her] husband" (ibid.) that she leaves to compose herself and he finds the picture in her papers still wet with tears: the physical evidence of an imaginative encounter, a particularly intense experience of transport before a work of art. Curiously, Montauban doesn't find among Julia's papers the letter to Maria that he interrupts, which not only describes but also enacts these experiences. It is this fantasizing to the moment that is the real proof of her adultery of the imagination.

These descriptions of the portrait are probably the most Rousseauian scenes in *Julia de Roubigné*. They are somewhat less excessive versions of the accounts of Julie's portrait in *La Nouvelle Héloïse*. Julie intends the portrait that she sends to St. Preux to operate as a "talisman" that will allow them to communicate across distance and absence. St. Preux opens the package containing the portrait, exclaiming, "Julie! . . . ô ma Julie! le voile est déchiré . . . je te vois . . . je vois tes divins attraits!" (Julie! . . . Oh my Julie! . . . the veil is torn away . . . I behold you . . . I behold your divine features!). He vacillates between moments of belief in "le magique effet de ces traits" (the magical effect of these features) and moments of disillusionment: "Je crois, en le voyant, te revoir encore" (When I look at it, I think I am beholding you once more) but "un instant me désabuse, toute la douleur de l'absence se ranime et s'aigrit en m'ôtant l'erreur qui l'a suspendue" (I am instantly disabused; all the pain of absence is reanimated and sharpened when it dispels the error that had relieved it). St. Preux's desire to "transmettre" to her senses the "délire et l'illusion" (transmit to your senses the delirium and the illusion of mine) that he experiences seems to succeed; Julie writes: "Je m'imagine que tu tiens mon portrait, et je suis si folle que je crois sentir l'impression des caresses que tu lui fais et des baisers que tu lui donnes" (I imagine that you are holding my portrait, and I am so crazy that I think I am feeling the touch of the caresses and the kisses you are giving it).[17] Julie's sensual hallucination of transcending distance and absence is actually a fantasy about St. Preux and her portrait. She imagines him kissing and caressing a painting, not herself.

Mackenzie reproduces this crucial scene from *Julie* in an abbreviated and miniature version; but the model of Julie's portrait shows us that Julia's real crime lies less in her impassioned viewing of Savillon's portrait than in her imagining that he is viewing her portrait in a moment of simultaneous fetishism. It is when she wonders, "Will he pardon my offences, and thus press it?" that she stops herself and writes: "I dare not: this bosom is the property of Montauban" (2: 121). Rousseau's model locates Julia's transgression in the realm of the aesthetic. When Montauban earlier overhears Julie speak Savillon's name in her sleep, he wonders "if some previous cause had impressed it on her imagination" (2: 103). At the end of the novel, he is said to have "revenged the imagined injury" (2: 200) of his wife's infidelity; and although the phrase "imagined injury" ostensibly refers to the fact that he has only imagined her adultery, that her infidelity is imaginary in the sense that it is a fiction of his imagination, it also suggests that the injury has been inflicted by imagination, and that this adultery of the imagination, mediated through the representations of papers and pictures, is enough to make Julia guilty.

This problem also returns us to the problem of plot in the novel. *Julie* is filled with scenes in which representations, images, dreams, memories, and imaginary events seem to have a greater effect than the actual experiences they recall or anticipate. Julie, for example, writes, "tout me retrace une scène imaginaire avec plus de force que les événements qui me sont réellement arrivés" (everything retraces to me an imaginary scene with more force than events that have really befallen me).[18] Montauban must revenge imagined injuries, not only because they have a force and reality of their own, but also because in the story of his life, in misery as in happiness, there are, so to speak, no real injuries. Nothing actually happens after his marriage until he murders Julia: of facts he has nothing to write. The consummation of the affair between Julia and Savillon takes place only in imagination (theirs as well as Montauban's), but adultery of the imagination is as bad as the real thing, because in this novel there is no other story—except for the ledger of accounting. When Julia remarks, "Comedies and romances, you know, always end with a marriage, because, after that, there is nothing to be said" (2: 79), neither she nor Montauban realizes that they are characters in a tragedy. Living with her parents in what Savillon pictures as "the remains of ancient Gothic magnificence" amidst a "scene . . . formed to create those Romantic illusions" (2: 10), Julia describes her disappointment after "cherishing romantic hopes" (94); and even Montauban concedes that he is not "such a man as the writer of a romance would have made a husband for Julia" (2: 94). Yet the source of the tragedy is not the disillusionment that comes when romantic illusions are replaced by facts. Ironically, one could say that Montauban's romantic illusions (and the "sense of honour" that he carries "to a very romantic height" [1: 32]) lead to the tragedy, but the novel takes up the plot of tragedy when he becomes witness to the illusions and delusions of Julia's sentimental and aesthetic experience.

The romantic experience of art inscribed in the story of sentiment is finally not an alternative to the story of business that seems to destroy sentiment. The transport of art and sympathy that might carry one to the time and place of a scene of suffering finally reminds the reader or beholder of the distance and absence that prevents more than an aesthetic response. This fundamental paradox of eighteenth-century aesthetics can make one hate the part one is obliged to perform in the world; or, in the Rousseauian view that Mackenzie elaborates in his *Lounger* essays, make one weep for Yambu in the theater while remaining impassive before the slave ship. Insofar as it is effective, however, in generating the transport of sympathy, the experience of art threatens to call up dangerous ideas, "emotions," as Savillon says in another context, that "would be dangerous to the peace of us all" (2: 142). In this sense, although he may reject anti-abolitionist arguments, Mackenzie also warns of "the dangerous consequences" of a "momentary ebullition of romantic humanity." Mackenzie's essays contain conventional warnings about novels, romances, and theater and "the dangers to which they sometimes expose their readers," explaining, "I am not, however, insensible of the value, perhaps but too sensible of the power, of these productions of fancy and of genius."[19] Yet if *Julia de Roubigné* suggests that the experience of art may be too intense, too difficult to control, it is more than a cautionary tale about the dangerous consequences of calling forth excessive passions and feelings. Art and sensibility seem both necessary and dangerous in the market economy of the novel, both too powerful and not powerful enough. To be sensible of their power, however, as well as their value, is to realize that the reader, implicated in the commercial transactions that both frame and structure the pervasive accounting of the characters, may also be compromised by the counterstory of aesthetic experience.

In Rousseau as in Richardson, the epistolary novel aims to use the very mediation of the letter form that puts the reader at two removes from the text's address to create the illusion of immediacy, the illusion that (in Julia's words in the first letter in Mackenzie's novel) "I will speak to you on paper when my heart is full, and you will answer me from the sympathy of yours" (1: 7). Such illusions, like Julia's "extasy" and "blissful delusion" and "enthusiastic rapture" (2: 178–79, 185) when she imitates on the organ music that she has heard in a dream, seem dangerously transgressive and even mad. The picture and papers stained with tears make Julia both look and feel guilty. If she is a victim of the fiscal transactions entered into between her father, her husband, and herself, she is also in some sense a victim of a transaction with art that is presented as a kind of accident. She finds the picture, originally drawn "by a painter who was accidentally in our neighbourhood," while "rummaging out a drawer," and guiltily wonders after turning her eye "involuntarily to the door of the apartment" whether she is guilty for "accidentally thinking of Savillon" (1: 175). This accidental encounter with a work of art recalls the "whimsical accident" (1: viii) through which the Frenchman's father acquires the letters that become the text of the novel. Accident or not, Julia's intense aesthetic experience mirrors the experience that the romantic reader of the novel of sensibility might be expected to have while reading her letters, while reading *Julia de Roubigné.*

If *Julia de Roubigné* asks the reader to consider what it means to buy the book, it also asks what it means to become the reader of an epistolary novel, to become a witness to "records of private life," "memoirs of sentiment, and suffering" (1: viii). Savillon suggests that aesthetic experience humanizes the mind and encourages sentiments of compassion and sympathy, but the novel suggests that if acts of imagination can seem too dangerously volatile among friends who have "exchanged resemblances" (1: 173), they can seem disconcertingly voyeuristic among strangers. In a unique epistolary appearance in the text (in a posthumous letter that evokes Julie's posthumous letter in *La Nouvelle Héloïse*), Julia's mother offers this advice about marriage: "Its sacredness is broken for ever, if third parties are made witnesses of its failings, or umpires of its disputes" (1: 188). What is the position of the reader, however, in purchasing and becoming witness to the scenes from a marriage that make up *Julia de Roubigné?* Early in the novel, Montauban fantasizes about becoming Julia's friend and then exclaims to his correspondent: "but friend is a word insignificant of the connexion—to have one soul, one fate with her! to participate her happiness, to share her griefs! to be that single Being to whom, the next to Divinity, she pours out the feelings of her heart" (1: 73).

This desire for sympathy and intimacy is somewhat out of character for Montauban, and in the context of the novel, it is highly improbable that he could ever fulfil it. Indeed, in this indirect and mediated epistolary narrative, in which Julia and Savillon remain mostly ignorant of the other's feelings, meet only once at the end of the book, barely exchange letters, and communicate almost entirely in the imagination, the only one who is in the privileged position that Montauban imagines is the reader. The reader, however, even in the person of the confidante and *destinatrice* Maria, whom Julia (in language that recalls Smith's *Theory of Moral Sentiments*) calls "my best monitor" (1: 175), can never really be more than a third party, a witness to the scene. Julia's promise at the beginning of the novel, "I will speak to you on paper when my heart is full, and you will answer me from the sympathy of yours" (1: 7), may seem to address the reader, but this fantasy on the part of both author and reader either in the correspondence or in the novel of sensibility is finally only a fantasy—if a powerful and dangerous one.

Montauban, of course, like Othello, is a bad witness who misconstrues appearances; he is a bad reader of Julia's story—at least of its plot, if not of its sentiments—even when he intercepts the correspondence of Julia and Savillon and actually assumes the more omniscient position of the reader of the novel. He is driven mad by the portrait he accidentally finds, by the epistolary exchange between Julia and Savillon of which he becomes a reader: by both his guilty knowledge and his mistaken belief in his ability when faced with Julia's "embarrassment of guilt" to "even without a key . . . read her soul to the bottom" (2: 130). Montauban first learns about Julia's past connection with Savillon when his servant leads the Roubigné family domestic Le Blanc to tell "the story. . . . He knew not that he was delivering the testimony of a witness—that the fate of his former mistress hung on it!" (2: 132). Le Blanc is introduced as a narrator in the second letter of the novel when he gives Julia and her father an "account" (1: 9), "narration" (1: 12), "recital" (1: 13), and "description" (1: 15) of their lost paternal estate. Given the preoccupation of the editor and the characters with the reduction of the narrative to nothing—with the desire to make the "history of this poor heart . . . a blank" (1: 172), with the status of the "blank" "property" (1: 165) of a future account that will be filled in by fate, with the way in which "life now fades into a blank, and is not worth the keeping" (2: 114)—it is not a coincidence that this witness and narrator is named Le Blanc. The one time we see Le Blanc reading, he is handed a "paper" by Roubigné, who, overcome by his impending financial ruin, wants to settle accounts with his faithful servant. Le Blanc narrates: "'Here are so much wages due to you, Le Blanc (said he, putting the paper in my hand). You shall receive the money now; for I know not how long these louis may be mine to give you.'—I could not read the figures, I am sure I could not: I was struck blind, as it were, while he spoke so" (1: 107).

At this emotional moment of accounting, the figures become blank, figuratively speaking; the paper becomes unreadable, the witness by his own testimony cannot see. As Le Blanc weeps, one might say that at least for a moment, sentiment destroys the narrative of accounting, although this white "domestic of a family" (2: 44), whom Savillon contrasts with a black slave, is in some sense appalled by seeing his familial relationship with his master reduced to wages. In the end, the narrative of accounting and the story of sentiment seem to cancel each other out, as do the plot of the novel and the events that take place only in the realm of the imaginary. The novel of sensibility, sold to a third party and transmitted at several removes, can account for sentiment and imagine sentiment only in a narrative that would seem to destroy sentiment—or produce a dangerous overabundance of it. At the end of the Introduction, the editor notes that he has gained an "advantage" from his work because "I often wandered from my own woe, in tracing the tale of another's affliction, and, at this moment, every sentence I write, I am but escaping a little farther from the pressure of sorrow" (1: xii). Unlike Julia's writing to the moment (her fantasy that "at this moment" the one with whom she has "exchanged resemblances" is "gazing thus on the resemblance" of herself as she is gazing on his image), this acknowledgement of woe escapes sentiment and suffering through the act of writing itself. As the editor traces the tale of another's affliction, the tracing itself seems to reduce his own story of sentiment and suffering to nothing—at least in the eyes of the reader, who is told of a story that will not be told. In this sense, the editor who stands in for Mackenzie at the opening of the book finally refuses to be "entirely accountable" (1: xii).

In the end, the reader is left with the problem of how to respond to both the account and the tale of another's affliction. The last letter is narrated by one minor character to another (Monsieur de Rouillé to Mademoiselle de Roncilles); its mostly third-person account of the tragedy's last scenes begins, "The writer of this letter has no title to address you, except that which common friendship and common calamity may give him" (2: 187) and ends, "I look on the body of Montauban—I weep over the pale corse of Julia!—I shudder at the sacrifices of mistaken honour, and lift up my hands to pity and justice!" (2: 202). Rouillé is the character who earlier leads Montauban to think about "characters" who are "small pieces of coin, which, though of less value than the large, are more current amongst men," while acknowledging that "a thousand of those *livres* do not constitute a *louis*" (2: 91–92). With no title to address us beyond the claim of a common calamity, he stands as a moved beholder to the business of tragedy: like the reader, not insensible of the value, but perhaps too sensible of the power, of books.

6 | *Writing Masters and "Masculine Exercises" in* The Female Quixote

Prove, therefore, that the books which I have hitherto read as Copies of Life, and Models of Conduct, are empty Fictions.

Charlotte Lennox, *The Female Quixote*

It is well known that the rise of the novel in the eighteenth century was accompanied by commentaries about the danger of reading novels; the authors of the works of fiction that we now call novels typically distinguish their narratives from works and genres that were seen as frivolous and false at best and immoral and corrupting at worst. Rousseau's warning in the 1761 preface to *Julie, ou La Nouvelle Héloïse*, "Jamais fille chaste n'a lu de romans" (A chaste girl never read novels), follows Richardson's less ironic efforts (as expressed in the 1740 preface to *Pamela*) to write a virtuous novel in a world that was "too much, as well as too early, debauched by pernicious *Novels*."[1] The danger of reading novels was seen to lie in bad examples; Richardson, Rousseau, and others sought to provide exemplary heroes and heroines to serve as models for their readers, although readers as diverse as Puritans and Henry Fielding found their stories of "virtue rewarded" to be disingenuous or hypocritical. Even virtuous heroes and heroines were seen to inflame the passions in readers whose sensibilities could become overstimulated. Fears about the risks of reading novels, however, even works whose content would not be considered harmful, are also reflected in the period's renewed interest in the figure of Don Quixote. Portrayed in the context of satire rather than sensibility, Don Quixote represented a cautionary story about the power of art and the dangers of blurring the boundaries between reality and fiction.[2]

Charlotte Lennox's *The Female Quixote, or The Adventures of Arabella,* published in 1752, tells the story of Arabella, a young woman who has read too many seventeenth-century French heroic romances, and who seems to believe that they are depictions of real life rather than fictions. Arabella is not so much naïve as literal-minded; and, like Don Quixote, she gets into trouble not because she reads romances as historical documents but because she looks at the world as if it were a romance. Arabella looks at the world through the frame of fiction. Governed by the rules of romance writing, she turns all those around her into characters in the plots that she is compelled to repeat and represent. Although a heroine in a satire rather than a sentimental novel, Arabella is like Rousseau's Julie and Mackenzie's Julia in that she inhabits a realm of likenesses, copies, patterns, simulacra, playacting, and representations—as both Arabella and her creator, Lennox, author plots that contain ghostly simulacra and echoes of prior models, images, and texts. In *The Female Quixote,* the paradigmatic Don Quixote plot dramatizes the dangerous power of art and the dangers of viewing the world as if it were art through Lennox's ambivalent investigation of female authorship and masculine authority. The problem of turning one's life into a copy or likeness of the model of fiction is seen both in the novel's anxieties about authority and in its inscription of its heroine in a crisis of literary imitation that also turns on the problematic relationship between models and copies. Arabella dramatizes the dangers of inhabiting a world of likeness as Lennox explores acts of literary impersonation in art and life that are also inscribed in the context of the novel's meditation on writing masters and its own problematic relation to prior authors and authorities.

In book 2 of *The Female Quixote, or The Adventures of Arabella,* the narrative of Arabella's history opens up to include the story of a character named Miss Groves. Arabella has entered into a year of mourning following the death of her father; and her uncle, Sir Charles, and her cousin, Glanville, have left for London, hoping for a "Reformation in her" that will cure her addiction to romances and her belief that they are "real Pictures of Life" (7). Contrary to the "Command" and "Will" of her father, Arabella has refused to consent to marry her cousin; and Glanville departs regretting "the little Power his Father had over her" (64–65). Following this departure, Arabella's books are said to be "the only Amusement she had left," but although she reads them with "Delight" and "more Eagerness than ever," she is lonely and melancholy. In this state, wishing for "an agreeable Companion of her own Sex and Rank," Arabella encounters a young lady at church who reminds her of a heroine from Scudéry's popular seventeenth-century French romances. She determines to make the acquaintance of "this Fair one" (67), a lady named Miss Groves.

Approaching her as a voracious reader would pick up a new book, Arabella is frustrated. She takes Miss Groves home and leads her "into the Gardens, supposing a Person, whose Uneasiness, as she did not doubt, proceeded from Love, would be pleased with the Sight of Groves and Streams, and be tempted to disclose her Misfortunes"; but even when faced with groves, Miss Groves will not be led into autobiographical disclosures. She maintains "Silence," betrays an "absence of Mind," and speaks "not at all in the manner of an afflicted Heroine." Determined "to know her Adventures," Arabella commands Mrs. Morris, Miss Groves's attendant, "to relate, her Lady's History to her" (68–69). The next chapter is almost entirely devoted to Mrs. Morris's "Narration" (77) of Miss Groves's scandalous story, which Arabella manages to translate into the conventions of romance in order to read its protagonist as an afflicted heroine rather than a sexually transgressive juvenile delinquent attracted to the wrong sort of men. Arabella's quixotic identification of Miss Groves with Cleopatra is both a comic gesture and an early warning to those readers who would mistake a cautionary tale for young women for a narrative of romantic adventures. The scene also fits into a pattern (remarked by critics) in which Arabella's interest in romance coincides with her investment in plots that turn upon erotic desire.[3] Yet we still might ask how Miss Groves's history relates to Arabella, and how the relation of her narrative might help us comprehend both Arabella's history and the narrative of *The Female Quixote*.

As told by Mrs. Morris, Miss Groves's life story includes a dangerous liaison at the age of fifteen, an affair with a rakish gentleman, two illegitimate children, and a secret marriage. The outline of this scandalous plot is all that is necessary to achieve the comic and didactic goals of the episode, but Lennox provides further details. According to Mrs. Morris, as a child, Miss Groves "delighted in masculine Exercises . . . and by those coarse Exercises, contract[ed] a masculine and robust Air not becoming her Sex, and tender years." These masculine exercises include "leaping over Hedges and Ditches," but we are told that they led to a different sort of sexual transgression when Miss Groves found "a Lover in the Person who taught her to write." Despite Arabella's assumption that this "Writing-master might have been some illustrious Person, whom Love had disguised," Mrs. Morris insists that he "was never discovered to be any thing better than a Writing-master," that he was dismissed "when the Intrigue was discovered," and that he "continues still to teach Writing" (71–72).[4]

Critics have focused on the problem of *reading* in *The Female Quixote;* but to understand the relation between women and romance, and the status of various forms of transgression in the realms of sexuality, gender, and authority, we also need to consider the problem of writing, especially as it relates to masters and mastery.[5] Although the instruction in penmanship of a minor character may not at first seem relevant to Arabella's story, in the context of the narrative, the terms of the episode are highly charged. When juxtaposed with other episodes in the novel, "The History of Miss *Groves*" (as the story is titled in the heading to chapter 5) can be placed in a constellation of concerns or associations that helps us to understand how the transgression of a young lady having a love affair with her writing master might be related to a preference for masculine exercises.

Arabella has also had a writing master. Her father, the Marquis, "took her from under the Direction of the Nurses and Women" when she was four and "taught her to read and write" (6). (Although the books that obsess Arabella originally were purchased by her mother, she encounters this "great Store of Romances"—which are "not in the original *French,* but very bad Translations" [7]—in her father's library, where they are transported after her mother's death.) Arabella's father acts as a writing master in another sense when he literally commands her to write after she refuses to marry Glanville (whom she suspects of wanting to "make himself Master of her Person") and commands him to leave in a rejection of "a tyrannical Exertion of parental Authority" (34–35). Although Glanville chooses not to take advantage of "her Father's Authority" (37), the Marquis exercises that authority by commanding her to write him an apology: "leading her to his Writing-Desk, [he] ordered her, instantly, to write to her Cousin." Arabella insists that her father "dictate what I must say" and she explains to Glanville in the letter she is forced to write that "it is in Obedience to my Father's absolute Commands, that you receive this Mandate from *Arabella*" (40), naming herself in the third person in this first-person impersonation.

Here, the writing master who has taught her to write commands her writing, dictates to her by dictating what she must say; he masters her person by controlling her words. As transgression is prevented, mastery of writing is identified with the authority of the father. Miss Groves's father also dies at the beginning of her story—hence, perhaps, her susceptibility to "the Person who taught her to write" (71). Arabella's writing master father dies shortly after failing to burn her books and dictate her choice of husband; Sir Charles and Glanville refrain from forcing her "to perform the Marquis's Will" (64) and marry. Arabella already has rejected one suitor, "who was Master of no great Elegance in Letter-writing" (13). At the moment in her life and narrative that she becomes acquainted with "The History of Miss *Groves*," it is uncertain what Arabella's relation will be to either writing masters or the mastery of writing.[6]

A later scene underlines Arabella's investment in the story of Miss Groves. In book 6, Arabella unsuccessfully orders a dressmaker in Bath to "make her a Robe after the same Model as the Princess *Julia's*" (269). The story of her conversation with the dressmaker, who is dismissed "because she did not understand the Fashions that prevail'd two thousand Years ago," becomes widely known and when Arabella appears wearing her new dress, she becomes commonly known as "the Princess *Julia*." Arabella speculates, "I fancy they either took me for some Princess of the Name of *Julia*, who is expected here to-Night, or else flatter me with some resemblance to the beautiful Daughter of *Augustus*." Mr. Selvin insists that the Princess Julia was a "licentious Lady" and "the most abandon'd Prostitute in *Rome*" and continues, "many of her Intrigues are recorded in History; but to mention only one, Was not her infamous Commerce with *Ovid*, the Cause of his Banishment?" Arabella defends the relationship between "that ingenious Poet" and the "absolutely chaste" Princess Julia as entirely "innocent, tho' a little indiscreet" (273) and she proceeds to defeat Mr. Selwin's sketchy knowledge of history with her extensive command of romance narratives.

The satire of the scene is evident, but what is striking here is the double parallel that identifies Julia with both Arabella and Miss Groves, thus establishing a further correspondence between Arabella and Miss Groves. Like Miss Groves in her "Intrigue" (72) with her writing master, Princess Julia is condemned for her licentious "Intrigues" (273) and, in particular, her affair with a master of writing: the ingenious poet Ovid. Arabella defends the reputation of the Princess, just as she defends the virtue of Miss Groves. (We are told that Arabella "would not have been astonished" if she had learned that Miss Groves was "the Daughter of a King" [68]—that is to say, a princess.) After Mrs. Morris recounts how Miss Groves "found a lover in the Person who taught her to write," Arabella responds that "it is not strange, that Love should produce such Metamorphoses" (71). She refers to her theory that the writing master was a disguised man of quality, but in the context of the parallels between Princess Julia and Miss Groves, the reference to "Metamorphoses" resonates next to the later reference to Ovid. Arabella's appearance dressed as Princess Julia in book 7—where she is named as Julia, identified as or with Julia—identifies her with a sexually transgressive woman who is scandalously involved with a male master of writing.

Another scene also centers on Arabella's identification with a woman who is described as a prostitute. In book 9, Arabella has an adventure in the public gardens in London: "An Officer of Rank in the Sea Service had brought his

Mistress disguis'd in a Suit of Man's or rather Boy's Cloaths, and a Hat and Feather, into the Gardens." When some of the people present begin "to suspect her sex," a man "pretending to be affronted at something she said, drew his Sword upon the disguis'd Fair One, which so alarm'd her, that she shriek'd out, She was a Woman, and ran for Protection to her Lover." When Arabella learns that "A Gentleman had drawn his sword upon a Lady disguis'd in a Man's Habit," she tries to help the woman, who is seated with her "antagonist . . . kneeling at her Feet, making Love to her in Mock-Heroicks for the Diversion of the Company." Having joined in the spectacle, to the astonishment of the crowd, demanding to know the "History" of the woman's "Misfortunes," Arabella is dragged away by Glanville, who thinks her mad to "make all this Rout about a Prostitute." He asks, "Do you see how every body stares at you?" (334–36).

Like the Princess Julia and Miss Groves (whom Arabella conducts "into the gardens"), the woman who has come "into the gardens" in masculine attire is identified with transgressive sexual behavior. She also becomes involved in what is at least a parody of a romantic scene in which a poet declares his love for her, as the gentleman "mak[es] Love to her in Mock-Heroicks." As if a parody of Miss Groves with her writing master or Julia with Ovid, the supposed prostitute receives the mock advances of a man who speaks in verse. Miss Groves is first described as "this Fair one" (67), just as the woman in the park is described as "the disguis'd Fair One" and "this unfortunate Fair One" (335). Furthermore, the prostitute's disguise in a man's or boy's clothes recalls the "masculine exercises" that caused Miss Groves to contract "a masculine and robust Air not becoming her Sex" (71).

Earlier, in arguing that the writing master was in disguise, Arabella recalls another episode of cross-dressing in which Orontes fell in love with the "Daughter of the Queen of the *Amazons* . . . and, knowing that the Entrance into that Country was forbid to Men, he dressed himself in Womens Apparel" (72). This, of course, is no ordinary cross-dressing, since to disguise himself as an Amazon, a man must disguise himself as a woman who engages in "masculine exercises." Arabella maintains that Amazonian "Women went to the Wars, and fought like Men" (204). In the gardens, Arabella (who has recently gone to the ball incognito) is herself virtually a "disguis'd Fair One," in that she is "covered with her Veil" (334).

The stories of both Miss Groves and the woman in the park are associated with Amazons, cross-dressing, and gender confusion as well as writing; Princess Julia (who, in her expression of desire, might also be associated with masculine prerogatives) fits into the pattern of women who have engaged in intrigues with men associated with writing through her licentious behaviour and her liaison with the author of the *Metamorphoses*. Obviously, these are not identical scenes with interchangeable characters; yet together they form a constellation of concerns and details that best make sense in juxtaposition. Most important, these characters and scenarios help us to situate Arabella. Through this network of associations, through the cross-references, parallels, and intratextual allusions that link these three scenes together, we see Arabella's attraction to and identification with women involved with cross-dressing, sexual and gender transgression, and the masculine province in which male writers are masters.

Despite the association of these women with masculine exercises, however, we might wonder how transgressive their transgression is if it still leaves men the masters of writing. Arabella displays an interest in the woman who takes "a Lover in the Person who taught her to write," but *The Female Quixote* might be seen as asking whether a woman (with or without a writing master) could learn how to write. Could a woman master the exercise of writing, appear in the person of a writing master, without engaging in cross-dressing? Could a woman assume control of her own story? Such questions are inevitably raised by the notorious penultimate chapter of the novel, entitled "*Being in the Author's Opinion, the best Chapter in this History*" (368). Here, like an Arabella who willingly takes dictation at her father's writing desk, Lennox seems to give over her narrative to a patriarchal writing master in an apparent abdication of female authorship and authority to either the person or the personification of Dr. Johnson. (There is no evidence that Johnson actually wrote the chapter, as some readers have supposed, but it is generally agreed that Lennox probably wrote the learned Doctor's part in Johnson's style.)[7] The questions that this chapter poses, however, are already present in the stories of and about women recounted in the narrative. The problem in reading these stories turns less on decoding the gender or even the status of *romance* (which cannot be assigned a stable position in relation to the *novel* or some other genre) than on understanding the narrative's complex and ambivalent interrogation of both the authorship and the plot of women's stories.

Mrs. Morris's "Narration" of Miss Groves's life story is unusual in the novel. It recounts a woman's story and it is the only extended narrative told by a woman that is represented for the reader. We do not read the version of "the History of her Life" (348) that Arabella tells to the supposed Princess of Gaul. This playacting Princess tells the story of her adventures in chapter 4 of book

9 but this story turns out to be a fiction authored by Sir George, a visiting Baronet who is a friend of Glanville and has become a suitor of Arabella. Miss Groves herself insists on "Silence" (67, 68) when Arabella solicits her story, and she is horrified when Mrs. Morris tells her "History" (77). Throughout the novel, as several commentators have noted, Arabella is told that women should not have stories.[8] Miss Glanville is shocked that Arabella expects to have a "History," but even Arabella expects that someone else will tell it: "I shall not write it . . . tho', questionless, it will be written after my Death" (110). She instructs her maid Lucy to "relate her History" to her cousins and Sir George, but Lucy protests: "How can I make a History about your Ladyship? . . . I never could tell how to repeat a Story when I have read it; and I know it is not such simple Girls as I can tell Histories." Although Arabella's order to perform as the omniscient narrator of her mistress's "History" leaves Lucy speechless, when she is called upon to narrate a later episode, her problem is not an overabundance of narrative facts. Rather, she feels that, like Miss Glanville, she has "nothing to tell, that would make an History" (110).

In book 7, when Arabella "command[s]" Lucy "to give her a Relation of what had happen'd" in what she thinks was an attempted abduction, Lucy insists: "I can't make a History out of nothing." Lucy's silence and her inability to narrate are said to bring Arabella to "a Full Stop" (304–5). What silences Arabella (and closes book 7) is less Lucy's refusal to speak than her insistence that she has no story to tell—that is to say, that Arabella's life has no plot to speak of. The end of the novel might be seen to concede this point. In her disputation with "the Doctor," Arabella recalls her plunge into the river to escape her supposed ravishers and asks: "Do you count my late Escape for nothing?" (379). Her renunciation of her role as a heroine in romance plots by the end of the chapter brings the novel to a full stop because it seems to convert the story of her life to nothing. *The Female Quixote* ends at this point because after her conversion and marriage, the heroine is no longer a heroine. *The Adventures of Arabella* must come to a close because, according to the terms of the novel, there can be no more adventures to narrate. In these terms, romance dramatizes the wish that women's lives will have plots, that women will have stories to tell.

In this sense, despite the homage that Lennox pays to Richardson, *The Female Quixote* is not a Richardsonian novel.[9] Although the novel begins with a daughter who rebels against "a tyrannical Exertion of parental Authority" (35) and refuses the husband her father intends for her, when her father dies and the executor of his will declines to enforce his "Will," the plot veers away from tragedy or melodrama into satire and farce.[10] Yet what makes *The Female Quixote* most unlike a novel by Richardson is its almost total rejection of autobiography. Despite her desire to have a story, Arabella does not tell her own story to either the other characters (except for her offstage narration to the Princess of Gaul) or the reader. Although she writes a few letters according to the dictates of paternal authority or romantic convention, she does not express herself in epistolary dialogue. The narrator may promise, for example, to "acquaint the Reader with what had passed in the Apartment; and also, following the Custom of the Romance and Novel-Writers, in the Heart, of our Heroine" (180), but the reader gets relatively little sense of Arabella's inner thoughts and motives apart from the mistakes she makes in interpreting the world around her. Arabella is unique in the novel because she believes that she has a story, but, as we have seen, she expects that someone else will tell or write the History that she cannot or will not give herself. The apparent reduction of Arabella's adventures to nothing by the end of the novel is related to her refusal of autobiography and her abdication of the mastery of authorship.

In its avoidance of the autobiographical mode of narration, the novel for the most part rejects the narrative device of the interpolated tale that is so common in romances and eighteenth-century fiction. The exceptions to this narrative strategy are the third-person account of Miss Groves and two acts of autobiographical fiction that are authored by Sir George. Arabella has other suitors in the course of the novel but Sir George is the only one who tries to draw her into intrigues by playing the role of a writing master. He is the only character in the novel who is presented as an author. When Glanville says, "It is pity you are not poor enough to be an Author; you would occupy a Garret in *Grub-street,* with great Fame to yourself, and Diversion to the Public," Sir George protests, "I have Stock enough by me, to set up for an Author Tomorrow, if I please." Presenting himself as a master of various forms and genres of writing—he boasts that he has "no less than Five Tragedies . . . Three or Four Essays on Virtue, Happiness, etc. Three thousand Lines of an Epic Poem; half a Dozen Epitaphs; a few Acrostics; and a long String of Puns" (252)—Sir George seems to pride himself on his particular mastery of the forms of romance. Like the Countess, Sir George is "perfectly well acquainted with the chief Characters in most of the *French* Romances" (130). However, whereas the Countess speaks "the Language of Romance" (325) to suggest to Arabella that this language is archaic, Sir George uses his "Knowledge of all the Extravagances and Peculiarities in those Books . . . to make his Addresses to *Arabella* in the Form they prescribed" (130). He draws Arabella into intrigues by playing the role of a writing master, writing to her "in the Style of Romance" (255), and he intervenes in the plot of the narrative specifically in the character of an author of romance fiction.

Sir George relates his "Adventures" (207) in book 6; beginning with a first chapter entitled, "*Containing the Beginning of Sir* George's *History in which the ingenious Relater has exactly copied the Stile of Romance*" (208), this first-person narrative continues almost uninterrupted for nearly ten chapters, complete with dialogue and interpolated letters in a pastiche of adventures that follow the formula of romance narratives. Sir George's design backfires when he inadvertently depicts his "Character" (at least in Arabella's eyes) as "Ungrateful and Unjust," and he ends "with Shame and Vexation at having conducted the latter Part of his Narration so ill." Book 6 comes to a close with Sir George's defense of his expertise as an "Author" to Glanville and Sir Charles; he regrets "that damn'd Slip I made at the latter end of my History" (250, 252).

The effect is comic as this author makes love to Arabella in his version of mock-heroics for the diversion of the company; just as Sir Charles finds in Sir George's narration entertainment and "Proof of the Felicity of his Invention," we can appreciate Lennox's command not only of satire but also of the form and style of romance. However, if (unlike Sir Charles) we are to "penetrate into the Meaning of Sir *George's* Story" (253–54), we should ask what it means that his autobiographical fiction virtually takes over the novel for the space of an entire book.[11] Although Lennox's antiromance demonstrates the deception of romance fiction, it seems to surrender its pages to the romantic intrigue of another writing master. The character of the narrator regains control over the narration as Sir George seems to run out of adventures, but Sir George's narration gets him in trouble when the plot of the romance narrative comes into conflict with the plot of the novel.

Despite this mistake (or perhaps because of it), Sir George conspires to take over the plot of the novel through another act of autobiographical fiction. This time his design is more elaborate: his narrative strategy involves other characters and he takes on the role of the invisible third-person narrator. In exercising this authority, he is able (at least temporarily) to play the role of the author of *The Female Quixote* (or at least *The Adventures of Arabella*). Soon after the scene with the woman disguised as a man in the public gardens in book 9, Arabella meets an afflicted heroine in an encounter that is "conformable to what she has read in Romances" and "more worthy indeed to be styl'd an Adventure than all our Fair Heroine had ever yet met with" (341). This chapter, turned over to the first-person narrative of "*the History of the Princess of* Gaul" (343), is the only story within the novel told about a woman besides that of Miss Groves and the only autobiographical narrative spoken by a woman.

The story of the Princess's life comes to an end at the conclusion of the chapter, but the plot she inaugurates continues throughout book 9 after she accuses Glanville of being her unfaithful lover Ariamenes. As the plot unfolds, Glanville suspects that "some Plot grounded on [Arabella's] Romantick Notions had been laid, to prepossess her against him" and he concludes that Sir George, known for "his plotting Talent," is "the Author of their present Misunderstanding" (354). Eventually, Glanville learns that Sir George had "brib'd a young Actress to personate a Princess forsaken by him; and had taught her all that Heap of Absurdity with which she had impos'd upon *Arabella*" (368). In the end, Sir George confesses "the ridiculous Farce he had invented to deceive her" (382). Once again, we see Sir George literally playing the role of author as he plots to take over the plot of the novel with the plot of a romance. This time his act of autobiographical fiction is written to be performed by someone else; writing as a playwright, he authors a script that goes beyond the bounds of the fictive autobiography he creates for his heroine by drawing the other characters into his scenario. His dramatic monologue hijacks the narrative of *The Female Quixote*, which then takes on the forms of romance. Miss Glanville detects his "Disguise" and "Artifice" and the "Plots" that he has entered into with a chambermaid. Disguised in one of Arabella's veils, she goes to meet Sir George. Impersonation and mistaken identity lead to a nearly fatal sword fight after Glanville apprehends Sir George delivering "a Speech he had study'd for his present Purpose" (365) to Miss Glanville, whom both mistake for Arabella.

Arabella's narration of "the History of her Life" to the Princess is said to contain "Events almost as Romantick and Incredible as any in her Romances" (348); as the plot of book 9 unfolds, it is not Arabella's misinterpretations or fancy that make the story seem romantic. The comedy of errors approaches tragedy rather than "Farce," and, as heroines appear in disguise, while heroes clash with their rivals in love, the plot of *The Female Quixote* comes to resemble the plot of a romance. Arabella is the victim in a complicated stratagem in which the writing master who would be her lover disguises himself and engages in "Heroicks" (365)—or at least Mock-Heroics. Miss Glanville, who previously ridiculed Arabella's view of the world, disguises herself in a veil and plays the role of Arabella in order to revenge herself on her unfaithful lover.

Glanville behaves "like a Madman" (357) and acts the part of a romantic hero. Sir George himself becomes a character in a dangerous farce that departs from his script and escapes his authority.

If Sir George loses control of his plot, one might wonder whether the same is true of Lennox, whose antiromance seems to assume the incredible form that her novel has disparaged. Although the events of book 9 dramatize the fraud and deceit of romance fiction (one could read Sir George's wound as a punishment for his romantic plotting), the irony is that the artifice of romance has become too real. As Laurie Langbauer argues, "the line between the novel and romance disappears."[12] Through his usurpation of authorship, Sir George seems to steal control of the narrative away from Lennox; yet paradoxically, the eventual loss of authority over the plot that Sir George experiences could be seen to figure the loss of authority that Lennox seems to suffer at his hands. As a mock-author, he stands as a parody of the author of romance fictions; yet as an author with "plotting Talent," whose intrigues and stratagems both enforce and escape his authority, he also stands in the place of Lennox.[13]

The story of Sir George returns us to the stories of writing masters, sexual transgression, gender confusion, princesses, and cross-dressing with which we began. When we learn that the character who appears to tell her life story as the Princess in book 9 is really a female impersonation created by the male author of romance plots and fictive autobiographies, we are reminded that, when we see Sir George take over the narrative in his efforts to become the master writer that Arabella falls in love with, we are really witnessing a female author disguising herself as a male storyteller. The Princess of Gaul is a male impersonation disguised as a female impersonation. Like the male actor playing the female Viola playing the male Cesario in an Elizabethan production of *Twelfth Night*, a female author plays a male author who writes an autobiographical fiction in the first person of a female character.[14]

This double cross-dressing reminds us that Arabella is continually mistaken in thinking that the romances written by Scudéry that form her master plots are by a man rather than a woman. Lennox and her readers would have known that although *Clelia* and *Cleopatra* and other romances were published under the name of Georges de Scudéry, his sister Madeleine was really the author.[15] Reading bad English translations of romances that she takes as histories, Arabella does not seem to know that Madeleine de Scudéry engaged in literary cross-dressing in publishing under her brother's name. As an author, Sir George—like Monsieur Georges—is really a woman in man's clothes.

In this context we might reconsider what it means that the penultimate chapter of the novel seems to have been written by or at least in the person of a male writer. Even if one rejects the theory that Dr. Johnson wrote this chapter, the appearance of a learned Doctor to effect Arabella's cure inscribes this question in the plot of the novel. At the end of book 8, the Countess is offered as the ideal person to "make a Convert of Lady *Bella*" (330) (as Arabella is sometimes called). Having been "deep read in Romances" when she was young, she herself is said to "likely have been as much a Heroine as Lady *Bella*" had not "an early Acquaintance with the World" and "other Studies" (323) cured her. Yet this mature and rational woman is abruptly removed from the scene of the novel because of an "Account she receiv'd of her Mother's Indisposition" (330). The sudden desertion of the benevolent Countess and the reference to her indisposed mother both recall the death of Arabella's mother three days after Arabella was born. Book 8 abruptly breaks off, and it is left to the deceptive romance author Sir George and the Johnsonian "worthy Divine" (366) to effect Arabella's cure and conversion in book 9. In this sense, the book ends with a double renunciation: Arabella's renunciation of romances *and* Lennox's apparent abdication of female authority and authorship—both in replacing the sensible and educated Countess by "the Pious and Learned Doctor" (366) and (perhaps) in turning over her narrative to the mastery of Dr. Johnson, or at least his masterful voice.[16]

This apparent act of literary ventriloquy might instead (or also) be seen, however, as a final act of cross-dressing. We might see Johnson playing the role of Lennox, as Sir George writes the script spoken by the actress playing the Princess; but we might also imagine Lennox disguised as the patriarchal writing master, just as she stands as the author behind Sir George when he stands as the author behind the Princess's autobiographical narrative. Arabella repeatedly insists that the man who taught Miss Groves to write was really someone else disguised as a writing master. At the end of the novel, where Miss Glanville appears in disguise, we should recall that her first name is Charlotte. Perhaps Charlotte Lennox also finds it necessary to appear in disguise: a transgressive woman dressed in the male persona of the writing master Dr. Johnson. The novel warns about the dangers of such disguises; but it also might tell us about their necessity. The plots and intrigues of the novel suggest that a woman might have to dress in man's clothes in order to engage in masculine exercises, that she might have to personate or impersonate a man in order to have the authority of authorship.

The question of authority and authorship is also raised in the novel's dedication, which should be read next to the penultimate chapter. Addressed to the earl of Middlesex, the dedication begins with the subject of power: "My Lord, such is the Power of Interest over almost every Mind, that no one is long without Arguments to prove any Position which is ardently wished to be true." Hoping that "this Book may, without Impropriety, be inscribed to Your Lordship," the author of the dedication acknowledges being uncertain that "my Reasons will have the same Force upon other Understandings" and worries that "They who see Your Lordship's Name prefixed to my Performance, will rather condemn my Presumption, than compassionate my Anxiety." Having appealed to the earl for "Protection" and then worried that the appeal will itself be condemned, the dedication ends (as it began) with the question of power: "How can Vanity be so completely gratified, as by the allowed Patronage of him whose Judgment has so long given a Standard to the National Taste?" The last paragraph is made up of three questions that somewhat strangely carry over into the space of its signature (fig. 3). We might ask what questions are asked by the question marks that punctuate even the (anonymous) name of the author, turning it into a question.

The dedication raises the question of whether it can inscribe the name of "*Your* Lordship," prefix his name to the author's "Performance," in its appeal to "powerfully suppress all Opposition." The speech act that would protect the writer, however, is not so much the inscription that addresses the text "to" the earl of Middlesex as the signature by which the author declares herself—or himself. Yet what has the author declared in "declaring myself / *My* Lord, / *Your* Lordship's / *Obliged and most Obedient Humble Servant,* / *The* Author?"? The enjambment allows one to read this declaration in different ways. The sense of the appeal is most obviously to invoke the lord's power and protection by declaring oneself to be his servant—paradoxically, to take on his power over others by making oneself subservient to him. (Indeed, in the momentary pause of this typographical signature's first line, the self-inscription almost seems to declare the author "*My* Lord"—to speak, as it were, in the name of the lord.) Ultimately, however, the syntax declares the author as "*The* Author": the "I" of the dedication can invoke and assume the lord's power "by declaring myself . . . *The* Author." In this sense, power would be seen to come not from inscribing or prefixing someone else's name but rather from the autobiographical act of naming oneself—of declaring oneself to be the author.[17]

However, the typographical signature of the name of the author in this self-declaration inevitably raises a question, since it declares the author speaking in

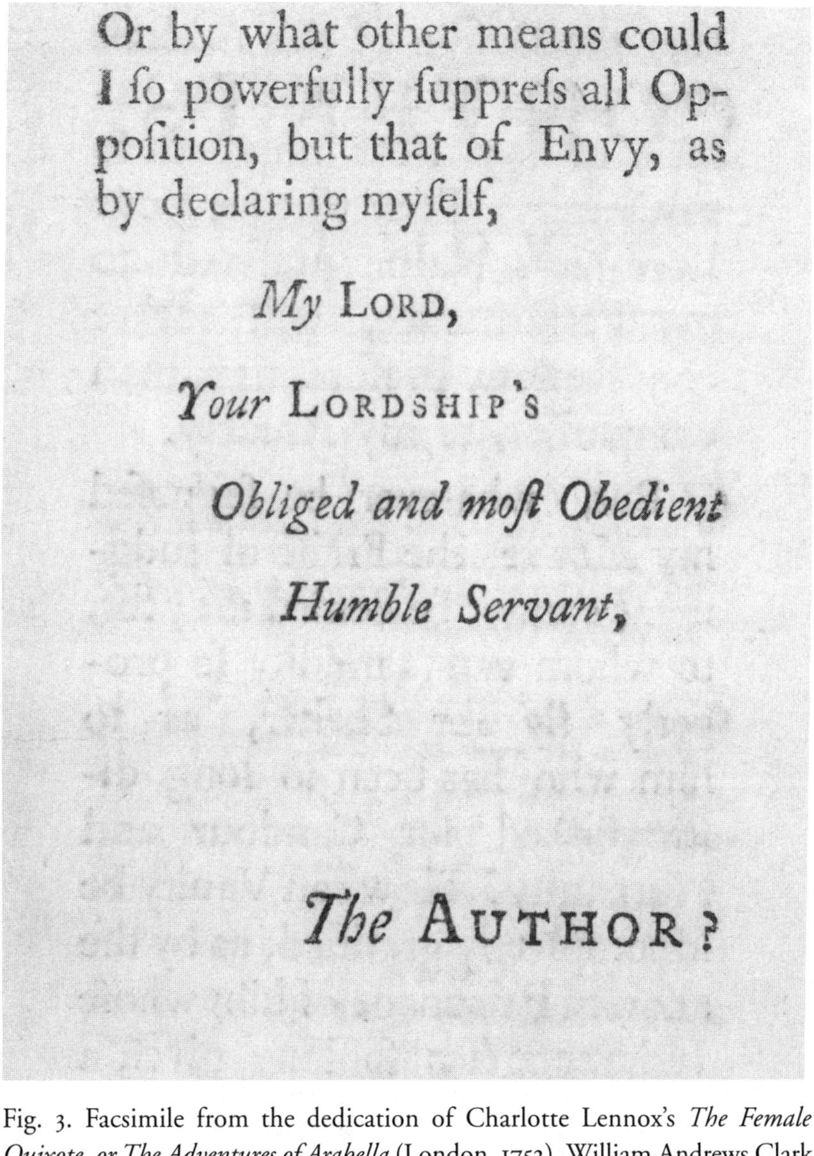

Or by what other means could I fo powerfully fupprefs all Oppofition, but that of Envy, as by declaring myfelf,

My LORD,

Your LORDSHIP'S

Obliged and moft Obedient

Humble Servant,

The AUTHOR?

Fig. 3. Facsimile from the dedication of Charlotte Lennox's *The Female Quixote, or The Adventures of Arabella* (London, 1752). William Andrews Clark Memorial Library, University of California, Los Angeles.

the first person as "*The* AUTHOR?" This interrogation should remind us that there *is* a question about both the self and the self-declaration of the author of the dedication: according to a tradition authorized by Boswell, the dedication is a "Performance" by Johnson, the man who actually offered his "Patronage" to the author of *The Female Quixote*. Although recent scholars, following Duncan Isles, have doubted the theory that Johnson wrote the Johnsonian chapter of Arabella's conversion, Boswell's attribution of the dedication has not been questioned, despite his lack of evidence and his mistakes in dating the novel.[18] We do not know who wrote the dedication or the circumstances of its composition; but, like the penultimate chapter, the question of authorship *about* the text highlights the question of authorship *in* the text. Both dedication and novel dramatize questions about authorship, power, and gender. The epistolary preface that begins the text anticipates a reading of the novel as it raises, and indeed enacts, these key questions. As it begins, *The Female Quixote, or The Adventures of Arabella*—after a title page on which (typically) the name of the author is absent—the dedication prepares us for a consideration of what it means to declare oneself as either "*the author*" or "*the author?*" Must a female author speak in the name of (the voice of, the guise or the disguise of) a male authority in order to speak with the power of a writing master? What would it mean to declare oneself as an author—or have someone else declare oneself as the author—in a novel in which powerful acts of autobiography are conspicuously absent and plots seem to derive their authority from unseen authors? The dedication to the earl of Middlesex might remind us of the ambiguous (perhaps *in-between*) gender of the author of such a novel.

Readers have noted that Arabella's investment in romance is related to her preoccupation with power.[19] Most of her adventures reiterate her insistence on the authority of her own *commands,* especially over men. Despite her apparent vulnerability to abductors, she expects or demands that her suitors be obedient and humble servants who show "Respect and Submission to my Commands" (18). Since she repeatedly expects her rejections to drive her suitors to death, she often must command them to live.[20] The "Authority" and "absolute Power" she claims in these scenes, however, are derived from the "Empire of Love," which, "like the Empire of Honour, is governed by laws of its own" (320). Consequently, a "strict Observer of romantic Forms" (13), Arabella is governed by "the Laws of Romance" (137). Her delusions, as the novel presents them, are based not only on her supposition that "romances were real Pictures of Life" (7) but also on her belief in what she describes as "the Authority of Custom" (44).

Custom is determined by the plots of romance narratives; Arabella finds it difficult to act without "searching the Records of her Memory for a Precedent" (12).[21] Although others find it ridiculous that Arabella is "governed by such antiquated Maxims" (45), she repeatedly pledges her allegiance to "the Laws of Gallantry" (32) and "the Rules prescribed by Romances" (181). Unwilling "to violate the Laws of Romance" (348), Arabella wants her life to be "exactly conformable to the Laws of Romance" (297). This means that Arabella can never have absolute power or authority. The power she repeatedly invokes itself depends upon laws, rules, and precedents that prescribe her actions—all of which are derived from the higher authority of texts written by others.

It makes sense that Arabella believes that others will recount her "History," since the plot of her story has always already been written by someone else about someone else. In the context of Arabella's submission to the laws of romance, we can see the implications of her (and the novel's) apparent avoidance of autobiography. Arabella's belief that her life has a plot is regulated by her refusal or inability to assume authority for the plot of her life. Consequently, a subject in the empire of romance, she can be a heroine but never an author; since the plot of her life has been prescribed, she does not appear to be capable of authoring her own life, of mastering her own story. The deception in which she stumbles into the plot scripted by Sir George is only one instance of the story of her life, in which fictions authored by others govern her every move. Arabella's absolute power is a fiction, a fantasy, because she is only a character in a prescribed plot that dictates her words and actions. In abdicating the authority of autobiography, in surrendering her life story, Arabella risks surrendering her life.

It is this obedience to the laws or rather the plots of romance that leads Arabella to plunge into the Thames in book 9. Thinking that she and her female companions are about to be abducted by some horsemen, she recalls a scene in Scudéry's *Clelia* that she has evoked twice previously in the narrative.[22] Addressing the ladies with her, she says:

> The Action we have it in our Power to perform will immortalize our Fame, and raise us to a Pitch of Glory equal to that of the renown'd Clelia herself.
>
> Like her, we may expect Statues erected to our Honour; Like her, be propos'd as Patterns to Heroines in ensuing Ages: And like her, perhaps, meet with Sceptres and Crowns for our Reward.
>
> What that beauteous *Roman* Lady perform'd to preserve herself from Violation by the impious Sextus, let us imitate to avoid the Violence our intended Ravishers yonder come to offer us.

After she calls upon her companions to "follow the Example I shall set you, and equal me with the *Roman Clelia*," Arabella "plung'd into the *Thames*, intending to swim over it, as *Clelia* did the *Tyber*" (363) (fig. 4). On one level, this experience functions as the symbolic death and rebirth that is the typical climax of a narrative of conversion: the "Thought" that inspires Arabella's leap is described as "worthy [of] those ingenious Books which gave it Birth," and when she is rescued from the water, she is described as "to all Appearances dead." In Adrien Perdou de Subligny's *Mock-Clelia* (which appears to have been a model for Lennox's mock romance), a deluded heroine makes a similar plunge "in imitation of *Clelia* whom she believed her self to be" and then is partly cured when "the water which she drank in the *Tyber*, had a little cooled the choler which fed her melancholy."[23] Arabella's cure must wait until her "Heart yields to the Force of Truth" (381) in conversation with the worthy Divine, but her conversion is in a sense anticipated and acted out in her baptism of fire and water.

To understand the character of Arabella's cure, however, we need to understand precisely what is wrong with her when she jumps into the river. As we have seen, the "Action" that she believes is in her "Power to perform" is an act of imitation only, a replay of the act that Clelia "perform'd" in a plot that has become a script that governs Arabella's life. Here her subservience to the authority and prescription of romantic forms almost kills her. With its repeated "Like her . . . Like her . . . And like her . . . ," Arabella's speech emphasizes that her will to power (and fame) is essentially a will to imitate. Yet it also reveals that Arabella's desire to be *like* Clelia is a desire to be like someone who is imitated: "Like her, we may expect Statues erected to our Honour; Like her, be propos'd as Patterns to Heroines in ensuing Ages."

Arabella imagines herself in the middle of a complex chain of imitations and likenesses. In Scudéry's original romance version of Clelia's adventures, Lucretia appears in a dream vision to warn Clelia that Sextus "has a design against your honour as he had against mine"; warned by a "Complotter" of the "Plot" against her, Clelia avoids a reenactment of Lucretia's fate by plunging into the Tiber and escaping to Rome with the other "fair Virgins" (who also have been sent to Porsenna as hostages) following her "example." To recognize her courage, the Senate resolves "that a Statue on Horse-back should be erected to *Clelia*"; Porsenna himself commissions a statue and, in verses inscribed on the pedestal, Anacreon describes her as a "new Venus."[24] Like Clelia's companions, Arabella follows the "example" of the heroine who becomes a new Venus rather than a new Lucretia and subsequently has works of

Fig. 4. Engraving by François Chauveau in M. de Scudéry (Madeleine de Scudéry), *Clélie, histoire romaine* (Paris, 1658–62), vol. 5. Beinecke Rare Book and Manuscript Library, Yale University.

art designed in her likeness. Like the statues, Arabella would be like Clelia—a new Clelia—but this also means that she herself would be imitated. Instructing her companions to "follow the Example I shall set you, and equal me with the *Roman Clelia,*" Arabella would be equal to Clelia in the sense that she, too, would be a "Pattern" for both works of art and subsequent heroines. In copying and performing the role of Clelia, Arabella hopes that she also will become a role that others will perform. This is perhaps the closest that Arabella—dependent throughout the novel upon the authority of "Precedent"—comes to imagining the power of authorizing future performances. It will be her last adventure as a heroine. Her companions, "who had listen'd with silent Astonishment at the long Speech" and "scream'd out aloud at this horrid Spectacle" (363), form an audience but do not imitate her performance or follow her example.

Arabella is clearly punished for her pride, but we also can recognize in the scene the culmination of her fundamental misreadings of likeness. Throughout her life, Arabella has insisted that romances are both likenesses and patterns: to her "romances were real Pictures of Life" (7) *and* precedents for her to imitate. When, a few pages before her plunge, she hopes that the Princess of Gaul "might be mistaken, thro' the great Resemblance that possibly was between *Ariamenes* and *Glanville,*" and recalls that "*Mandana* had been deceiv'd by the Likeness *of Cyrus* to *Spitridates*" (356), Arabella might suggest the terms for her own predicament: she is mistaken by resemblance and deceived by likeness. Her disputation with the Doctor to a great extent turns upon this question. Declaring that the "great End of History, is to shew how much human Nature can endure or perform," Arabella challenges the Doctor to prove that the books she has read "as Copies of Life, and Models of Conduct, are empty Fictions" (376–77). He insists on the right to decide "in some Measure authoritatively, whether Life is truly described in those books; the Likeness of a Picture can only be determined by a Knowledge of the Original. . . . nothing is more different from a human Being, than Heroes and Heroines" (379–80). Invoking the authority of his authority, the Doctor asserts that the pictures of romances cannot be models because they are not copies. At the moment that Arabella tries to copy a model in a performance that will allow her to be a model as well as a copy, she finds that she has copied an empty fiction; as a likeness of a likeness, she seems to be like nothing. In a sense, Arabella herself has become an empty fiction—a statue of Clelia or even a reproduction of a statue.

Of course, Arabella is an empty fiction: a character in a satirical novel that with its Fieldingesque chapter headings and references to "our Heroine" makes few claims to be realistic. Indeed, Lennox's decision to make this scene the climax of Arabella's adventures and the prelude to her disillusionment serves to locate Arabella in a chain of fictions and imitations. Lennox seems to be imitating Subligny's *Mock-Clelia* here as she makes her heroine plunge into the river in imitation of Clelia, just as Subligny follows Scudéry's plot about a woman whose heroic stance is reproduced by artistic imitations. Arabella's imitation of a literary model mirrors Lennox's own acts of literary imitation in following the pattern of Subligny's imitation of Scudéry—although Arabella does not understand how the repetition of heroic history has led to the "ridiculous Farce" (382) acknowledged at the end of the novel. Lennox's reminder of the ways in which Scudéry's plot itself involves apparitions, doubles, examples, patterns, reproductions, and copies underlines the overdetermined character of these acts of literary imitation.

This scene also reminds us that *The Female Quixote* (like *The Mock-Clelia: Being a Comical History of French Gallantries, and Novels, in Imitation of Dom Quixote*) is an imitation of Cervantes's famous novel.[25] The female Quixote is a new Quixote; ironically, despite her efforts to model herself on literary characters, Arabella (like Leopold Bloom) is modeled on a famous character without knowing it. In following this pattern, Lennox also follows the example of previous imitators such as Subligny and (closer to home) Fielding, who not only declared on the title page of *Joseph Andrews* that his novel was "Written in Imitation of the Manner of Cervantes, Author of *Don Quixote*" but also wrote a play called *Don Quixote in England.* Fielding himself reviewed *The Female Quixote* in *The Covent-Garden Journal,* evaluating the novel mostly by comparing Cervantes's "Original" with Lennox's "Imitation" or "Copy."[26] Lennox is imitating and copying both Cervantes and other imitators of Cervantes. Obviously, the issue here is not originality or authorship—except insofar as "Quixotic Imitations" are by definition *about* originality and imitation. We have seen that Lennox's story about a character who copies and imitates the plots, characters, and precedents of the books she has read raises questions about authority and imitation not only for the heroine but also for the author, who at key moments may or may not speak in her own voice or abdicate authority for the authorship of the novel.

As these questions come up in the contexts of Arabella's complex imitation of Clelia and the subsequent conversion of her adventures to nothing by the Doctor, who appears to speak with or by the authority of Dr. Johnson, we should recognize that these scenes also return us to acts of cross-dressing. In Scudéry's romance, as Clelia makes her heroic escape across the Tiber, we read:

"On the side of *Rome,* they who perceiv'd a Woman upon a Horse swimming in the middle of the River . . . knew not at first whether these were not men disguised in the habits of women."[27] Furthermore, in Subligny's quixotic version of this scene, immediately before the heroine takes her plunge in imitation of Clelia, she and her companions dress themselves as Amazons.[28] As the courageous heroine of Scudéry's romance displays masculine valor and leads her companions on horseback, she appears to be a man disguised as a woman rather than a woman acting like a man; in the mock-heroic version, the heroine really is dressed like a man, or rather dressed like women who dress and behave like men. We might recall that in arguing that Miss Groves's writing master was in disguise, Arabella describes how Orontes "dressed himself in Womens Apparel" (72) in order to gain entrance to the country of the Amazons. Arabella's investment in Clelia is related to her interest in Amazonian women—who, she insists, "went to the Wars, and fought like Men," despite her incredulous uncle's assertion that it would be "shameful" to "offer a Woman the Command of an Army!" (204–5).

In her last act as the heroine of *The Adventures of Arabella,* Arabella inscribes herself in a line of women engaged in masculine exercises. This line includes not only Clelia, Miss Groves, and the prostitute in the park but also, as we have seen, the author. The echoes of disguise and cross-dressing that resonate in the reproduction of Clelia's action evoke the authorial disguises that layer the narration of the final chapters of the novel. In this sense, Arabella as Clelia exemplifies (whether as model or copy) the ambiguous identity of the author a moment before the authority of the Doctor seems to take over control of the text. Arabella's Amazonian pose supports the possibility that the Doctor's subsequent performance is an act of literary imitation in which Lennox and not Johnson engages in cross-dressing.

Dr. Johnson is actually identified by name in the novel's penultimate chapter. Having rejected "the Authority of Scribblers, not only of Fictions, but of senseless Fictions; which at once vitiate the Mind, and pervert the Understanding" (374), the Doctor assures Arabella (and the reader) that it is not necessary to renounce all fiction. In a paragraph punctuated with the markers of footnotes that inscribe the names "*Richardson,*" "*Clarissa,*" and "The Author of the Rambler" at the bottom of the page, he remarks: "Truth is not always injured by Fiction. An admirable * Writer of our own Time, has found the Way to convey the most solid Instructions, the noblest Sentiments, and the most exalted Piety, in the pleasing Dress of a † Novel, and, to use the Words of the greatest ‡ Genius in the present Age, 'Has taught the Passions to move at the Command of Virtue'" (377).[29] In typographical gestures that disrupt the narrative's mimetic surface, the text identifies the "admirable Writer" as "Richardson" and the "Novel" as "*Clarissa,*" while "the greatest Genius" is identified only as "The Author of the Rambler." Although Glanville has earlier referred to "the productions of a *Young,* a *Richardson,* or a *Johnson*" as well as "the *Rambler*" (253), here the Doctor reintroduces the character of "the author" we met in the dedication. We may believe that "the author" of the dedication is "the author of the Rambler." Yet in posing the question of "the author?" once again, we might ask: who is the author of the *Rambler?*

The question is not as odd as it might seem; the praise of Richardson by Johnson that the chapter cites in quotation marks does appear in the opening lines of Number 97 of the *Rambler,* but "the author" of the essay in this issue turns out to be Samuel Richardson, not Samuel Johnson. After the introductory lines inform the reader that "this day's entertainment" is owed to "an author" who has "taught the passions to move at the command of virtue," the text is turned over to a guest author who (beginning with the common epistolary address "To THE RAMBLER. SIR . . . ") takes on the role of the author of the *Rambler.*[30] At the moment that the author of the chapter evokes the example of Richardson—a model for the author who would write novels rather than romances—and cites the words and the authority of the author of the *Rambler,* she or he alludes to an instance in which "the author" has transferred the authority for his text to another author.

In naming authors and citing authorities in order to declare its own generic identity, *The Female Quixote* gestures to a moment of authorial exchange. The character of the Doctor who represents either Johnson taking over Lennox's role or Lennox disguised as Johnson evokes a moment in which naming "the author" is particularly complicated: "the author's" praise of "an author" signals a moment in which Samuel Richardson takes over Samuel Johnson's role. The reference to "the greatest Genius in the present Age" in the course of what is described as "*in the Author's Opinion, the best Chapter in this History*" ironically suggests that the author's identity and even authority may be less stable than they appear. The reference to "the pleasing Dress of a Novel" reminds us that novels, too, also can appear in costume. One of the prefaces to *Pamela* speaks of the work appearing "under the modest disguise of a *novel*"; presented as a "standard or pattern for this kind of writing," it supposedly "borrows none of its excellencies from the romantic flights of unnatural fancy, its being founded in truth and nature."[31] As we wonder whether the Doctor is disguised as the novelist or the novelist is disguised as the Doctor, our attention is drawn to the status of *The Female Quixote* as a novel disguised as a romance *and* a romance disguised as a novel.

As the audience for the textual masquerade of *The Female Quixote,* we should note that the issue of the *Rambler* that the Doctor brings to our attention in citing its author's praise of a novelist is largely devoted to criticizing the behavior of women. The author (apparently Richardson standing in for the author) praises the *Rambler* for continuing the *Spectator*'s tradition of exposing women's "manners"; he imagines that in the future "the *Spectators* may shew to the rising generation what were the fashionable follies of their grandmothers, the *Rambler* of their mothers, and that from both they may draw instruction and warning." Focusing on the *Spectator*'s exposés of "the misbehaviour of young women at church by which they vainly hope to attract admirers," the essay bemoans the even worse manners and morals of contemporary women and concludes with the insight that "even fine faces, often seen, are less regarded than new faces, the proper punishment of showy girls, for rendering themselves so impoliticly cheap."[32]

The author of the *Rambler,* apparently encouraged by the praise offered by his guest author in Number 97, continued the tradition of showing women their follies in a series of satirical portraits in Numbers 113 and 115 written in the person of "Hymenaeus," who admits to being "considered as an adversary by half the female world." Number 115 contains the portrait of Imperia, who, "having spent the early part of her life in the perusal of romances, brought with her into the gay world all the pride of Cleopatra . . . and thought her charms dishonoured, and her power infringed, by the smallest transgression of her commands." Readers have recognized Imperia as a prototype of Arabella, although Duncan Isles suggests that by 1751 Lennox would have "discussed her idea with Johnson, who paid it the compliment of imitation."[33] The possibility that the author of the *Rambler* was imitating the author of *The Female Quixote* multiplies and complicates the already overdetermined layers of personation, impersonation, imitation, and authorial cross-dressing that we have seen at play in Lennox's novel.

The gallery of rejected female types that the *Rambler* displays, however, also raises the possibility that Lennox's character appears in Number 113, where the author describes "a lady of great eminence for learning and philosophy" identified as "the deep-read Misothea": "The queen of the Amazons was only to be gained by the hero who could conquer her in single combat; and Misothea's heart was only to bless the scholar who could overpower her by disputation.

Amidst the fondest transports of courtship she could call for a definition of terms, and treated every argument with contempt that could not be reduced to regular syllogism. You may easily imagine that I wished this courtship at an end."[34] Regardless of who is imitating whom in these intertextual dialogues, it seems clear that, in *The Female Quixote*'s penultimate chapter, Arabella is a composite of the characters of Imperia and Misothea. She is deeply read in romances rather than books of learning and philosophy, and the Doctor is not there for courtship; but it is precisely in the scholastic court of disputation that Arabella, earlier so invested in the Queen of the Amazons, follows Misothea's precedent in debating the "laws of Conference," "the Terms of the Question and Answer," and proofs about fiction and truth. The Doctor says he hesitates entering into "a Dispute with your Ladyship" because he is "accustom'd to speak to Scholars with Scholastick Ruggedness" (371); Arabella seems at home in this discourse and challenges him "to prove" (374) his accusations about her Histories. By the end of the "Controversy" and "Confutation" (368), like the woman whose "heart was only to bless the scholar who could overpower her by disputation," Arabella concedes his "Proof" and "Position" (375) and declares: "my Heart yields to the Force of Truth" (381). Although Hymenaeus decides that it would take too much time to cure Imperia, the Doctor proves to be the scholar who can overpower Arabella by disputation and thus (on behalf of Glanville) conquer her heart.

These terms also resonate next to the dedication. Although the author of the dedication to *The Female Quixote* worries that "SUCH is the Power of Interest over almost every Mind, that no one is long without Arguments to prove any Position which is ardently wished to be true," the Doctor does manage to "powerfully suppress all Opposition" on the part of Arabella. Although the author feels uncertain "that my Reasons will have the same Force upon other Understandings" (3), in the end Arabella's "Heart yields to the Force of Truth" (381). Having told the Doctor to "exert the Authority of your Function" and promised "on my Part, Sincerity and Submission" (370), Arabella must finally yield to him when he pronounces "authoritatively, whether Life is truly described in those Books" (379). It is this authority that is opposed to the authority of romance authors, which finally is rejected as "the Authority of Scribblers, not only of Fictions, but of senseless Fictions" (374). This position finally brings Arabella to a full stop and ends the novel.

The terms of this debate and the conflation of the characters of Imperia, Misothea, and Arabella in the penultimate chapter must once again raise the question of the author's identity—not just who the author is but also *where* the author is in this gallery. We know that Johnson admired, respected, and promoted Lennox.[35] Yet it is difficult to imagine that any "lady of great eminence for learning and philosophy" would not have identified with or at least felt addressed by the intellectual Queen of the Amazons depicted by Johnson. We have seen the paths of Arabella and Lennox intersect throughout the novel, particularly in their acts of literary imitation; these apparent allusions to the *Rambler* in *The Female Quixote* would seem to inscribe Lennox in Arabella's position as she is overpowered.

It is difficult to know how to read the complicated intertextual dialogues and overdetermined acts of literary imitation, impersonation, and appropriation that Lennox seems engaged in with Johnson. The evocation of Misothea in the chapter of Arabella's cure both casts the chapter in an ironic light and raises the stakes of Arabella's renunciation of romance. In aligning her heroine with Johnson's character of Misothea, Lennox further aligns herself with her heroine. The reappropriation of Johnson's "lady of great eminence for learning and philosophy" (following, perhaps, Johnson's appropriation of the then unpublished Arabella in his portrait of Imperia) in a sense saves both characters from rejection and rewrites them as a woman whose "noble Powers of Reason" (382) are finally appreciated. If the Doctor gets to play the role of the Divine who performs a "Miracle" (382), it is because, unlike Hymenaeus, he does not decide to let Arabella "grow wise at leisure, or to continue in error at her own expense." In acting on behalf of Arabella's suitor Glanville, he does not "wish this courtship at an end," and consequently Lennox's version of the story will not end "in frozen celibacy,"[36] like that of Hymenaeus.

Although the Doctor replaces the Countess as the character who cures Arabella, the reinscription of the "deep-read Misothea" holds out the possibility that Arabella might come to resemble the woman who "among her own Sex had no Superior in Wit, Elegance, and Ease, [and] was inferior to very few of the other in Sense, Learning, and Judgment" despite the fact that she was "deep read in Romances" (323–23). Imperia and Misothea are rehabilitated as Arabella comes to resemble the Countess, who might resemble the author of the work. It is not clear who conquers whom in the single combat of this intertextual dialogue, especially if we imagine Lennox engaging in Amazonian exercises and disguising herself in order to gain entrance into that republic of letters where writing masters are in command.

When seen in the context of these allusions to the *Rambler,* however, the renunciation of romance that ends the novel is doubly problematic. It has been noted that the novel begins with a restaging of *The Tempest,* as the Marquis falls victim to Court "Plots" (5) and retires with his daughter to a remote and artificial paradise.[37] At the end of the novel, Lennox might be seen to renounce her art; and just as Prospero breaks his staff and drowns his book in his and Shakespeare's renunciation of art, Lennox in a sense drowns Arabella. Early in the narrative, a maid carrying several of Scudéry's romances is described as "sinking under the Weight of those voluminous Romances" (49). Later, after agreeing to stop encouraging Arabella's "romantic Ideas," Sir George insists, "I must quit my Heroics by Degrees, and sink with Decency into my own Character" (197). Arabella is pulled from the river almost dead after sinking under the weight of romances, but we must ask whether she has a character of her "own" to sink into when she abandons the "Rules of Heroick Virtue" (368). What does Lennox renounce in renouncing the heroine of *The Adventures of Arabella*?

In Scudéry's romance, when the Roman Senate decides to erect a statue to honor Clelia for her courageous escape, it also decides to return her and the other "fair Virgins" to Porsenna with the instructions that he take better care of his hostages.[38] To what extent is Arabella sent back as a hostage to Johnson and Richardson as Lennox, with their advice, ends her book? Lennox aligns her closing portrait of Arabella with the Theophrastan characters of women contained in the *Rambler* and the tradition of criticizing the manners and morals of women that Richardson traces back to the *Spectator*. If, as Richardson suggests, "the *Spectators* may shew to the rising generation what were the fashionable follies of their grandmothers, the *Rambler* of their mothers, and . . . from both they may draw instruction and warning," one might wonder what sort of instruction or warning daughters and granddaughters were meant to receive from *The Female Quixote*. Although Arabella is not guilty of the sort of behavior that Richardson condemns, the novel might be said to illustrate in a different context "the proper punishment of showy girls." In this sense, Lennox's apparent impersonation of Johnson in the penultimate chapter would not represent an act of self-empowerment; rather, through an internalization of the authority of the writing master, Lennox plays Johnson to her own Arabella (and Misothea) and in doing so stages an act of surrender and perhaps self-sacrifice in which she shows herself overpowered in single combat.

Sir George is brought back onto the stage of the novel in the final chapter to share in both the authority for curing Arabella and the punishment for staging shows. Following the Doctor's "Miracle," Glanville decides that while Arabella's "Mind was labouring under the force of Conviction," the introduction of Sir George "confessing the ridiculous Farce he had invented to deceive her" and "all the Artifices her Deception by Romances had given him Encouragement to use upon her" would "add to the Doctor's solid Arguments the poignant Sting of Ridicule which she would then perceive she had incurred" (382). In this confession, we see both the punishment of the romance author, who (with less grace than Prospero) must "submissively" ask his reader's "Pardon" (383), and the humiliation of the reader, who has believed the empty fictions of this unseen author.

However, we also see Sir George's role in Arabella's conversion. This unwitting collaboration between the Doctor and Sir George, between the force of truth and the force of farce, reminds us of Sir George's role as "the author" in the novel. When Arabella yields submissively before the authority of the Doctor, this apparent surrender repeats her abdication of authority to the prescribing authority of romance. Sir George's submissive confession reveals the authority that he has had over Arabella and her plot; perhaps it suggests the price of abdicating authority for one's own story and one's own character. In the last paragraphs, "entangled in his own Artifices" (383), Sir George must marry Miss Glanville. As Charlotte Lennox's self-parodic double, it is only appropriate that the character named Charlotte should end the novel by entering into an uneasy alliance with Sir George. Entangled in her own artifices, Charlotte Lennox must end by declaring her collaboration with George—and consequently with Georges (that is to say, Madeleine) de Scudéry. Perhaps this is "the proper punishment of showy girls."

The *Spectator* essays that Richardson recalls while playing the role of the author of the *Rambler* focus on young women who make spectacles of themselves in church in hoping "to attract admirers." The author laments that, bad as "the misbehaviour of young women at church" was in the past, contemporary ladies "frequent those publick places" (such as "gaming tables") and "are not ashamed to shew their faces wherever men dare go."[39] The only young woman to behave in this manner in *The Female Quixote* is Miss Groves. According to Mrs. Morris, Miss Groves "frequented all public Places," "lavished away large Sums at Gaming," and became "the Object of general Admiration" (74) in Court. We are introduced to her when she goes to church, where she catches the eye not of those distracted young men described in the *Spectator* but rather of Arabella, whose "Attention was immediately engaged by the Appearance of this Stranger, who was very magnificently dressed" (67). Miss Groves, as we have seen, seems to be punished for her showy behavior, her masculine exercises, and her intrigue with her writing master. However, we are still left with the question of what we are to make of Arabella's attraction to and investment in the figure of Miss Groves and what warning and instruction daughters and granddaughters should receive from her story.

We saw that when Arabella went to London, she "refus'd to make her Appearance at Court" although finally "she condescended to go *incog.* to the Gallery on a Ball Night" (333). Within a few days, she has the adventure in the gardens in which "a Gentleman had drawn his Sword upon a Lady disguis'd in a Man's Habit," only to kneel "at her Feet, making Love to her in Mock-Heroicks" (335). Perhaps "showy girls" who want to avoid punishment for appearing in the public places where men dare to go must appear incognito, disguised in a man's habit. A woman who published herself in this manner might find herself wooed with a sword like Hippolyta, the "queen of the Amazons [who] was only to be gained by the hero who could conquer her in single combat." Or she might find herself engaged in masculine exercises, disguised in the habit of a writing master: the author of a narrative disguised in the modest dress of a novel.

7 Arguing by Analogy
Hume's Standard of Taste

But the greatest thing by far is to be a master of metaphor. It is the one thing that cannot be learnt from others; and it is also a sign of genius, since a good metaphor implies an intuitive perception of the similarity in dissimilars.

Aristotle, *Poetics*

Thus although critics, as Hume says, are able to reason more plausibly than cooks, they must still share the same fate.

Kant, *The Critique of Judgement*

Hume's essay, "Of the Standard of Taste," begins with this declaration: "The great variety of Taste, as well as of opinion, which prevails in the world, is too obvious not to have fallen under every one's observation."[1] I take this sentence to be a philosophical joke, or if not a joke, at least an ironic announcement of the key terms in Hume's investigation of the standard of taste. Hume begins with what is obvious and observed by everyone, but in a paradox that resonates throughout the essays, what presents itself to everyone's eyes is the variety of taste and opinions. We all agree that we do not all agree. This is merely common sense, and Hume suggests that "this variety of taste is obvious to the most careless enquirer" (227). But the tension suggested in Hume's observation about "every one's observation" is already implied in the term "standard," which ambiguously vacillates between a sense of what is common, average, and shared by all and the identification of a unique—or at least authoritative—exemplar. This vacillation raises the question of the differences between standard taste and a standard of taste, between a standard of taste and *the* standard of taste. By focusing his enquiry into taste on the question of the standard, Hume enters into the central dilemma about taste that emerges in eighteenth-century aesthetics, although the "Of" in the title warns us that Hume might not posit, or even define, such a standard. Our view of the standard of taste—what we mean when we speak of the standard of taste—depends on our view of the uniformity or the variety of our opinions.

The possibility of a standard of taste is explicitly or implicitly central to discussions of taste in eighteenth-century aesthetics.[2] It is well known that in the first decades of the eighteenth century, the neoclassical practice of judging works of art according to their adherence to a priori rules and principles was challenged by a focus on the effects of the work. Like Addison, who drew upon Locke to inaugurate a psychological or empirical aesthetics, and Du Bos, who proclaimed, "Everyone possesses the rule or the compass applicable to my reasonings,"[3] critics increasingly emphasized the subjective response and experience of readers and beholders.[4] Shaftesbury, whose notion of an internal moral sense would be elaborated into an aesthetic sense by Du Bos, Francis Hutcheson, and others, and who was the first to formulate the concept of aesthetic disinterestedness,[5] is concerned that wholly subjective criteria would lead to false and capricious judgments, subjecting taste to the whims of irregular fancy. He is contemptuous of the uninformed fancy he calls "the *je ne sais quoi* to which idiots and the ignorant would reduce everything."[6]

If the standard, rule, and measure within each person may be uninformed and unreliable, or if the validation of subjective responses leads to an unacceptably skeptical position that denies works any value in themselves and turns all judgment into accidental fancy, then an external standard of taste must be found if one is to judge works of art without appeal to a priori rules.[7] One way to ground a standard of taste and regulate capricious subjectivities is to assume that there is, after all, universal agreement about good and bad art. If there generally is, or at least has been, universal agreement (or what passes for universal agreement) about the value of works of art, then the principle that there is good and bad art is established, and individual examples can be recognized and identified, at least eventually. In his essay on taste in Number 409 of *The Spectator* (an important model for Hume's essay), Addison expresses confidence in the normative consensus established by works "which have stood the Test of so many different Ages and Countries." He recommends in *Spectator* Number 29 that the arts "deduce their Laws and Rules from the general Sense and Taste of Mankind, and not from the Principles of those Arts themselves; or in other Words, the Taste is not to conform to the Art, but the Art to the Taste."[8] Reynolds would later declare: "What has pleased, and continues to please, is likely to please again: hence are derived the rules of art, and on this immoveable foundation they must ever stand."[9]

If, however, there is no standard in the sense of what is common, average, and shared by all, then the standard of taste must be located in an exemplar or authority: an acknowledged judge who will determine and set the standard of taste, who will interpret, adjudicate, and perhaps legislate the laws and rules of art. Hume's essay on taste (published in January 1757) rejects the "principle of the natural equality of tastes" (231). Insisting on the variety of taste, Hume entertains, yet finally resists, the relativist, skeptical position; and although he posits "general rules of art" founded "on experience and on the observation of the common sentiments of human nature" (232), he finally locates the standard of taste in characteristics of true judgment and delicacy found only in very rare critics.[10] He seems to displace the problem of the standard of taste by appealing to the authority of such judges. The trajectory of Hume's enquiry can be seen in miniature in the declaration most often cited from the essay: "It is natural for us to seek a *Standard of Taste;* a rule, by which the various sentiments of men may be reconciled; at least, a decision, afforded, confirming one sentiment, and condemning another" (229).

The argument of Hume's essay follows the narrative suggested in this sentence. Modified retroactively by an "at least," it is a narrative of diminishing hopes or expectations. A standard of taste should in one sense be what is obvious; a rule implies an effort to proscribe variety; a decision confirms or condemns, conceding the lack of unanimity, uniformity, universal consent, and even reconciliation. This narrative would seem gradually to relinquish claims to a standard of taste that is standard because it is obvious and to move toward a standard imposed by authority, embodied in an exemplary judge or critic. "It is sufficient, for our present purpose," Hume writes, "if we have proved, that the taste of all individuals is not upon an equal footing" (242). Although he follows both Shaftesbury and Addison in delineating the qualities that would enable a "true judge" to establish "the true standard of taste and beauty"—"Strong sense, united to delicate sentiment, improved by practice, perfected by comparison, and cleared of all prejudice" (241)—Hume's formulation and advocation of these characteristics has been seen as his major contribution to eighteenth-century discussions of taste.[11]

Yet all the terms in Hume's formulation about our search for the standard of taste—the obvious standard, the normative rules, and the regulating decision—depend on an appeal to universal consent. Indeed, to say that *it is natural* for us to seek a standard, a rule, or at least a decision in the realm of taste, is from the outset to inscribe this search in the central predicament of the essay: the possibility of asserting what is standard or (in this sense) common to all. In examining this predicament, we need to consider how one could *prove* anything about taste, which is to ask what it would mean to prove either what is evident or what is not evident. This consideration also requires an examination of the status of argument in the essay, especially the rhetoric of empiricism generally regarded as central to Hume's test of taste. What is at stake is not just the possibility of ascertaining and demonstrating the standard of taste. "Of the Standard of Taste" is finally about the position of critics.

At the end of the first book of *A Treatise of Human Nature*, Hume insists that it is "natural" even for skeptics to feel "assurance" in "an exact and full survey of an object." He explains: "On such an occasion we are apt not only to forget our scepticism, but even our modesty too; and make use of such terms as these, *'tis evident, 'tis certain, 'tis undeniable;* which a due deference to the public ought, perhaps, to prevent." Conceding that he "may have fallen into this fault after the example of others," Hume insists: "such expressions were extorted from me by the present view of the object, and imply no dogmatical spirit, nor conceited idea of my own judgment, which are sentiments that I am sensible can become no body, and a sceptic still less than any other."[12] Yet in "Of the Standard of Taste," an essay that considers the idea that one should form of one's own judgment, Hume repeatedly asserts with certainty what is evident, what is natural, and, most important, what is obvious. Throughout the essay, as he evaluates the possibility of finding the standard, rule, or decision that we naturally seek in spite of the variety of taste that is too obvious to have escaped our attention, Hume begins declarations, sentences, and often paragraphs with constructions such as "It is evident . . . " (231), "It is natural . . . " (229), "It is very natural . . . " (230), "It is well known . . . " (240), "It is acknowledged . . . " (236), "Though it be certain . . . " (235), "it must be allowed . . . " (235), and "It is indeed obvious . . . " (228).

Repeatedly, Hume emphasizes what he takes to be obvious, describing, for example, the "variety of taste" that "is obvious to the most careless observer" (227); "the most obvious and grossest impropriety"; what is "obvious" (228) in Homer; and "one obvious cause, why many feel not the proper sentiment of beauty" (234). On one level, it is obvious that these are merely common expressions, but the essay turns on the question of what is obvious—or more specifically, what is recognized as obvious, what is obviously obvious. After noting the obvious variety of taste, Hume considers "terms in every language" about which "all men . . . must agree" (227), "unanimity" about moral precepts (228), "what has been universally found to please in all countries and in all ages" (231), "universal experience" (231), "uniformity of sentiment" (234), decisions in which "the sentiments of all mankind are agreed" (236), "models and principles, which have been established by the uniform consent and experience of nations and ages" (237), and principles of taste that are "universal" (241) and "uniform in human nature" (244). However, insofar as the essay is about the possibility of the standard of taste, it is about the possibility of universality and uniformity. It must address the question of what it would mean to seek to establish anything by proclaiming its obviousness or by appealing to universal consent.

To consider this question, we should look more closely at the terms and strategies of Hume's argument, especially as he seems to shift from standard to rule to decision, replacing the search for a standard with the search for a judge who will determine the standard. Here we arrive at the notoriously circular trajectory of the essay. Various commentators have tried to delineate what Peter Kivy describes as "a vicious circle whereby good art is defined in terms of the good critic and the good critic in terms of good art."[13] I suggest that both the logic and the illogic of the essay turn less on a circle than on a series of repetitions through which Hume both shifts the terms of his argument and falls back upon the terms that he appears to be rejecting. One way to trace this trajectory is to focus on what is perhaps the most astonishing turn of the essay: the moment when Hume confronts what is not certain. It is here that the essay threatens to break down.

After positing the variety of taste and opinion and rejecting both relativism and a priori rules, Hume acknowledges the existence of some "general rules of art," which are said to be "founded only on experience and on the observation of the common sentiments of human nature" (232). He concludes: "It appears then, that, amidst all the variety and caprice of taste, there are certain general principles of approbation or blame, whose influence a careful eye may trace in all operations of the mind" (233). Hume goes on to posit "particular forms or qualities, from the original structure of the internal fabric," which are "calculated to please" or "to displease" (233), but instead of identifying these forms or qualities or describing how they are calculated, he shifts his focus to the perfection or imperfection of our organs of perception and considers the importance of possessing delicacy of taste. It is at this point, in offering "a more accurate definition of delicacy"—the only definition offered in the essay—that Hume tells the story from *Don Quixote* about the kinsmen of Sancho Panza who are expert wine tasters. One pronounces some wine good except for a taste of leather; the other pronounces it good except for a taste of iron; both are ridiculed until "an old key with a leathern thong" (235) is discovered at the bottom of the hogshead. Interpreting and extrapolating from this story, Hume insists that some judges will be able to demonstrate their superiority over other "pretended judges" (236) and prevail in disputes of taste; and, returning to the delicacy of taste, he enumerates the characteristics that will enable and authorize some few critics "to give judgment on any work of art, or to establish their own sentiment as the standard of beauty" (241).

However, at this point, acting as if "the principles of taste [are] universal," identifying the composite characteristics that make the "true judge" and the ideal "verdict," Hume acknowledges the difficulty of finding the critics who can "establish their own sentiment as the standard of beauty." Suddenly, just as he does twenty-seven times in the essay, and seven times in the next five paragraphs, Hume interrupts himself with a "But . . ." that qualifies, complicates, or even challenges the assertion he has just made.[14] Here he interrupts his arrival at "the true standard of taste and beauty" with an acknowledgement of uncertainty. He inquires: "But where are such critics to be found? By what marks are they to be known? How distinguish them from pretenders? These questions are embarrassing; and seem to throw us back into the same uncertainty, from which, during the course of this essay, we have endeavoured to extricate ourselves" (241).

But what precisely is the embarrassing uncertainty from which Hume (and his readers) must extricate themselves? Ostensibly, the embarrassing questions raised by the problem of identifying the standard of taste are raised by the problem of identifying the judge who will establish the standard. But Hume's attempt to extricate himself is revealing. Rather than falling back on the characteristics of a good judge or insisting that the character of a good judge should be acknowledged to exist in general even if one cannot be found in particular, he acknowledges that "whether any particular person be endowed with good sense and a delicate imagination, free from prejudice, may often be the subject of dispute, and be liable to great discussion and enquiry"; but he goes on to insist: "But that such a character is valuable and estimable will be agreed in by all mankind." He then suggests that in disputes, men will have to "produce the best arguments" and "acknowledge a true and decisive standard to exist somewhere, to wit, real existence and matter of fact"; and he somewhat disingenuously concludes, "it is sufficient for our present purpose, if we have proved" that "some men in general, however difficult to be particularly pitched upon, will be acknowledged by universal sentiment to have a preference above others" (242). Hume makes a similar move earlier when he asserts that "a delicate taste of wit or beauty must always be a desirable quality. . . . In this decision the sentiments of all mankind are agreed" and then concludes that one "can ascertain a delicacy of taste" by ascertaining the "models and principles, which have been established by the uniform consent and experience of nations and ages" (236–37).

It is odd to see the author of *Dialogues Concerning Natural Religion* assert that the true judge must exist because it is desirable, valuable, and estimable that such a judge should exist. Hume tries to extricate himself from his uncertainty by insisting that we would all agree that there is a standard of taste because we would all agree that some critics will determine a standard of taste because we would all agree that it would be good if such critics existed. It might have been sufficient to have proven that some people will be acknowledged by most people to be better judges, or that most people would agree on the characteristics that would make a good judge; but lacking universal agreement, Hume falls back upon universal agreement. He replaces universal agreement in matters of taste with critics whose taste will set the standard; the verdict of these critics is based on rules established by universal sentiment and the uniform consent and experience of all nations and ages, and authorized by the universal sentiment that good critics exist—which is itself authorized by the universal sentiment that it would be good if such critics existed. Although the variety of taste strikes him as obvious, and he argues emphatically that tastes are not equal, in his argument both the general rules of beauty and the decisions of judges that would set the standard of taste are authorized by various acts of universal agreement. In other words, the uncertainty that Hume seeks to extricate himself from is uncertainty itself; not uncertainty about something (such as the question of where standards or critics are to be found) but rather the possibility that we might not be able to say: "'*tis evident, 'tis certain, 'tis undeniable.*" Furthermore, the "same uncertainty, from which, during the course of this essay, we have endeavoured to extricate ourselves," is finally uncertainty about sameness: uncertainty about the agreement and universal consent that would guarantee what is obvious, certain, and evident.[15]

Here we should return to the embarrassing question of what Hume proves in his essay and consider what it would mean for an essay about what is obvious and universally acknowledged to need to prove something about the standard of taste. This question returns us to the status of argument in the essay (both Hume's argument and the argument that he argues is instrumental in setting the standard of taste) and to the status of evidence in Hume's search for what is evident in articulating a standard of taste. These questions return us to Hume's retelling of the story about Sancho Panza's wine-tasting relatives and the key with the leathern thong. It is obvious that on one level this is a story about empiricism; indeed, the episode dramatizes the etymological relation between taste and test, trial, and touch. Critics have emphasized the "experimental method" at the center of Hume's theory of taste and the contribution of the essay in advancing a "method based on fact and observation," a "method of practical criticism and verification."[16] However, if this story about a test of taste is about the role of empiricism in establishing the standard of taste, this is not just because it displays the empirical methods of judges as they exercise their powers of examination and their fine delicacy of taste. The story is really about the possibility of using empirical methods to judge the judges. It is the judges' taste and not the wine that is put to the test here. Sancho's kinsmen prevail in their dispute about taste because the evidence proves both of their verdicts correct.

But this is precisely where Hume's proof and his parable about empiricism break down. The problem is not simply that Sancho's kinsmen prove only that each can detect different chemical properties in wine and not that the wine is good except for traces of leather or iron.[17] Hume asserts that to produce "general rules or avowed patterns of composition is like finding the key with the leathern thong"; but in the realm of aesthetic taste, is the production of rules or patterns really like finding the key with the thong? Can anything be produced that is like the key with the thong? Would it really be enough to produce something that is merely like the key with the thong? The problem here is whether judges of art can produce evidence that will prove their verdicts; and, furthermore, how Hume might produce evidence to prove his argument about judgments of taste. Once again we need to retrace the turns of Hume's argument at a crucial juncture of the essay. Hume uses the story from *Don Quixote* to claim that even if beauty and deformity are not themselves qualities in objects, "it must be allowed, that there are certain qualities in objects, which are fitted by nature to produce those particular feelings" and that these are especially discernible by those with delicacy of taste. In the realm of art, these qualities seem to take the form of "general rules of beauty" that are "drawn from established models, and from the observation of what pleases or displeases." Hume insists on the *likeness* between "these general rules or avowed patterns of composition" and "the key with the leathern thong; which justified the verdict of SANCHO's kinsmen"; and although he acknowledges that it is more difficult to prove one's case in the realm of art, he insists that when, in a dispute about taste, we "show" our "antagonist" an "avowed principle of art," "illustrate this principle by examples," and then "prove, that the principle may be applied to the present case," the "pretended judge" finally "must conclude" (235–36) that he is wrong.

We can recognize the pattern in which Hume seeks to authorize the verdict of judges by appealing to universal consent, which here takes the form of general rules, general principles, established and acknowledged models, the observation of what pleases, avowed patterns, and avowed principles. What is different here is that like the hypothetical judge he describes, Hume seeks to prove his argument through the application of a principle and an illustration. After telling the story, Hume tries to teach us how to apply it; or, rather, he writes: "The great resemblance between mental and bodily taste will easily teach us to apply this story" (235). Critics agree that the story operates as a parable or an allegory in Hume's essay, although they don't all agree on what lesson it teaches us. I would argue that the key lesson of this illustration lies in what it teaches us about the problem of resemblance for a theory of taste. It is the perception of resemblance, Hume argues, the perception of likeness, that will teach us how to apply the story.

In "Of the Immortality of the Soul," Hume enquires, "By what arguments or analogies can we prove any state of existence, which no one ever saw, and which no wise resembles any that ever was seen?" (598). He asks what we can "conclude from analogy" (591), what we can prove by analogy. For example, he claims that the "*physical* arguments from the analogy of nature" are "the only philosophical arguments, which ought to be admitted with regard to this question, or indeed any question of fact" (596). In seeking to extricate himself from the uncertainty about judges in his essay on the standard of taste, Hume insists that "these are questions of fact, not of sentiment" (242); but his arguments about taste are crucially arguments by analogy, arguments about likeness. In explaining the application of his story by declaring, "To produce these general rules or avowed patterns of composition is like finding the key with the leathern thong," he follows his metaphor with a simile. He goes on to say that just as Sancho's kinsmen would have been right if the key with the thong had never been produced, "In like manner, though the beauties of writing had never been methodized . . . the different degrees of taste would still have subsisted"; and just as a "good palate is not tried by strong flavours. . . . In like manner, a quick and acute perception of beauty and deformity must be the perfection of our mental taste" (236). The phrase "in like manner" (234, 239) also appears before and after this section, which is followed by a reference to "a like reason" (244). Hume's argument by analogy operates by continually pointing out likeness.[18]

Hume must proceed by analogy precisely because his arguments (like the arguments of the critic or judge) must prove what no one ever saw. This is to say that he must prove something that merely resembles something that has been seen; which is to say that what he must prove (by analogy) is precisely resemblance itself: he must prove that something resembles or is like something else. At the center of his analogy, his effort to argue in the like manner, is a metaphor. "The great resemblance between mental and bodily taste will easily teach us to apply this story," he writes, and he goes on to describe what "we call delicacy of taste, whether we employ these terms in the literal or metaphorical sense" (235). It is this metaphor (and the subsequent simile of the key with the thong) that will teach us how to apply the allegory; arguing by analogy, resemblance will teach us how to understand likeness. Hume's argument depends on our belief in the resemblance between mental and bodily taste, our acceptance of his claim that it does not matter whether we employ these terms in the literal or metaphorical sense. Taste in the figurative sense, he asserts, is like taste in the literal sense.

Now this may seem obvious; the word "taste" has long been used as a metaphor to describe the faculties of perception and judgment that evaluate and respond to works of art. In the eighteenth century, however, the status of taste as a metaphor was not necessarily evident, certain, or obvious; at the least, it called for comment or even explanation. For example, in *Spectator* Number 409, Addison explains: "Most Languages make use of this Metaphor, to express that Faculty of Mind, which distinguishes all the most concealed Faults and nicest Perfections in Writing. We may be sure this Metaphor would not have been so general in all Tongues, had there not been a very great Conformity between that mental Taste, which is the Subject of this Paper, and that Sensitive Taste which gives us a Relish of every different Flavour that affects the Palate."[19] In an article on taste that appeared in the *Encyclopédie* around the same time as Hume's essay, Voltaire notes that the sense we use to discern food "has produced in all known languages [*dans toutes les langues connues*] the metaphor that expresses by the word *taste* the sentiment of beauty and deformity in all the arts: it is an immediate discernment like that of the tongue and the palate [*comme celui de la langue & du palais*]."[20] Addison and Voltaire both begin their essays on taste with an observation about universal agreement; and the object of agreement is what Burke in a related context describes as the "consent of all men in the metaphors which are taken from the sense of Taste."[21]

Hume eschews the Lockean gesture of clearing the ground of his enquiry by defining key terms such as "taste" or "standard," and he does not explicitly acknowledge the metaphor of taste in beginning his essay. But the paradoxical account of the obviousness of the variety of taste that prefaces his investigation is mostly a discussion of language. Hume observes that we "call *barbarous* whatever departs widely from our own taste and apprehension." Suggesting that the variety of taste is even "greater in reality than in appearance," he notes that the "sentiments of men often differ with regard to beauty and deformity of all kinds, even while their general discourse is the same." He continues: "There are certain terms in every language, which import blame, and others praise; and all men, who use the same tongue, must agree in their application of them. Every voice is united in applauding elegance, propriety, simplicity, spirit in writing; and in blaming fustian, affectation, coldness, and a false brilliancy: But when critics come to particulars, this seeming unanimity vanishes; and it is found, that they had affixed a very different meaning to their expressions" (227). Language, in this sense, masks differences.

Although Hume remarks that an "explanation of the terms" usually resolves disputes "of opinion and science," he describes matters of "sentiment" and "morality" in which "unanimity is real" but "some part of the seeming harmony in morals may be accounted for from the very nature of language." For example, the "word *virtue,* with its equivalent in every tongue, implies praise, as that of vice does blame," but Homer's Ulysses "delights in lies and fictions," whereas Fenelon's hero (in his 1699 French epic) always tells the truth. In the same manner, the Koran is said to use Arabic terms of approbation that, "from the constant use of that tongue, must always be taken in a good sense," but Muhammad is said to apply them to treachery and inhumanity. Asserting that expressions that "imply a degree either of blame or approbation, are the least liable to be perverted or mistaken," Hume concludes this discussion of "moral virtues" and "terms themselves" (228–29) somewhat inconclusively. He moves on to his consideration of our natural search for a standard, a rule, or at least a decision in what often is treated as the real beginning of the essay, although it is uncertain whether he has solved a problem or reached an impasse.

As we have seen, however, neither the question of language in general nor the metaphor of taste in particular is left behind. This is because Hume enters the key metaphors taken from the sense of taste from the moment that he first raises the question of language and agreement. Like Voltaire, who seems to echo Addison's assertion about the presence of the metaphor "in all Tongues" in naming the metaphor produced "dans toutes les langues connues [in all known languages (*langues*)]" to describe "un discernment prompt comme celui de la langue & du palais [an immediate discernment like that of the tongue (*langue*) and the palette]," Hume declares: "There are certain terms in every language, which import blame, and others praise; and all men, who use the same tongue, must agree in their application of them." (The use of the word "language" right before the word "tongue" demonstrates that Hume had another word available to him.) In fact, Hume repeats the metaphor in each of the next two paragraphs, speaking of the "word *virtue*, with its equivalent in every tongue" and Arabic words that "from the constant use of that tongue, must always be taken in a good sense." By beginning his essay on taste with a discussion of tongues, by underlining the dual meaning of "tongue" as language and organ of taste, Hume brings together two sets of metaphors that compel us to consider what it means to "employ these terms in the literal or metaphorical sense" (235). Together, they doubly recall the status of taste as a metaphor and the importance of language in the theory of taste.

We have seen that Hume's argument depends on an analogy between mental and bodily taste, an exchange between the literal and the figurative senses of the terms of taste. The status of the word "tongue," however, suggests that the terms of the exchange are not entirely stable. Following Addison, Hume in three instances uses the word "tongue" in its figurative sense—it seems to function here as a synecdoche for language—but the word's association with the subject of the essay depends on its role in the literal sense of taste. Paradoxically, although the essay depends on an analogy that takes the terms of taste figuratively, by drawing our attention to the metaphors taken from the sense of taste, it often leads us to read in the opposite direction and take the terms literally. These terms, which in another context might not attract attention, are set in play by a network of figures that rise to the surface once we have the key to the metaphoric code.

For example, in Hume's characterization of the skeptical position, he cites the opinion that to "seek the real beauty, or real deformity, is as fruitless an enquiry, as to pretend to ascertain the real sweet or real bitter" and then cites the "proverb" that it is "fruitless to dispute concerning taste." It is at this point that he comes close to acknowledging the terms of the metaphor that Addison begins with: "It is very natural, and even quite necessary, to extend this axiom to mental, as well as bodily taste" (230). But what does it mean to call an enquiry or dispute "fruitless" just as one acknowledges that one's enquiry into taste depends on an analogy with food and taste buds? Whether such moments reflect Hume's playfulness or his anxiety, they operate more as symptoms than as jokes, because they point to fundamental problems with Hume's governing analogy. The analogy, based on the resemblance between mental and bodily taste, threatens to break down precisely because disputes about taste in art are fruitless. The skeptical reader might ask: where's the fruit?

Or one might ask: where's the tongue? The central parable from *Don Quixote,* which makes explicit the terms of resemblance and literal or metaphorical sense, is also touched by the essay's subtle wordplay. Hume suggests that he offers Cervantes's story about a disputed "judgment in wine" so as "not to draw our philosophy from too profound a source" (234) and then, in an essay that began by asking whether disputants "at bottom . . . agreed in their judgment" (227), he proceeds to tell a story about "what was found at the bottom" of a hogshead of wine. If one lets the terms of taste resonate further, this story takes on the characteristics of a dream or hallucination. In focusing on the key found in the hogshead, critics have ignored half of the evidence. What is twice referred to as a "hogshead" produces not just a key but also a "thong" that proves the wine tasters' sense of taste. It is as if the *thong,* the vindicating piece of evidence produced in the hogshead, is the *tongue* itself in a grotesque vision of a displaced and disembodied organ of taste. Hume follows this story with his extended account of what constitutes the organs of taste in matters of beauty and art. But his parable of empiricism threatens to break down, and not only because the judge lacks the key piece of evidence that would prove his verdict. In the realm of aesthetic taste, the tongue is also missing. It can't be produced to authorize one's sense of taste any more than the physical properties of beauty can be produced.[22]

We have seen that the status of the tongue as metaphor, synecdoche, and literal body part is set in play from the outset of the essay as it develops a network of verbal associations and slippages between the literal and the figurative; we are introduced to "terms in every language" that "all men, who use the same tongue, must agree in their application of" but the application of these terms is suspended between the literal and the figurative precisely when the definition of taste is evoked. What is at stake in Hume's essay—what is at stake in any consideration of the possibility of a standard of taste—is the question of what it would mean *to use the same tongue:* what it would mean to share both language and sensation. Hume addresses the question of whether one tongue is like another—whether we can, so to speak, taste with the same tongue. When he first mentions the resemblance between mental and bodily taste in his skeptical account of the skeptical position, Hume claims that the passing of the "axiom" that it is "fruitless to dispute concerning taste" into a "proverb" has the "sanction of common sense," although, he adds, there is "a species of common sense which opposes it" (230). Obviously a key concept for eighteenth-century philosophers, common sense is related to the question of what is obvious; but in the context of Hume's discussion of the standard of taste, it is also another expression for and of the central problem of the essay. The essay is about the possibility of common sense, in the sense of Kant's idea of a *Gemeinsinn* or *sensus communis*;[23] it is about the possibility of sense being common, in several senses. Even as it suggests that its claims are self-evident, it asks whether we can share both sense (in the sense of meaning) and sensation. In asking what we have in common, it asks whether any of us really use the same tongue.

These senses of common sense indicate the resemblance between the problem of language and the problem of taste in Hume's essay; both turn upon the possibility of likeness. Unlike Addison, Hume does not emphasize the conformity in all languages that authorizes the conformity of mental and bodily taste; but his discussion of the tendency of language to mask the variety of taste and sentiments and create an illusion that all who use the same tongue must agree raises the question of the "consent of all men in the metaphors which are taken from the sense of Taste." Here we see that the problem of the standard is from the outset inscribed in the very terms of taste. Like the standard, the metaphor itself seems to depend upon universal consent; it must be authorized by the agreement of all languages. In claiming that "this Metaphor would not have been so general in all Tongues, had there not been a very great Conformity between that mental Taste . . . and that Sensitive Taste," Addison seems to naturalize the metaphor. Hume says of the "proverb" about disputes concerning taste, "It is very natural, and even quite necessary, to extend this axiom to mental, as well as bodily taste" (230). He acknowledges this extension to be a metaphor a few pages later.

Although he suggests that language reveals variety of opinion rather than uniformity, Hume describes the metaphor of taste as a kind of catachresis. Although it seems to lack a proper name, it stands as a perception of resemblance that is too obvious not to have fallen under everyone's observation. On the next page, in discussing what "has been universally found to please in all countries and in all ages," he writes: "Many of the beauties of poetry and even of eloquence are founded on falsehood and fiction, on hyperboles, metaphors, and an abuse or perversion of terms from their natural meaning" (231). If the metaphor of taste represents an abuse or perversion of terms from their natural meaning, it is nonetheless natural to use it, just as it "is natural for us to seek a Standard of Taste" (229). At the same time, however, Hume seems to find it necessary to explain his metaphor and to support his argument by analogy.

Despite the Lockean overtones in Hume's acknowledgement that poetry and eloquence are founded on falsehoods, metaphors, and perversions of natural meaning, Hume does not seem concerned that his speculations might be founded on fiction; indeed, his philosophical essay draws several examples from literature. Hume claims to introduce the "more accurate definition of delicacy" contained in Sancho's wine-tasting story to "mingle some light of the understanding with the feelings of sentiment." In the preceding paragraph, in arguing that organs of perception such as the eye and the palate can offer "a true standard of taste and sentiment," he writes: "If, in the sound state of the organ, there be an entire or a considerable uniformity of sentiment among men, we may then derive an idea of the perfect beauty; in like manner as the appearance of objects in day-light, to the eye of a man in health, is denominated their true and real colour, even while colour is allowed to be merely a phantasm of the senses" (234). The truth of the standard and the standard of truth may be founded on a phantasm of the senses, as long as there is an entire or *at least a considerable* uniformity of sentiment. Hume asks that we see in like manner—that we share in the sense of his metaphors and the collective hallucination of senses that turns a phantasm into a true and real standard.

Paradoxically, however, if we agree to see in like manner, to see the resemblance that guarantees Hume's necessary metaphor and renders his argument by analogy merely obvious, we must conclude that there is no "natural equality of tastes" (231). From the moment we consent to the phantasm of senses—either that contained in the metaphors taken from the sense of taste or that provided by our organs of perception—we enter into the phantasm of likeness that governs the standard of taste. Likeness is so important in "Of the Standard of Taste" not merely because the essay is preoccupied with the resemblance structuring both its central metaphors and its argument by analogy, but also because, sharing the eighteenth-century preoccupation with sympathy, it is about the possibility of likeness between readers or spectators.[24] It asks whether one can draw an analogy between one's own senses and those of others, whether one's own sentiments are like those of others, whether one's own judgment is equal to that of others. Insofar as these are epistemological questions, and insofar as he is a skeptic, Hume knows that we cannot answer them—and he knows that this itself is an answer. However, his discussion of the possibility of the standard of taste, which seeks to deny the equality of tastes while basing its arguments on universal agreement, produces ambivalent—or perhaps merely paradoxical—answers to these questions. Despite his privileging of the ideal critic's faculties of judgment and perception, Hume locates the critic's authority in shared experience and opinions.

This tension in Hume's argument is related to a tension in the essay's privileging of the effects of the work of art and our responses to it rather than rules and formulas. As we have seen, the subsequent emphasis on subjectivity and individuality makes the search for a standard of taste more difficult and more necessary. Hume both encourages and discredits subjective responses, just as he demands universal agreement to establish the authority of the judge who would stand as the exemplar of taste. At the beginning of the essay, in speculating about terms used by all who use the same tongue, Hume observes that "Every voice is united in applauding" or "blaming" various characteristics "in writing. . . . But when critics come to particulars, this seeming unanimity vanishes." The explanation may be that "they had affixed a very different meaning to their expressions" (227) but the problem that remains is not merely a problem of language. In the end, we must ask how people who cannot taste with the same tongue, or speak in the same tongue, could be united in one voice. Hume finally suggests that one voice or tongue could speak for others, and his essay finally speaks for the voice of the critic.

Hume argues that the standard of taste and the authority of judges ultimately depend on the ability of the "true judge" (241) to "silence the bad critic, who might always insist on his particular sentiment, and refuse to submit to his antagonist" (236) unless he is confronted with the avowed rules and principles that constitute the evidence for the judge's verdict. Yet despite his belief in the analogy suggesting that a judge of art could produce physical evidence like the key with the thong, Hume states that in disputes about taste, "men can do no more than . . . produce the best arguments, that their invention suggests to them," while acknowledging "a true and decisive standard to exist somewhere." He even suggests that "they must have indulgence to such as differ from them in their appeals to this standard" (242). Despite this indulgence, however, in the absence of a judge who would be recognized by universal consent or who could prove his verdict with irrefutable evidence, the judge who establishes the standard—whatever admirable qualities this judge may embody—seems finally to be the critic who can silence other critics. Perhaps the bad critic is merely the critic who can be silenced. It might not take an argument to leave one silent or silenced, however; silence might result from deferring to someone else's voice or tongue, letting someone else either speak or taste in one's place.

From the first paragraph of "Of the Standard of Taste," which begins with what is "too obvious" (226), the character of the essay's narrator (I will continue to call him "Hume") speaks almost entirely in the first-person plural. Indeed, the first time we encounter the first-person singular in the essay, it is not Hume speaking but rather the voice of Sancho Panza: "I pretend to have a judgment in wine," he says, basing his authority on that of his two wine-tasting kinsmen. Hume speaks in the first-person singular in only two places. More than halfway into the essay, he argues that as a critic of a work "addressed to the public, though I should have a friendship or enmity with the author, I must depart from this situation; and considering myself as a man in general, forget, if possible, my individual being" (239). Later, after referring to "my opinion" (245), he asserts that if a poet condones vicious manners, "I cannot, nor is it proper I should, enter into such sentiments; and however I may excuse the poet, on account of the manners of his age, I never can relish the composition" (246).

It is perhaps appropriate that an essay that advances the cause of aesthetic disinterestedness should seem to efface the voice of the author. The first appearance of the first-person singular in Sancho's mouth as he attests to the powers of his tongue ironizes not only his pretense of judgment but also Hume's own authority as he supports his argument with a fiction about an iron key and a leathern thong. When Hume subsequently appears to speak in his own voice, he either insists on an act of sympathy with an imagined audience that results in a forgetting of "my individual being" or suggests that the boundaries of the self might prevent one from entering into the sentiments of someone else. It is as if he fears conveying a conceited idea of his own judgment (a sentiment that "can become no body, and a sceptic still less than any other"). Instead of asserting his individual voice, Hume creates a persona that represents a united voice, a sympathetic sharing of voice, sentiment, and tongue. But it is precisely this first-person plural, the "we" that stands for common sense and consensus, that must silence the reader. Just as the standard of taste depends on the forgetting of "my individual being"—in deference either to universal sentiment or to an authoritative judge—the argument of the essay depends on Hume's ability to speak in the *first-person plural* rather than the first-person singular. He must speak for us in asserting what is natural, evident, and obvious even as he questions the possibility of making such an assertion. In the end, Hume's best argument must persuade us that his premises are too obvious not to have fallen under everyone's observation. Like any good critic, he must persuade his silent readers that he speaks for them, not that he speaks with unique authority.

This may be the critic's greatest power. When Sir Joshua Reynolds writes about taste some twenty years later, he stresses the normative force of consensus. Following Adam Smith's stoical *Theory of Moral Sentiments* as well as his precursors on taste, Reynolds insists that "we must regulate our affections of every kind by that of others. The well-disciplined mind acknowledges this authority, and submits its own opinion to the publick voice." Although his *Discourses on Art* seek to turn his audience of artists into critical authorities, Reynolds argues that "a general union of minds, like a general combination of the forces of all mankind, makes a strength that is irresistible"; and he warns that a "man who thinks he is guarding himself against prejudices by resisting the authority of others, leaves open every avenue to singularity, vanity, self-conceit, obstinacy, and many other vices, all tending to warp the judgment. . . . This submission to others is a deference which we owe, and indeed are forced involuntarily to pay."[25] Hume emphasizes the authority of those singular judges who will set the standard of taste. In Hume's depiction of disputes about taste, the frequent emphasis on the judge who sets the standard of taste by using the best argument to "silence the bad critic" (236) often gives the impression that Hume advocates a court of appeals or a supreme court of taste.[26] However, Reynolds's combination of Hume's *agon* of taste and authority with Addison's "Test of so many different Ages and Countries" draws Hume's theory and his rhetorical strategies to their logical conclusion: the most irresistible authority is derived from the power to speak in the public voice. The critic may claim merely to articulate universally avowed and shared principles, but his power comes from speaking as the public. By forcing singular opinions to submit to uniformity, the standard of taste silences everyone. The standard of taste is potentially most authoritarian when it stands for the unspoken phantasm of the public voice, when it bases its decision confirming one sentiment and condemning another on what is merely common to all.[27]

It is well known that Hume had a reputation for "guarding himself against prejudices by resisting the authority of others." To conclude my analysis of Hume's ambivalent investment in authority and his predicament in writing about the standard of taste, I would like to recall the dedication that prefaces Hume's *Four Dissertations,* the volume in which "Of the Standard of Taste" first appeared.[28] Dated January 1757, and inscribing the volume to Hume's kinsman John Home, a clergyman and "Author of DOUGLAS, A Tragedy," this preface not only echoes some of the key terms and positions at play in the essay on taste; it stands as an ironic postscript that places the authority of the critic—and in particular, Hume's authority as a critic—in a different light. The events surrounding both John Home and David Hume in 1757 are too complicated to explain fully here, but they inflect "Of the Standard of Taste." Even before it opened in Edinburgh on December 14, 1756, *Douglas* was regarded as a triumph of Scottish literary nationalism. It was, however, soon at the center of a vociferous pamphlet war after being denounced by antitheatrical officials of the Scottish clergy who objected to ministers writing plays, and even to ministers attending the theater. Hume's extravagant praise of the play in the preface to *Four Dissertations* drew him into the controversy, and some felt that he did John Home more harm than good.

Hume's own book already was marked by controversy; it was known that Hume had been forced to suppress two of the volume's essays. He replaced "Of the Immortality of the Soul" and "Of Suicide" with "Of the Standard of Taste" after what was then called *Five Dissertations* was already in proofs. Some contemporary attacks on *Douglas* link the two controversies, suggesting that Hume's praise of the tragedy is meant to stand in for his suppressed essay on suicide, since *Douglas* ends with the suicide of its heroine.[29] The preface might be seen to acknowledge the controversy that silenced Hume by forcing him to write "Of the Standard of Taste" to replace his two censored essays. In like manner, it may anticipate the controversy about *Douglas,* which uncannily recalls the essay's concluding discussion about how differences in taste are produced by differences in national identity and religion.[30] What is most striking, however, is that the preface follows, anticipates, and comments on "Of the Standard of Taste." While praising *Douglas* as a great work of art and (like the essay) advocating tolerance, the preface repeatedly returns to the question of the variety of opinion. Hume—who here writes in the first-person singular as "David Hume, Esq."—emphasizes at some length that his friendship with "The Reverend Mr. Hume" has been characterized by "differences of opinion." What is at stake, however, is his ambivalent relation to public opinion and his authority as a judge of art. Acknowledging that his "professions of friendship" might cause him to be "accused of partiality" toward his cousin and namesake, he finds in the audience's unanimous approval of the play "incontestible proofs" of the author's genius. He invokes "the unfeigned tears which flowed from every eye, in the numerous representations which were made of it on this theatre" and "the unparalleled command, which you appeared to have over every affection of the human breast." At the same time, however, from the moment he confesses his "ambition to be the first who shall in public express his admiration" for the tragedy, Hume acknowledges and indeed asserts his singularity. He writes: "My enemies, you know, and, I own, even sometimes my friends, have reproached me with the love of paradoxes and singular opinions; and I expect to be exposed to the same imputation, on account of the character, which I have given of your DOUGLAS. I shall be told, no doubt, that I had artfully chosen the only time, when this high esteem of that piece could be regarded as a paradox; to wit, before its publication; and that not being able to contradict in this particular the sentiments of the public, I have, at least, resolved to go before them."

Shortly after writing "Of the Standard of Taste," in the preface to the volume that contains both that essay and "Of Tragedy," Hume offers his critical opinion—proven and authorized by every eye in the theater—that the author of *Douglas* possesses "the true theatric genius of *Shakespear* and *Otway*" (inadvertently proving, perhaps, in pairing the now obscure Thomas Otway with Shakespeare, that there is no accounting for taste).[31] Yet at the moment that he seems to pronounce the standard of taste, Hume inscribes himself in a paradoxical position: literally paradoxical, he suggests, because he contradicts the *doxa,* stands against public opinion; yet paradoxically not really paradoxical, since the reading public will share his opinion when it has sentiments of its own. Hume's self-deprecatory gesture both recalls and anticipates his singularity, his disapproval by the public, and his willingness to contradict general opinion and common sense. Yet, in assuming that the public will view the play in a like manner, it also suggests that Hume will not finally contradict the public voice. In this sense, Hume both undermines and underlines his authority as a critic, regarding his own stance with irony while preempting the voice of his still silent audience by speaking before them and commanding their consent.

Finally, however, as if remembering his "individual being," Hume proclaims his "love of paradoxes and singular opinions" and acknowledges his "enemies" (recalling the last sentence of the essay, which alludes to Boccaccio's defense "against his enemies" [249]). He seems to choose the contradiction implicit in paradox rather than the submission to others that would be recommended by Reynolds, or the reconciliation of singular opinions with universal agreement that would be sought by Kant. In *The Critique of Judgement,* insisting that one "cannot be talked into" a judgment of taste "by any grounds of proof," Kant would declare: "Thus although critics, as Hume says, are able to reason more plausibly than cooks, they must still share the same fate." Although Hume might prefer to avoid argument by leading us to believe that his assertions are obvious, or by speaking as a critic with irresistible authority, he ultimately insists that it is not fruitless to dispute concerning tastes. He is interested in what Kant calls "the force of demonstrations,"[32] even if these demonstrations can be only arguments by analogy, arguments about likeness. In Hume's view, all who seek the standard of taste must enter into argument, especially those who would use the same tongue.

Acknowledgments

This book frames and is framed by a history of dialogues: conversations that took place with students, colleagues, lecture audiences, readers, and friends in classes, conferences, hallways, kitchens, letters, footnotes. Some of the texts and issues that form and inform these chapters have preoccupied me for many years—at least since I took a seminar in graduate school called "Writing about Art" with Michael Fried. Michael Fried and Louis Marin first introduced me to eighteenth-century aesthetics and became models of intellectual inquiry and engagement through their teaching and writing.

I am especially grateful to the students in classes that I taught at Yale University, who for many years allowed me to test and work out the readings that evolved into these chapters. Of particular importance to me as I developed these ideas were talks that I designed for the Yale Center for British Art in 1980 and 1983, the English Institute at Harvard University in 1988, the UCLA Center for Seventeenth- and Eighteenth-Century Studies and the William Andrews Clark Memorial Library in 1995, and the Eighteenth-Century Scottish Studies Society in Grenoble in 1996. Frances Ferguson and Ronald Paulson invited me to present two seminars to an NEH Summer Institute on eighteenth-century aesthetics at Johns Hopkins University in 1990. The responses I received in these and many other venues helped me to articulate my arguments.

In New Haven, I benefited from conversations with Jean-Christophe Agnew, Norton Batkin, Paul Fry, Brigitte Peucker, Patricia Meyer Spacks, and Candace Waid, as well as Peter Brooks, Jill Campbell, Margaret Ferguson, David Hensley, Geoffrey Hartman, Michael Holquist, John Merriman, Claude Rawson, Karen Valihora, Blakey Vermeule, and Jennifer Wicke. I was fortunate to find in the English Department of the University of California, Santa Barbara, a remarkable group of eighteenth-century scholars: Elizabeth Heckendorn Cook, Robert Erickson, William Warner, and especially Everett Zimmerman. Others who have allowed me to draw them into dialogue about this book over the years include Porter Abbott, Ann Bermingman, John Bender, Karen Bowie, Robert Darnton, Jody Enders, Robert Folkenflik, Bernadette

Acknowledgments

Fort, Randall Garr, Jamie Gracer, Dick Hebdige, Victoria Kahn, Laura Kalman, Deborah Kaplan, Rhoda McGraw, Mark Rose, Neil Saccamano, Judy Shanks, and Muriel Zimmerman. Paul Hernadi and Simon Williams graciously arranged for me to have a place to write as a Visiting Fellow at the UC Santa Barbara Interdisciplinary Humanities Center in 1996–97; I didn't expect to return.

I would not have been able to reanimate this project without the support of Chancellor Henry Yang and the colleagues in my office: Lisa Daniels, Kim Coonen, Susan Stanfield, Claudia Kashin, Nicole Klanfer, Leslie Gray, Elizabeth Heckendorn Cook, and Chuck Wolfe. Steve Nichols kindly solicited this book for the Parallax series. The editors and staff at the Johns Hopkins University Press have been cooperative and professional. Randy Schiff and Maggie Sloan helped me prepare the manuscript and proofs with a calming competence.

While writing parts of this book, I was generously supported by a fellowship from the John Simon Guggenheim Foundation and sabbatical leave from Yale University. I was fortunate to have the resources of the Bibliothèque nationale de France, the Yale University Library, the Yale Center for British Art, and the Donald C. Davidson Library and the Arts Library at UC Santa Barbara. For reproductions and permission to reprint the illustrations used here, I am grateful to the Bibliothèque nationale, the Beinecke Rare Book and Manuscript Library at Yale University, the British Museum, and the William Andrews Clark Memorial Library of the University of California, Los Angeles.

Earlier versions of parts of this book appeared in the following publications: *Eighteenth-Century Fiction* 5 (1993); *Eighteenth-Century Studies* 28 (1995); *Eighteenth-Century Studies* 35 (2002); *Passionate Encounters in a Time of Sensibility*, ed. Maximilian E. Novak and Anne Mellor (Newark: University of Delaware Press, 2000); *Clarissa and Her Readers: New Essays for the* Clarissa *Project,* ed. Carol Houlihan Flynn and Edward Copeland (New York: AMS Press, 1999); *The Cambridge History of Literary Criticism*, vol. 4: *The Eighteenth Century* (Cambridge University Press, 1997), ed. H. B. Nisbet and Claude Rawson; and the *Yale Journal of Criticism* 3 (Fall 1989). I thank the editors and publishers for their encouragement and cooperation.

My sisters, Cindy Marshall and Karen Marshall, and their families have provided sustenance over the years. This book is dedicated to my parents, Helene and Arthur Marshall, who first introduced me to aesthetic experience, and everything that followed. Candace Waid's presence as my interlocutor and reader can be felt throughout these pages. Finally, I am grateful to Daniel Waid Marshall for his daily conversation and for teaching me to play basketball.

Notes

Introduction: The Problem of Aesthetic Experience

1. The examples listed here for the most part are taken from the books discussed in the following chapters. The tableaux of spectators in the theater and related examples are discussed in the context of Diderot's work in the chapter "Forgetting Theater" in my book *The Surprising Effects of Sympathy: Marivaux, Diderot, Rousseau, and Mary Shelley* (Chicago: University of Chicago Press, 1988), 105–34.

2. See Alexander Gottlieb Baumgarten, *Aesthetica* (Frankfurt a/O, 1750; facs. rpt., Hildesheim: Olms, 1961). Hans Reiss provides a useful account of the term "aesthetic" in "The Rise of Aesthetics from Baumgarten to Humboldt," in *The Cambridge History of Literary Criticism,* vol. 4, *The Eighteenth Century,* ed. H. B. Nisbet and Claude Rawson (Cambridge: Cambridge University Press, 1997), 658–80. Reiss notes that Baumgarten used the term "aesthetic" as early as his 1743 master's dissertation, and that by the time he published his *Aesthetica* in 1750, the term and many of his ideas had already been "popularized (and misrepresented) by his pupil Georg Friedrich Meier" in a treatise written in German (Reiss, "Rise of Aesthetics," 658). The *Oxford English Dictionary* cites an 1842 complaint about the importation of the word "aesthetic" into English and notes that its adoption was "long opposed" in the nineteenth century. See also Jeffrey Barnouw, "Feeling in Enlightenment Aesthetics," *Studies in Eighteenth-Century Culture* 18 (1988): 323–42.

3. Richard Steele, Joseph Addison, Jonathan Swift, et al., *The Tatler,* ed. Donald F. Bond, 3 vols. (Oxford: Clarendon Press, 1987); Anthony Ashley Cooper, Lord Shaftesbury, *Characteristics of Men, Manners, Opinions, Times,* ed. John M. Robertson, 2 vols. (1900; rpt. Gloucester, Mass.: Peter Smith, 1963); id., *Second Characters or The Language of Forms,* ed. Benjamin Rand (New York: Greenwood Press, 1969). See David Marshall, *The Figure of Theater: Shaftesbury, Defoe, Adam Smith, and George Eliot* (New York: Columbia University Press, 1986); and id., "Shaftesbury and Addison: Criticism and the Public Taste," in *Cambridge History of Literary Criticism* 4: 633–57.

4. Approaching a different set of texts with a different approach, Ronald Paulson describes a "countertradition" to "the modern category of the aesthetic," writing: "The official tradition was that which issued in the writings of Shaftesbury on taste and which flowered in the elaborate theorizing of the Sublime at the end of the century. The countertradition developed Addison's interest in the Beautiful,

the Novel, and the Strange, and found its chief exponent in the practice of Hogarth" (Paulson, *The Beautiful, Novel, and Strange: Aesthetics and Heterodoxy* [Baltimore: Johns Hopkins University Press, 1996], xviii). Although these works focus on the sublime, provocative reconsiderations of some of the key terms of eighteenth-century aesthetic theory are included in Frances Ferguson, *Solitude and the Sublime: Romanticism and the Aesthetics of Individuation* (New York: Routledge, 1992), and Peter de Bolla, *The Discourse of the Sublime: History, Aesthetics, and the Subject* (New York: Basil Blackwell, 1989). G. Gabrielle Starr comments on the recent "reexamination and revaluation of the aesthetic" in "Ethics, Meaning, and the Work of Beauty," *Eighteenth-Century Studies* 35, 3 (2002): 361–78. This special issue of *Eighteenth-Century Studies,* edited by Peter Fenves, is titled "Aesthetics and the Disciplines." See also the essays in *Eighteenth-Century Aesthetics and the Reconstruction of Art,* ed. Paul Mattick (Cambridge: Cambridge University Press, 1993). Obviously, there is extensive scholarship and commentary on the concepts of disinterestedness and aesthetic judgment, especially in relation to Kant. Some helpful accounts can be found in *Essays in Kant's Aesthetics,* ed. Ted Cohen and Paul Guyer (Chicago: University of Chicago Press, 1982), and Howard Caygill, *Art of Judgement* (Oxford: Basil Blackwell, 1989). See also John Guillory, *Cultural Capital: The Problem of Literary Canon Formation* (Chicago: University of Chicago Press, 1993), 269–340.

5. M. H. Abrams, "Art-as-Such: The Sociology of Modern Aesthetics," in *Doing Things with Texts: Essays in Criticism and Critical Theory,* ed. Michael Fischer (New York: Norton, 1990), 139. See also Abrams, "From Addison to Kant: Modern Aesthetics and the Exemplary Art," in *Studies in Eighteenth-Century British Art and Aesthetics,* ed. Ralph Cohen (Berkeley: University of California Press, 1985), 16–48, and "Kant and the Theology of Art," *Notre Dame English Journal* 13 (1981): 75–106.

6. Jerome Stolnitz, "On the Origins of Aesthetic Disinterestedness," *Journal of Aesthetics and Art Criticism* 20 (1961): 138. See also id., "On the Significance of Lord Shaftesbury in Modern Aesthetic Theory," *Philosophical Quarterly* 11 (1961): 97–113. Dabney Townsend offers a revision of Stolnitz's account of Shaftesbury in "Shaftesbury's Aesthetic Theory," *Journal of Aesthetics and Art Criticism* 41 (1982): 205–13. See also Townsend, "From Shaftesbury to Kant: The Development of the Concept of Aesthetic Disinterestedness," *Journal of the History of Ideas* 48 (1987): 287–306.

7. "A work of art may or may not be true to the world or serve practical ends or have moral effects, but such considerations are held to be supervenient upon (or, in some views, destructive of) the defining experience—that is, the absorbed and disinterested contemplation of the product for itself, simply as a work of art" (Abrams, "Art-as-Such," 135).

8. Ibid., 136.

9. Abrams, "Art and Such," 158.

10. See Susan Staves, "Don Quixote in Eighteenth-Century England," *Comparative Literature* 24 (1972): 193–215, and Ronald Paulson, *Don Quixote in England* (Baltimore: Johns Hopkins University Press, 1998).

11. "Combien de fois ne me suis-je pas surpris, comme il est arrive à des enfants qu'on avait menés au spectacle pour la première fois, criant: *Ne le croyez pas, il vous trompe"* (How many times haven't I been surprised, as happens to children taken to the theater for the first time, crying: *Don't believe him, he is deceiving you*) (Denis Diderot, "Éloge de Richardson," in *Oeuvres esthétiques,* ed. Paul Vernière [Paris: Garnier, 1975], 30).

12. Stolnitz, "Origins," 137. In "On the Significance of Lord Shaftesbury in Modern Aesthetic Theory," Stolnitz writes that "the chief impulse in the modern period is to establish the autonomy of the aesthetic" (100). Martha Woodmansee, in "The Interests in Disinterestedness: Karl Phillip Moritz and the Emergence of the Theory of Aesthetic Autonomy in Eighteenth-Century Germany," *Modern Language Quarterly* 45 (1984): 24, suggests that "[i]n an important sense Art is an invention of the eighteenth century."

13. Reiss, "Rise of Aesthetics," 659.

14. Stolnitz, "Origins," 142.

15. Joseph Addison and Richard Steele, *The Spectator,* ed. Donald F. Bond, 5 vols. (Oxford: Clarendon Press, 1965), No. 414, June 25, 1712; No. 413, June 24, 1712.

16. Richard Payne Knight, *An Analytical Inquiry into the Principles of Taste* (London, 1805; 4th ed., 1808), 154.

17. Ernst Cassirer, *The Philosophy of the Enlightenment,* trans. Fritz C. A. Koelln and James P. Pettegrove (Princeton: Princeton University Press, 1951), 323–24. See also Jean-Baptiste Du Bos, *Réflexions critiques sur la poésie et sur la peinture,* 3 vols. (1732–36), 4th ed. (Paris: Chez P.-J. Mariette, 1740).

18. See Marshall, *Surprising Effects of Sympathy,* 9–27.

19. Louis Marin, "The Frame of Representation and Some of Its Figures," trans. Wendy Waring, in *The Rhetoric of the Frame: Essays on the Boundaries of the Artwork,* ed. Paul Duro (Cambridge: Cambridge University Press, 1996), 82. In this passage, Marin cites Jacques Derrida's discussion of "le parergon" in *La Vérité en peinture* (Paris: Flammarion, 1978).

20. Uvedale Price, *Essays on the Picturesque as Compared with the Sublime and the Beautiful; and, on the Use of Studying Pictures, for the Purpose of Improving Real Landscape* 3 vols. (London: J. Mawman, 1810), 1: 338–39.

21. William Gilpin, *An Essay upon Prints, Containing Remarks upon the Principles of Picturesque Beauty* (London, 1768), 2; id., *Three Essays: On Picturesque Beauty; on Picturesque Travel; and on Sketching Landscape* (London, 1792), 1.

22. Humphry Repton, *The Landscape Gardening and Landscape Architecture of the Late Humphry Repton, Esq,* ed. J. C. Loudon (London, 1840), 114, 105.

23. I borrow this phrase from Ronald Paulson, *Emblem and Expression: Mean-

ing in English Art of the Eighteenth Century (Cambridge: Cambridge University Press, 1975), 20.

24. Obviously, other examples of fiction could have been included. In addition to some of the works that I have discussed in other publications, there are numerous other Enlightenment texts in which characters have intense or complicated experiences with novels, letters, paintings, plays, and music, as well as the simulacra of dreams, visions, and hallucinations, or are described interacting with other characters as if they were figures in a painting, actors in a play, or characters in a novel. I would be surprised if the reader cannot think of other literary tableaux that could have been added to the variety of aesthetic experiences discussed in this book. The texts discussed in this book were, for the most part, written after 1750, and there are certainly earlier examples of the sort of scenes and preoccupations that I am discussing. One could argue that the epistolary novel displays, dramatizes, and thematizes readers responding to literary texts; French writers, such as Marivaux and Du Bos, are especially concerned with the effects of the work of art at the beginning of the century. However, in the second half of the eighteenth century, especially in England, the development of the novel following Richardson and Fielding, and the development of a discourse of criticism and what we would today call aesthetics, along with the rise of the picturesque, give a self-consciousness and urgency to these concerns.

25. Geoffrey Hartman uses the phrase "representation-compulsion" in a different context in "The Interpreter: A Self-Analysis," in *The Fate of Reading and Other Essays* (Chicago: University of Chicago Press, 1975), 8.

26. In an article focused on the couplet, J. Paul Hunter reflects on "what is now a generation-old critique of the Enlightenment deriving from Horkheimer and Adorno, a position usually identified with the Frankfurt School and carried on now mainly under the banners of national or empire studies." He continues: "This critique has made some telling and legitimate historical points . . . [b]ut it also badly misrepresents a number of features of the Enlightenment that the couplet is then made to symbolize, including accounts of the mindset of the eighteenth century generally—and of English texts in particular—as acquisitive, rigid, righteous, and ruthlessly rationalistic" (Hunter, "Sleeping Beauties: Are Historical Aesthetics Worth Recovering," *Eighteenth-Century Studies* 34, 1 [2000]: 3). See Terry Eagleton's influential *The Ideology of the Aesthetic* (Cambridge: Basil Blackwell, 1990). Eagleton acknowledges: "The very emergence of the aesthetic marks in this sense a certain crisis of traditional reason, and a potentially liberating or utopian trend of thought. By the end of the eighteenth century, such appeals to feeling will have become identified as dangerously radical." He suggests, however, that the "clear bold light of republican rationalism, and the intimate affective depths of the poetic, come to figure throughout the nineteenth century as effective antinomies" (60–61). See also *Aesthetics and Ideology,* ed. George Levine (New Brunswick, N.J.: Rutgers University Press, 1994), esp. Levine's essay, "Reclaiming the Aesthetic" (1–32).

27. My interpretations are not inconsistent with interpretations that would foreground ideology, class, gender, race, and other topics that have become central to the field of eighteenth-century studies. Questions about ideology, gender, or political context are often important in the texts that I discuss—the problem of mastery and authority for female authors, the consolidation of landownership and aristocratic power, the abolition of slavery, the institution of marriage, the economics of inheritance laws, the specter of revolution, the ideological role of the critic as an authoritative arbiter or of taste, to name a few examples—but these questions are not usually my primary focus. The other stories that one could tell about these texts do not contradict or undermine the stories that I want to tell. Indeed, the fact that the persistent preoccupations that I trace here exist somewhere "below" plot, theme, and ostensible subject matter underlines their significance. The problem of aesthetic experience that I seek to frame—my argument that it is indeed a problem—cannot be explained away by other often important interpretations that place these texts in social or historical contexts. It is my methodological and ideological prejudice, having been trained in the techniques of close reading and the skeptical strategies of literary hermeneutics, that the text (and its reflections on representation and signification) can never be explained away, rendered transparent, or translated into a pure reflection of social realities. The problematic experience of art remains, leaving its persistent trace.

28. Among various relevant studies, see, e.g.: J. Paul Hunter, *Before Novels: The Cultural Contexts of Eighteenth Century English Fiction* (New York: Norton, 1990; John Brewer, *The Pleasures of the Imagination: English Culture in the Eighteenth Century* (New York: Farrar Straus Giroux, 1997); and William B. Warner, *Licensing Entertainment: The Elevation of Novel Reading in Britain, 1684–1750* (Berkeley: University of California Press, 1998).

Chapter 1   The Problem of the Picturesque

1. Uvedale Price, *Essays on the Picturesque as Compared with the Sublime and the Beautiful; and on the Use of Studying Pictures, for the Purpose of Improving Real Landscape,* 3 vols. (1794–98; London: J. Mawman, 1810), 1: 338–39. See also David Solkin, *Richard Wilson: The Landscape of Reaction* (London: Tate Gallery, 1982).

2. William Gilpin, *An Essay upon Prints, Containing Remarks upon the Principles of Picturesque Beauty* (London, 1768), 2; id., *Three Essays: On Picturesque Beauty; on Picturesque Travel; and on Sketching Landscape* (London, 1792), 1.

3. Raymond Williams, *The Country and the City* (1973; St. Albans, Herts, U.K.: Paladin, 1975), 149, 154. The word "scenery" seems to have been applied to the landscape for the first time (at least in print) in 1784 in William Cowper's "The Task." See also John Barrell, *The Idea of Landscape and the Sense of Place, 1730–1840: An Approach to the Poetry of John Clare* (Cambridge: Cambridge University Press, 1972), 23–24; and John Brewer, *The Pleasures of the Imagination: Eng-*

lish Culture in the Eighteenth Century (New York: Farrar Straus Giroux, 1997), 615–24.

4. Price, *Essays,* 1: 9–10; 3: 247–48. Gilpin writes: "The account I have here given of the forest-vista is the sober result of frequent examination. A transcript of the first feelings would have been rhapsody; which no description should indulge. The describer imagines that his own feelings of a natural scene can be conveyed by warm expressions. Whereas nothing but the *scene itself* can convey his *feelings*" (William Gilpin, *Remarks on Forest Scenery, and Other Woodland Views, Relative Chiefly to Picturesque Beauty,* 2 vols. [London, 1791; facs. rpt., Richmond, Surrey, U.K.: Richmond Publishing Co., 1973], 2: 69). Price refers to "the arrangement of real scenery" when speaking of the "difference between looking at nature merely with a view to making pictures, and looking at pictures with a view to the improvement of our ideas of nature" (1: 9–10). He also refers to "a piece of natural scenery" in writing that "whether it be confined or extensive, a wood, a river, or a distant view, every eye is more or less pleased, with a happy combination of forms, colours, lights, and shadows" (3: 247–48). See Frances Ferguson, *Solitude and the Sublime: Romanticism and the Aesthetics of Individuation* (New York: Routledge, 1992), 129–45. Michael Fried's *Absorption and Theatricality: Painting and Beholder in the Age of Diderot* (Berkeley: University of California Press, 1980) discusses the stakes of theatricality for Diderot and eighteenth-century French painting in terms that have proved important for our understanding of many eighteenth-century writers.

5. Jane Austen, *Mansfield Park: A Novel,* in *The Novels of Jane Austen,* ed. R. W. Chapman, 5 vols. (Oxford, 1923; rpt. 1966), 3: 209; 113; 108. See my chapter 3, 72–90. On the picturesque and Austen, see Martin Price, "The Picturesque Moment," in *From Sensibility to Romanticism: Essays Presented to Frederick A. Pottle,* ed. Frederick W. Hilles and Harold Bloom (New York: Norton, 1965) and *Forms of Life: Character and Moral Imagination in the Novel* (New Haven: Yale University Press, 1983), 65–89. See also Alistair M. Duckworth, *The Improvement of the Estate: A Study of Jane Austen's Novel* (Baltimore: Johns Hopkins University Press, 1971), 35–80.

6. Goethe's *Elective Affinities* depicts characters engaged in extensive discussions of prospects, point of view, and landscape design (there is even an English count who spends his time "catching the picturesque views of the park in his portable *camera obscura* and in making drawings of these" [die malerischen Aussichten des Parks in einer tragbaren dunklen Kammer aufzufangen und zu zeichnen]), and it dramatizes them posing in *tableaux vivants* in which they "represent well-known paintings" (Johann Wolfgang von Goethe, *Elective Affinities,* trans. Elizabeth Mayer and Louise Bogan [South Bend, Ind.: Gateway Editions, 1963], 230, 185; German citations are from *Die Wahlverwandtshaften* [Stuttgart: Reclam, 1977], 198). The theatrical performances in *Elective Affinities* underline a perspective that has been present from the opening pages; for instance: "At the door Charlotte welcomed her husband and led him to a seat where he could take in at a sin-

gle glance, through door and windows, the different views of the landscape, as though set in frames" (An der Türe empfing Charlotte ihren Gamahl und ließ ihn dergestalt niedersitzen, daß er durch Tür und Fenster die verschiedenen Bilder, welche die Landschaft gleichsam im Rahmen zeigten, auf einen Blick übersehen konnte) (4).

7. James Dallaway, "Supplementary Anecdotes of Gardening in England," in his 1826–28 edition of Horace Walpole's *Anecdotes of Painting in England*; rpt. in *The English Landscape Garden,* ed. John Dixon Hunt (New York, 1982), 18: 301. Dabney Townsend discusses aesthetic distance and relates the picturesque to aesthetic theories in "The Picturesque," *Journal of Aesthetics and Art Criticism* 55 (1997): 365–76.

8. Price, *Essays,* 1: 37, 39. Price seeks to define the picturesque by distinguishing it from the sublime and the beautiful; he intends his treatise to be a kind of pendant to Burke's *Enquiry,* hoping to show "that the picturesque has a character not less separate and distinct than either the sublime or the beautiful, nor less independent of the art of painting" (ibid., 40). Despite or perhaps because of its pervasiveness, there are discussions of the problem of defining the term "picturesque" as late as the 1820s, along with explanations of etymology and translation, laments about ambiguity, complaints about jargon, and recourses to neologisms—all of which point to an uncertainty about the referent. This suggests that what is at stake here is not so much the refinement of a term or definition as the invention and evolution of a concept. Price himself suggests that it is only after painters "first illustrated, and brought into notice and general observation" certain objects that were "neither grand, nor beautiful, nor ugly" that "it was very natural that such a word should be invented, and soon be commonly made use of, which discriminated the character of such objects, by their relation to the artist himself, or to his work." He continues: "we find accordingly that the Italians, among whom painting most flourished, invented the word *pittoresco,* which marks the relation to the painter, and which the French, with a slight change, have adopted; while the English use the word *picturesque,* as related to the production" (ibid., 218). It is not clear what it would mean for the invention of the word "picturesque" to be natural. The word "has not been considered as perfectly naturalized among us," Richard Payne Knight writes (*An Analytical Inquiry into the Principles of Taste,* 4th ed. [London, 1805–8], 148–49). It seems that the problem of defining the picturesque is from the outset one of defining an idea; and to define the idea, one must describe what the picturesque is like: one must be able to recognize it. Pope is said to have inaugurated the use of the word in the context of descriptions of nature. In a letter in 1712, he describes lines of verse as being "what the French call very picturesque" (cited in Morris R. Brownell, *Alexander Pope and the Arts of Georgian England* [Oxford: Clarendon Press, 1978], 104). Christopher Hussey notes that "the French Academy did not admit *pittoresque* till 1732" (Hussey, *The Picturesque: Studies in a Point of View* [1927; rpt. London: Cass, 1967], 32). See Wil

Munsters, *La poétique du pittoresque en France de 1700 à 1830* (Geneva: Droz, 1991), 22–79.

9. Gilpin, *Three Essays*, 36, 1. Describing "picturesque beauty," Gilpin writes: "This great object we pursue through the scenery of nature; and examine it by the rules of painting" (42) Distinguishing between the beautiful and the picturesque, Gilpin makes a distinction between objects "which please the eye in their *natural state;* and those, which please from some quality, capable of being *illustrated in painting*" (1). He remarks that "the picturesque eye is not merely restricted to nature. It ranges through the limits of art. The picture, the statue, and the garden are all objects of its attention" (45).

10. Ibid., 5–8, 46.

11. Martin Price, "Picturesque Moment," 259.

12. Barrell, *Idea of Landscape*, 50, 59. Barrell argues that the eighteenth-century English connoisseur developed a "way of looking at landscape" that "expressed itself in a specialized vocabulary, and a grammar, as it were, of landscape patterns and structures" (ibid., 7). "[T]he picturesque was a *language,* and a language apparently needed with some urgency at that 'moment,'" John Dixon Hunt argues ("Ut Pictura Poesis, Ut Pictura Hortus, and the Picturesque," *Word and Image* 1 [1985]: 87), citing an 1807 letter from Robert Southey that refers to the picturesque as "a new science for which a new language has been formed." It became an "amalgam of pictorial-poetic-grammatical principles," Christopher Hussey writes, referring to Capability Brown's landscape design (Hussey, *Picturesque*, 138).

13. Knight, *Analytical Inquiry,* 154.

14. If the history of the picturesque intersects with the literary history of gardening, these developments in painting, literature, aesthetics, and landscape design themselves intersect with the social and political history of eighteenth-century England. It is outside the scope of this chapter to discuss the variety of influences and enabling conditions that coincided to form both the literal and the figurative grounds on which the picturesque would be developed and cultivated. Painting gained new prestige and this interest in the visual arts extended to literature as theories of *ut pictura poesis* were reinvigorated and descriptive poetry became popular. Claude, Rosa, and Poussin were considered ideal landscape painters, and artists such as Wilson and Constable developed their own versions of English landscape painting. The popularity of the Grand Tour, which introduced the British aristocracy to both the Alps and Italian landscape painting, encouraged a taste for landscape, and connoisseurs carried out their acquisition of landscape art outside as well as inside their country houses. This taste for particular forms and styles of landscapes extended from the descriptions imaged in poetry and the perspectives framed on their walls to the prospects framed by their windows and experienced from the privileged points of view enjoyed by landowners who walked through their grounds as beholders. An agricultural revolution and the enclosure acts permitted landowners to consolidate their property into large single blocks of land

with the house and park at the center. A great deal of attention has been devoted to the social, political, and ideological valences of the picturesque in recent years. See John Barrell, *The Dark Side of the Landscape: Rural Poor in English Painting, 1730–1840* (New York: Cambridge University Press, 1980); John Dixon Hunt and Peter Willis, *The Genius of the Place: The English Landscape Garden, 1620–1820* (London: Elek, 1975); Ann Bermingham, *Landscape and Ideology: The English Rustic Tradition, 1760–1860* (Berkeley: University of California Press, 1986), and *Learning to Draw: Studies in the Cultural History of a Polite and Useful Art* (New Haven: Yale University Press, 2000), 77–126; and Alan Liu, *Wordsworth: The Sense of History* (Stanford: Stanford University Press, 1989), in addition to Barrell, *Idea of Landscape,* Hussey, *Picturesque,* and Williams, *Country and the City.* Three collections of essays are also noteworthy: *The Iconography of Landscape: Essays on the Symbolic Representation, Design, and Use of Past Environments,* ed. Denis Cosgrove and Stephen Daniels (Cambridge: Cambridge University Press, 1988); *The Politics of the Picturesque: Literature, Landscape and Aesthetics since 1770,* ed. Stephen Copley and Peter Garside (Cambridge: Cambridge University Press, 1994); and *Prospects for the Nation: Recent Essays in British Landscape, 1750–1880,* ed. Michael Rosenthal, Christiana Payne, and Scott Wilcox (New Haven: Yale University Press, 1997).

15. Joseph Spence, *Observations, Anecdotes, and Characters of Books and Men,* ed. James M. Osborn, 2 vols. (Oxford: Oxford University Press, 1966), 1: 252. Brownell describes the estate as "the paradigm of the picturesque landscape" (*Alexander Pope,* 133). "By gardening, I mean that sort of it more peculiarly denoted by the epithet Picturesque," George Mason wrote in *An Essay on Design in Gardening* (London, 1768), 4. Gilpin's *Essay upon Prints* appeared the same year.

16. Walpole, *Anecdotes of Painting in England,* ed. Dallaway, 280, 271.

17. William Shenstone, *The Works in Verse and Prose of William Shenstone, Esq.,* 2 vols. (London, 1764); rpt. in *The English Landscape Garden,* ed. John Dixon Hunt (New York: Garland, 1982], 17: 129.

18. Anthony Ashley Cooper, Lord Shaftesbury, *Characteristics of Men, Manners, Opinions, Times, etc.,* ed. John M. Robertson, 2 vols. (1900; rpt. Gloucester, Mass.: Peter Smith, 1963), 2: 122, 125, 98. Pope's 1713 essay in *The Guardian* privileges "unadorned Nature" over "the modern Practice of Gardening" in which we "recede from Nature, not only in the various Tonsure of Greens into the most regular and formal Shapes, but even in monstrous Attempts beyond the reach of the Art it self: We run into Sculpture, and are yet better pleas'd to have our Trees in the most awkward Figures of Men and Animals, than in the most regular of their own" (quoted in Hunt and Willis, *Genius of the Place,* 205, 207.) Yet even in his influential 1731 Epistle to the architect Lord Burlington ("To build, to plant, whatever you intend, / To rear the Column, or the Arch to bend, / To swell the Terras, or to sink the Grot; / In all, let Nature never be forgot. / Consult the Genius of the Place in all"), Pope's declaration in favor of the natural is expressed in the

terms of art. His "Genius of the Place" "scoops in circling Theatres the Vale," "varies Shades from Shades," and "Paints as you plant, and as you work, Designs." (*The Twickenham Edition of the Poems of Alexander Pope,* ed. John Butt, 10 vols. [London: Methuen, 1939–67], 3.2: 137–39). For Brownell, "the idea of the picturesque is implicit" in these lines (*Alexander Pope,* 109).

19. Joseph Addison and Richard Steele, *The Spectator,* ed. Donald F. Bond, 5 vols. (Oxford: Clarendon Press, 1965), 3: 550 (No. 414, June 25, 1712).

20. Ibid., 560 (No. 416, June 27, 1712).

21. Ronald Paulson, *Emblem and Expression: Meaning in English Art of the Eighteenth Century* (Cambridge: Cambridge University Press, 1975), 20.

22. The language of such gardens required a knowledge of iconography and allusions, as well as the intellectual ability and the sensibility to reflect on death, virtue, liberty, solitude, or whatever topos or theme was suggested. It also employed puns and sophisticated intertextual references. For example, Hunt and Willis describe the temples at Stowe as "a determined visual pun on the family motto—*Templa quam dilecta* (How delightful are thy temples!)—which was itself a verbal play with Cobham's family name of Temple" (Hunt and Willis, *Genius of the Place,* 26). See also Paulson, *Emblem and Expression,* 27.

23. In the chapter on "The Association of Ideas" added to the fourth edition of the *Essay Concerning Human Understanding,* Locke writes: "Some of our Ideas have a natural Correspondence and Connexion one with another: It is the Office and Excellency of our Reason to trace these, and hold them together in that Union and Correspondence which is founded in their peculiar Beings. Besides this, there is another Connexion of Ideas wholly owing to Chance or Custom" (*An Essay Concerning Human Understanding,* ed. Peter H. Nidditch [Oxford: Oxford University Press, 1975], 395). Hunt and Willis describe the "ambitious scheme of associations" presented by the Elysian Fields at Stowe, which "require a visitor to compare ancient virtue with its modern counterpart (a ruined and Gothic Temple of Modern Virtue was established nearby), to register the political significance of the British Worthies, which in its turn involved noticing that a line was missing from a Virgilian quotation, and to appreciate that the Temple of Ancient Virtue called to mind the Roman temple of Vesta (the so-called Sybil's Temple) at Tivoli, and the Temple of British Worthies some other modern Italian examples" (*Genius of the Place,* 33–34). Hunt shrewdly observes that the popularity of Joseph Spence's *Polymetis* (1747) itself suggests that such "classical learning, especially its visual/verbal configurations . . . was fast becoming a lost language" and that Spence's "academic picturesque" is accompanied by a "scepticism with the old iconographical languages it usually employed." Hunt cites Du Bos's complaint that Rubens's allegorical figures in his paintings of Marie de Médicis are "des chiffres, dont personne n'a le clef, et même peu de gens la cherchent" (ciphers for which no one has the key, and few people even try to find it) (Hunt, "Ut Pictura Poesis," 100–101, 98).

24. Gilpin insists that it is not from "*scientifical* employment, that we derive

our chief pleasure. We are most delighted, when some grand scene, tho perhaps of incorrect composition, rising before the eye, strikes us beyond the power of thought—when the *vox faucibus haeret;* and every mental operation is suspended. In this pause of intellect," he asserts, "this *deliquium* of the soul, an enthusiastic sensation of pleasure overspreads it, previous to any examination by the rules of art. The general idea of the scene makes an impression, before any appeal is made to the judgment. We rather *feel,* than *survey* it" (Gilpin, *Three Essays,* 49–50). Gilpin is here concerned with the danger of being too preoccupied with the principles of painting when looking with a picturesque eye; but it is clear that there was no pause of intellect among the emblems of the poetic garden.

25. Thomas Whately, *Observations on Modern Gardening . . . to which is added An Essay on the Different Natural Situations of Gardens. With notes by Horace (Late) Earl of Orford* (London, 1801), 83–84.

26. "So closely did he copy nature," declared an obituary of Capability Brown cited by Barrell, "that his work will not be mistaken" (*Idea of Landscape,* 49).

27. Cited in Hussey, *Picturesque,* 138.

28. This codification and standardization of lines and forms may have coincided with changes in convention and perception that altered the sense of what was natural. In the history of literature and painting, changes in the conventions of representation can deny previously effective works of art the power of conviction and thereby necessitate new forms that will either fulfill or challenge new notions of verisimilitude. Perhaps what at first seemed radically natural in Brown's gardens came to feel artificial to a later generation, just as the once natural-seeming qualities of the poetic garden had begun to feel increasingly archaic and unnatural earlier in the century. For more on debates about landscape gardening and competing theories and practices of picturesque aesthetics (in addition to works cited in other notes), see David Watkin, *The English Vision: The Picturesque in Architecture, Landscape, and Garden Design* (New York: Harper and Row, 1982); John Dixon Hunt, *Gardens and the Picturesque: Studies in the History of Landscape Architecture* (Cambridge, Mass.: MIT Press, 1992). See also Kim Ian Michasiw, "Nine Revisionist Theses on the Picturesque," *Representations* 38 (1992): 76–100, and Sidney K. Robinson, *Inquiry into the Picturesque* (Chicago: University of Chicago Press, 1991). For a discussion of Knight's arguments with both the improvers and Price, see Andrew Ballantyne, *Architecture, Landscape, and Liberty: Richard Payne Knight and the Picturesque* (Cambridge: Cambridge University Press, 1997), 138–239. A useful collection of documents and excerpts from key texts in the debates is *The Picturesque,* ed. Malcolm Andrews, 3 vols. (Mountfield, East Sussex, U.K.: Helm Information, 1994).

29. Richard Payne Knight, *The Landscape: A Didactic Poem. In Three Books. Addressed to Uvedale Price, Esq.,* 2d ed. (London, 1795), 17–18n. In *Sketches and Hints on Landscape Painting* (1795), Repton defiantly repeated in his response to Knight: "I do not hesitate to acknowledge, that I once supposed the two arts to be

more intimately connected, than my practice and experience have since confirmed" (Humphry Repton, *The Landscape Gardening and Landscape Architecture of the Late Humphry Repton, Esq,* ed. J. C. Loudon [London, 1840], 99).

30. Knight, *Landscape,* 2d ed., 101.

31. Richard Payne Knight, *The Landscape, A Didactic Poem. In Three Books. Addressed to Uvedale Price, Esq.,* 1st ed. (London, 1794), 1. Knight attacks the improvers in terms that recall Addison and Pope: "Nature in all rejects the pedant's chain; / Which binding beauty in its waving line, / Destroys the charm it vainly would refine; / For nature still irregular and free, / Acts not by lines, but gen'ral sympathy. / The path that moves in even serpentine, / Is still less nat'ral than the pointed line."

32. Knight, *Landscape,* 2d ed., 99–101; Price, *Essays,* 1: 243–44.

33. Repton, *Sketches in Landscape Gardening* (in ed. cited in n. 29 above), 99. Underlining his concern with comfort and convenience rather than picturesque effects, Repton cites William Wyndham: "A scene of a cavern, with banditti sitting by it, is the favourite subject of Salvator Rosa; but are we therefore to live in caves, or encourage the neighborhood of banditti? Gainsborough's country girl is a more picturesque object than a child neatly dressed in a white frock; but is that a reason why our children are to go in rags?" (115).

34. Repton, *Sketches in Landscape Gardening,* 114, 104.

35. Defensive about the relative positions of art and nature in his theory, Price denies that he recommends "the study of pictures in preference to that of nature, much less to the exclusion of it" (*Essays,* 3). In the first edition of the *Essay on the Picturesque,* he speaks of a "painter, or whoever views objects with a painter's eye," and he elaborates that by "painter" he means "any man (artist or not) of a liberal mind, with a strong sense of feeling for nature as well as art, who has the gift of comparing both together" (Price, *Essay on the Picturesque as Compared with the Sublime and the Beautiful; and on the Use of Studying Pictures, for the Purpose of Improving Real Landscape* [London, 1794], 9). Gilpin also denies having declared "*all beauty* to consist in *picturesque beauty*—and the face of nature to be examined *only by the rules of painting.*" He claims to "speak a different language. We speak of the grand scenes of nature, tho uninteresting in a *picturesque light,* as having a strong effect on the imagination." In responding to nature, Gilpin writes, "We every where make a distinction between scenes, that are *beautiful* and *amusing;* and scenes that are *picturesque.* We examine, and admire both" (Gilpin, *Three Essays,* ii). However, the problem lies in a language that itself pictures nature in scenes, in a point of view that seems to alter the face of nature by designing or merely illuminating it with the rules of painting.

36. Whately, *Observations,* 81.

37. Price, *Essays,* 1: 5.

38. Whately, *Observations,* 1.

39. Cited in Malcolm Andrews, *The Search for the Picturesque: Landscape Aes-*

thetics and Tourism in Britain, 1760–1800 (Aldershot, Hants, U.K.: Scholar's Press, 1989), 34.

40. The most enthusiastic appeals to the beauty of nature still praised its spectacles and scenes. In *Ichnographia Rustica, or, The Nobleman, Gentleman, and Gardner's Recreation* (London: D. Browne, 1718), 153, Stephen Switzer speaks of "Theatres of Wood and Corn" and suggests that "if we have not such by Nature," we should "create them by Art, by digging a Hole in one place, to make a Hill in another." Gilpin describes "an Ampitheatre of Mountains" (cited in Hunt and Willis, *Genius of the Place,* 153, 257). Whately describes the view from a bridge as "a perfect opera scene" (Whately, *Observations,* 113), and William Stukeley describes mountains arranged "like scenes at a playhouse" (cited in Andrews, *Search for the Picturesque,* 29). Garden and landscape designers consciously incorporated not only the architectural forms and perspectives of theater but even theaters and amphitheaters themselves. Noting that "the garden and the theatre have been closely connected at various points in their history," Hunt and Willis write that "the Italian Renaissance garden often contained a theatre, where plays and operas were performed, and this in its turn the English garden imitated with theatres or amphiteatres at Rousham, Claremont and Stowe; Pope's garden at Twickenham had its 'Bridgemannick Theatre'. From placing theatres in gardens it was but a short step to thinking of the whole garden in theatrical terms. Thus Pope at Rousham, for example, admired 'the prettiest place for water-falls, jetts, ponds inclosed with beautiful scenes of green and hanging wood'—and his use of scenes surely implies a sense of places contrived like the theatre sets of Thornhill" (Hunt and Willis, *Genius of the Place,* 36–37). Hunt writes: "it is clear that the early eighteenth-century gardenists saw their designs in terms of the theatre: Pope and visitors to Twickenham referred to the 'scenes of [his] little garden', while Pope on his travels saw the actual topography of the Avon Gorge at Bristol as 'the broken Scenes behind one another in a Playhouse.' . . . Not only were gardens organized in perspectival views like stage sets, but like those in the theatre their scenes were unthinkable except as stages for human action" (Hunt, "Ut Pictura Poesis," 93). See also id., "Theaters, Gardens, and Garden Theaters," in *Gardens and the Picturesque,* 49–74.

41. "An Epistolary Description of the Late Mr. Pope's House and Garden at Twickenham" (1747), published in *The General Magazine* (Newcastle) in January 1748 and reprinted in Hunt and Willis, *Genius of the Place,* 249–50.

42. Brownell, *Alexander Pope,* 129.

43. Gilpin, *A Dialogue upon the Gardens of the Right Honorable the Lord Viscount Cobham at Stow in Buckinghamshire* (1748), cited in Hunt and Willis, *Genius of the Place,* 256.

44. Anonymous, *Gentleman's Magazine,* quoted in Hunt and Willis, *Genius of the Place,* 250.

45. Ibid., 249.

46. Addison, Steele, et al., *Spectator,* ed. Bond, 3: 550–51 (No. 414).

47. Andrews, *Search for the Picturesque,* 68; Barrell, *Idea of Landscape,* 23. Andrews traces the Claude-glass back "to the studio mirrors used by Renaissance painters, and to instruments such as the *camera obscura.*" He notes that "William Mason thought the Claude Glass 'perhaps the best and most convenient substitute for a Camera Obscura, of anything that has hitherto been invented'" (Andrews, *Search for the Picturesque,* 68–69).

48. Quoted in Andrews, *Search for the Picturesque,* 68. See also Hunt, "Picturesque Mirrors and the Ruins of the Past," in *Gardens and the Picturesque,* 171, passim; Brewer, *Pleasures of the Imagination,* 634–35; Bermingham, *Learning to Draw,* 101–3; and Susan Sloman, *Gainsborough in Bath* (New Haven: Yale University Press, 2002), 137–40.

49. Barrell cites a novel by Susanna Harvey Keir in which "the heroine, out walking, comes to 'a height commanding one of the grandest prospects' she had ever beheld, and immediately takes out her pocket volume of Thompson—who would go for a walk without one?—and finds in it 'a lively description of the whole surrounding scenery'" (Barrell, *Idea of Landscape,* 43). Thomas Jefferson, who made a tour of English gardens "to estimate the expence of making and maintaining a garden in that style," made his visits while reading Whately's descriptions of them. "I always walked over the gardens with his book in my hand, examined with attention the particular spots he described, found them so justly characterised by him as to be easily recognized, and saw with wonder that his fine imagination had never been able to seduce him from the truth" ("Memorandums Made on a Tour to Some of the Gardens in England" [1786], cited in Hunt and Willis, *Genius of the Place,* 333). More romantic observers were less concerned with truth and seduction. Samuel Monk complains that "throughout the picturesque phase nature was frequently scarcely seen at all, for the lover of the picturesque was bent upon discovering not the world as it is, but the world as it might have been had the Creator been an Italian artist of the seventeenth century. Shut up in the Palace of Art, he could look out only through stained-glass windows which falsely colored the natural world." Monk suggests, however, that "Wordsworth would never have seen God through nature, had not the generations which preceded him seen nature through Claude and Salvator" (Samuel H. Monk, *The Sublime: A Study of Critical Theories in XVIII-Century England* [Ann Arbor: University of Michigan Press, 1962], 204).

50. Gilpin, *Observations, Relative Chiefly to Picturesque Beauty, Made in the Year 1776, on Several Parts of Great Britain* (London, 1789), 2 vols., 1: 124. Gilpin writes: "Coloured glasses may be amusing; but I should rather wish to have them hung up in frames with handles to be used at pleasure, than fixed in a window, and to impose the necessity of looking through them" (123–24).

51. Gilpin, *Remarks on Forest Scenery,* 2: 235, 233–34.

52. Knight, *Analytical Inquiry,* 1: 196.

53. Gilpin states that there is a "difference" since "the camera represents objects as they really are; while the imagination, impressed with the most beautiful scenes, and chastened by the rules of art, forms its pictures, not only from the most admirable parts of nature; but in the best taste" (*Three Essays*, 52).

54. Gilpin, *Three Essays*, 57.

55. Repton, *Observations on the Theory and Practice of Landscape Gardening* (1803), in id., *Landscape Gardening*, 222.

56. Whately, *Observations*, 1.

57. No author, title, or reference is provided in Repton's text. See René Louis de Gérardin, *De la Composition des paysages, ou Des Moyens d'embellir la Nature autour des Habitations, en joignant l'agréable à l'utile* (Geneva, 1777).

58. *Ibid.*, 7, xii–xiii, 9, 8, 20. In his *Sketches and Hints*, Repton declares that "Monsieur Gerardin is greatly mistaken, when he directs, that no scene in nature should be attempted till it has first been painted" (Repton, *Landscape Gardening*, 97). See Dora Wiebenson, *The Picturesque Garden in France* (Princeton: Princeton University Press, 1978); and Munsters, *Poétique du pittoresque*.

59. Knight, *Landscape*, 2d ed., 47–48.

60. Ibid., 49.

61. Ibid., 49–50.

62. Joshua Reynolds, *Discourses on Art*, ed. Robert R. Wark (New Haven: Yale University Press, 1975), 239.

63. Henry Fielding, *The History of Tom Jones, a Foundling* (New York: Modern Library, 1950), 759. For a discussion of the mirroring of passions and sentiments that takes place in an act of sympathy, see David Marshall, "Adam Smith and the Theatricality of Moral Sentiments," in *The Figure of Theater: Shaftesbury, Defoe, Adam Smith, and George Eliot* (New York: Columbia University Press, 1986).

64. Knight, *Landscape*, 50.

65. Ibid., 50.

66. Fielding, *Tom Jones*, 757, 761.

67. Knight discusses Reynolds's theories in a review of *The Life of Sir Joshua Reynolds, late President of the Royal Academy, &c*, by James Northcote, *Edinburgh Review* 23 (1814): 263–92. See Ballantyne, *Architecture*, 145–70.

68. Reynolds, *Discourses*, 232, 235.

69. Ibid., 233.

70. Ibid., 237–38.

71. Ibid., 241, 29, 95, 204, 224.

72. Ibid., 239–40.

73. Ibid., 240.

74. Whately, *Observations*, 84–85.

75. Cited in Hunt and Willis, *Genius of the Place*, 268.

76. Shenstone, *Works*, 136.

77. Repton, *Landscape Gardening*, 162, 84.

78. Richard Payne Knight, *The Landscape: A Didactic Poem. In Three Books. Addressed to Uvedale Price,* Esq., 1st ed. (London: W. Bulmer & Co., 1794), 1.

79. Price, *Essays,* 334–35.

80. Price, *Essay,* 287. Price cites Tasso's line "L'arte che tutto fa, nulla si scopre" in the concluding chapter to his *Essays on the Picturesque* and adds, "although no precept be more generally admitted in theory than that of concealing the art which is employed, none has been less observed in practice" (Price, *Essays,* 334). Cf. Tasso, *Gerusalemme liberata* 16.9.8, in *Opere,* ed. Bortolo Tommaso Sozzi (Turin: Unione tipografico, 1955), 449, and Aristotle, *Poetics,* trans. Ingram Bywater, in *Rhetoric and Poetics of Aristotle* (New York: Modern Library, 1954), 258.

81. Price, *Essays,* 1: 344–45.

82. Knight, *Analytical Inquiry,* 152–53. Cf. Price: "All external objects affect us in two different ways; by the impression they make on the senses, and by the reflections they suggest to the mind. These two modes, though very distinct in their operations, often unite in producing one effect; the reflections of the mind, either strengthening, weakening, or giving new direction to the impression received by the eye" (Price, *An Essay on Architecture and Buildings, as Connected with Scenery,* in *Essays,* 2: 247).

83. Knight, *Analytic Inquiry,* 196.

84. Ibid.

85. Gilpin, *A Dialogue upon the Gardens of the Right Honorable the Lord Viscount Cobham at Stow in Buckinghamshire* (1748), cited in Hunt and Willis, *Genius of the Place,* 258. Addison writes: "A Man of Polite Imagination is let into a great many Pleasures, that the Vulgar are not capable of receiving. He can converse with a Picture, and find an agreeable Companion in a Statue. . . . So that he looks upon the World, as it were, in another Light, and discovers in it a Multitude of Charms, that conceal themselves from the generality of Mankind" (Addison and Steele, *Spectator,* ed. Bond, 3: 541 [No. 411, June 21, 1712]). Knight's theories of associationism are influenced by Archibald Alison's *Essay on the Principles of Taste* (Edinburgh, 1790). For more on the critic and taste, see my chapter 7, 176–96.

86. Knight, *Analytic Inquiry,* 143.

87. Ibid., 146.

88. Ibid., 144, 197.

89. Denis Diderot, *Oeuvres esthétiques* (Paris: Hermann, 1975–), 10: 78. For an extensive discussion of these situations in Diderot's work, see "Forgetting Theater," in David Marshall, *The Surprising Effects of Sympathy: Marivaux, Diderot, Rousseau, and Mary Shelley* (Chicago: University of Chicago Press, 1988), 105–34.

90. Fanny Burney, *Evelina, or the History of a Young Lady's Entrance into the World* (1778; New York: Signet, 1992), 24.

91. Fielding, *Tom Jones,* 761.

92. Knight, *Landscape,* 50.

93. Knight, *Analytical Inquiry,* 153.

94. Fielding, *Tom Jones,* 759.

95. Hunt, *Figure in the Landscape,* 6. According to Hunt, "we know that landowners sought to employ others to do their meditation for them. Charles Hamilton advertised for a hermit at Paine's Hill in Surrey and built him a hermitage where his contract required him to remain for seven years—'with a Bible, optical glasses, a mat for his feet, a hassock for his pillow, an hourglass for his timepiece, water for his beverage, and food from the house. He must wear a camel robe, and never, under any circumstances, must he cut his hair, beard, or nails, stray beyond the limits of Mr. Hamilton's grounds, or exchange one word with the servants.' Another sat in a cave 'with an hourglass in his hand, and a beard belonging to a goat . . . with orders to accept no half-crowns from visitors, but to behave like Giordano Bruno'. This last survived apparently for fourteen years; the first fled after three weeks" (8). David Streatfield describes an estate where for picturesque effect a fire was "kept alight in a cottage on the outlying part" from the eighteenth century until "the beginning of World War II" (Streatfield, "Art and Nature in the English Landscape Garden: Design Theory and Practice, 1700–1818," in *Landscape in the Gardens and Literature of the Eighteenth Century* [Berkeley: University of California Press, 1981], 69).

Chapter 2   The Impossible Work of Art

1. Edmund Burke, *A Philosophical Enquiry into the Origin of Our Ideas of the Sublime and the Beautiful,* ed. James T. Boulton (Notre Dame, Ind.: University of Notre Dame Press, 1968), 167, 170. For discussions of Burke's empiricism and the status of mental images, see W. J. T. Mitchell, *Iconology: Image, Text, Ideology* (Chicago: University of Chicago Press, 1986), esp. 7–46 and 116–49, and Frances Ferguson, *Solitude and the Sublime: Romanticism and the Aesthetics of Individuation* (New York: Routledge, 1992), 37–96.

2. Gotthold Ephraim Lessing, *Laocoön: An Essay on the Limits of Painting and Poetry,* trans. Edward Allen McCormick (Indianapolis: Bobbs-Merrill, 1962), 5. German citations, when given, refer to Lessing, *Laokoon, oder Über die Grenzen der Malerei und Poesie* (Stuttgart: Philipp Reclam, 1971). Parenthetical citations of Lessing, unless otherwise noted, refer to these editions.

3. Horace, *Ars Poetica* in *Satires, Epistles, Ars Poetica,* trans. H. Rushton Fairclough (Cambridge, 1966), v. 361. The term "poetry" in eighteenth-century comparisons generally was used in the way we would use "literature"; it could refer to dramatic as well as epic poetry, as well as lyric modes. It also gradually encompassed the novel, although most treatises on aesthetics did not find it decorous to discuss novels.

4. The scholarship on the traditions of the sister arts, the parallels between the literature and painting, literary pictorialism, descriptive poetry, and *ut pictura poesis* is extensive. Important and relevant discussions include Jean Hagstrum, *The*

Sister Arts: The Tradition of Literary Pictorialism and English Poetry from Dryden to Gray (Chicago: University of Chicago Press, 1958); John B. Bender, *Spenser and Literary Pictorialism* (Princeton: Princeton University Press, 1972); and Lawrence Lipking, "Quick Poetic Eyes: Another Look at Literary Pictorialism," in *Articulate Images: The Sister Arts from Hogarth to Tennyson,* ed. Richard Wendorf (Minneapolis: University of Minnesota Press, 1983), 3–25 (in addition to other useful essays, this volume also provides a "Checklist of Modern Scholarship in the Sister Arts," 251–52). See also Ralph Cohen, *The Art of Discrimination: Thomson's The Seasons and the Language of Criticism* (Berkeley: University of California Press, 1964); Patricia Meyer Spacks, *The Poetry of Vision: Five Eighteenth-Century Poets* (Cambridge, Mass.: Harvard University Press, 1967); Rensselaer W. Lee, "Ut Pictura Poesis: The Humanistic Theory of Painting," *Art Bulletin* 22 (1940): 197–269 (rpt. New York: Norton, 1967); William G. Howard, "Ut Pictura Poesis," *PMLA* 24 (1909): 43–71; and Cicely Davies, "Ut Pictura Poesis," *Modern Language Review* 30 (1935): 159–69. W. J. T. Mitchell has made important contributions to our current understanding about the critical and theoretical dimensions of these traditions. See Mitchell, *Iconology: Image, Text, Ideology;* id., "Ekphrasis and the Other," in *Picture Theory* (Chicago: University of Chicago Press, 1994), 151–82; and *The Language of Images,* ed. id. (Chicago: University of Chicago Press, 1974).

5. On *enargeia* and *energeia,* see Hagstrum, *Sister Arts,* 11–12. Noting the "combination of ancient aesthetic principle and modern scientific psychology," Hagstrum suggests that *ut pictura poesis* "rested on English empiricism—on Lockean epistemology and the related aesthetic tradition that ran from Hobbes to Addison" (ibid., 136, 150). Addison's 1712 *Spectator* essays on the pleasures of imagination are seen as the definitive English version of the doctrine of *enargeia.* See also William K. Wimsatt Jr. and Cleanth Brooks, *Literary Criticism: A Short History* (New York: Knopf, 1959), 254–62, and Bender, *Spenser,* 8–10. Words "ought to set the scene before our eyes," Aristotle declares, and he praises "expressions which set things before the eyes" (*Rhetoric,* trans. J. H. Freese [Cambridge, 1959], 3.10.399, 405). In terms echoed by many eighteenth-century commentators on *ut pictura poesis,* esp. Kames, Aristotle advises the poet to "put the actual scenes as far as possible before his eyes. In this way, seeing everything with the vividness of an eye-witness as it were, he will devise what is appropriate" (*Poetics,* trans. W. Hamilton Fyfe [Cambridge, 1973], 17.1.65). According to Cicero, "every metaphor, provided it be a good one, has a direct appeal to the senses, especially the sense of sight, which is the keenest." He instructs the orator that "the metaphors drawn from the sense of sight are much more vivid, virtually placing within the range of our mental vision objects not actually visible to our sight" (Cicero, *De oratore,* in *Cicero,* trans. H. Rackham, Loeb Classical Library, 28 vols. [Cambridge, Mass.: Harvard University Press, 1968], 3: 127). One could speculate that the growth of epistemology and theories of perception in the early eighteenth century contributed to the revival or at least the revitalization of aesthetic theories about the

importance of images in literary works. The relation between the philosophical and nascent scientific investigations of the time and contemporary endorsements of *ut pictura poesis* may be less a sign of influence than an indication of related concerns and preoccupations. Yet the speculations of writers such as Locke and Hume were clearly important to the theorists of *ut pictura poesis,* at least in part because of the centrality of the status of images to Enlightenment epistemology and a preoccupation with acts of imagination, mimesis, and representation.

6. See Hagstrum, *Sister Arts,* 18n. See also John Hollander, "The Poetics of *Ekphrasis,*" *Word and Image* (1988), 209–19; Murray Krieger, *Ekphrasis: The Illusion of the Natural Sign* (Baltimore: Johns Hopkins University Press, 1992); James A. W. Heffernan, *Museum of Words: The Poetics of Ekphrasis from Homer to Ashbery* (Chicago: University of Chicago Press, 1993).

7. See Jean-Baptiste Du Bos, *Réflexions critiques sur la poesie et sur la peinture,* 3 vols., 4th ed. (Paris, 1740).

8. Charles Batteux, *Les Beaux Arts réduits à un même principe* (Paris, 1747), 247.

9. See Wendy Steiner, *The Colors of Rhetoric: Problems in the Relation Between Modern Literature and Painting* (Chicago: University of Chicago Press, 1982). For a discussion of how these issues are played out in the context of film, see Brigitte Peucker, *Incorporating Images: Film and the Rival Arts* (Princeton: Princeton University Press, 1995).

10. In "Quick Poetic Eyes: Another Look at Literary Pictorialism," Lipking tries to take seriously "eighteenth-century ways of seeing" in poetry. He argues: "The vast majority of modern readers are blind to eighteenth-century poetry. We do not see poems well; we do not make the pictures in our minds that the poets direct and excite us to make; and we are often so complacent about our ways of reading that we blame the poem for our own failure to notice its signals" (23, 5). In an interesting early twentieth-century critique of Lessing, Frank Egbert Bryant invokes William James to discuss "Lessing's Psychology of Vision" and "The Nature of Mental Imagery" ("Lessing's Laocoon," in *A History of English Balladry and Other Studies* [Boston: Four Seas Company, 1919], 223–385).

11. Henry Home, Lord Kames, *Elements of Criticism,* 3 vols. (Edinburgh, 1762); New York: Campbell & Son, 1823), 2 vols., 1: 87. The text cited here is the 4th American ed., from the 8th London ed.; references refer to this text unless otherwise noted. For a discussion of *Elements of Criticism,* see Peter de Bolla, *The Discourse of the Sublime: History, Aesthetics, and the Subject* (New York: Basil Blackwell, 1989), esp. 92–102. See also Ian Simpson Ross, *Lord Kames and the Scotland of His Day* (Oxford: Oxford University Press, 1972), 378–80; and Robert L. Montgomery, *Terms of Response: Language and Audience in Seventeenth- and Eighteenth-Century Theory* (University Park: Pennsylvania State University Press, 1992), 119–25.

12. Du Bos, *Réflexions critiques,* 1: 278, 273, 274–75.

13. *The Works of Dionysius Longinus, On the Sublime: or, A Treatise Concerning*

the Sovereign Perfection of Writing, trans. Leonard Welsted (London, 1712, 1724), 183. In addition to Ferguson and De Bolla, see Samuel H. Monk, *The Sublime: A Study of Critical Theories in XVIII-Century England* (Ann Arbor: University of Michigan Press, 1962); Thomas Weiskel, *The Romantic Sublime: Studies in the Structure and Psychology of Transcendence* (Baltimore: Johns Hopkins University Press, 1976). Neil Hertz, *The End of the Line: Essays on Psychoanalysis and the Sublime* (New York: Columbia University Press, 1985); Ronald Paulson, *Representations of Revolution, 1789–1820* (New Haven: Yale University Press, 1983); Jonathan Lamb, "The Sublime," in *The Cambridge History of Literary Criticism,* vol. 4: *The Eighteenth Century,* ed. H. B. Nisbet and Claude Rawson (Cambridge: Cambridge University Press, 1997), 394–416.

14. Roger de Piles, *Cours de peinture par principes* (Paris, 1708), trans. "by a Painter" as *The Principles of Painting* (London: J. Osborn, 1743), 257–58.

15. Augustine, *Confessions,* 2 vols., trans. William Watts (London: William Heinemann, 1912), 1: 463–64.

16. This passage is from the third edition of Kames's *Elements of Criticism* (Edinburgh, 1765), 85.

17. This phrase also appears in ibid., 79.

18. In the First Exercise of *Spiritual Exercises,* Ignatius instructs the exercitant: "The first prelude is a mental image of the place. It should be noted at this point that when the meditation or contemplation is on a visible object, for example, contemplating Christ our Lord during His life on earth, the image will consist of seeing with the mind's eye the physical place where the object that we wish to contemplate is present" (*The Spiritual Exercises of St. Ignatius,* trans. Anthony Mottola [New York: Image Books, 1964], 54). See Louis L. Martz, *The Poetry of Meditation: A Study in English Religious Literature of the Seventeenth Century* (New Haven: Yale University Press, 1954).

19. "Every one is sensible, that describing a past event as present, has a fine effect in language: for what other reason than that it aids the conception of ideal presence?" Kames observes (*Elements of Criticism,* 1: 90).

20. "What we call 'poetic pictures' [*poetische Gemälde*] were *phantasiae* to the ancients. . . . And what we call 'illusion,' the deceptive element of these pictures, they termed *enargia,*" Lessing complains in a note to *Laocoön.* He argues that "modern treatises on poetry" should have adopted Plutarch's use of the phrase "waking dreams" and "dropped the word 'picture' altogether," in which case "poetical *phantasiae* would not have been so readily confined to the limits of a material painting" (*Laocoön,* 208; *Laokoon,* 111).

21. Kames, *Elements of Criticism,* 3d ed., 504.

22. Thomas Hobbes, *Leviathan; or, The Matter, Forme and Power of a Commonwealth Ecclesiasticall and Civil,* ed. Michael Oakeshott (New York: Collier, 1978), 15–16.

23. George Berkeley, *Principles, Dialogues, and Philosophical Correspondence,* ed. Colin Murray Turbayne (Indianapolis: Bobbs-Merrill, 1965), 38, 36.

24. Every thought, writes Hobbes in his definition of sense in the *Leviathan,* is "a *representation* or *appearance,* of some quality, or other accident of a body without us, which is commonly called an *object.* . . . this *seeming,* or *fancy,* is that which men call *sense;* and consisteth, as to the eye, in a *light,* or *colour figured.*" Imagination accounts for the presence of an image of the object after the object is gone: "After the object is removed, or the eye shut, we still retain an image of the thing seen, though more obscure than when we see it. And this is it, the Latins call *imagination,* from the image made in seeing. . . . But the Greeks call it *fancy;* which signifies *appearance,* and is as proper to one sense, as to another. IMAGINATION therefore is nothing but *decaying sense;* and is found in men, and many other living creatures, as well sleeping, as waking" (*Leviathan,* 15–16).

25. Locke, *Essay Concerning Human Understanding,* ed. Alexander Campbell Fraser, 2 vols. (New York: Dover, 1959), 1: 152, 149.

26. Joseph Addison and Richard Steele, *The Spectator,* ed. Donald F. Bond, 5 vols. (Oxford: Clarendon Press, 1965), 3: 537 (No. 411, Saturday, June 21, 1712). Cf. Wimsatt and Brooks, *Literary Criticism,* 255n.

27. Addison suggests that the "reason, probably, may be, because in the Survey of any object, we have only so much of it painted on the Imagination, as comes in at the Eye; but in its Description, the Poet gives us as free a View of it as he pleases" (Addiso and Steele, *Spectator,* ed. Bond, 3: 559–61 [No. 416, Friday, June 27, 1712]).

28. David Hume, *Enquiries Concerning Human Understanding and Concerning the Principles of Morals,* ed. L. A. Selby-Bigge (Oxford: Clarendon Press, 1975), § 12, pt. 1: 151.

29. Ibid., § 2: 17.

30. Ibid., § 5, pt. 2: 47, 49.

31. Ibid., 49.

32. The phrase "fictions of the imagination" appears in the third (1765) and fourth (1769) editions of Kames's *Elements of Criticism,* but not in later editions. For an account of Kames's somewhat ambivalent relations with Hume and the *Enquiry,* see Arthur E. McGuinness, "Hume and Kames: The Burdens of Friendship," *Studies in Scottish Literature* 6 (1969): 3–19.

33. Kames makes concessions to common sense, of course, but recalling "an object of sight in that manner," he changed the third edition's "it appears to me precisely same as in the original survey, only more faint and obscure" (2: 504) to "it appears to me precisely the same as in the original survey, only less distinct" (2: 359).

34. Hume, *Enquiry,* 52.

35. Du Bos, *Réflexions critiques,* 1: 402.

36. Ibid., 274–75.

37. Ibid., 387–88.

38. Hume, *Enquiry,* 49.

39. Charles-Alphonse Dufresnoy, *De arte graphica* (Paris, 1668), translated under the title *The Art of Painting. . . with an original Preface, containing a Parallel between Painting and Poetry, By Mr. Dryden* (London, 1750), iv, xlvii, li, liv.

40. Alexander Pope, "Preface" to *The Iliad of Homer,* in *Works,* ed. Maynard Mack (New Haven: Yale University Press, 1967), 358. Further citations of Pope's "Preface" refer to this text. See Hagstrum, *Sister Arts,* 229; 210–42; Robert W. Williams, "Alexander Pope and *Ut Pictura Poesis,*" *Sydney Studies in English* 10 (1984): 61–75; and Morris R. Brownell, *Alexander Pope and the Arts of Georgian England* (Oxford: Oxford University Press, 1978), 39–70.

41. Homer, *Iliad* (19.565–710), trans. Robert Fagles (Harmondsworth, U.K.: Penguin Books, 1990), 483. Further citations of the *Iliad* refer to this translation.

42. W. J. T. Mitchell describes Homer's description as "a utopian site that is both a space within the narrative, and an ornamented frame around it, a threshold across which the reader may enter and withdraw from the text at will." He sees the shield as "an imagetext that displays rather than concealing its own suturing of space and time, description and narration, materiality and illusionist representation." Critics have quarreled with Lessing's argument. Citing Jean Hagstrum's claim that Homer's description is "not, as Lessing believed, the presentation of an action or a process," Mitchell suggests that Homer's text "can be mobilized to support either Lessing or Hagstrum" (Mitchell, *Picture Theory,* 177–78; see Hagstrum, *Sister Arts,* 19).

43. Hagstrum defends the Anacreonitic tradition, insisting that poems by Anacreon and later Rochester "may be said to achieve the *enargeia* that ancient critics and rhetoricians were almost unanimous in requiring" (*Sister Arts,* 25).

44. My translation is taken from the Appendix to Patricia A. Rosenmeyer, *The Poetics of Imitation: Anacreon and the Anacreontic Tradition* (Cambridge: Cambridge University Press, 1992), 246. Lessing cites the Greek.

45. Lucian, *Essays in Portraiture,* in *Lucian,* trans. A. M. Harmon, Loeb Classical Library, 8 vols. (London: William Heinemann, 1925), 4: 271.

46. "Picture a woman dyeing ivory blood red . . . / a Carian or Maeonian staining a horse's cheekpiece, / and it's stored away in a vault and troops of riders / long to sport the ornament, true, but there it lies / as a king's splendor, kept and prized twice over— / his team's adornment, his driver's pride and glory. / So now, Menelaus, the fresh blood went staining down / your sturdy thighs, your shins and well-turned ankles" (*Iliad* [4.160–67], 150). For a related discussion of Homeric similes, see David Marshall, "Similes and Delay," in *Modern Critical Views: Homer,* ed. Harold Bloom (New York: Chelsea House, 1986), 233–36.

47. Lucian, *Essays in Portraiture Defended,* 309.

48. Ibid., 333, 327.

49. Lucian, *Essays in Portraiture,* 279, 285.

50. Ibid., 261, 257, 259.

51. Ibid., 275–76.

52. Rosenmeyer, *Poetics of Imitation,* 247.

53. Lucian, *Essays in Portraiture,* 263.

54. See my chapter 1, 16–39.

55. See David Marshall, *The Figure of Theater: Shaftesbury, Defoe, Adam Smith, and George Eliot* (New York: Columbia University Press, 1986).

56. To some extent, drama was seen as an alternative to this impasse of descriptive writing. Theater offered a model for and a literalization of the ideals of *ut pictura poesis* inasmuch as it embodied literary texts in a visual medium. Jonathan Richardson, in comparing writing and painting, notes that the "Theatre gives us Representations of Things different from both these, and a kind of Composition of both: There we see a sort of moving, speaking Pictures." Not surprisingly, he concludes that painting is superior: "but these are transient; whereas Painting remains, and is always at hand. And what is more considerable, the Stage never represents things truly, especially if the Scene be remote, and the Story ancient" (Richardson, *An Essay on the Theory of Painting* [London, 1715], 7). Du Bos sees dramatic poetry as possessing an advantage over painting, since a tragedy "renferme une infinité de tableaux." The poet, he writes, "nous présente successivement, pour ainsi dire, cinquante tableaux" (Du Bos, *Réflexions critiques,* 1: 396). In his article on "Composition" in the *Encyclopédie,* Diderot writes: "Un bon tableau ne fournira guere qu'un sujet, ou même qu'une scene de drame; & un seul drame peut fournir matiere à cent tableaux différens" (Denis Diderot and Jean le Rond d'Alembert, *Encyclopédie, ou Dictionnaire raisonné des sciences, des arts et des métiers,* vol. 3 [Paris, 1753], 773). Diderot (who attacked the use of "portraits" in novels) argued in his *Entretiens sur le fils naturel* and *Essai de la poèsie dramatique* that plays should learn from painting and present tableaux to the spectators in the audience. (Denis Diderot, *Oeuvres complètes,* 33 vols. [Paris: Hermann, 1975–], vol. 10.) See Diderot's description of the poet as a painter in the *Salon de 1767.* See also Michael Fried, *Absorption and Theatricality: Painting and Beholder in the Age of Diderot* (Berkeley: University of California Press, 1979). For Kames, drama enacts the situation that he demands from literature by embodying a text that literally presents a scene before an audience. Following Shaftesbury, he praises "dialogue-writing" (1: 355), in which (in Shaftesbury's formulation) "the author is annihilated, and the reader, being no way applied to, stands for nobody. . . . The scene presents itself as by chance and undesigned" (Anthony Ashley Cooper, Lord Shaftesbury, *Characteristics of Men, Manners, Opinions, Times, etc.,* ed. John M. Robertson, 2 vols. [1900; rpt. Gloucester, Mass.: Peter Smith, 1963], 1: 132). Kames speaks of the writer, who "annihilating himself, can thus become another person" (1: 354). Not only does Kames advocate the annihilation of the author, he also wants the text to disappear. "Painting seems to possess a middle place between reading and acting,"

he says; "theatrical representation is the most powerful" of "all the means for making an impression of ideal presence." An epic poem (which "employs narration") or a "narrative poem is a story told by another" whereas "tragedy represents its facts as passing in our sight" (1: 89–90; 2: 262). Even drama, however, must avoid what Kames calls the "descriptive manner of representing passion"; the "descriptive tragedy" that conveys only "cold description in the language of a bystander" (1: 355–56) will place only the language of description before our eyes.

57. Hugh Blair, *Lectures on Rhetoric and Belles Lettres,* ed. Harold F. Harding, 2 vols. (Carbondale: Southern Illinois University Press, 1965), 2: 383–84, 371.

58. Cited in René Wellek, *A History of Modern Criticism, 1750–1950,* 4 vols. (New Haven: Yale University Press, 1966) 1: 164–65. See also David Wellbery, *Lessing's Laocoön: Semiotics and Aesthetics in the Age of Reason* (Cambridge: Cambridge University Press, 1984), 225–27. For other relevant discussions of Lessing and the problem of language and representation, in addition to Wellbery, see Carol Jacobs, *Telling Time: Lévi-Strauss, Ford, Lessing, Benjamin, de Man, Wordsworth, Rilke* (Baltimore: Johns Hopkins University Press, 1993), 95–127; Benjamin Bennett, *Beyond Theory: Eighteenth-Century German Literature and the Poetics of Irony* (Ithaca, N.Y.: Cornell University Press, 1993), 116–61; Tzvetan Todorov, *Theories of the Symbol,* trans. Catherine Porter (Ithaca, N.Y.: Cornell University Press, 1982), 137–46; and Claudia Brodsky Lacour, "'Is that Helen?' Contemporary Pictorialism, Lessing, and Kant," *Comparative Literature* 45, 3 (Summer 1993): 230–57.

59. Ludwig Wittgenstein, *Philosophical Investigations,* trans. G. E. M. Anscombe (1953; 2d ed., New York: Macmillan, 1958), 48.

60. Ibid., 47.

61. Ibid., v, 48.

62. Ibid., 28.

Chapter 3 *True Acting and the Language of Real Feeling*

1. Lionel Trilling, *The Opposing Self: Nine Essays in Criticism* (New York: Viking, 1955), 218. For Jonas Barish, "the theatricals come charged with a mysterious iniquity that challenges explanation" (*The Antitheatrical Prejudice* [Berkeley: University of California Press, 1981], 301). I would like to thank Patricia Meyer Spacks, Candace Waid, and Deborah Kaplan for valuable responses to the first version of this chapter.

2. Trilling, *Opposing Self,* 218. See also Lionel Trilling, *Sincerity and Authenticity* (Cambridge, Mass.: Harvard University Press, 1971), 73–80. For some discussions of *Lovers' Vows,* see Penelope Gay, "Theatricals and Theatricality in *Mansfield Park,*" *Sydney Studies in English* 13 (1987–88): 61–73; William Reitzel, "*Mansfield Park* and *Lovers' Vows,*" *Review of English Studies* 9 (1933): 451–56; Sybil Rosenfeld, "Jane Austen and Private Theatricals," *Essays and Studies* 15 (1962): 40–51; Madeline Hummel, "Emblematic Charades and the Observant Woman in Mansfield

Park," *Texas Studies in Literature and Language* 15 (1973): 251–65; Dvora Zelicovici, "The Inefficacy of Lovers' Vows," *ELH* 50 (1983): 531–40; Elaine Jordan, "Pulpit, Stage, and Novel: *Mansfield Park* and Mrs. Inchbald's *Lovers' Vows*," *Novel* 20 (1987): 138–48; E. M. Butler, "*Mansfield Park* and Kotzebue's *Lovers' Vows*," *MLR* 28 (1933): 326–37; H. Winifred Husbands, "*Mansfield Park* and *Lovers' Vows*: A Reply," *MLR* 29 (1934): 176–79.

3. Trilling speaks of Austen's regard of "self-sufficiency, self-definition, and sincerity" as well as Fanny's "single-mindedness and sincerity" (*Sincerity and Authenticity*, 73, 75). In his introduction to the novel, Tony Tanner describes *Mansfield Park* as "a place where you must be true to your best self"; he writes: "role-playing must make against stability and fixity." Edmund's acting "involves an abdication of his true self" (Introduction, Jane Austen, *Mansfield Park* [Harmondsworth, U.K.: Penguin Books, 1980], 27–31; further citations, unless otherwise noted, refer to this text.) For other examples of this view, see C. Knatchbull Bevan, "Personal Identity in *Mansfield Park*: Forms, Fictions, Role-Play, and Reality," *Studies in English Literature* 27 (1987): 595–608, and A. Walton Litz, *Jane Austen: A Study of Her Artistic Development* (New York: Oxford University Press, 1965), 119–28.

4. Litz, *Jane Austen*, 127.

5. See, e.g., ibid., 126. Barish, who cites Litz, writes: "As in the case of Cordelia, the inability to feign becomes an emblem of rectitude" (306). Fanny's "utter incapacity to act, especially to act across gender-lines, emblematically confirms her integrity: Fanny can represent no one but herself," according to Ruth Bernard Yeazell, "The Boundaries of *Mansfield Park*," *Representations* 7 (1984): 138.

6. Jane Austen, *Sense and Sensibility* (New York: Bantam Books, 1983), 84.

7. Not even Martin Price, who has written astutely about both Uvedale Price and Fanny Price, has even suggested that there is a coincidence here—although he is the only one who has a good excuse. See Martin Price, "The Picturesque Moment," in *From Sensibility to Romanticism: Essays Presented to Frederick A. Pottle*, ed. Frederick W Hilles and Harold Bloom (New York: Oxford University Press, 1965), 259–92, and id., *Forms of Life: Character and Moral Imagination in the Novel* (New Haven: Yale University Press, 1983), 65–89. See also Alistair M. Duckworth, *The Improvement of the Estate: A Study of Jane Austen's Novels* (Baltimore: Johns Hopkins University Press, 1971), 35–80; and for another helpful discussion, John Barrell, *The Idea of Landscape and the Sense of Place, 1730–1840* (Cambridge: Cambridge University Press, 1972), 1–63. See my chapter 1, 16–39, for an extended analysis of theories of the picturesque.

8. Uvedale Price, *Essays on the Picturesque, as Compared with the Sublime and the Beautiful; and on the Use of Studying Pictures, for the Purpose of Improving Real Landscape*, 3 vols. (1794–98; London: J. Mawman, 1810).

9. In *Northanger Abbey*, the impressionable Catherine Morland witnesses the Tilneys as they "were viewing the country with the eyes of persons accustomed to drawing, and decided on its capability of being formed into pictures, with all the

eagerness of real taste." They also have been discussing "instruction" and what follows is called "a lecture on the picturesque"; Catherine, who convinces her friends of her "natural taste," is described as "so hopeful a scholar that . . . she voluntarily rejected the whole city of Bath as unworthy to make part of a landscape" (Jane Austen, *Northanger Abbey* [New York: Bantam Books, 1985], 89–90). In *Sense and Sensibility,* we read a discussion of "the picturesque" and people "who pretend to more admiration of the beauties of nature than they really feel." Marianne complains that "admiration of landscape scenery is become a mere jargon. Everybody pretends to feel and tries to describe with the taste and elegance of him who first defined what picturesque beauty was." She continues: "I detest jargon of every kind, and sometimes I have kept my feelings to myself because I could find no language to describe them in but what was worn and hackneyed out of all sense and meaning." Edward, who insists he knows "nothing of the picturesque" and does not admire fine prospects "on picturesque principles," tells Marianne that he is convinced "that you really feel all the delight in a fine prospect which you profess to feel" (83–84). "Fanny's Romantic rhapsodies on star-gazing or shrubberies are treated with gentle irony," Penelope Gay notes ("Theatricals and Theatricality in *Mansfield Park*," 64). I am suggesting that the irony is less than gentle (see Price, *Forms of Life,* 89).

10. The assertion that the moral problem with the theatricals is that the actors do not really act but rather are expressing their real feelings is often made in objection to Trilling's claims about the dangers of losing the self in impersonation. See Marilyn Butler, *Jane Austen and the War of Ideas* (Oxford: Oxford University Press, 1975), 232; Stuart M. Tave, *Some Words of Jane Austen* (Chicago: University of Chicago Press, 1973), 184; and Thomas R. Edwards Jr., "The Difficult Beauty of *Mansfield Park*," *Nineteenth-Century Fiction* 20 (1965): 61.

11. Mrs. Inchbald, *Lovers' Vows: A Play in Five Acts,* from the German of Kotzebue, 5th ed. (London, 1798), 506.

12. See, e.g., Margaret Kirkham, *Jane Austen, Feminism and Fiction* (Brighton, Sussex, U.K.: Harvester Press, 1983), 107–19.

13. Shakespeare, *Measure for Measure,* 5.1.211.

14. Johann Wolfgang von Goethe, *Elective Affinities,* trans. Elizabeth Mayer and Louis Bogan (South Bend, Ind.: Gateway Editions, 1963), 173, 273–74, 35. *Die Wahlverwandtschaften* was published in 1809. Reviews of the novel, along with brief excerpts, appeared in 1812 in the *Monthly Review; or Literary Journal* (68: 540–43) and *Monthly Magazine, or British Register* (33: 40–41). A French translation by Jean-Baptiste-Joseph Breton de la Martinière was titled *Ottilie, ou Le Pouvoir de la sympathie* (Paris: Vve Le Petit, 1810).

15. Goethe, *Elective Affinities,* 97, 261, 248.

16. Leo Bersani, *A Future for Astyanax: Character and Desire in Literature* (New York: Columbia University Press, 1984), 76; D. A. Miller, *Narrative and Its Discontents: Problems of Closure in the Traditional Novel* (Princeton: Princeton Uni-

versity Press, 1981), 21; Joseph Litvak, "The Infection of Acting: Theatricals and Theatricality in Mansfield Park," *ELH* 53 (1986): 345. See Litvak's subsequent *Caught in the Act: Theatricality in the Nineteenth-Century English Novel* (Berkeley: University of California Press, 1992), 1–26; as well as D. A. Miller, *Jane Austen; or, the Secret of Style* (Princeton: Princeton University Press, 2003).

17. Since Fanny at this point knows nothing about Henry's unfaithfulness and adultery, "it was impossible for her to understand much of this strange letter" (426), but I think that the verbal echoes in Mary's litany, "hear nothing, surmise nothing, whisper nothing," ask us to imagine Fanny responding with Leontes' questions about adultery in *The Winter's Tale:* "Is whispering nothing?" he asks, and then, after a list of accusations, "Is this nothing? / Why, then the world is nothing and all that's in't is nothing, / The covering sky is nothing, Bohemia nothing, / My wife is nothing, nor nothing have these nothings, / If this be nothing" (1.2.283–94). Cf. *Macbeth:* "Life's but a walking shadow, a poor player / that struts and frets his hour upon the stage / And then is heard no more. It is a tale / Told by an idiot, full of sound and fury / Signifying nothing" (5.5.24–28). In *King Lear,* when called upon to declare her love for her father, Cordelia says, "Nothing," and Lear responds, "Nothing will come of nothing" (1.1.89–92).

18. Tony Tanner, Introduction to *Mansfield Park,* 30. See Litvak, "Infection of Acting," 345. For discussions of eighteenth-century theories of acting, many of which claimed that the ideal actor would forget himself and become the part he was playing, see my *The Surprising Effects of Sympathy: Marivaux, Diderot, Rousseau, and Mary Shelley* (Chicago: University of Chicago Press, 1988), esp. chaps. 5 and 6. See also Walter Jackson Bate, "The Sympathetic Imagination in Eighteenth-Century English Criticism," *ELH* 12 (1945): 144–64; and Earl R. Wasserman, "The Sympathetic Imagination in Eighteenth-Century Theories of Acting," *Journal of English and Germanic Philology* 46 (1947): 264–72. For a discussion of theories of acting and how *Mansfield Park* "engages the language of elocution and connects elocution's influence on acting and on speech," see Pamela Howell Michaelson, *Speaking Volumes: Women, Reading, and Speech in the Age of Austen* (Stanford: Stanford University Press, 2002), 128.

19. Cf. *King Lear* 2.3.21: "Edgar I nothing am."

20. See, e.g., Miller, *Jane Austen,* 77–83, and Litz, *Jane Austen,* 129.

21. Samuel Richardson, *Pamela, or Virtue Rewarded* (1740–42; New York: New American Library, 1980), 386–87.

22. Aristotle, *Poetics,* trans. Ingram Bywater, in *Rhetoric and Poetics of Aristotle* (New York: Modern Library, 1954), 258.

23. Bersani, *Future for Astyanax,* 76–77. See Trilling, *Opposing Self,* 225–28, and *Sincerity and Authenticity,* 75–78; Litz, *Jane Austen,* 128–29; and Butler, *Jane Austen,* 230–49.

24. See, e.g., John Halperin, "The Novelist as Heroine in *Mansfield Park:* A Study in Autobiography," *MLQ* 44 (1983): 154.

Chapter 4   Fatal Letters

Epigraph: "Everything retraces to me an imaginary scene with more force than the events that have really befallen me" (*Julie, or the New Heloise,* trans. Philip Stewart and Jean Vaché [Hanover, N.H.: University Press of New England, 1997], 270). Parenthetical page references in the text refer to Jean-Jacques Rousseau, *Julie ou La Nouvelle Héloïse,* ed. René Pomeau (Paris: Garnier, 1960), 309. Translations with page references refer to the English version by Stewart and Vaché cited above; some of these have been modified in order to convey key words in Rousseau's text, and passages in which there is more than slight modification are indicated. Translations without page references are my own.

1. Samuel Richardson, *Lettres angloises, ou Histoire de Miss Clarisse Harlove,* trans. Antonine-François Prévost, 6 vols. (London: Nourse, 1751). The illustration appears as plate 7 in the second part of the sixth volume between pages 238 and 239. The illustration appears between pages 2 and 3 of volume 13 in *Lettres angloises, ou Histoire de Miss Clarisse Harlove,* 13 vols. (Paris: Libraires Associés, 1774). Citations of Prévost's translation in this chapter refer to this edition; the translations of Prévost's text are my own. In addition to citing Prévost's text, I provide Richardson's text. Because my argument often turns upon close reading and the textual similarities between Rousseau's text and Prévost's text, I cite the French text throughout as well as that of Richardson. This means that for the benefit of the reader who does not read French, I sometimes translate Prévost's (sometimes approximate) French translation of Richardson's English back into my own English. I am interested in the play of meanings and echoes among these texts and translations. Citations of Richardson refer first to Samuel Richardson, *Clarissa. Or, The History of a Young Lady,* 8 vols. (3d ed., London, 1751; reprint, New York: AMS Press, 1990), although for the convenience of readers, I also provide references to the Penguin reprint of the first edition (1746–48), *Clarissa or The History of a Young Lady,* ed. Angus Ross (Harmondsworth, U.K.: Penguin Books, 1985). The first page number cites the AMS edition and the second page number cites the Penguin edition. Prévost translated the first edition of *Clarissa,* but in the passages discussed here, there are no significant differences between the first and third editions. Richardson did not include illustrations when he published *Clarissa.* See T. C. Duncan-Eaves, "Graphic Illustration of the Novels of Samuel Richardson, 1740–1810," *Huntington Library Quarterly* 14 (1950–51): 349–83.

2. Richardson, *Lettres angloises,* trans. Prévost, 13: 2; Richardson, *Clarissa:* "I will give thee the woeful scene that presented itself to me, as I approached the bed" (8: 4/1361]).

3. Because Rousseau launched the project of illustrating his novel somewhat late in its production, the first edition does not contain any illustrations. See *Lettres de Deux Amans, Habitans d'une petite Ville au pied des Alpes Recuillies et publiées par J. J. Rousseau,* 6 vols. (Amsterdam: Marc Michel Rey, 1761). Gravelot's en-

gravings were first published separately along with Rousseau's textual descriptions, "Sujets d'estampes," as *Recueil d'estampes pour la Nouvelle Héloïse* (Paris: Duchesne, 1761). They were included in subsequent editions and in some cases were bound into copies of the first edition. The illustrations are reproduced in both the Garnier text and the Stewart and Vaché translation cited.

4. Richardson, *Lettres angloises,* trans. Prévost, 13: 2.

5. This surrogate also paradoxically screens the beholder out, thereby neutralizing the theatrical situation staged within the scene. See Michael Fried, *Absorption and Theatricality: Painting and Beholder in the Age of Diderot* (Berkeley: University of California Press, 1980).

6. See Pomeau, Introduction to *Julie ou La Nouvelle Héloïse,* vi.

7. "He has, in every respect, proposed Mr. Richardson, the author of Clarissa and Pamela, for his model: he has, in a former work, given his opinion of our countryman's merit, and here confirms his applause by actual imitation. . . . It is natural to compare a copyist with the original; and to do both justice, they each separately excell," a generally favorable reviewer of Rousseau wrote in the *Critical Review; or, Annals of Literature* 11, art. 13 (January 1761): 65–66. A long review of the English translation of *Julie* that compares Rousseau and Richardson, beginning with the observation that Rousseau "has formed his Eloisa on the plan of the celebrated Clarissa," appeared in the *Critical Review* of September 1761 (12, art. 8: 203–11) and was translated under the title "Parallele entre la Clarice de Richardson & la nouvelle Eloïse de M. Rousseau" in the *Journal étranger* in December 1761 (art. 11: 184–95). The death of Richardson in July 1761 revived interest in him in France, inspiring Diderot's "Éloge de Richardson," first published in the *Journal étranger* of January 1762 (Rousseau's novel is conspicuously absent from Diderot's discussion.) See Thomas O. Beebee, *Clarissa on the Continent* (University Park: Pennsylvania State University Press, 1990), and Georges May, "The Influence of English Fiction on the French Mid-Eighteenth-Century Novel," in *Aspects of the Eighteenth Century,* ed. Earl R. Wasserman (Baltimore: Johns Hopkins Press, 1965), 265–80.

8. References in Rousseau's letters suggest that he knew some but not much English. On August 28, 1761, Rousseau sent Mme de Luxembourg a copy of "la Julie Angloise" and asked for her observations on this English translation of his novel in preparation for a new edition, explaining: "je n'entends pas assés la langue pour me fier aux miennes" (*Correspondance complète de Jean Jacques Rousseau,* ed. R. A. Leigh [Geneva: Institut et Musée Voltaire, 1965–98]], 9: 106). In a letter written on May 25, 1764, Rousseau declined an invitation to abridge Richardson's works, writing: "D'ailleurs, n'entendant pas l'Anglois, il me faudroit toutes les traductions qui ont été faites pour les comparer et choisir, et tout cela est embarrassant pour vous [et] pour moi, ou plutot pour tous les deux" (ibid., 20: 85–86).

9. The *Journal étranger* of March 1762 included a translation of Morden's letters describing the burial (126–38) and subsequent editions included some version

of this supplement (see Beebee, *Clarissa on the Continent*, 187, 207). See also Frank Howard Wilcox, "Prévost's Translations of Richardson's Novels," *Modern Philology* 12 (1925–26): 341–411.

10. When the first part of Prévost's translation of *Sir Charles Grandison* was published, Grimm wrote: "Il faut avoir bonne opinion de soi pour se faire ainsi sculpteur du marbre de M. Richardson" (January 15, 1756); when the last part appeared, he wrote: "M. l'abbé Prévost, qui avait déjà fort tronqué les derniers volumes de *Clarisse* dont il n'y avait pas un mot à perdre, a absolument estropié le roman de *Grandisson*" (August 1, 1758) (*Correspondance littéraire, philosophique et critique, par Grimm, Diderot, Raynal, Meister, etc.,* ed. Maurice Tourneux, 16 vols. [Paris: Garnier, 1877–82], 3: 161; 4: 24–25). In 1751, when the translation of *Clarissa* first appeared, Grimm wrote: "Ce long ouvrage, dont il ne parait encore que la moitié, fait beaucoup de bruit à Paris qu'il n'y a de succès. . . . J'ai éprouvé dans la lecture de ce livre une chose qui n'est pas ordinaire, le plaisir le plus vif et l'ennui le plus assommant" (January 25, 1751; 2: 24–25). Marmontel praises Prévost's talents as a translator in the *Mercure de France* of August 1758. Diderot, who read *Clarissa* in English, castigated Prévost in his "Éloge de Richardson": "Vous qui n'avez lu les ouvrages de Richardson que dans votre élégante traduction française, et qui croyez les connaître, vous vous trompez" (Diderot, *Oeuvres esthétiques,* ed. Paul Vernière [Paris: Garnier, 1968], 36). Although Diderot and Rousseau had broken off relations by the time the "Éloge" was published in 1762, Rousseau obviously might have heard Diderot talk about or read the Testament and burial scenes between 1751 and 1758.

11. In *Jean-Jacques Rousseau and the Cosmopolitan Spirit,* trans. J. W. Matthews (New York: Burt Franklin, 1965), Joseph Texte notes that Rousseau saw Prévost frequently during 1751, and he suggests that Rousseau may have read Prévost's translation of *Clarissa* in manuscript (ibid., 111, 161, 227). In trying to explain why Prévost abridged the last volume of *Clarissa,* Jean Sgard suggests that his publisher may have forced him to make cuts; and he argues further that Rousseau may have influenced Prévost to abridge Richardson's text (Sgard, *Prévost romancier* [Paris: Librairie José Corti, 1968], 544). (When asked by Charles-Joseph Panckoucke to abridge Richardson's works in 1764, Rousseau wrote: "Ceux de Richardson en ont besoin incontestablement. . . . J'oserais tenter de faire ce que vous me proposez" [*Correspondance complète de Jean Jacques Rousseau,* ed. Leigh, 20: 85–86].) Rousseau includes Prévost among his friends at this time, calling him an "homme très aimable et très simple, dont le coeur vivifiait ses écrits, digne de l'immortalité, et qui n'avait rien dans l'humeur, ni dans sa société, du sombre coloris qu'il donnait à ses ouvrages" (Rousseau, *Confessions* [Paris: Garnier, 1964], 443). It is possible that some of the excised letters concerning Clarissa's corpse and funeral were present in an early version of the translation and that Rousseau saw them in the original manuscript or that he had discussions with Prévost about the English text and the translation when Prévost was trying to decide which letters to cut. Henri Rod-

dier argues that Prévost's translation of *Grandisson* had a significant influence on Rousseau when he was writing *La Nouvelle Héloïse* (Roddier, *L'Abbé Prévost: L'Homme et l'oeuvre* [Paris: Hatier-Boivin, 1955], 172–76).

12. In the *Lettre à d'Alembert sur les spectacles,* the composition of which over-lapped with that of *La Nouvelle Héloïse,* Rousseau praises *Pamela* in one footnote and in another writes, "On n'a jamais fait encore, en quelque langage que ce soit, de roman égal à *Clarisse,* ni même approchant" (Rousseau, *Du contract social et autres oeuvres politiques* [Paris: Garnier, 1975], 166, 189). *Julie* contains a footnote that quarrels with Richardson's opinion of love at first sight (319), as well as some-what derogatory allusions to Richardson in the final footnote and in the second preface (733, 750). In the *Confessions,* Rousseau seems defensive about Richardson; after discussing the publication of *Julie,* he complains about Diderot's "Éloge de Richardson" and writes: "si, toute chose égale, la simplicité du sujet ajoute à la beauté de l'ouvrage, les romans de Richardson, supérieurs en tant d'autres choses, ne sauraient, sur cet article, entrer en parallèle avec le mien" (if, all things being equal, the simplicity of the subject adds to beauty of the work, then Richardson's novels, superior in so many other things, would not on this article be able to be on a par with mine) (Rousseau, *Confessions,* 645).

13. See Duncan-Eaves, "Graphic Illustration of the Novels of Samuel Richard-son, 1740–1810"; Vera Salomons, *Gravelot* (London: John & Edward Bumpus, 1911); and Robert Halsbard, "The Rococo in England: Book Illustrators, Mainly Gravelot and Bentley," *Burlington Magazine* 127 (1985): 870–80.

14. Rousseau "left nothing to the artist's judgement" and the illustrations are "mere dictations," Salomons claims (*Gravelot,* 30). Rousseau's comments are very detailed, specifying (for example) the angle of a character, clothing, the shape of a face, and the size of his heroines' breasts: "Je trouve dans les desseins que Julie et Claire ont le sein trop plat. Les Suissesses ne l'ont pas ainsi. Probablement M. Coindet n'ignore pas que les femmes de nôtre pays ont plus de tétons que les Parisiennes" (November 5, 1760, in *Correspondance complète de Jean Jacques Rousseau,* ed. Leigh, 7: 295; see also letters of October 31, 1760 [7: 274], November 11, 1760 [7: 309–10], and December 7, 1760 [7: 341]). On January 1, 1761 Rousseau wrote a long letter criticizing and demanding changes in "la dernière estampe," the tableau of the deathbed scene (ibid., 8: 12–13). See Maurice Cranston, *The Noble Savage: Jean-Jacques Rousseau, 1754–1762* (London: Penguin Press), 154, 167, 235–36, 260. For discussions of the illustrations in *Julie* and the relations between image and text in the novel and "Sujets d'estampes," see Philip Stewart, "*Julie* et ses légendes," *Studies on Voltaire and the Eighteenth Century* 260 (1989): 257–78; Philip Stewart, *Engraven Desire: Eros, Image, and Text in the French Eighteenth Cen-tury* (Durham, N.C.: Duke University Press, 1992), 19–21; and Claude Labrosse, *Lire au XVIIIe siècle: "La Nouvelle Héloïse" et ses lecteurs* (Lyon: Presses universi-taires de Lyon; Paris: C.N.R.S., 1985), 209–40.

15. Some recent critical discussions about the relation between *Clarissa* and

Julie have tried to go beyond a concern with influence. Bryon R. Wells, for example, in pursuing what he calls "parallel readings" of the two novels, argues that "the debate on the question of influence which Richardson's novel(s) may have had in the writing of *La Nouvelle Héloïse* is fundamentally unproductive and essentially moot." Yet Wells's insistence that "to read a strong Richardsonian intertext in Rousseau's novel" is "to undermine the latter's originality" still reflects the anxiety of earlier critics that evidence about influence would somehow diminish Rousseau's originality or genius (Wells, *Clarissa and La Nouvelle Héloïse: Dialectics of Struggle with Self and Others* [Ravenna: Longo Editore, 1985], 148–49). Although this chapter is not about the question of influence, I suggest that once released from this critical anxiety about influence and originality, it should be possible to find the question of *Clarissa*'s presence in the text of *Julie* interesting and important to an understanding of the novel. I suggest further that the likelihood that Rousseau read Richardson's novel in translation does not weaken the link between the two novels; rather, it means that we may need to attend to Prévost's as well as Richardson's language in order to hear the echoes that resonate between *Clarissa* and *Julie*. For an interesting discussion of *Julie* as an inversion of *Clarissa*, see Gregory L. Ulmer, "*Clarissa* and *La Nouvelle Héloïse*," *Comparative Literature* 4 (1972): 289–308. Two comparisons that focus on the death scenes are Roseann Runte, "Dying Words: The Vocabulary of Death in Three Eighteenth-Century English and French Novels," *Canadian Review of Comparative Literature* 6 (1979): 360–68; and Julie A. Strome, "'An Exit so Happy': The Deaths of Julie and Clarissa," *Canadian Review of Comparative Literature* 10 (1987): 192–210. See also the paired readings of the novels in Nancy K. Miller, *The Heroine's Text: Readings in the French and English Novel, 1722–1782* (New York: Columbia University Press, 1980), 83–115.

16. Rousseau, *Julie*, 731: "It is no longer I who speak to thee; I am already in death's embrace. When thou seeth this Letter, worms will gnaw thy lover's face, and her heart where thou shalt no longer dwell" (610).

17. Richardson, *Clarissa*, 8: 97–98/1413.

18. Ibid., 7: 212/1253; 7: 336/1319.

19. Ibid., 5: 312–13/895–96.

20. Ibid., 7: 331/1316.

21. Ibid., 8: 98/1413.

22. Ibid., 5: 303–4/890. See Catherine Gallagher, *Nobody's Story: The Vanishing Acts of Women in the Marketplace, 1670–1820* (Berkeley: University of California Press, 1994), esp. 203–56.

23. Ibid., 5: 352/916.

24. Ibid., 8: 44, 46/1384. She does write: "I will not, on any account, that it be opened; and it is my desire, that it shall not be touched but by those of my own Sex" (ibid., 8: 97/1413).

25. Ibid., 8: 125/1427.

26. Ibid., 8: 182/1457.

27. Ibid., 7: 422/1357.

28. Ibid., 7: 412/1351.

29. Ibid., 5: 330/904. Lovelace's voyeuristic interest in "half of one pretty foot only visible" when he beholds her "sleepy lifelessness" distinguishes his acts of beholding from those of Morden and Belford. One can detect in these scenes the influence of similar moments in Marivaux, esp. in *La Vie de Marianne*.

30. Ibid., 8: 3–5/1360–61.

31. Ibid., 8: 14/1367.

32. Clarissa concedes that "if he come while I *can* see, I *will* see him," ordering the screen to be placed so "he might not see what was behind it" (Ibid., 7: 412–16/1351–53).

33. Ibid., 8: 6/1361.

34. Ibid., 8: 5/1361.

35. In "Thomas Edwards and the Dialectics of Clarissa's Death Scene" (*Eighteenth-Century Life* 16 [1992]: 130–52), David C. Hensley, following Margaret Doody and Mark Kinkead-Weekes, notes that Clarissa's death "is above all an *inner* process in which Clarissa rejoices that she can at last withdraw from 'beholders eyes.'" Hensley argues: "Though mediated by Belford's still rakishly theatricalizing gaze, Clarissa's death is the ultimate antitheatrical event in the novel. This paradox is underscored by her failing eyesight, a figural fulfillment of her stubborn non-ocular ideal of integrity" (146). I would emphasize the paradox in what Hensley calls "Richardson's paradoxical antitheatrical views" (149). For a comprehensive analysis of the ways in which eighteenth-century French painters and art critics use strategies to neutralize or deny the inherent theatricality of their compositions—for example, in making a centrally displayed figure blind or asleep or dying—see Fried, *Absorption and Theatricality: Painting and Beholder in the Age of Diderot*. I discuss the problem of theatricality in the eighteenth-century novel in *The Figure of Theater: Shaftesbury, Defoe, Adam Smith, and George Eliot* (New York: Columbia University Press, 1986) and *The Surprising Effects of Sympathy: Marivaux, Diderot, Rousseau, and Mary Shelley* (Chicago: University of Chicago Press, 1988). Stewart discusses the "sleeping figure" in eighteenth-century French engravings and illustrations in *Engraven Desire*, 175–98. For related discussions of Clarissa's death, see Margaret Ann Doody, *A Natural Passion: A Study of the Novels of Samuel Richardson* (Oxford: Clarendon, 1974), 151–87; Mark Kinkead-Weekes, *Samuel Richardson: Dramatic Novelist* (London: Methuen, 1973), 259–73. See also Carol Houlihan Flynn, *Samuel Richardson: A Man of Letters* (Princeton: Princeton University Press, 1982), 39–45; William Warner, *Reading Clarissa: The Struggles of Interpretation* (New Haven: Yale University Press, 1979), 63–87; and Ira Konigsberg, *Samuel Richardson and the Dramatic Novel* (Lexington: University of Kentucky Press, 1968), 74–94. Terry Eagleton discusses the death as a public event in *The Rape of Clarissa* (Minneapolis: University of Minnesota Press, 1982), 74.

36. For a useful discussion about Clarissa as body, portrait, and visual representation, see Janet E. Aikins, "Richardson's 'speaking pictures,'" in *Samuel Richardson: Tercentary Essays,* ed. Margaret Ann Doody and Peter Sabor (Cambridge: Cambridge University Press, 1989), 146–66. For a discussion of the status of the visual image in Richardson's work, see Doody, *Natural Passion,* 216–40.

37. Richardson, *Clarissa,* 8: 90/1409.

38. Ibid., 8: 70/1398. Castle describes the coffin as "a literalization of that hermeneutic situation which has conditioned Clarissa's tragedy." She emphasizes the death of the author here—"the disappearance of the authorial body"—to suggest that it undermines authority and introduces indeterminacy (Terry Castle, *Clarissa's Ciphers: Meaning and Disruption in Richardson's "Clarissa"* [Ithaca, N.Y.: Cornell University Press, 1982], 145). See also Elizabeth Bronfen, *Over Her Dead Body: Death, Femininity, and the Aesthetic* (Manchester: University Press, 1992), 146–50; Garrett Stewart, *Death Sentences: Styles of Dying in British Fiction* (Cambridge, Mass.: Harvard University Press, 1984).

39. Richardson, *Clarissa,* 8: 70/1398.

40. Ibid., 8: 87/1406.

41. Ibid., 8: 20/1370.

42. Ibid., 2: 264–65/343; 2: 182/299. Richardson, *Lettres angloises,* trans. Prévost: "Mais pourquoi m'arrêter à des maux imaginaires, lorsque j'en ai de si réels à combattre?" (4: 131); "Je lui ai répondu que tout ce qu'on s'imagine fortement produit dans le temps plus d'effet qu'une simple imagination, quoique les autres puissent n'en pas juger de même" (4: 6).

43. Richardson, *Clarissa,* 8: 8/1363.

44. Richardson, *Lettres angloises,* trans. Prévost, 13: 7. According to the translation, the time is "quatre minutes précises après six heures."

45. I have altered the translation to preserve the Richardsonian present tense.

46. Richardson, *Clarissa,* 8: 79/1403; id., *Lettres angloises,* trans. Prévost, 13: 142. The letter recounting Anna Howe's experience with the corpse did not appear in the French translation until 1762. See my discussion of the publication history in nn. 9, 10, and 11, above.

47. Ibid., 8: 78/1402; Richardson, *Lettres angloises,* trans. Prévost, 13: 140.

48. I have adapted the translation to preserve the Richardsonian present tense and key terms.

49. My translation.

50. I have adapted parts of the translation in this paragraph. For discussions of the veil, see Jean Starobinski, *Jean-Jacques Rousseau: La Transparence et l'obstacle* (Paris: Gallimard, 1971), 139–48; John Lechte, "Woman and the Veil—Or Rousseau's Fictive Body," *French Studies,* 423–39; and Paul Pelckmans, "Le rêve du voile dans *La Nouvelle Héloïse," Revue Romane,* 86–97.

51. See Candace Waid, *Edith Wharton's Letters from the Underworld: Fictions of*

Women and Writing (Chapel Hill: University of North Carolina Press, 1991), 17–49. As Waid observes, Wharton first intended to name her heroine Juliet. Lily's final deathbed tableau recalls and in some ways repeats the *tableau vivant* that she has performed as Reynolds's "Mrs. Lloyd." Waid links Lily's death to *Clarissa* in "The Building of *The House of Mirth*," in *Writing the American Classics, Part Two*, ed. Tom Quirk (Columbia: University of Missouri Press, 1996), 160–86.

52. Diderot, *Oeuvres esthétiques*, 868–69.

53. Richardson, *Clarissa*, 8: 78/1402; id., *Lettres angloises*, trans. Prévost, 13: 141.

54. Richardson, *Lettres angloises*, trans. Prévost, 13: 5–6. Richardson: "And down sunk her head upon her pillow, she fainting away, and drawing from us her hands. We thought she was gone; and each gave way to a violent burst of grief. But soon shewing signs of returning life, our attention was again engaged" (8: 6/1362).

55. Claire herself writes earlier: "Je sais bien qu'un songe n'amène pas un événement, mais j'ai toujours peur que l'événement n'arrive à sa suite" (632) (I know full well a dream does not bring about an event, but I always fear the event will come to pass as a consequence [530]).

56. Lovelace writes: "Me pardonneras-tu, de t'entretenir d'une misérable vision? Tu en concluras du moins, que la nuit comme le jour, ma Clarisse m'est toujours présente" (Richardson, *Lettres angloises*, trans. Prévost, 12: 67–69). In the English text, Lovelace describes how he "found wrapt in my arms her azure robe (all stuck thick with stars of embossed silver) which I had caught hold of in hopes of detaining her; but that was all that was left me of my beloved Clarissa. . . . I awakened in a panic; and was as effectually disordered for half an hour, as if my dream had been a reality. Wilt thou forgive me troubling thee with such visionary stuff? Thou wilt see by it, only, that sleeping or waking, my Clarissa is always present with me" (7: 148/1218).

57. Richardson, *Lettres angloises*, trans. Prévost, 12: 94.

58. Ibid., 4: 130–31; Richardson: "I awoke in a cold sweat, trembling, and in agonies; and still the frightful images raised by it, remain upon my memory. But why should I, who have such *real* evils to contend with, regard *imaginary* ones? This, no doubt, was owing to my disturbed imagination" (2: 264–65 [343]).

59. As Carol Flynn notes, Clarissa's death is in some sense prefigured in the first pages of the novel when she refers to a near-fatal illness. In her first letter in the book, Clarissa writes: "I have sometimes wished, that it had pleased God to have taken me in my last fever" (1: 5/41). After Clarissa's misfortunes, Mrs. Norton remarks, "When at Nine years old, and afterwards at Eleven, you had a dangerous fever, how incessantly did we all grieve, and pray. . . . Yet *now*, my dear, as it had proved . . . what a much more desirable event, both for you, and for us, would it have been, had we *then* lost you!" (7: 30/1154). See Flynn, *Samuel Richardson*, 39. Writing to Lovelace at the time of Belton's death that "thou hast not quite cured me of the Metaphorical," Belford presents an "Allegory" that begins: "We are apt

to hope too much, not considering that the Seeds of Death are sown in us when we begin to love, and grow up, till, like rampant Weeds, they choak the tender flower of life, which declines in us, as those Weeds flourish" (7: 189/1240).

60. Richardson, *Lettres angloises,* trans. Prévost, 4: 6. Richardson, *Clarissa:* "I said that whatever we strongly imagined was, in its effects, at the time, *more* than imaginary, although to others it might not appear so" (2: 182/299).

61. Rousseau, *Julie,* 699: "Whatever role one may have played in life, one must not playact at one's death" (584).

62. For an insightful discussion of the portrait and related scenes that shares many of the concerns of this reading, see Françoise Meltzer, *Salomé and the Dance of Writing: Portraits of Mimesis in Literature* (Chicago: University of Chicago Press, 1987), 127–58. Paul de Man discusses the status of "portrait" and "tableau" in his reading of the second preface in *Allegories of Reading: Figural Language in Rousseau, Nietzsche, Rilke, and Proust* (New Haven: Yale University Press, 1979), 188–220. See also Dorothea E. Von Mücke, *Virtue and the Veil of Illusion: Generic Innovation and the Pedagogical Project in Eighteenth-Century Literature* (Stanford: Stanford University Press, 1991), 115–60.

63. Richardson, *Clarissa,* 8: 44/1383; id., *Lettres angloises,* trans. Prévost, 13: 38.

64. Richardson, *Lettres angloises,* trans. Prévost, 13: 24. Richardson, *Clarissa:* "Nor had death, which changed all things, a power to alter her lovely features!" (8: 20/1370).

65. Richardson, *Clarissa,* 8: 74/1400.

66. Ibid., 8: 52/1388.

67. Richardson, *Lettres angloises,* trans. Prévost, 13: 44–45.

68. Julie also seems to come back to life in the last letter in which Claire cites the words that she imagines Julie's voice calling to her. We might see in Clarissa's ten posthumous letters, her will, and the emblems and inscriptions on the lid of her coffin—all of which keep her talking or at least being read for many pages after her death—Richardson's efforts to preserve Clarissa or at least his refusal to let her die.

69. Geoffrey Hartman uses the phrase "representation-compulsion" in a different context in "The Interpreter: A Self-Analysis," in id., *The Fate of Reading and Other Essays* (Chicago: University of Chicago Press, 1975), 8.

70. See the discussion of this scene and related issues in Marshall, *Surprising Effects of Sympathy,* 105–34.

71. Rousseau, *Julie,* 725: "The event is not predicted because it will happen; but it happens because it was predicted" (606).

72. For a discussion of this tradition, see Rensselaer W. Lee, *Writing on Trees: Ariosto into Art* (Princeton: Princeton University Press, 1977).

73. Richardson, *Clarissa,* 8: 20/1370; id., *Lettres angloises,* trans. Prévost, 13: 24.

74. See the end of the fourth book of the *Confessions:* "Comme en général les objets font moins d'impression sur moi que leurs souvenirs, et que toutes mes

idées sont en images, les premiers traits qui se sont gravés dans ma tête y sont de-meurés, et ceux qui s'y sont empreints dans la suite se sont plutôt combinés avec eux qu'ils ne les ont effacés" (198) (As, in general, objects make less of an impres-sion on me than do memories, and all my ideas are in images, the first traits that engraved themselves in my head have remained there, and those which were sub-sequently imprinted have combined with rather than effaced them). For a discus-sion of these images in relation to autobiography and sympathy, see Marshall, *Sur-prising Effects of Sympathy,* 166–77.

75. Peter Brooks discusses the fetishistic aspect of this letter, as well as the rela-tion between Julie's body and writing, in *Body Work: Objects of Desire in Modern Narrative* (Cambridge, Mass.: Harvard University Press, 1993), 43–47. For another account of the body in eighteenth-century literature, see Carol Houlihan Flynn, *The Body in Swift and Defoe* (Cambridge: Cambridge University Press, 1990).

76. Richardson, *Clarissa,* 4: 39. Richardson, *Lettres angloises,* trans. Prévost: "& que je ne suis, en quelque sorte, qu'un *zero* pour le *faire valoir* & pour *grossir la somme de mes douleurs*" (7: 152).

77. The note to the letter, which takes issue with Richardson by name, ob-serves that "M. Richardson se moque beaucoup de ces attachemens nés de la pre-mière vue" (319) (Mr. Richardson makes great fun of these attachments born of first sight [280]). In the preface, a complaint about works addressed to young girls identifies "les modernes romans anglais" (750) (modern English novels [17]).

78. St. Preux himself alludes to "les lettres d'Héloïse et d'Abélard" (60) (the letters of Heloise and Abelard [70]) early in the narrative. For a discussion of the significance of this story in the novel, see Peggy Kamuf, *Fictions of Feminine De-sire: Disclosures of Heloise* (Lincoln: University of Nebraska Press, 1982), 97–122.

Chapter 5 The Business of Tragedy

1. Unless otherwise noted, citations refer to the first edition, Henry Macken-zie, *Julia de Roubigné, a Tale. In a Series of Letters. Published by the Author of The Man of Feeling and The Man of the World,* 2 vols. (London, 1777).

2. Mackenzie explains that the description of a minor character is included be-cause "the picture it exhibited pleased myself" (2: 46). On the opposition of nar-rative and sentiment, see Timothy Dykstal, "The Sentimental Novel as Moral Phi-losophy: The Case of Henry Mackenzie," *Genre* 27 (1994): 59–81.

3. "Poetry and Business: A Moral Tale," in *The Works of Henry Mackenzie, Esq.,* 8 vols. (Edinburgh, 1808), 8: 24–33. For some background, see Gillian Skinner, *Sensibility and Economics in the Novel, 1740–1800: The Price of a Tear* (New York: St. Martin's Press, 1999), although the discussion of Mackenzie (91–116) does not mention *Julia de Roubigné.*

4. He notes of the "bundle of little episodes, put together without art," that "had the name of Marmontel, or a Richardson, been on the title-page—'tis odds

that I would have wept" (Henry Mackenzie, *The Man of Feeling* [1771; New York: Norton, 1958], n.p.).

5. Anthony Ashley Cooper, Lord Shaftesbury, *Characteristics of Men, Manners, Opinions, Times, etc.*, ed. John M. Robertson, 2 vols. (1900; rpt. Gloucester, Mass.: Peter Smith, 1963), 1: 198. See David Marshall, *The Figure of Theater: Shaftesbury, Defoe, Adam Smith, and George Eliot* (New York: Columbia University Press, 1986), 9–70.

6. "It appears, accordingly, from the experience of all ages and nations, I believe, that the work done by freemen comes much cheaper in the end than that performed by slaves," Adam Smith writes in *The Wealth of Nations* (1776; New York: Random House, 1937, 81), which appeared in 1776, one year before the publication of *Julia de Roubigné*. See also the discussion of the use of "metayers" among slave cultivators (366–68).

7. Noting that Scottish writers in the eighteenth century were "pretty well agreed in opposing slavery," Harold William Thompson writes: "Just before the publication of Mackenzie's *Julia* the Scottish nation had been stirred by the case of Joseph Knight, an African negro purchased in Jamaica by a Scottish gentleman and brought to Scotland where the slave claimed a right to liberty. Three of Mackenzie's friends—Dundas, Maclaurin, and Maconochie—argued for the negro; another friend, Cullen, spoke for the master. The Lords of Session decided in favor of the negro" (Thompson, *A Scottish Man of Feeling: Some Account of Henry Mackenzie, Esq., of Edinburgh and of the Golden Age of Burns and Scott* [London: Oxford University Press, 1931], 151). See also Reginald Coupland, *The British Anti-Slavery Movement* (London: Frank Cass, 1933); and Bruce Lenman, *Integration, Enlightenment, and Industrialization: Scotland, 1746–1832* (Toronto: University of Toronto Press, 1991). Mary Wollstonecraft frequently compares the situation of women to that of slaves in *Vindication of the Rights of Woman;* for example, citing Knox's *Essays,* she writes: "Supposing that women are voluntary slaves—slavery of any kind is unfavourable to human happiness and improvement," she asks: "who can tell, how many generations may be necessary to give vigour to the virtue and talents of the freed posterity of abject slaves?" (Wollstonecraft, *Vindication of the Rights of Woman* [Harmondsworth, U.K.: Penguin Books, 1985], 171–72).

8. Mackenzie in *The Lounger,* No. 27 (August 6, 1785), in *Works of Henry Mackenzie,* 5: 229.

9. Mackenzie, *A Review of the Principal Proceedings of the Parliament of 1784,* in *Works of Henry Mackenzie,* 7: 362.

10. John Wesley's *Thoughts upon Slavery* (published in 1774, based on *Some Historical Accounts of Guinea,* published in Philadelphia in 1771 by Anthony Benezet) at one point directly addresses "captains, merchants, or planters" and asks: "Are you a man? Then you should have an human heart. But have you indeed? What is your heart made of? Is there no such principle as compassion there? Do you never feel another's pain? Have you no sympathy, no sense of human woe,

no pity for the miserable? When you saw the flowing eyes, the heaving breasts, or the bleeding sides and tortured limbs of your fellow-creatures, was you a stone, or a brute? Did you look upon them with the eyes of a tiger? When you squeezed the agonizing creatures down in the ship, or when you threw their poor mangled remains into the sea, had you no relenting? Did not one tear drop from your eye, one sigh escape from your breast? Do you feel no relenting now? If you do not, you must go on, till the measure of your iniquities is full. Then will the great God deal with you as you have dealt with them, and require all their blood at your hands" (*The Works of John Wesley*, ed. Thomas Jackson [1872], 11: 59–79).

11. For a discussion of Adam Smith's *Theory of Moral Sentiments* and eighteenth-century theories of sympathy, see Marshall, *Figure of Theater*, 165–92. See also David Marshall, *The Surprising Effects of Sympathy: Marivaux, Rousseau, Diderot, and Mary Shelley* (Chicago: University of Chicago Press, 1988). For relevant discussions of Mackenzie, see Elaine Ware, "Charitable Actions Reevaluated in the Novels of Henry Mackenzie," *Studies in Scottish Literature* 22 (1987): 132–41; G. A. Starr, "Sentimental Novels of the Later Eighteenth Century," in *The Columbia History of the British Novel*, ed. John Richetti (New York: Columbia University Press, 1994), 181–98; John Mullan, "The Language of Sentiment: Hume, Smith, and Henry Mackenzie," in *The History of Scottish Literature*, ed. Andrew Hook (Aberdeen: Aberdeen University Press, 1987), 273–89; John Dwyer, "Enlightened Spectators and Classical Moralists: Sympathetic Relations in Eighteenth-Century Scotland," in *Sociability and Society in Eighteenth-Century Scotland*, ed. John Dwyer and Richard B. Sher (Baltimore: Johns Hopkins University Press, 1991; reprint, Edinburgh: Mercat Press, 1993), 96–118; and Maureen Harkin, "Mackenzie's *Man of Feeling*: Embalming Sensibility," *ELH* 61 (1994): 317–40.

12. Mackenzie in *The Lounger* 28 (August 13, 1785), in *Works of Henry Mackenzie*, 5: 243–45.

13. Jean-Jacques Rousseau, *Lettre à M. d'Alembert sur les spectacles,* in *Du Contract social et autres oeuvres politiques* (Paris: Garnier Frères, 1975), 141 (my translation). See Marshall, *Surprising Effects of Sympathy*, 135–77.

14. Mackenzie in *The Lounger*, No. 28 (August 13, 1785), in *Works of Henry Mackenzie*, 5: 232–33.

15. Mackenzie in *The Lounger*, No. 20 (June 18, 1785), in *Works of Henry Mackenzie*, 5: 182–83.

16. These passions and feelings are said to be "in themselves blameless, nay, praiseworthy, but which, encouraged to a morbid excess, and coming into fatal though fortuitous concourse with each other, lead to the most disastrous consequence" (Scott cited in Thompson, *Scottish Man of Feeling*, 158). For an account of the influence of *Julia de Roubigné* on Scott, see Harry E. Shaw, "Scott, Mackenzie, and Structure in *The Bride of Lammermoor*," *Studies in the Novel* 13 (1981): 349–66.

17. Jean-Jacques Rousseau, *Julie ou La Nouvelle Héloïse*, ed. René Pomeau (Paris: Garnier, 1966), 258, 268. Translations are from *Julie, or the New Heloise,*

trans. Philip Stewart and Jean Vaché (Hanover, N.H.: University Press of New England, 1997), 228–29, 236. For a related discussion of these passages in *Julie,* see my chapter 5, 127–46. Kim Ian Michasiw discusses Mackenzie's reworking of *Julie* in "Imitation and Ideology: Henry Mackenzie's Rousseau," *Eighteenth-Century Fiction* 5 (1993): 153–76.

18. Rousseau, *Julie,* 270 (309 in translation).

19. Mackenzie in *The Lounger,* No. 28 (August 13, 1785), in *Works of Henry Mackenzie,* 5: 243. In *The Mirror,* No. 101 (April 25, 1780), a "reader" writes: "In books, whether moral or amusing, there are no passages more captivating both to the writer and the reader, than those delicate strokes of sentimental morality, which refer our actions to the determination of feeling. In these the poet, the novel-writer, and the essayist, have always delighted; you are not, therefore, singular, for having dedicated so much of the *Mirror* to sentiment and sensibility. I imagine, however, Sir, there is much danger in pushing these qualities too far; the rules of conduct should be founded on a basis more solid, if they are to guide us through the various situations of life; but the young enthusiast of sentiment and feeling is apt to despise those lessons of vulgar virtue and prudence, which would confine the movements of a soul formed to regulate itself by finer impulses" (*Works of Henry Mackenzie,* 5: 3–4). See also *The Lounger,* No. 20 (June 18, 1785): "The principal danger of novels, as forming a mistaken and pernicious system of morality, seems to me to arise from that contrast between one virtue or excellence and another, that war of duties which is to be found in many of them, particularly in that species called the sentimental. These have been chiefly borrowed from our neighbours the French, whose style of manners, and the very powers of whose language, give them a great advantage in the delineation of that nicety, that subtilty of feeling, those entanglements of delicacy, which are so much interwoven with the characters and conduct of the chief personages in many of their most celebrated novels" (*Works of Henry Mackenzie,* 5: 181). See also John Mullan, *Sentiment and Sociability: The Language of Feeling in the Eighteenth-Century* (Oxford: Clarendon Press, 1988), 114–46; John Dwyer, *Virtuous Discourse: Sensibility and Community in Late Eighteenth-Century Scotland* (Edinburgh: John Donald Publishers, 1987), 141–67; and Barbara M. Benedict, *Framing Feeling: Sentiment and Style in English Prose Fiction, 1745–1800* (New York: AMS Press, 1994), 117–32.

Chapter 6   Writing Masters and "Masculine Exercises" in The Female Quixote

Epigraph: Charlotte Lennox, *The Female Quixote, or The Adventures of Arabella* (London, 1752), ed. Margaret Dalziel, with an Introduction by Margaret Anne Doody and a Chronology of Charlotte Lennox and Appendix on "Johnson, Richardson, and *The Female Quixote*" by Duncan Isles (New York: Oxford University Press, 1989), 377. References are to this edition unless otherwise noted.

1. Rousseau's preface goes on to warn that any girl who dared to read even a

single page is ruined ("une fille perdue"), although once she has begun, "qu'elle achève de lire: elle n'a plus rien à risquer" (let her finish reading: she has nothing more to risk) (Jean-Jacques Rousseau, *Julie ou La Nouvelle Héloïse,* ed. René Pomeau [Paris: Garnier, 1960], 4; Samuel Richardson, *Pamela, or Virtue Rewarded* [New York: New American Library, 1980], 27).

2. See Ronald Paulson, *Don Quixote in England: The Aesthetics of Laughter* (Baltimore: Johns Hopkins University Press, 1998); Susan Staves, "Don Quixote in Eighteenth-Century England," *Comparative Literature* 24 (1972): 193–215. Michael McKeon discusses the significance of Cervantes, as well as the transformations of the romance tradition, in *The Origin of the English Novel, 1660–1740* (Baltimore: Johns Hopkins University Press, 1987).

3. See Doody, Introduction to Lennox, *Female Quixote,* ed. Dalziel, xxix; Patricia Meyer Spacks, *Desire and Truth: Functions of Plot in Eighteenth-Century Novels* (Chicago: University of Chicago Press, 1990), 24; Laurie Langbauer, *Women and Romance: The Consolations of Gender in the English Novel* (Ithaca, N.Y.: Cornell University Press, 1990), 79; and Deborah Ross, "Mirror, Mirror: The Didactic Dilemma of *The Female Quixote,*" *Studies in English Literature* 27 (1987): 462.

4. These details are repeated in book 4: Arabella declares that Charlotte makes a "ridiculous Mistake" in taking "a Nobleman for a Writing-master only because his Love put him upon such a Stratagem to obtain his Mistress," insisting that the "Writing master was some noble Stranger in Disguise" (Lennox, *Female Quixote,* ed. Dalziel, 142).

5. My focus on this problem is informed by Candace Waid's accounts of related issues in the fiction of Edith Wharton. See *Edith Wharton's Letters from the Underworld: Fictions of Women and Writing* (Chapel Hill: University of North Carolina Press, 1991). I also have benefited from Jill Campbell's discussions of gender and cross-dressing in *"Natural Masques": Gender, Identity, and Power in Fielding's Early Works* (Stanford: Stanford University Press, 1995). When I published this essay in article form in 1993, I did not have the benefit of Catherine Gallagher's important reading, "Fiction, Gender, and Authorial Property in the Career of Charlotte Lennox," in *Nobody's Story: The Vanishing Acts of Women Writers in the Marketplace, 1670–1820* (Berkeley: University of California Press, 1994), 145–202.

6. Although Arabella's early writing master is her father rather than her lover, soon after he dies she imagines that her uncle—that is, her father's brother, who replaces her father as the authority responsible for her—has incestuous desires for her. Later, Sir George, who is presented as a master of writing, becomes her suitor.

7. The theory that Johnson actually wrote the chapter (first argued by John Mitford in 1843 and endorsed by Miriam Small in her 1935 biography of Lennox) is based on stylistic similarities and it attests to Lennox's success in writing in Johnson's voice. See Mitford, *Gentleman's Magazine,* n.s., 20 (1843): 132–33; Miriam Rossiter Small, *Charlotte Ramsay Lennox: An Eighteenth-Century Lady of Letters* (New Haven: Yale University Press, 1935), 79–82. Spacks sums up the debate by as-

serting that "it hardly matters whether Johnson actually wrote the crucial chapter. . . . If not literally, at least metaphorically, Dr Johnson articulates the view of the world that persuades Arabella to abandon her dream of creating meaning and interest beyond the domestic sphere" (Spacks, *Desire and Truth*, 15). For Langbauer, "just as Arabella, once in this sphere, loses her voice, when Lennox calls on it in the penultimate chapter of *The Female Quixote,* so does she. Like Arabella's voice with the Doctor's, Lennox's blends with Dr Johnson's, so much so that it is impossible to know who really wrote the chapter—but whether Dr Johnson wrote it or whether he influenced a most faithful pastiche is immaterial" (Langbauer, *Women and Romance,* 82). See also Duncan Isles's very sensible discussion in "Johnson, Richardson, and *The Female Quixote,*" which appears as the Appendix to the Oxford edition, 419–28, esp. 422. In a recent analysis of typesetting and "signatures" as well as style, O. M. Brack Jr. and Susan Carlile argue "that the bibliographical evidence does not support intervention by an external agent and that, in fact, the entire work was written by Lennox herself" (Brack and Carlile, "Samuel Johnson's Contributions to Charlotte Lennox's *The Female Quixote,*" *Yale University Library Gazette* 77, 3–4 [2003]: 167).

8. See, e.g., Doody in Lennox, *Female Quixote,* ed. Dalziel, x, xxvii, and Spacks, *Desire and Truth,* 15. Glanville's sister arrives on the scene in the chapter following the adventure with Miss Groves and although her life has not been scandalous, she is also offended when Arabella requests a "Recital" of her "Adventures"; she accuses Arabella of trying to "draw [her] into a Confession" (89). Asked by Arabella to recount her "History" at the beginning of book 3, Miss Glanville insists, "It would not be worth your hearing; for really I have nothing to tell, that would make an History" (110). The countess whom Arabella meets at the end of book 8, who has great skill in "Poetry, Painting, and Musick" (322–23), resists Arabella's request for "the Recital of her Adventures" (327) in the same terms. Despite her fluency in "the Language of Romance" (325), she seems offended by the word "Adventures" and insists that in recounting the mere facts of her birth, christening, education, and marriage, "I have told you all the material Passages of my Life" (327).

9. Joseph F. Bartolomeo, "'Feminine' Tragedy and Quixotic Comedy," in *Matched Pairs: Gender and Intertextual Dialogue in Eighteenth-Century Fiction* (Newark: University of Delaware Press, 2002), 90–122, argues that *The Female Quixote* can be read as a satire of *Clarissa.*

10. Unlike Lennox's *The Life of Harriot Stuart* (1750), this novel does not seem to take seriously the threat of rape that preoccupies Arabella throughout the novel. Doody argues in relation to the Doctor's claims that "it is nonsense to tell a young woman that rape and abduction are only fictions. The novel itself has presented such dangers as distinctly possible in contemporary real life" (Lennox, *Female Quixote,* ed. Dalziel, xxx). Lennox's original plans for the ending of her novel may have involved *Clarissa;* see Isles, "Johnson, Richardson, and *The Female Quixote,*" 425–26.

11. Doody notes that "Sir George seizes the narrative in his own parodic mock-history" (Lennox, *Female Quixote,* ed. Dalziel, xxvii).

12. Langbauer, *Women and Romance,* 67.

13. "Instead of being in control of romance, the novel is drawn into and repeats it," Langbauer argues with a somewhat different emphasis (ibid.).

14. Of course, Lennox enters a tradition in which male authors from the beginning of the novel wrote fictitious first-person autobiographies of women.

15. Doody notes that Pierre Daniel Huet's 1670 *Traité de l'origine des romans* (translated into English in 1672 and 1715) "emphasizes the fact that the important novels *(romans)* of Scudéry were written by a woman" (Lennox, *Female Quixote,* ed. Dalziel, xvii). Huet writes: "None can, without Amazement, read those which a Maid, as Illustrious in her Modesty, as her Merit, has published under a Borrowed Name. . . . But Time has done her that Justice, which She denied her self; and has informed us, that the *Illustrious Bassa, Grand Cyrus,* and *Claelia,* are the Performances of Madam *de Scudery*" (Pierre Daniel Huet, *The History of Romances: An Enquiry into their Original,* trans. Stephen Lewis [1715], excerpted in *Novel and Romance, 1700–1800: A Documentary Record,* ed. Ioan Williams [New York: Barnes & Noble, 1970], 54).

16. My sense of the countess's role in the novel is indebted to conversations with Jill Campbell.

17. For a discussion of Shaftesbury's fictions, stances, and typography of dedications, see David Marshall, "The Characters of Books and Readers," in *The Figure of Theater: Shaftesbury, Defoe, Adam Smith, and George Eliot* (New York: Columbia University Press, 1986), 13–33.

18. In his account of the year 1762, Boswell writes, "He [Johnson] this year wrote also the Dedication to the Earl of Middlesex of Mrs. Lennox's 'Female Quixote,' and the Preface to the 'Catalogue of the Artists' Exhibition'" *(Boswell's Life of Johnson,* ed. George Birkbeck Hill, rev. L. F. Powell, 6 vols. [Oxford: Clarendon Press, 1934], 1: 367). The novel, of course, was published ten years earlier, in 1752. In the "Chronological Catalogue" of Johnson's prose works that prefaces the volume, the dedication appears under the year 1751 and is attributed to Johnson on the basis of "*inter. evid.*" (internal evidence) (19). The 1788 Stockdale supplement to Hawkins's edition of Johnson's *Works* includes the text of the dedication under the heading: "Dedication to the Female Quixote. By Mrs. Lennox. Published 1752" (*The Works of Samuel Johnson, LL.D.* [London, 1788], 14: 476–77). The inclusion of the texts in this volume is also said to be based on "internal evidence" (2). In his 1937 edition of *Samuel Johnson's Prefaces and Dedications,* writing at a time when Lennox's works are said to be "read only by literary antiquarians," A. T. Hazen attributes six of the dedications prefacing Lennox's works to Johnson. Hazen includes these six dedications while admitting his complete lack of "external evidence" (except for Boswell's indication that Johnson "acknowledged" the dedication to *Shakespear Illustrated*) (*Samuel Johnson's Prefaces and Dedications*

[New Haven: Yale University Press, 1937], 89, 107). It is certainly possible that Johnson wrote the dedication. However, even if Johnson were the author, Lennox might have had a hand in the composition, revision, or punctuation of the text. Perhaps Johnson wrote the dedication in a gesture of ironic symmetry, mirroring Lennox's concluding impersonation of him with his preemptive impersonation of her. Perhaps Lennox completed the penultimate chapter after the dedication was prepared. The dedication is equally suggestive if we imagine either Lennox or Johnson as the author—and perhaps most suggestive if we read it in the context of the textual dialogue that they seem to be conducting across and through the novel.

19. See, e.g., Doody in Lennox, *Female Quixote,* ed. Dalziel, xxv; Langbauer, *Women and Romance,* 88.

20. When Glanville becomes ill, Arabella instructs: "By all the Power I have over you, I command you to live" (134). She tells Sir Charles that "nothing is more common, than for a Gentleman, though ever so sick, to recover in Obedience to the Commands of that Person, who has an absolute Power over his Life" (145–46). These discussions about "her Power" (147) take on a more serious tone when the Doctor hopes "that no Life was ever lost by your Incitement" and Arabella, who feels guilty of "encouraging Violence and Revenge," considers "how nearly I have approached the Brink of Murder" (381).

21. Langbauer describes Arabella's "relation to romance" as "a form of repetition compulsion; she forever re-enacts the same romance conventions in the face of wildly different experiences" (Langbauer, *Women and Romance,* 73); see also Ronald Paulson, *Satire and the Novel in Eighteenth-Century England* (New Haven: Yale University Press, 1967), 276.

22. See Lennox, *Female Quixote,* ed. Dalziel, 62, 277.

23. [Adrien Perdou de Subligny,] *The Mock-Clelia: Being a Comical History of French Gallantries, and Novels, in Imitation of Dom Quixote* (London, 1678), 267. In the French: "elle se jetta pour le passer à la nage à l'imitation de celle qu'elle croyoit estre" *(La Fausse Clélie: Histoire Françoise, Galante et Comique* [Amsterdam, 1671], 207). In her Introduction to the novel, Margaret Dalziel notes that Subligny's novel "may have influenced" Lennox's "choice of events, since it ends with the heroine's riding her horse into a canal in imitation of Clelia's swimming the Tiber" *(The Female Quixote* [London: Oxford University Press, 1970], xvi).

24. [Madeleine de Scudéry,] *Clelia, An Excellent New Romance, Dedicated to Mademoiselle de Longeville. Written in French by the Exquisite Pen of Monsieur de Scudéry* (London, 1678), 691–94, 736. See *Clélie, Histoire Romaine. Par Mr. de Scudéry* (Paris, 1658–62), 5, 2 (1661): 903–34, 1324. Different verses appear in the original French.

25. We should recall that the narrator of *Don Quixote* claims at least initially to be translating the "History of Don Quixote of La Mancha, written by Cide Hamete Benengeli, Arabian historian" (Miguel de Cervantes Saavedra, *Don*

Quixote of la Mancha, trans. Walter Starkie [New York: New American Library, 1964]), 108.

26. "The Covent-Garden Journal, Number 24," in [Henry Fielding,] *The Covent-Garden Journal,* ed. Gerard Edward Jensen (New Haven: Yale University Press, 1915), 1: 279–80. Johnson notes in his brief account of *The Female Quixote* in *Gentleman's Magazine* that "Fielding, however emulous of Cervantes, and jealous of a rival, acknowledges in his paper of the 24th, that in many instances this copy excels the original" (March 1752; 22: 146). For more on Quixotism, see Small, *Charlotte Ramsay Lennox,* 64–117; Susan Staves, "Don Quixote in Eighteenth-Century England," *Comparative Literature* 24 (1972): 193–215; and Paulson, *Satire and the Novel in Eighteenth-Century England,* 115–21, and *Don Quixote in England,* 169–77.

27. Scudéry, *Clelia,* 693; *Clélie,* 920.

28. [Subligny,] *Mock-Clelia,* 267; *Fausse Clelie,* 206.

29. Commentators such as Small, who believe that Johnson wrote this chapter, find it necessary to interrupt their thesis at this point to suggest that Lennox inserted this extravagant praise of her patron into Johnson's text (Small, *Charlotte Ramsay Lennox,* 80).

30. Samuel Johnson, *The Rambler,* ed. Walter Jackson Bate and Albrecht B. Strauss (New Haven: Yale University Press, 1969), 2: 153. See the editor's note on p. 153 regarding Richardson's authorship of No. 97.

31. Samuel Richardson, *Pamela* (New York: New American Library, 1980), 29, 23.

32. Johnson, *Rambler,* 154–59.

33. Isles, Appendix, in Lennox, *Female Quixote,* ed. Dalziel, 420.

34. Johnson, *Rambler,* 239.

35. According to an account by John Hawkins (*The Works of Samuel Johnson* [London, 1787], 1: 285–86), Johnson organized a "whole night spent in festivity" to celebrate (in his words) "Mrs. Lennox's first literary child"; he "prepared for her a crown of laurel, with which, but not till he had invoked the muses by some ceremonies of his own invention, he encircled her brows." In his description of the night, Hawkins remarks on "the resemblance it bore to a debauch" (cited in Small, *Charlotte Ramsay Lennox,* 10–11).

36. Johnson, *Rambler,* 252, 239, 252.

37. See Ross, 458.

38. Scudéry, *Clelia,* 694; *Clélie,* 934.

39. Johnson, *Rambler,* 154, 158. The guest author of the *Rambler* probably refers to such numbers of the *Spectator* as No. 53 (1 May 1711), No. 129 (28 July 1711), No. 158 (31 August 1711), and No. 460 (18 August 1712). For more on the problem of theatricality in eighteenth-century literature, see my *The Figure of Theater: Shaftesbury, Defoe, Adam Smith, and George Eliot,* and *The Surprising Effects of Sympathy: Marivaux Diderot, Rousseau, and Mary Shelley* (Chicago: University of Chicago Press, 1988).

Chapter 7   Arguing by Analogy

1. David Hume, *Essays Moral, Political, and Literary,* ed. Eugene F. Miller (Indianapolis: Liberty Classics, 1985), 226. All further citations, unless otherwise noted, refer to this edition.

2. For background on taste and eighteenth-century aesthetics, see Peter Kivy, *The Seventh Sense: A Study of Francis Hutcheson's Aesthetics* (New York: Burt Franklin, 1976); Philip Flynn, "Scottish Aesthetics and the Search for a Standard of Taste," *Dalhousie Review* 60 (1980): 5–19; Samuel H. Monk, *The Sublime: A Study of Critical Theories in XVIII-Century England* (Ann Arbor: University of Michigan Press, 1960); Walter Jackson Bate, *From Classic to Romantic: Premises of Taste in Eighteenth-Century England* (Cambridge, Mass.: Harvard University Press, 1946); George Dickie, *The Century of Taste: The Philosophical Odyssey of Taste in the Eighteenth Century* (New York: Oxford University Press, 1996). For some discussions of Hume and taste not mentioned elsewhere, see Olivier Brunet, *Philosophie et esthetique chez David Hume* (Paris: A.-G. Nizet, 1965), 666–795; Teddy Brunius, *David Hume on Criticism* (Stockholm: Almquist & Wiksell, 1953), 74–90; Peter Jones, "Cause, Reason, and Objectivity in Hume's Aesthetics," *Hume: A Re-evaluation,* ed. Donald W. Livingston and James T. King (New York: Fordham University Press, 1976), 323–41; and Peter Kivy, "Hume's Neighbour's Wife: An Essay on the Evolution of Hume's Aesthetics," *British Journal of Aesthetics* 23 (1983): 195–208.

3. "Chacun a chez lui la règle ou le compas applicable à mes raisonnemens." Jean-Baptiste Du Bos, *Réflexions critiques sur la poésie et sur la peinture,* 3 vols. (1732–36), 4th ed. (Paris: Chez P.-J. Mariette, 1740) 2: 326.

4. Although still in the shadow of classical and neoclassical criticism, Addison condemns the critic who, "without entering into the soul of an author, has a few general rules, which, like mechanical instruments, he applies to the works of every writer." Richard Steele, Joseph Addison, Jonathan Swift, et al., *The Tatler,* ed. Donald F. Bond, 3 vols. (Oxford: Clarendon Press, 1987), 2: 149 (No. 165, April 29, 1710).

5. See R. L. Brett, *The Third Earl of Shaftesbury: A Study in Eighteenth-Century Literary Theory* (London: Hutchinson's University Library, 1951), 123–44; Jerome Stolnitz, "On the Origins of 'Aesthetic Disinterestedness,'" *Journal of Aesthetics and Art Criticism* 20 (1961–62): 131–43; Ernst Cassirer, *The Philosophy of the Enlightenment,* trans. Fritz C. A. Koelln and James P. Pettegrove (Princeton: Princeton University Press, 1951), 325. See my discussion and notes in the Introduction. Shaftesbury writes: "Reasons why a gentleman's taste if practical and empirical necessarily false: First Reason. Becomes interested, makes himself a party, espouses a manner, style" (*Second Characters or The Language of Forms,* ed. Benjamin Rand [New York: Greenwood Press, 1969], 112). For important background, see Lawrence E. Klein, *Shaftesbury and the Culture of Politeness* (Cambridge: Cambridge University Press, 1994).

6. Shaftesbury, *Second Characters,* 144. See Cassirer, *Philosophy of the Enlight-*

enment, 312–27. Shaftesbury writes in the *Characteristics* that the *je ne sais quoi* is "the unintelligible or the I know not what" that most people responding to a work of art, "feeling only by the effect whilst ignorant of the cause . . . suppose to be a kind of charm or enchantment of which the artist himself can give no account" (Anthony Ashley Cooper, Lord Shaftesbury, *Characteristics of Men, Manners, Opinions, Times,* ed. John M. Robertson, 2 vols. [1900; rpt. Gloucester, Mass.: Peter Smith, 1963], 1: 214). A character in Shaftesbury's *The Moralists* says, "All own the standard, rule and measure: but in applying it to things disorder arises, ignorance prevails, interest and passion breed disturbance" (2: 138). In his characterization of the skeptical position on taste, Hume reiterates the declaration in *The Moralists,* "there can be no such thing as real valuableness or worth; nothing in itself is estimable or amiable, odious or shameful. All is opinion. 'Tis opinion which makes beauty, and unmakes it. . . . Opinion is the law and measure" (2: 139).

7. This problem seems to have been especially pressing for eighteenth-century writers because the invention of the reading public in and by published books and periodicals contributed to a perceived crisis in public taste. In seeking to reform public taste, authors such as Addison and Steele were responding to a crisis that they helped to create through the proliferation of print and print culture. Writing in a somewhat different context about Addison's aim to "establish . . . a Taste of polite Writing," Neil Saccamano notes: "The 'great and only End' of *The Spectator* was to institute the very cultural subject to which it was supposedly addressed" ("The Consolations of Ambivalence: Habermas and the Public Sphere," *MLN* 106 [1991]: 695). See also Saccamano, "Authority and Publication: The Works of 'Swift,'" *Eighteenth Century* 25 (1984): 241–62.

8. Joseph Addison and Richard Steele, *The Spectator,* ed. Donald F. Bond, 5 vols. (Oxford: Clarendon Press, 1965), 3: 528 (No. 409, June 19, 1712) 1: 123 (No. 29, April 3, 1711). For more on Addison and taste, see Lee Andrew Elioseff, *The Cultural Milieu of Addison's Literary Criticism* (Austin: University of Texas Press, 1963), 181–88; and David Marshall, "Shaftesbury and Addison: Criticism and the Public Taste," in *The Cambridge History of Literary Criticism,* vol. 4: *The Eighteenth Century,* ed. H. B. Nisbet and Claude Rawson (Cambridge: Cambridge University Press, 1997), 633–57.

9. Joshua Reynolds, *Discourses on Art,* ed. Robert R. Work (New Haven: Yale University Press, 1975), 133 (Seventh Discourse).

10. Hume's characterization of the skeptical position rehearses some of the formulations contained in "The Sceptic" (159–80). Cf. "Of the Delicacy of Taste and Passion" (3–8). At the beginning of *An Enquiry Concerning the Principles of Morals,* Hume writes: "Truth is disputable; not taste: what exists in the nature of things is the standard of our judgement; what each man feels within himself in the standard of sentiment" (*Enquiries Concerning Human Understanding and Concerning the Principles of Morals,* ed. L. A. Selby-Bigge, 3d ed. rev. P. H. Nidditch [Oxford: Clarendon Press, 1975], 171).

11. In the "Pleasures of the Imagination" series, discussing differences in "Taste," Addison explains that "to have a true Relish, and form a right judgment of a Description, a Man should be born with a good Imagination, and must have weighed the Force and Energy that lie in the several Words of a Language." He adds, "The fancy must be warm, to retain the Print of those Images it hath received from outward Objects; and the judgment discerning" (Addison and Steele, *Spectator,* 3: 561 [No. 416, June 27, 1712]). Recall Shaftesbury's warnings about "ignorance . . . interest and passion" in the application of "the standard, rule and measure" that one carries within (Shaftesbury, *Characteristics,* 2: 138). In *Miscellaneous Reflections,* Shaftesbury declares, "A legitimate and just taste can neither be begotten, made, conceived, or produced without the antecedent labour and pains of criticism" (2: 257).

12. David Hume, *A Treatise of Human Nature,* ed. L. A. Selby-Bigge, 2d ed. rev. P. H. Nidditch (Oxford: Clarendon Press, 1978), 274.

13. Peter Kivy, "Hume's Standard of Taste: Breaking the Circle," *British Journal of Aesthetics* 7 (1967): 60. Kivy suggests that Hume's argument is not completely circular. See also Kivy, *Seventh Sense,* 143. Jeffrey Wieand observes that Hume would have us identify the ideal judge by examining "his verdicts to see if he consistently identifies beautiful and deformed things correctly. Yet we cannot do this because we only know what is beautiful and deformed on the basis of what the true judges say" (Wieand, "Hume's Two Standards of Taste," *Philosophical Quarterly* 34 [1983]: 139). James Noxon notes that "the aesthetically valuable" is identified by "the authoritative judgments of connoisseurs" whereas the connoisseur establishes his authority by "his ability to recognize the aesthetically valuable" (Noxon, "Hume's Opinion of Critics," *Journal of Aesthetics and Art Criticism* 20 [1961]: 160). Noxon also suggests that Hume's logic might be better than it at first appears. Stuart Brown considers the argument of the essay to be circular because Hume claims that "a standard of taste exists because the common sense and common sentiment of all ages are in agreement in judging certain authors, and they agree because there is a standard of taste upon which their judgments have been formed" (Brown, "Observations on Hume's Theory of Taste," *English Studies* 20 [1938]: 196). See also Noel Carroll, "Hume's Standard of Taste," *Journal of Aesthetics and Art Criticism* 43 (1984): 189–92.

14. Noting that Hume's essay "appears to be deeply at odds with itself," Barbara Hernstein Smith also remarks: "The *buts* that recur at the beginning of a good number of the paragraphs quoted above are characteristic of the entire essay, which moves repeatedly from some strong general statement to an acknowledgment and examination of the exceptions and thence to a qualified but highly unstable recovery of the initial generalization, requiring further acknowledgment and accounting for (or discounting of) further exceptions, and so on" (*Contingencies of Value: Alternative Perspectives for Critical Theory* [Cambridge, Mass.: Harvard University Press, 1988], 64). Mary Mothersill notes that a "careful reading" of the

essay "discovers odd discontinuities and inconsequences in Hume's interpretation—as if paragraphs, even whole pages, had simply been omitted. He will advance a claim, conspicuously fail to establish it, and then proceed as if it had been established" (Mothersill, *Beauty Restored* [Oxford: Clarendon Press, 1984], 180). On the question of the consistency of Hume's aesthetic theories, see Carolyn Korsmeyer, "Hume and the Foundations of Taste," *Journal of Aesthetics and Art Criticism* 35 (1976): 201–15. Christopher MacLachlan tries to account for the "inconsistencies, even contradictions, in Hume's argument" in terms of "the irony which Hume seems to use" (MacLachlan, "Hume and the Standard of Taste," *Hume Studies* 12 [1986]: 18). On the question of Hume's ironic style, see M. A. Box, *The Suasive Art of David Hume* (Princeton: Princeton University Press, 1990), 206–25.

15. In the *Enquiry Concerning Human Understanding,* discussing liberty and necessity, Hume declares: "It is universally acknowledged that there is a great uniformity among the actions of men, in all nations and ages, and that human nature remains still the same, in its principles and operations. The same motives always produce the same actions: The same events follow from the same causes." He argues here that we must make inferences based on expectations of similarity: "It seems evident that, if all the scenes of nature were continually shifted in such a manner that no two events bore any resemblance to each other, but every object was entirely new, without any similitude to whatever had been seen before, we should never, in that case, have attained the least idea of necessity, or of a connexion among objects" (82–83).

16. Ralph Cohen, "David Hume's Experimental Method and the Theory of Taste," *ELH* 25 (1958): 288; Redding S. Sugg Jr., "Hume's Search for the Key with the Leathern Thong," *Journal of Aesthetics and Art Criticism* 16 (1957): 101. For other comments on Hume's empirical method in this context, see Ernest Campbell Mossner, "Hume's 'Of Criticism,'" in *Studies in Criticism and Aesthetics, 1660–1800,* ed. Howard Anderson and John S. Shea (Minneapolis: University of Minnesota Press, 1967), 239.

17. In "Hume and the Standard of Taste," MacLachlan describes the subtle changes Hume makes in the story from *Don Quixote* and remarks that Hume uses "the story not just to define delicacy of taste but also to relate it to the problem of aesthetic judgment and the standard of taste" (19). Arguing that Hume writes with irony throughout the essay, he argues that the "story as a whole suggests the crucial difference between the physical tasting and aesthetic taste, while purporting to use this analogy conventionally" (30). Steven Sverdlik notes "how very misleading the story really is. It is natural to take the moral of the story to be that in aesthetic disagreements, extrinsic causal evidence can rationally decide the matter. In fact, however, the point is to show how criticism rests upon principles and effective criticism consists in noticing how generally avowed principles apply to a disputed case" ("Hume's Key and Aesthetic Rationality," *Journal of Aesthetics and Art Criticism* 45 [1986]: 72–73). "There is clearly something amiss with Hume's parallel

and the mistake is subtle and interesting," Mothersill notes (*Beauty Restored,* 194). See also Marcus Hester, "Hume on Principles and Perceptual Ability," *Journal of Aesthetics and Art Criticism* 37 (1979): 295–302, and Sugg, "Hume's Search for the Key with the Leathern Thong," 96–102.

18. Reasoning and probability "deriv'd from analogy" play an important role in *A Treatise of Human Nature,* where analogy depends on degrees of resemblance. (See *Treatise,* 142–47, 209, 624–25.) For some relevant background on arguments by analogy, see Victoria Kahn, *Rhetoric, Prudence, and Skepticism in the Renaissance* (Ithaca, N.Y.: Cornell University Press, 1985).

19. Addison and Steele, *Spectator,* ed. Bond, 3: 528 (No. 409, June 19, 1712).

20. "Ce sens, ce don de discerner nos alimens, a produit dans toutes les langues connues, la métaphore qui exprime par le mot *gout,* le sentiment des beautés & des défauts dans tous les arts: c'est un discernment prompt comme celui de la langue & du palais" (Voltaire in Denis Diderot and Jean le Rond d'Alembert, *Encyclopédie, ou Dictionnaire raisonné des sciences, des arts et des métiers,* vol. 7 [Paris, 1757], 761).

21. Edmund Burke, *A Philosophical Enquiry into the Origin of Our Ideas of the Sublime and Beautiful,* ed. James T. Boulton (Notre Dame, Ind.: University of Notre Dame Press), 14.

22. Hume alters the novel to emphasize the act of tasting. He recounts: "One of them tastes it; considers it; and after mature reflection pronounces the wine to be good, were it not for a small taste of leather. The other after using the same precautions, gives also his verdict in favour of the wine; but with the reserve of a taste of iron" (234–35). The novel reads: "one of them tasted it with the tip of his tongue; the other did no more but clap it to his nose; the first said the wine tasted of iron; the other affirmed it had a twang of goats leather" (*The History of the Renowned Don Quixote,* trans. T. Smollett, 2 vols. [London, 1755], 2: 72). In *An Essay Concerning Human Understanding,* Locke also alludes to Sancho Panza in a discussion that relates language and taste. Making the point that words as arbitrary signs can only communicate "by that voluntary connexion which is known to be between them and those simple ideas which common use has made them signs of," Locke declares: "He that thinks otherwise, let him try if any words can give him the taste of a pine-apple, and make him have the true idea of the relish of that celebrated delicious fruit. So far as he is told it has a resemblance with any tastes whereof he has the ideas already in his memory, imprinted there by sensible objects, not strangers to his palate, so far he may approach that resemblance in his mind. But this is not giving us that idea by a definition, but exciting in us other simple ideas by their known names; which will be still very different from the true taste of that fruit itself." Sounds cannot communicate such ideas, claims Locke: "For to hope to produce an idea of light or colour by a sound" is as much to say "that we might taste, smell, and see by the ears: a sort of philosophy worthy only of Sancho Pança, who had the faculty to see Dulcinea by hearsay" (*An Essay Con-*

cerning Human Understanding, ed. Alexander Campbell Fraser, 2 vols. [New York: Dover, 1959], 2: 37–38). See *Don Quixote,* pt. 2, bk. 1, chap. 9. As Fraser points out, Hume repeats part of this passage at the beginning of the *Treatise:* "We cannot form to ourselves a just idea of the taste of a pineapple, without having actually tasted it" (5). For an interpretation of Rilke's account of these questions, see David Marshall, "Reading Tasting," *Glyph Textual Studies* 6 (1979): 123–40. For a recent discussion of Hume's use of *Don Quixote,* see Ronald Paulson, *Don Quixote in England* (Baltimore: Johns Hopkins University Press, 1998), 83–107.

23. See esp. the "Analytic of the Beautiful," §§ 20–22, and the "Analytic of the Sublime," § 40, in Immanuel Kant, *The Critique of Judgement,* trans. James Creed Meredith (Oxford: Clarendon Press, 1991), 82–85, 150–54. For a relevant account of the question of a shared sense in relation to taste in Kant's *Critique,* see Jean-François Lyotard, *Leçons sur l'Analytique du sublime: Kant, critique de la faculté de juger,* [§§] 23–29 (Paris: Galilée, 1991), 231–68. For some useful discussions of Kant and the standard of taste in relation to Hume, see Ted Cohen, "An Emendation in Kant's Theory of Taste," *Nous* 24 (1990): 137–45; Stanley Cavell, "Aesthetic Problems of Modern Philosophy," in id., *Must We Mean What We Say?* (New York: Scribner, 1969), 86–96; H. Osborne, "Hume's Standard and the Diversity of Aesthetic Taste," *British Journal of Aesthetics* 7 (1967): 50–56; and Mothersill, *Beauty Restored,* 209–46. See also Paul Guyer, *Kant and the Claims of Taste* (Cambridge, Mass.: Harvard University Press, 1979); Ted Cohen and Paul Guyer, eds., *Essays in Kant's Aesthetics* (Chicago: University of Chicago Press, 1982); Howard Caygill, *Art of Judgement* (Oxford: Basil Blackwell, 1989). For a discussion of Burke, see Joel C. Weinsheimer, *Eighteenth-Century Hermeneutics: Philosophy of Interpretation in England from Locke to Burke* (New Haven: Yale University Press, 1993), 195–224. As usual, many of these questions are anticipated by Shaftesbury. See his brief discussion of the "appeal to common sense" and the problem of defining "common sense" in "*Sensus Communis:* An Essay on the Freedom of Wit and Humour": "If by the word sense we were to understand opinion and judgment, and by the word common the generality or any considerable part of mankind, 'twould be hard, he said, to discover where the subject of common sense could lie. For that which was according to the sense of one part of mankind, was against the sense of another. . . . *Common* sense was as hard still to determine as *catholic* or *orthodox*" (Shaftesbury, *Characteristics,* 1: 54–55).

24. See David Marshall, "Adam Smith and the Theatricality of Moral Sentiments," in *The Figure of Theater: Shaftesbury, Defoe, Adam Smith, and George Eliot* (New York: Columbia University Press, 1986), 167–92; and id., *The Surprising Effects of Sympathy: Marivaux, Rousseau, Diderot, and Mary Shelley* (Chicago: University of Chicago Press, 1988). For an account of Hume's concept of sympathy, see Norman Kemp Smith, *The Philosophy of David Hume: A Critical Study of its Origins and Central Doctrines* (London: Macmillan, 1960), 169–74.

25. Reynolds, *Discourses on Art,* 132–33.

26. See, e.g., Wieand, "Hume's Two Standards of Taste."

27. In an unpublished paper entitled "'Yielding at last': The Dynamics of Aesthetic Sentiment in Hume's 'Of the Standard of Taste,'" Neil Saccamano discusses the political implications of Hume's effort to speak for a "we" and posit a standard that would demand submission to the authoritative judgments of critics who would speak for all. I have benefited from conversations with Saccamano about Hume as well as from reading his work on the relations among rhetoric, politics, and aesthetics in Hume and other eighteenth-century authors. Saccamano emphasizes Hume's desire to bypass argument altogether. In "Of Eloquence," Hume imagines the power of a rhetoric that would not have to convince its audience: "ancient eloquence, that is, the sublime and the passionate, is of a much juster taste than the modern, or the argumentative and rational; and, if properly executed, will always have more command and authority over mankind" (108). (Hume discusses "disputes with men" and "arguments" at the beginning of the *Enquiry Concerning the Principles of Morals.*) In "Of the Scandal of Taste: Social Privilege as Nature in the Aesthetic Theories of Hume and Kant," Richard Shusterman discusses the problem of the standard of taste in the context of a "dilemma of liberalism" that seeks to "establish or legitimate an authoritative standard for consensus beyond the individual, which will not be seen as an unjustified imposition on his freedom as subject." He concludes that Hume's privileging of the critic solves the "liberalist paradox of authority and personal freedom. Personal freedom of sentiment is preserved as expressed in the free decision to submit one's taste to the authoritative standard set by those recognized as superior, the elect" (*Philosophical Forum* 20 [1989]: 216, 220). See also Frances Ferguson's discussion of Burke and Kant in "Legislating the Sublime," in *Studies in Eighteenth-Century British Art and Aesthetics,* ed. Ralph Cohen (Berkeley: University of California Press, 1985), 128–47; as well as Ferguson, *Solitude and the Sublime: Romanticism and the Aesthetics of Individuation* (New York: Routledge, 1992); and Terry Eagleton, *The Ideology of the Aesthetic* (Oxford: Basil Blackwell, 1990), 31–69.

28. David Hume, *Four Dissertations* (London: A. Millar, 1757), i–v. The volume contains "The Natural History of Religion," "Of the Passions," "Of Tragedy," and "Of the Standard of Taste." In a letter dated May 3, 1757, Hume described this dedication as "the only one I ever wrote, or probably shall ever write, during the Course of my Life" (*New Letters of David Hume,* ed. Raymond Klibansky and Ernest C. Mossner [New York: Garland, 1983], 38). For accounts of the complicated publication history of *Four Dissertations* and Hume's role in the controversies surrounding John Home's *Douglas,* see David Mossner, *The Life of David Hume* (Oxford: Clarendon Press, 1980), 321–32, 356–79; and James S. Malek, Introduction to John Home, *The Plays of John Home* (New York: Garland, 1980), ix–xi. MacLachlan comments briefly on Hume's role as a critic in relation to John Home ("Hume and the Standard of Taste," 35). For an insightful account of Hume's stance as a writer, see Jerome Christensen, *Practicing Enlightenment: Hume*

and the Formation of a Literary Career (Madison: University of Wisconsin Press, 1987). In "Of Essay Writing," Hume describes himself as "a Kind of Resident Ambassador from the Dominions of Learning to those of Conversation" (535). In this essay, he declares "Women of Sense and Education" to be "much better Judges of all polite Writing than Men of the same Degree of Understanding"; their "Delicacy of Taste, tho' unguided by Rules" is said to be preferable to "all the dull Labours of Pedants and Commentators" although their "tender and amorous Disposition . . . perverts their judgment" and leads to a "false taste" (536–37).

29. Mossner cites a pamphlet entitled *The Usefulness of the Edinburgh Stage Seriously Considered:* "The public need not now lament the suppression of his celebrated essay on the *lawfulness of suicide:* This is more beautifully represented in the character of *Lady Barnet,* who now throws herself over a rock with more than *Roman* courage. Nor need we mourn the loss of his incomparable treatise on the *mortality* of the soul, while viewing Glenalvon *risking eternal fire*" (Mossner, *Life of David Hume,* 327).

30. Obviously there were conflicting and overdetermined forces influencing Hume as aesthetic and personal issues became affairs of both church and state. He actually succumbed to pressure to suppress the dedication when the book went to press, but he changed his mind four days later and insisted that it be restored, although eight hundred copies already had been sold without it (see Mossner, *Life of David Hume,* 361–62). For Hume's own contradictory instructions to his publisher and his accounts of the publication of the dedication, see Hume's letters to Andrew Millar of January 11 and January 20, 1757, his letter to William Mure in February, and his letter to Adam Smith in February or March (*The Letters of David Hume,* ed. J. Y. T. Greig, 2 vols. [Oxford: Clarendon Press, 1932], 1: 238–46). In addition to alluding to matters of religion, by inscribing his book in a literary event so much associated with Scottish national identity (*Douglas* was produced in Edinburgh after being declared "totally unfit for the stage" by Garrick), Hume associates himself with what he calls in the essay one of the "two sources of variation" to his claim that the "general principles of taste are uniform in human nature": "the particular manners and opinions of our age and country" (243).

31. Hume, *Four Dissertations,* iii–vi.

32. Kant, *Critique of Judgement,* trans. Meredith, 141.

Index